The Complete Book of

Sight Hounds, Longdogs and Lurchers

Also by D. Brian Plummer

Non-fiction

Diary of a Hunter
The Fell Terrier
The Complete Jack Russell Terrier
Omega
Merle
Modern Ferreting
Adventures of an Artisan Hunter
The Working Terrier
Tales of a Rat-Hunting Man
The Complete Lurcher
Rogues and Running Dogs
Hunters All
Off the Beaten Track
North and North Again
The Cottage at the Edge of the World
Practical Lurcher Breeding

Fiction

Trog: A Novel
Lepus
Nathan

The Complete Book of

Sight Hounds, Longdogs and Lurchers

by

D. Brian Plummer

Robinson Publishing
London

Robinson Publishing
11 Shepherd House
Shepherd Street
London W1Y 7LD

First published by Robinson Publishing 1991

Copyright © 1991 by D. Brian Plummer. The right of D. Brian Plummer to be identified as author of this work has been asserted by him in accordance with the Copyright, Designs and Patents Act 1988.

All rights reserved.

A copy of the British Library Cataloguing in Publication Data is available from the British Library
ISBN 1 85487 096 3

Printed in Great Britain by
Mackays of Chatham PLC

Dedication

To Curtis Price and Paul Moore
in the hope that they will
continue with the work to which
I have dedicated my life.

CONTENTS

1	The Sight Hound Breeds	1
	The Afghan Hound	5
	The Greyhound	16
	The Whippet	54
	The Scottish Deerhound	88
	The Irish Wolfhound	102
	The Saluki	118
	The Borzoi	142
2	Rare Breeds	155
	The Pharaoh Hound	155
	The Ibizan Hound	158
	The Sloughi	162
3	Longdogs	165
4	Lurchers	176
5	Sight Hounds, Longdogs and Lurchers – A Summary	184
6	Choosing a Puppy	190
7	Rearing a Puppy	200
8	Rudimentary Training	209
9	Breaking to Livestock	231
10	Jumping	236
11	Quarry	244
	The Rabbit	246
	The Hare	254
	The Fox	262
	Deer	270

CONTENTS

12	Lamping	280
13	Coursing	313
14	Ferreting	326
15	Exhibiting Sight Hounds	337
16	First Aid	352
	Index	371

1. The Sight Hound Breeds

Each and every book concerned with the origin of sight hounds attributes the place of origin of these long-legged, keen-eyed, rather remote animals to Egypt or countries adjacent to that area. Most books offer, as proof of this theory, that the earliest illustrations of these hounds are to be found on ancient monuments and tombs which have been excavated along the Nile. A closer look at these drawings casts some doubt on this theory, however. True, long-legged prick-eared dogs are depicted, but these dogs might equally well be long-legged hunting dogs of any type and many of these representations show dogs little different from the rather lean Basenji or the allied Niam Niam-type hunting dogs. The illustrations indicate that the Egyptians knew of, and probably kept, long-legged dogs which may have been used to hunt game.

Likewise, because such monuments sport carvings and paintings of dogs which may or may not have been dogs of the greyhound type, it does not automatically follow that this kind of dog originated in that country. For instance should a group of American soldiers, the majority of which could be negroes, be killed by an act of terrorism in Berlin, and should the act receive the publicity expected, regarding such atrocities, would future researchers, delving into the photographs and data concerning the demise of the soldiers, be correct in assuming that because the Berlin newspapers sported photographs of the negro victims,

Berlin or countries adjacent to Germany were the places where negroes or negroid races originated?

At the time when the great monuments of Egypt were erected, the natives of Egypt had a fairly exact calendar (most ancient Mediterranean civilisations tended to favour a 360-day calendar, indeed Velikovsky believes that a year during antideluvian times may well have been only 360 days in duration and that since that time the earth has moved fractionally further from the sun) as well as a very exact knowledge of astronomy and a fairly good working knowledge of the geography of the lands around the Mediterranean. Trade with adjacent countries was flourishing together with the wars, which inevitably accompany successful trading, being successfully waged. Perhaps long-legged hounds may have been amongst the trade goods and booty brought from distant lands, rather than being taken from Egypt to those distant lands—and very distant lands at that, for it has been advanced, although again without conclusive proof, that the Egyptians knew of the existence of a continent to the south-east of Africa, and may even have explored Australasia.

Thus, while it is likely that the greyhound type may have originated in Egypt, or the Levant, it is by no means certain that the sight hounds owe their place of origin to the Middle East. An interesting and heretical theory is offered by Zeuner (*History of Domestication*). Zeuner considers it possible, but no more than possible, that the sight hound types may have originated independently in various parts of the world. It is possible that various primitive nomadic races domesticated wild dogs of different types and, by dint of selective breeding, produced types of dogs which not only hunted by sight rather than scent, but also developed long legs and a racy build so as to enable them to run down quarry. On first appearances this theory may carry little credibility as every breed of sight hound has almost exactly the same type of frame and the same slightly intractable disposition, which may suggest that the breeds have a common origin. However, on closer examination of the theory of multiple points of origin of sight hounds, the suggestion becomes slightly less absurd. Similar types of animal do develop independently yet still develop similar build, structure and, in some cases, coloration—the jaguar, the llamas of the Americas and the leopard and the camels of the Old World indicate this. Indeed so similarly do some types develop, even independently, that there is a school of scientific writers which believes that the bug-eyed monsters of pre-1950 science fiction are not only horrific and ludicrous but highly unlikely, and if life forms exist on other planetary systems, those life forms would almost exactly replicate the life forms on earth.

Many insist that the somewhat remote and intractable nature of all sight hounds would indicate that a common stock spawned all breeds of sight hound, but this theory too does not stand up to examination under a strong light. It can be said that the willingness to please of some breeds of dog is a quality that has been deliberately bred into them—wolves and wild dogs are not naturally biddable or innately willing to adapt to the tasks man requires of a dog. Primitive tribes, functioning independently of each other, may well simply have required a great turn of speed, coupled with catching ability in their hounds and may not have held the opinion that extreme pliancy, such as is found in shepherding and gun dog breeds, was a particularly desirable or necessary quality, particularly if the breed type had been developed by pre-pastoral nomadic groups who would have required a hound to bring down all edible quarry—and to primitive hunter-gatherers, relatively free of the taboos of the more civilised pastoral and agrarian races, most wild animals would have been considered edible.

If the sight hound types are not related or only slightly related, how can one allot the various breeds to groups and where do the divisions between the various types occur? Once again conjecture rather than plain fact must come into play. Popular opinion amongst cynologists suggests two main types of sight hound may exist: the Middle Eastern type; and the Celtic hounds, and possibly these types could be slightly related or totally unrelated. Between both types, intermediate forms derived from the mingling of both types of sight hound.

Celtic Hounds

Now extinct Great Irish hound
Irish wolfhound
Scottish deerhound
Now extinct Scottish greyhound
(almost certainly a lurcher or longdog type)
The modern greyhound, show, coursing and racing
The whippet
The Italian greyhound
Some lurcher and longdog types

Middle Eastern Hounds

Berber sloughi
Tuareg sloughi
Saluki
Afghan hound
Varieties of Baluchi hounds
Rampur hound

Intermediate Forms

The Ibizan hound
The Pharaoh hound
The borzoi—both types
Various Mediterranean types
such as the mongrel Chalo
Galgos similar in type to
British lurchers
Many longdog types

The chart indicates avant-garde thinking of a sort that would certainly be considered heretical by many, particularly those breed enthusiasts who claim wondrous but totally unsubstantiated antique origins for their hounds. Each and every sight hound breed book repeats, with monotonous similarity one should add, that their particular breed is the oldest breed in the world—a theory which is incidentally hotly contested by owners of Norwegian elkhounds and similar Spitz type breeds—and that their particular breed of sight hound is a direct descendant of the type of dog depicted on the tombs of the long dead Egyptian Pharaohs. There is little evidence to substantiate any of these claims, one might add, apart from drawings of animals which resemble either a very long-legged jackal type dog or perhaps, just perhaps, a dog of sight hound type. Why the opinion that antiquity of a breed type should place a dog head and shoulders above more modern strains is equally baffling, particularly as some of the more modern breeds of dog, such as the modern greyhound—a statement which will be clarified later—are faster, stronger and more adept at coming up on and catching game than their more primitive relatives.

Thus throughout this entire lengthy book while tales of the origin, or supposed origin of the various types are included in the text, they have been used purely for their entertainment value and should not be regarded as authentic evidence as to the origin of any type.

The Afghan Hound

Whether or not the Afghan hound is the world's most beautiful dog, as a journalist writing for an American magazine once described it, is questionable and anyway only a matter of opinion. However, the breed must surely be a contender for the title of the world's most enigmatic breed or, more accurately perhaps, the breed with the most baffling and enigmatic history.

Basically there are three theories as to the origin of this silky-coated hound that is clearly of the greyhound or sight hound type.

It is possible, just possible, that as Zeuner believes, the breed may have arisen independently from amongst the pariah type dogs which forage around the villages in the Transoxianic Knot, and that the breed is unrelated or at the best only slightly related to the saluki or other greyhound types. Few of the books concerned with the Afghan hound or allied breeds are prepared to accept this theory, or even mention it but it is possible that a breed type could have arisen in this area or further north in Central Asia and have been developed for its speed and long, cold resistant, hirsute jacket.

The majority of Afghan hound breed books suggest that the hound is simply a form of the saluki type desert greyhound and there is, in fact, evidence to suggest that intermediate forms twixt the saluki and the Afghan hound exist between the Fertile Crescent, Afghanistan and northern India. Indeed a form not unlike a hybrid between the saluki and the Afghan hound, the Rampur hound, is still hunted by the nomadic Banjari tribes, tribes similar in language, custom and appearance to the European gypsies or Romanies. Such hounds, unstandardized and very variable in type, were often bought by British soldiers serving in India prior to World War II, and there is ample evidence to suggest such dogs may still exist amongst the nomadic people of northern India. E G Walsh, author of *Lurchers and Longdogs*, purchased a hybrid between a Rampur hound and a saluki, bred by an army sergeant, and hunted it as a lurcher or longdog, running a variety of ground game from jackal to the gazelle.

The theory that the Afghan hound is a form of saluki and was imported to northern India and adjacent countries by either traders or by the armies of conquering Islamic warriors is lent support by the fact that the term Tazi hound is synonymous with Afghan hound and perhaps could mean that the hound may have originated in Taiz in Yemen, though the word 'tazi' is also said to be an Afghani dialect term for 'swift sprinter' or 'fast hound,' or, in certain dialects, simply white (cream or pale hounds were favoured in some districts in some districts of Afghanistan). Dr Van der Beck of the Smithsonian Institute is however of the opinion that there was social intercourse between the merchants of Taiz and the Indus River, the northernmost tributaries of which arise in Afghanistan. Likewise, the Hon. Mountstuart Elphinstone, author of *An Account of the Kingdom of Cabul and its Dependencies* (1815), describes a trip to Afghanistan and tells briefly of the hounds found there. More important still he mentions that a strain of horse, with obvious Arab characteristics, was bred by certain tribesmen and referred to as Tauzee horses, though once again the term may well mean swift or sprinter when applied to horses.

Yet another hypothesis has been offered to explain the origin of this mysterious hound. Jackson Sandford, an American breed enthusiast, writing in the *Afghan Hound Club of America Bulletin* (1942), suggests that he had evidence to prove the Afghan hound was the oldest true breed of dog on earth and suggests that the type originated in Central Asia 100,000 years ago, although how Mr Jackson Sandford arrived at such a conclusion is as mystifying as the origin of the Afghan hound itself. Jackson Sandford suggests that a Turko–Mongoloid tribe, the Yucchi, brought the dog from Central Asia when in 126 BC the tribe migrated to Afghanistan. He quotes a Chinese manuscript which makes mention of the hound.

> *These dogs are as large as foals, black and exceedingly fierce. The hair on them is long and on the ear is of such texture that the women shear them as sheep. When they hunt no animal stands before the ferocity of the hounds and horsemen are hard pressed to keep these hounds in view.*

The hounds described may have been Afghans or a type closely related to them. Similarly, and this seems more likely, the reference may be to one of the mastiff type dogs which are common in Central Asia and were probably related to the large and ferocious Tibetan mastiff.

Sandford also refers to a fourteenth century document which refers to a race of hounds living in the Transoxianic Knot. One such hound was shot and later examined by a Chinese surgeon who found that the dog's stomach was under the great rib. The hound so dissected was described as having a long tangled coat and the natives hunted them alongside hawks (after the manner of the Franks) and in conjunction with leopards, the hounds being amazingly fleet. Sandford clearly believed that the hound originated in Central Asia and spread south and west to become the saluki and the less hirsute hound types.

There is a tendency for those who keep these long-haired exotic hounds to suggest that these dogs were the property of the nobility and that lesser ranks were not allowed to own them—a state reminiscent of the Forest Law said to have been passed by Canute in 1016, 'no mean man might own a greyhound', but there is no evidence to support this, although the breed has certainly been linked with various dignitaries, particularly warlike and conquering rulers.

A tale is told that Saladin, a contemporary of our own twelfth century Richard I, incurred the wrath of Sinan, the Assassin chieftain whose fortress he was in the process of besieging. Despite the security which surrounded the Turkish chieftain, he awoke to find a warm flat cake of the type baked by the Assassins at his bedside and a dagger dipped in a potent poison resting on top of the cake. The message was clear to Saladin that in spite of stringent security, Sinan could have him killed when and where he wished. It appears that Saladin experienced something akin to a nervous breakdown, and begged forgiveness from the Old Man of the Mountains. Legend also has it that Saladin trained two Afghan hounds, feeding them from his own hand, allowing no-one to touch or talk to them to ensure their loyalty, for whereas human guards could be bribed, dogs so treated offer unquestionable loyalty to their owner and trainer. The fact that Saladin did lay siege to the Assassin fortress is recorded by both Runciman and Henry Treece in their histories of the crusades. Likewise the fact that Saladin experienced an illness akin to a nervous breakdown is well recorded. There is however little or no evidence to suggest that he trained a pair of Afghan hounds as guards, though the account makes a pretty tale.

Lt. Colonel Kullmar of the American Embassy in Kabul unearthed a similar type of story concerning the association of the breed with noble conquerors. Mahmoud the Gaznavid, who ruled from 988 was a great iconoclast and invaded India twelve times to spread Islamic learnings and to destroy the idols of the Hindu. He is said to have popularised the Tazi or Afghan hound and used them as hunting dogs, couriers and guards. It is said that a district near Kandahar was named Tazi province because of the Gaznavids' love of the hounds.

Tales of this nature surround the Afghan hound though no evidence exists to suggest that the ownership of such a hound was the sole prerogative of the nobility. Indeed many of the wandering bands, who knew nothing of frontiers and political boundaries, often kept superb specimens of Tazi hound and used them in much the same way as Romany gypsies and tinkers used the less aristocratic lurchers and longdogs. It is indeed a bad mistake to attribute false values to any of these Middle Eastern hounds and while it may be true that the most impoverished tribesmen refuse to sell their hounds, it must also be said that few Norfolk poachers, equally down at heel and impoverished, would consider selling an adult lurcher. Indeed refusal to part with any dog regardless of price indicates affinity with the dog rather than any taboo or custom concerning the sale of the creature. So much hogwash has been written on this subject, hogwash perhaps inspired by the status enjoyed by the British greyhound during the Middle Ages, that it is necessary to discount these tales. Afghan hounds, like salukis, sloughis or any of the desert greyhound breeds were kept by nobility and common alike, although it seems likely that for obvious reasons the very best types of hound may well have been bred by those who were financially well endowed.

Legend aside, a Major Amps of the British Army was stationed in Kabul in 1919, a time which marked the end of the long and bitter Afghan Wars. His wife, Mary Amps displayed a great interest in these long-haired Baluchi hounds and established a nucleus of good quality dogs, calling the establishment the Ghazni Kennels. The accounts of how Mrs Amps acquired the nucleus of these kennels are both legion and fascinating and she did much to debunk the supposed nobility of the breed type. She tells how she saw hounds which simply became restless at sundown and set out to forage, scrounge or hunt food.

Mrs Amps, writing in Croxton Smith's *Hounds and Dogs* (1932), gives an accurate account of chirk hawking with hound and saker falcon (though the shabbaz, a large type of goshawk was as frequently used). Mrs Amps records that the hounds and hawks were fed only on the flesh of a fast agile deer called the Ahu Dashti, a beast so fast that an eulogy is afforded it;

> *On the day it is born a man can outrun it*
> *On the second day a swift hound*
> *But on the third day only Allah.*

Major Amps was concerned with the coursing qualities of his hounds as much as with their aesthetic appeal and ran his hounds against greyhounds while on a visit to the Maharaja of Patiala in India. The hounds displayed none of the initial speed of the British greyhound, but were better at turning and easily outlasted the British dogs. Amps remarked that the country was as flat as a lawn and that if the Afghan hounds had been running over rocks and undulating plains, they may have performed much better than the greyhounds.

At the time when Major Amps was collecting specimens of the breed type, he believed that many hunters were crossing true Afghan hounds with salukis in order to reduce coat and produce animals which were more suitable for coursing in hotter climes. In all probability there were several types of hound, for the dogs were bred for their coursing merit irrespective of their long, hirsute or short coats, nor were native breeders aware of any standard of excellence for the breed type. In any event coat should be of minor importance to the owner of a hound bred for coursing.

This however is not the case today. The modern Afghan hound has levelled out as a dog measuring between 24–29 in. at the shoulder—roughly speaking, a dog of the same size as a modern coursing greyhound, and probably of the same proportions and construction as the dogs which accompanied early Afghani conquerors on their marches into India. What has changed, however, is the length and texture of coat. Modern Afghan hounds are far too profuse of coat to be of much use in the coursing field, particularly in temperate climes where coursing is conducted in winter with its associated snow and rain. The coat of the modern Afghan hound would absorb many pounds of water, mud and plant detritus during a day's coursing in Britain, and hence render the dog less than useful in the coursing field.

This fact is at least reflected in the attitude of club members to coursing events involving Afghan hounds. In recent years there has been a revival of interest in exploiting the natural ability of various breeds of sight hound—a revival which has prompted breed associations such as the Deerhound, the Whippet and the Saluki Clubs, to run coursing meets. Little enthusiasm to organise similar events has been forthcoming from any of the Afghan hound groups in Europe, although there is now some evidence that various American groups are staging coursing events in which Afghans are competing.

American fanciers, in fact, do far more with their sight hounds than their counterparts in Britain, as the interest in obtaining obedience qualifications with such unlikely candidates as Afghan hounds attests. It should be noted, however, that while Afghan hounds may perform well within the confines of a building or surrounded by a ring of spectators they seldom perform with the same alacrity when presented with situations in the field. Afghans, in common with most sight hounds, one should add, have an incredibly low attention span and a will to chase and pursue quarry well in excess of a desire to please their owners. The sight of a flapping leaf, or a piece of paper shifted by the wind will usually destroy any concentration in all but the most exceptional Afghan hound, and to expect hounds to remain steady while quarry is being flushed is usually asking too much of them. Sight hounds, despite the totally unscientific hokum found in breed books, are not easily trained, not intelligent and certainly not the ideal breeds for a beginner to try to train. It is a good policy to remember that all sight hounds are dual-personality dogs. On the lead or surrounded by a wall of spectators they may behave impeccably. Off the lead and in the field, the all too strong hunting instinct of these hounds makes them not only intractable but positive liabilities where other livestock is concerned. It is worthy of note that certain insurance companies are reluctant to issue third party insurances to cover the damage which may be caused by greyhound type dogs—Afghans, salukis, borzois etc, and some refuse to issue cover to owners of the far more tractable lurchers.

Thus it is all the more commendable that circus troupes manage to train Afghan hounds to a high standard of obedience and in situations where other livestock—ducks, sheep, pigs etc, take part in the act. The great beauty of these hounds, the startling elegance made manifest by their movement and their coats which complement their flowing gait, makes the hound ideal for exotic-looking public appearances, though in point of fact Afghan hounds are the very devil to train. Mrs Frank Burger, a more than merely competitive dog trainer, uses twenty dogs in her circus act, eight of which are pure-bred Afghan hounds. She comments that Afghans cannot be forced to learn tricks but respond to training when they are 'good and ready'. Mrs Burger remarks that while a terrier or a poodle can be trained from scratch in two months, it often takes over a year to train an Afghan hound to a similar level of proficiency.

Miller and Gilbert in their comprehensive book, *The New Complete Afghan Hound* (Howell Book House), comment on the fact that while jumping, scaling and hurdling are easily learned by the hounds, the act of retrieving either the dummy or captured quarry seems alien to them, and it requires great patience to teach these hounds to return objects or game to hand. The coursing purist, the typical *aficionado* of sight hound breeds, will usually accept this peculiarity and in fact it is fair to say that most pure-bred sight hounds show a similar reluctance to retrieve. However with patience, admittedly with great patience, most Afghans can be taught rudimentary retrieving, but it is wise to remember that, while an Afghan hound may perform tolerably well in a confined space, in the field with its obvious distractions the dog may well behave less well, for like all sight hounds Afghan hounds have a relatively low concentration span. Miller and Gilbert make special note of the capricious nature of the Afghan hound during training, and special mention of the control of the Afghan hound in the field has been made in the articles by American dog trainer Shelley Hennessey who has not only won well in classes where the aesthetic qualities of the dog have been of primary importance, but has also coursed and obedience trained her Afghan hounds.

Regardless of the difficulties a trainer will encounter, no Afghan hound should remain untrained. Sadly the glamorous appearance of the dog and the exotic ethos that surrounds it does tend to attract unsuitable, image-seeking owners who, because of their inability to understand the machinations of the sight hound mentality, tend to produce biological time bombs rather than trained dogs. Such is the hunting instinct of these hounds—and it must be borne in mind that prior to the 1920s they had been bred exclusively for hunting and that their hunting instinct had been finely honed for several thousand years. Thus, despite the fact that few of the modern hounds are coursed, the instinct to run quarry is still very strong. This makes an uncontrollable dog a serious problem in urban areas and a positively frightening prospect in a rural situation, for sheep are the perfect animals to stimulate the coursing instinct in any dog, since they are large, noisy, seldom able to retaliate, and prone to run rather than stand ground if pursued.

To say that Afghan hounds benefit from obedience training is magnificent meiosis. The fact is that unless this type of dog is given a lengthy period of obedience training, specimens are likely to become more of a liability than a pleasure to own. This becomes all too apparent when an Afghan hound slips its leash at a large dog show and needs to be caught up again. Scenes which smack of total training incompetence often result, and if many breeders and exhibitors told the truth they would admit to the fact that their dogs are nearly impossible to catch in such circumstances. Breeders selling puppies would do well to ensure that the would-be purchaser agrees to attend obedience classes with the hound, or at least arranges to take some measure to ensure that it becomes trained rather than simply being kept as a potentially dangerous ornament.

Coursing instinct is something to exploit rather than suppress and the Afghan hound still has it in plenty. In the Middle East, desert greyhound type dogs are still used to hunt game, though the perfection of the high-powered rifle has reduced most game to small numbers except in the most isolated areas. Young hounds are allowed to course jerboas, small but swift desert rodents which move with a hopping action similar to that of the kangaroo and which, when pressed, have the ability to vanish down a convenient hole, thus evading the hounds pursuing them. Young hounds probably find these rodents testing quarry and as Middle Eastern greyhounds are amongst the slowest of sight hounds to learn the technique of picking up fleeing quarry, this kangaroo rat tests the ability of the sapling to the full.

Sooner or later the hounds are slipped at desert hares and no more fleet or testing quarry exists. The hare, a similar species to the European brown hare uses the desert terrain to the full to evade a pursuer, springing over rocky zeugen and yardang, leaping over obstacles and pitfalls in a similar manner to that in which a Scottish blue hare chooses to evade a lurcher. Hares are the ultimate test of a dog's speed, stamina and picking-up ability, but the natives of Central Asia consider the speed, agility and stamina considerably inferior to that of a species of black buck known as the Ahu Dashti. So swift is this gazelle that the Asiatic tribes, irreverent as hunters are apt to be, state that only Allah can outpace it.

A pair of hounds are often used to course this swift gazelle but even these are often outpaced by the creature. Thus the Afghani resorts to chirk hawking to bring down the gazelle, working in much the same way as the Saudi or Bedouin saluki owner, but while the saluki owner tends to favour the use of the saker falcon to bring down its prey, the Afghani prefers the shabbaz, a strong powerfully built goshawk found in the forests of northern India, some females of which are nearly the size of a small male Bonelli's eagle. These hawks bind to the horns of the gazelle, flapping wildly and clawing for a purchase hold and the gazelle, thus confused and terrified, is slowed down to such an extent that the hounds are able to bring it down. Hounds to be used for this spectacular hunting technique are quartered and fed with the hawks from the day of their weaning and thus become accustomed to working with them.

To the British falconer, accustomed as he is to the spaniel and pointer working in conjunction with hawks and falcons to secure game, the art of chirk hawking must appear no great feat. Nothing could be further from the truth. Pointers and spaniels seldom lay claim to the quarry brought down by the hawk or falcon, but such is the disposition of any sight hound and such is the sport of the pursuit of the gazelle that a perfect understanding must exist between the hawk and the hounds, a true symbiotic existence which must be tested to the full by the predatory and fractious disposition of both Shabbaz and Afghan hound.

There are reports of hounds being used to bring down large dangerous quarry such as boar and even leopard, though both beasts are more than a match for a pair of hounds. The Indian species of wild pig rivals the Prussian boar in size and ferocity. Few hounds relish the prospect of tackling any species of pig, for the courage of the boar is legendary. It is worthy of note that the early Indo-European warriors adopted a crested helmet so that its shape might resemble the crested spine of the boar and perhaps confer some of the courage of boar to the wearer of the helmet. It is also worthy of note that the Nordic surname Eberhard means brave as a boar. No animal is more dangerous when hard pressed, wounded or cornered. When brought to bay it seeks protection for its rear amongst trees or rocks and wreaks havoc with its long, bevelled-edged tushes, tushes which are so stained and filthy that Shakespeare was correct in stating

And where he strikes his hooked tushes slay

for the hound, if not disembowelled by the first slashes of the tushes, often dies of tetanus induced by the wounds.

Sight hounds can outstrip the fleeing boar, though pigs of any species are remarkably fast when pursued, but once the boar is brought to bay, discretion is of more importance than speed or blind courage. No hound is capable of dispatching a boar unaided. Indeed until the invention of the modern longbow and the bodkin-headed arrow, this must have been an almost impregnable adversary. Hounds bring the boar to bay quite easily, as pigs need little encouragement to stand and fight rather than run, but once it stands its ground, hounds must keep it at bay by nipping, barking and tormenting the pig rather than indulging in a suicidal headlong tackle.

Leopards are also hunted by native Tazi or Afghan hounds, and once again the task of the hounds is to run the leopard and tree it or bring it to bay amongst rocks but not to tackle the cat. There is, however, a tale of a Major Mackenzie who owned a large, powerful male

Afghan hound which gave pursuit to a nearly full-grown leopard and, after a hard and testing battle, killed it. As to the veracity of the tale it is impossible to make a fair and valid comment, sufficient to say that no dog of any breed is a match for a healthy adult leopard.

There seems scant interest in working or coursing the Afghan hound in Britain, possibly because the long silky coat of this hound is irreparably damaged by the mud and dirt of the British countryside. Private coursing meets arranged by some enthusiasts are poorly attended and the hounds seldom perform well. However I must disagree with Frank Sheardown, *The Working Longdog*, who believes that the instinct has been bred out of the Afghan hound. Sagar, the saluki coursing enthusiast comments on the capricious performances put up by many salukis in the field, and believes that if a saluki is run in a state of mental and physical readiness, it is seldom capricious and unreliable, but adds that few people are capable of understanding the complex mental make-up of the saluki. Might this also be true of the more hirsute Afghan hound and perhaps the hound really awaits the coming of a trainer who understands its mental and physical requirements.

Jackson Sandford who hunted Afghans in America notes that the hound is as a whole not very reliable in the field and only one in ten males—and no bitches (which is curious as bitch sight hounds often make very persistent coursers) is of any use in the field, but adds that some hounds have successfully hunted rabbit, hare, fox, puma, lynx and house (feral, at least one hopes the writer means feral) cats.

As a breed, however, one must feel that the potential of the Afghan hound has not been fully exploited in either Britain or America.

The Greyhound

It is almost impossible not to eulogise on the subject of the greyhound. It is the fastest of dogs despite ludicrous tales that Afghan hounds are faster. It is the most elegant of dogs—for nothing has the poise and dignity of a top class greyhound. Above all it is the most physically perfect of breeds. Hereditary faults are seldom encountered, physical exaggeration which has dogged breeds such as the bulldog, the chow chow, and even that gigantic sight hound, the Irish wolfhound, are not met with in the greyhound. The dog is a triumph of genetic manipulation and whereas most other breeds of dog tend to physically deteriorate with each and every generation of the breed, each successive generation of greyhounds is faster than the last, more powerful, more durable, more physically perfect. In half a century the greyhound's speed has improved beyond belief, so much so in fact that the times of track legends of the 1920s would look ridiculously slow on the meanest unlicenced tracks of today—and the times of 1920s stars are nowadays bettered by greyhound blooded longdogs and lurchers.

Where the greyhound originated, is the subject of much debate, but the type is old, very old, older perhaps than cynologists or archaeologists could imagine. Archaeological evidence indicates that the breed or a similar, if not identical type, is depicted on the walls of tombs of ancient Egypt, but there is every possibility that the breed was an ancient one before primitive man decided to settle on that thin strip of fertile land along the banks of the Nile. The type appears as though specifically designed, engineered as a dog to pursue swift and elusive quarry. Such a type would seem oddly out of place in the deltaic marshlands of ancient Egypt, conditions that would be unlikely to have produced the greyhound. Thus if the Middle East was the place where the greyhound type evolved—and there is precious little evidence to suggest that it is—in all probability the type would have originated in the arid scrublands that lie adjacent to the fertile valley of the Nile, in country more conducive to the production of a fleet type of hunting dog.

A popular theory among cynologists is that the greyhound, or to be less specific, a greyhound type originated from the domestication of the Arabian wolf, a sub-species of the Palearctic wolf, but rangier, leggier, more sparse of flesh than its northern counterpart. Advocates of this theory claim that this dolichocephalic wolf is the obvious ancestor of the greyhound type, but there is precious little evidence to suggest that any species of wolf is the ancestor of the greyhound. Zeuner suggests that while the wolf seems the most logical of ancestors of any breed of dog, domesticated dogs may equally well claim descent from the semi-wild type of dog typified by the Australian dingo or perhaps an even more primitive wild dog which in its truly wild state is extinct. Likewise Zeuner postulates that while Egypt or the adjacent arid areas may well have been the birthplace of a greyhound type, it is also feasible that the various types of greyhound could have arisen independently in various localities. Thus the greyhound, the saluki, the deerhound, the borzoi could be unrelated or perhaps only slightly related. It is indeed an interesting theory and one that writers of breed books concerning sight hounds should explore rather than slavishly adhering to the theory that all greyhound types originated in the Middle East. True, drawings and paintings of long sleek racy hunting dogs are found in very ancient Egyptian tombs, but it should also be pointed out that nomadic tribes, inhabitants of the arid plains in which the greyhound may have originated, erected no such ornate tombs and hence the development of a greyhound type of dog amongst these desert peoples would have remained unrecorded. Thus the greyhound type may have originated millenia before the Egyptians decided to decorate tombs with designs incorporating greyhound-like dogs.

Whatever its exact origin, the greyhound type was widely known in the Middle East many centuries before the advent of the Christian Era. The Bible makes scant reference to dogs in general—except in contempt for the dietary and sanitary habits of the species. This is curious for whereas it seems likely that the greyhound may have been developed amongst the nomadic races of the earth, there is a strange distaste for dogs amongst the nomadic races which spawned both Judaism and Islam. Perhaps, just perhaps, the taboos which were carried on from the pastoral way of life to the settled dwellers in towns were preceded by equally persistent race memories which originated when man forsook the hunter-gatherer type existence and began to domesticate sheep, cattle and goats. Perhaps the domestication of nervous bovine, ovine and caprine beasts made the presence of dogs a little less desirable although to the western keeper of herds and flocks the control of stock without dogs seems impossible. Dogs, however, are seldom used by Middle Eastern nomads to move and restrict flocks, and hence dogs are usually considered undesirable amongst Middle Eastern livestock.

For some reason the greyhound type is not included in the taboos of Islamic and Judaic cultures and they possibly enjoy an unique status. Solomon makes mention of the fleetness of the hound perhaps, but it is possible that Solomon was simply an acute observer of natural history rather than a canophile. Certainly there are many references to the much abused 'and Solomon spoke many things of birds and animals', quote, in both Judaic and Islamic literature, but whether the reference to the greyhound refers to the greyhound as we know it today, or to the desert hounds such as the saluki, the Afghan and the sloughi, will probably never be determined, and anyway is of little consequence.

The appearance of the greyhound type in Europe occurred much later, though there are tales that the Phoenicians introduced a type of fleet hunting dog to the Balearic Islands and later to Spain. Such theories are questioned throughout this book however as perhaps being the product of romantic delusions rather than hard factual evidence. There is no evidence that there existed any dog in Southern Europe capable of running down a hare, until the invasion of the Celts in the third century BC but there is considerable evidence that the Celts introduced the greyhound or greyhound type to Europe. Whether or not the Balearic type hounds, the galgo or the Pharaoh hound, can trace their ancestry to imports from Africa or are the results of imports of Celtic greyhounds from Europe is also debatable.

The Celts, prior to their invasion of the Mediterranean lands, were natives of central Europe, although there is every indication from the analyses of various existing Celtic languages, Gaelic, Welsh etc, that the race or group of races had their origins further to the east. Apparently the Celts were great dog lovers, for poodles as well as greyhounds and other breeds accompanied them on their migrations. However it would seem unlikely that the greyhound type which accompanied the Celts would have been identical to the stock competing in today's Greyhound Derby. In all probability a variety of types accompanied the invading Celts, types varying in shape, size and coat, from dogs similar to the whippet, to outrageously huge dogs the size of small ponies. The smaller dogs might have been used to secure small game such as hares (rabbits at this period in time would have been confined to the land around the south west of Europe and North Africa and had not yet spread to the rest of Europe and Asia), and birds up to the size of cranes or bustards, while the large hounds were able to pull down wolf, deer, elk and possibly boar, for boar was certainly hunted; tales of these hunts, much embroidered by Gallic use of hyperbole, appear in Celtic legends. Medieval carvings and drawings of wild boar hunts show heavily armoured mastiff type dogs engaged in bringing their quarry to bay. However references to boar hunts in the *Mabinogion* seem to indicate that the large greyhound type dogs—possibly the ancestors of Irish wolfhounds and Scottish deerhounds, were responsible for bringing down wild boars, the bravest of all animals. Some indication that the type can be used to hunt wild pig is given by accounts of Queensland hunters who use kangaroo hounds, mixtures of a longdog type, to turn boar and then resort to the use of pit bull terriers or hybrids between pit bull terriers and collies to hold the cornered pig. Even though the feral pig of Queensland is not a Prussian boar, being simply a descendant of escapee pigs, the fighting prowess of any species of wild or feral pig should never be underestimated. Both feral pigs and truly wild pigs present 400 pounds of solid muscle together with a thick hide capable of turning a spear, arrow or lance, let alone a dog's teeth.

There are many references to the greyhound in Celtic British literature, despite the fact that the invasion of the Anglo–Saxon races following the departure of the Roman Legions must have destroyed copious amounts of literature concerning the type. Yet the Saxons too had a great fondness for these hounds. Whether or not they were acquired from Celtic breeders or imported from their native Germany has yet to be determined, but it is likely that the hound would have been fairly well established in Germany prior to the migrations of the Anglo–Saxons and Jutish invaders. In the eighth century the Duke of Mercia, the greatly troubled Elfric, kept a kennel of greyhounds, but once again it must be remembered that the term greyhound is an all embracing one and could have referred to enormous brutes the size of Irish wolfhounds as well as to diminutive whippet-sized dogs of varying coat and size. The Cotton Library, however, offers more conclusive proof of the type of hound kept by these hunters, for a ninth-century manuscript depicts a Saxon chieftain accompanied by his huntsman with a pair of lurcher-sized dogs of greyhound type.

Later still, immediately prior to the Norman Conquest, Edward the Confessor—'more priest than king' was reputed to follow 'swift hounds'—though swift hounds may indicate greyhounds or possibly some other breed of hound, for few types of Anglo–Saxon hunting dog would have been unable to keep pace with a heavy horse and qualify for the title 'swift'. It is also worth noting that Edward had considerable contact with Norman France, where entirely different breeds of scent-hunting hounds were being developed.

It is commonly believed that Canute, the son of Sweyn Forkbeard and first Viking King of England, passed the first of the oppressive Forest Laws in 1016 when he decreed 'No mean man might own a greyhound', no mean man being someone without a certain income. Most books concerning the sight hound quote this edict and further state that there were similar moves afoot in Normandy where a similar Nordic race had settled and social codes concerning hunting had already begun to develop. In point of fact it is believed that this so called first Forest Law is in fact a twelfth-century forgery, an act perpetrated perhaps to lessen the public feeling for the atrocities which were to follow when Norman kings came to the throne. In point of fact, Canute's only edict concerning hunting was a statement that every man had a right to hunt on his own land. Canute, in point of fact, seems not to have made mention of the greyhound.

The Norman Conquest and its hunting-orientated kings, which followed on the heels of the death of Edward the Confessor, was to be far more stringent in its laws governing the use of greyhounds or greyhound type dogs to capture game. The passions of the Norman kings were warring and the chase, skills at which they excelled. Areas were cleared of population to 'let in the Forest', so that beasts of the chase could run free and prosper. Deer must have abounded before the Conquest, but after it, afforded protection by the savage Forest Laws, they flourished. Contrary to what most history books tell us, the Anglo–Saxon peasantry displayed no great interest in the chase and hence regulations prohibiting the hunting of deer probably failed to be particularly restrictive, but regulations and laws once passed frequently seem to be meant to be broken, man being a perverse animal and so poachers, those who set out deliberately to defy the laws of the Forest, began to appear. Hence, to deter poaching, punishments by today's standards disproportionate to the crime, were meted out.

William Rufus, who followed hot on the heels of the Conqueror, was said to be particularly harsh in his enforcement of the Forest Laws and decreed that offenders should be branded, maimed or castrated. To evaluate the impact that such an edict must have had, it should be remembered that in Anglo–Saxon times, capital or corporal punishment was rarely used to deter offenders and fines called weregild (or man money) would have been the punishment for a crime even as heinous as manslaughter. Thus to be maimed or castrated for the pursuit of game must have seemed just as outrageous to the native Britisher then as it is now.

Even more draconian was the edict that all dogs living near the forest (greyhounds would have been particularly singled out by law enforcers) were to be lawed—two toes of the dog's feet were to be struck off to inhibit the speed of the dog. Chevenix Trench compares this mutilation merely to the docking of tails as practised today, but the comparison is clearly ludicrous. A docked tail is usually amputated before the puppy is ten days old whereas the lawing of toes would have been far more painful and would have resulted in the production of a permanently crippled animal. However William Rufus may well have been one of those kings whom history has deliberately wronged. He was never popular with the clerics of the time since he was a flamboyant homosexual and an advocate of the Cathar heresy—a crusade against the Cathars was to be conducted nearly a century later. Thus if history has wronged Canute who probably never uttered the words 'No mean man might own a greyhound' perhaps it also did less then justice to the unfortunate William Rufus.

His successor, Henry I, passed even harsher edicts to deter the poacher, although it should be remembered that between the reign of Rufus and Henry I, a civil war had ravaged the land and perhaps harsh laws were necessary to prevent the chaos of the times of the Stephen and Matilda conflict from continuing. Henry I, like Canute, gave every man the right to hunt on his own land, a curious right by today's standards perhaps, but made trespass in the Royal forests and pursuit of deer an extremely dangerous pursuit. For causing a deer to run until it panted a freeman would be fined ten shillings, a colossal sum at the time, but a serf, who would never have owned such a sum, was to be savagely whipped. It the beast was a Royal Stag the punishment was stepped up, a freeman being imprisoned for a year and a serf outlawed for life (any man might kill an outlaw without fear of punishment). Should however the deer die as a result of being coursed, an offending freeman would lose his freedom and a serf his life. Truly the lot of the owner of a greyhound or of this type of dog was a dangerous one, and it became the dog of the aristocrat, the dog of literally, the 'landed' gentry.

The role of the greyhound prior to the Norman Conquest needs to be fully understood. Far from being the specialist coursing dog of today, the greyhound of Anglo-Saxon times would have occupied the role of the present-day lurcher, and may perhaps have had a similar appearance. It would have been predominantly a pot filler, a provider of fresh meat during a winter of salt meat, meat sometimes nearing a state of putrefaction as the winter came to a close. Rabbits would not appear as wild animals (perhaps feral animals would be more accurate) for several hundred years, but hares, both blue and brown abounded in open country. Deer, however, would have been the principal quarry of the Anglo-Saxon greyhound, and both roe and red were abundant in the forests of Britain at that time. Lest the reader imagine that a larger type of greyhound would have been required to take such quarry there seems little evidence to suggest that deerhound-sized greyhounds were more common than the more typical greyhounds seen today. Drawings, carvings and brief descriptions of pre-Norman Conquest greyhounds indicate that dogs smaller than the coursing greyhounds of today were common. Despite the opinion of Pattison, in *Coursing* (Standfast Press,) that lurchers are incapable of taking deer, whippet-sized hounds regularly bring down roe and in those days it would have been the practice to slip a brace or trio of dogs to secure the larger, more powerful red deer—and there is some evidence that the red deer of the Anglo-Saxon forests were larger than the moorland bred red deer of Scotland and Dartmoor. Forest deer would have been better nourished on the regular supplies of food which were more accessible and hence would have grown accordingly. In all probability fox, wildcat, wolf and marten would also have been considered quarry for the greyhound at this time. The greyhound would thus have been the ideal sporting dog for the Anglo-Saxon landowner, but its use would have become more and more restricted after the invasion of the Normans.

The fact that the keeping of greyhounds was now the prerogative of the ruling classes represented no great social revolution throughout the rest of Europe however, though it was something quite new in Britain. Similar systems had been introduced on the continent, particularly in France although many weak Parisian kings were unable to enforce such laws. In Normandy which at times functioned quite independently of the rest of France, quite severe laws had long been implemented and rigorously enforced, but Europe was not alone in the implementation of laws prohibiting commoners the right to keep swift hounds. In Tartary, the successors of Ghengis Khan forbad persons of lower rank keeping hounds and hawks, and in the vicinity of the camp of Ghengis Khan even nobles required special dispensations to be allowed to keep greyhounds, or perhaps dogs of that type might be a more accurate expression. Gibbon in *The Decline and Fall of the Roman Empire* explains the reasons for these regulations quite succinctly. Hunting was regarded as a preparation for war, a type of training for combat, and indeed such ideas persisted even into the early twentieth century where pig sticking in India provided useful experience for the actual work of the light cavalry. Throughout Europe and Asia a warrior class had begun to emerge and it became an elite to which even the most adept members of the peasantry seemed unlikely to aspire. Hence hunting and the training required by this warrior caste as preparation for war was not regarded as a pursuit which was suitable for the peasantry. The greyhound itself was not singled out and regarded as the symbol of the aristocrat, it was simply that the active pursuit of game by any means whatsoever was now the prerogative of the ruling warrior classes. Reference to the types of hawk to be kept by persons of various ranks in Abbess Juliana Berner's *Book of St Albans* indicates that hunting of any sort was the prerogative of men of property and title and undercurrents of this philosophy still prevail to this day amongst many of the sporting aristocracy.

Despite the expansion of the forests under the Normans and Angevin kings and the ravages of the plague during the late fourteenth century the population of Britain rose steadily and the pressures of improved farming methods caused a proportionate decline in wildlife. The wolf became the denizen of the more isolated spots of Britain, the bear had become extinct before the Norman Conquest and the boar was a creature kept in specially made up parks to be hunted only on specific occasions. Despite the preserves established by Norman kings, the population of red deer shrank slowly, although there is some indication that fallow deer were increasing in number and it was said that during the seventeenth century any one county in Britain held more fallow deer than the whole of Europe though few of such deer could be regarded as totally wild animals and most were kept in parks enclosed by pales of wood.

Reclamation of wasteland for pasture and the utilisation of good corn land for sheep and cattle may have given rise to an increase in the population of the brown hare, however, despite the fact that these creatures were afforded little protection under the Forest Laws. In 1269 the notorious Chief Forester, Peter De Neville, was taken to task for keeping a team of greyhounds which were probably used to catch deer. He claimed that the dogs were kept to catch hares, foxes and wildcat, and pleaded that such was his zeal at upholding the game laws of the time that he had imprisoned one Peter of Liddington for two days and nights, binding him in iron chains in a cell so damp that the said Peter paid the jailor two pence for the use of a wooden bench to raise him above the waters in his cell. The Nevilles were notorious reprobates who flouted all law and human decency and did exactly as they pleased. However for exploiting the law and yet staying within its parameters even the Nevilles could not hold a candle to the notorious Hugh, a forester of Staffordshire who fined people at a whim. If a greyhound had been lamed by amputation of the toes of the right foot Hugh fined the owner for not having amputated the toes of the left instead, and should the luckless owner have lawed all feet he was fined for being overzealous as only one foot should be lawed.

It would be incorrect, nevertheless to suppose that every commoner's greyhound was lawed or subject to the Forest Laws, though even the King of Scotland kept unmutilated dogs only by special dispensation. The clergy regulated and governed by the more lenient laws of the church, often cocked a snoot at the foresters (though clergy were certainly subject to arrest for offences in the forest) who were helpless to enforce their regulations against a man of the cloth. Chaucer makes mention of a monk who kept greyhounds as swift as birds to hunt hare and Abbess Juliana Berner was so conversant concerning hounds of the chase that she describes the Greyhound thus in her *Book of St Albans 1486*

> *Headed like a snake*
> *Necked like a drake*
> *Back like a beam*
> *Side like a bream*
> *Footed like a cat*
> *Tail like a rat*

The Abbess clearly ran and hunted unlawed greyhounds and in her rather unpleasant 'seven ages of a greyhound' section of the book she mentions that by its seventh year a greyhound had long outlived its usefulness and should be

THE SIGHT HOUND BREEDS

sent to a tanner who might make use at least of the dog's hide.

There is some difference of opinion concerning the variation of type which some allege to have taken place in the greyhound around the beginning of the sixteenth century. Johannes Caius 1576 in his unlikely and fanciful *British Dogs* suggests that two types were emerging from the common greyhound stock, larger rough-coated dogs better physically equipped to run deer, and smaller smooth-coated dogs favoured by those wishing to take hares, but it is likely that this difference in type had always existed.

It is said that in the eighteenth century Lord Orford finally caused the breeding out of rough coats in greyhounds by introducing bulldog blood into the breed, but this is a ridiculous oversimplification of matters. Orford was an inspired meddler rather than a practising eugenist and experimented widely with the breeding of coursing greyhounds. He was in a very favourable position to conduct his experiments since he was inordinately rich and was known and respected by every owner of suitable stud dogs in the Eastern counties of England. Furthermore he had no regard for convention and was an inveterate eccentric, at one time driving a phaeton drawn by two couples of red deer stags.

Orford kept a standing kennels of over a hundred greyhounds and such was his desire to win that he used all his resources to produce the required greyhounds. He mated small and delicate Italian greyhounds (E G Walsh, *The English Whippet*, considers this type of dog to be simply a diminutive greyhound rather than a distinct breed) to reduce the bulk of his dogs, and according to Taplin used various types of lurcher to improve the hunting prowess of his hounds. His most successful cross, however, seems to have been the mating of pit bulldogs (dogs similar to today's American pit bull terrier) to greyhounds, which gave the cross courage—referred to as 'bottom' by Orford's contemporaries—to persist with the course when discomfort through the exertion caused most dogs to visibly 'wilt'. It is said that infusion of blood introduced a small rose ear, a smooth almost naked coat and possibly brindle colouring to the greyhound, though Orford's most successful hound, Czarina, who ran forty-seven courses and was never beaten, was perhaps a mere one-sixteenth part bulldog and was also Italian greyhound bred—a cross used to improve and give elasticity to the cloddy shape produced by the bulldog hybrid.

However, Orford's bulldog cross probably made little impact on the greyhound as a whole. In Czarina the blood had been much diluted and would be diluted still further by Thornton, a prodigal who continued the bloodline from Czarina via her son, Claret, and the even more famous grandchild, Snowball. Thus the amount of bulldog blood found in the modern greyhound must be infinitesimally small and it might be suggested that if Orford had not performed his experiments in greyhound breeding others might have produced similar improvements by the selective breeding of existing pure-bred greyhounds rather than by outcrossing. The time was at hand for improvement generally in livestock. Better sheep, cattle, horses and pigs had begun to evolve by judicious selection as much as by outcrossing.

Orford's death was as bizarre as his life. He was plagued with some form of insanity—and during his second spell of madness he escaped from his 'keeper' to watch Czarina, his favourite hound, course. Mounted on his piebald pony 'as broad as it was long' he rode to the meet, and as Czarina came up on her hare he became wildly excited and fell from his mount, breaking his neck and dying instantly.

After Orford's death, Colonel Thornton bought Czarina along with other hounds at Tattershalls, purchasing them for a mere thirty to fifty guineas each, a pathetic sum, for as Carson Ritchie in *The History of the British Dog*, comments, a Cumberland-bred greyhound (a very fine type had begun to develop in Cumbria in the late eighteenth century) would fetch 150 guineas. Thornton was not particularly enamoured of these Norfolk-bred dogs, who did not fare well against the local greyhounds, which were used to running over hilly terrain and were more heavily built. In all probability Thornton's greyhound stock was descended from the Wolds-bred dogs of Flixton, Staxton and Folkton, dogs which had been used to hunt down the last remaining English wolves. The hybrid stock from the Yorkshire greyhounds mated to the Norfolk type bred by Orford produced, according to Taplin, the three best greyhounds ever bred in one litter, namely Major, who was sketched by Reinagle, foremost dog artist of the time, Sylvia, an unbeaten bitch, and the famous Snowball who won forty courses against other good-class greyhounds, all of them second generation from Czarina who had whelped their sire Claret in her thirteenth year. Thornton died in 1819 beggared by his passion for the chase and the wild excesses of his later life. Towards his later years he became as eccentric as Orford and at one time flew cormorants to fish and hunted captive deer which had ribbons flowing from their antlers. He died in exile in France to escape his debtors, an embarrassment to his coursing contemporaries.

Judicious selection had produced the greatest coursing hounds in the world, the pedigrees of which had been produced by some of the greatest and most flamboyant eccentrics ever. Thornton's wife had encouraged women to the coursing field, though fox-hunting was to be denied women until the 1850s, and many of the greatest followers of coursing were, and still are, ladies such as Miss Ann Richards of Compton Beauchamp who regularly walked twenty-five miles to a meet. Thus it was that in 1858 the National Coursing Club had been set up, and in 1882 *The Greyhound Stud Book* was commenced which carefully recorded the pedigrees of greyhounds and gave details of their ownership.

However shortly after the death of Thornton there had been a surge of interest in coursing and the quality of competition at these coursing meets had begun to improve dramatically. Orford had founded the Swaffham Club in 1776, and Ashdown Park beloved by Ann Richards was established in 1780. In 1825 Lord Molyneux founded the Altcar Club, where, such was the quality of sportsmanship amongst the members, no official judge was appointed for several years and members acted as umpires for each other. The evolution of the club and the origin of the Waterloo Cup has been dealt with in the chapter entitled *Coursing*, but to omit mention of the event and the description of the coursing meet would be a gross oversight for any writer.

Britain is famous for its sporting fixtures, the Derby, the equally prestigious Greyhound Derby, the Oxford v Cambridge Boat Race and the Grand National all of which have distinctive sporting character, character which foreigners visiting Britain are wont to experience before returning home. However few sporting fixtures can be quite as distinctive as the Waterloo Cup, run near Liverpool early in the year and open to sixty-four of the finest coursing greyhounds in the world. No event can match the meet for its unique atmosphere; *aficionados* of coursing, enthusiasts of greyhound breeding, and curious sightseers congregate as well as those who would gleefully see the sport of coursing brought to an end. The meet has in recent years brought with it a host of people who seem determined to ban coursing, so that nowadays the presence of such bands of outraged, and often outrageous, League Against Cruel Sports supporters has become as much a part of the event as the coursing itself.

The event is unique and has rightly been described as the ultimate trial of a greyhound. Sixty-four dogs come together at Withans for the traditional first-day meet, and such is the thinning out process that by the middle of the third day only two dogs are left to compete for the coveted Waterloo Cup. Speed, stamina and speed again are tested in this arduous three day event and the victor can justly be described as the best coursing greyhound in the world.

The coursing field at Withans is long and fairly narrow and the area abundantly stocked with strong winter hares, a test for any dog for hares driven onto this field by beaters are well aware that they can find safety and sanctuary in the famous rhododendron bushes at the end of the field. The field at Withans is a test of pure speed and coursing style for the dog and on the opening day no slow dog, no matter how game and tenacious it may be, seems to fare well. Courses of longer than forty seconds are rare, and on day one the first thirty-two courses of the Cup and the sixteen second round courses are run. Here also takes place the sixteen first-round courses for The Purse, an event open to all first-round losers. By the end of day one, only sixteen of the fastest coursing dogs in the world are left to compete for the second leg of the meet which is run at Lydiate.

Speed alone is not enough to win at Lydiate. At Withans a course rarely lasts for more than a minute, but at Lydiate the meet is staged on a huge field which stretches as far as the eye can see. Courses last for upwards of ninety seconds, ninety seconds run at a gruelling 30 miles an hour pursuing the world's greatest athlete, the British brown hare. Courses of over three-quarters of a mile are not unknown and the Lydiate day is truly a test of both stamina and speed. No speed merchant which has speed as its only quality can survive such a meet and dogs which have insufficient stamina begin to wilt visibly after the first course at Lydiate. Coursing skill is tested to the utmost, stamina and tenacity are of paramount importance on this ground. Here fast imports from the track, dogs famous for their early pace come to grief and the Lydiate wilt, as one sports commentator describes the 'burn out' of dogs which live by speed alone, is very real indeed.

On the third day when speed and stamina have already been tested to breaking point the final four competitors return to Withans for the last leg of the event and this day also sees the finals of The Purse, and The Plate for second-round losers.

Again not only speed is tested but also constitution for no dog which is not perfectly conditioned can survive to compete in this last taxing day's events, a day made all the more difficult by the effects of the efforts of the two previous days. Four dogs quickly become two and the final course is electric with tension from slippers, owners and spectators alike. It is a miracle of coursing prowess that emerges as overall winner of this most testing of coursing events in greyhound history.

At the time of writing, the price of admission is £5 per day and there are few events which give such value for money. By day three the spectators are oblivious to the shouts of derision from the League Against Cruel Sports, oblivious to the biting chill of the air and the stinging, icy sleet which somehow always manages to put in the moment or so's appearance on the day of the Cup. The meet is difficult to match for pageant, spectacle and above all, a test of a greyhound's constitution. To ban such a spectacle would be almost sacrilegious for it is as much a part of the British way of life as Wimbledon, Epsom, Ascot, or even the right to belong to the League Against Cruel Sports.

The foundation of the *Coursing Stud Book* in 1882 paved the way for rapid improvement in the performance of the coursing greyhound, for the registration of stock and for the keeping of accurate pedigrees which is essential for the eugenic advancement of livestock of any sort.

Lord Lurgan's fabulous greyhound, Master McGrath, sired by Dervock and out of Lady Sarah, was whelped before the foundation of the stud book. The Master was a slightly less than middle-sized dog, black in colour and typical of the standards of his age. Along with Fullerton, McGrath is ranked as one of the greatest greyhounds of all time. The dog was not particularly fashionably bred and was a rank outsider, when as a puppy he was entered for the Waterloo Cup in 1868. He faced a star-studded field including the great Bab-at-the-Bowster and the tenacious Lobelia, the 1867 cup winner. Thus it was surprising that the Master toppled Lobelia in the semi-finals and went on to win the Blue Riband.

When the Master returned to compete again in 1869 it was as a folk hero rather than an outsider. He had won many prizes since his triumph of the previous year and went on to win in a hotly contested final against Bab-at-the-Bowster. In 1870 he attempted a hat trick but was trounced by a finely built bitch, Lady Lyons, and nearly drowned when he toppled into the ice-covered River Alt. It was a disappointment to Lord Lurgan who retired the dog to stud for eight months, but decided to bring the Master out of retirement for one last attempt at the hat trick in 1871. This time McGrath drew Pretender in the final and won handsomely. Dublin went wild the night of the final and even Queen Victoria asked to see the hound. At stud the Master was less than successful and though he mated many bitches, he bred little of worth, let alone anything to better him.

A saying amongst many coursing enthusiasts is that, in the field dogs are favoured, but a good bitch is really difficult to beat. Lobelia and Bed of Stone come instantly to mind to illustrate this fact, but first and foremost Coomasie must be considered. Coomasie, a rather pale fawn bitch, was scarcely bigger than a large track whippet. In 1877 just prior to the founding of the *Stud Book* she won the Cup, scaling in at a mere forty-two pounds, and was a mere two pounds heavier when she toppled Zarel to achieve her second honour. A sense of purpose seemed to characterise this bitch, a single-mindedness seldom found in young greyhounds. Speed she had and early pace, but such qualities are seldom sufficient to win the Cup. Coomasie also seemed to have a tenacity unequalled in her competitors. Classic line breeding, had conspired to produce this fragile-looking bitch and her size and physique should disprove the supposition that only powerful and robust animals can win at Altcar.

Another bitch deserving of a place of honour in the greyhound hall of fame was Miss Glendyne who divided the honours with Bit of Fashion in 1885, but in 1886 won the coveted award outright by overmatching Penelope II. Yet it was to be as a brood that the top class performer, Bit of Fashion, was to achieve fame. Once again rather loose line breeding came into the production of her two famous sons, Troughend, and the most famous greyhound of all time, Fullerton, both sired by the capricious dog Greenstick. Fullerton shared honours with his litter mate, Troughend, at the Barbican in a rather ragged course, but that year he defeated Hershel for the Cup. Unlike Fullerton, Hershel was not only a great dog in the field, but a prepotent sire who not only fathered a great number of top class coursing dogs until late in the 1890s, but features in the tails of the majority of pedigrees of later winners.

Fullerton went from strength to strength to win four Waterloo Cup awards, three outright, one divided, thirty-one out of thirty-three courses. He was a failure at stud and his line passes into the mists of oblivion although his memory certainly lives on. In 1989, to commemorate the centenary of Fullerton's first Cup success, organisers of coursing events staged a special Fullerton exhibition at Altcar with photographs, awards etc to illustrate the brilliant career of this dog.

Whether or not the true value of a greyhound should be assessed by the dog's perfomance in the field or track or by the quality of its progeny is a moot point. Clearly from the point of view of coursing performances at Altcar,

Master McGrath and Fullerton must be classed as the most important greyhounds of their day but neither proved prepotent sires. Dee Rock, winner of the 1935 Cup, proved one of the most influential sires in coursing history. He was fairly loosely bred to FF breeding—Farndon Ferry, Fiery Foe etc—and once mated to suitable bitches he produced a spate of winners including the persistent Dutton Rock, Delightful Devon (1939 W Cup), Dee Flint (1940), Swinging Light (1941 and 1942), String (runner-up 1943). Not only was Dee Rock an important sire, but some of his progeny were equally prepotent so perhaps one can safely include Dee Rock in the list of Stars of the Leash.

A male, being polygamous, has a great deal more chance of producing a spate of champions than a bitch which will seldom whelp more than fifty puppies in her entire life as a brood. A male can produce the gametes for siring this quantity of puppies in a matter of days. Just now and again however a bitch is prepotent enough to produce a large number of top class offspring. Two such bitches come instantly to mind, the first Just Coming who whelped Shortcoming (1921 Cup Winner) and the equally prepotent Latto (1923 Cup Winner), Letisia—a daughter of the Solar Prince son, Bauhus, also gave birth to two cup winners Minnesota Miller 1976, and Minnesota Yank 1977. In both cases the sires were unrelated or only slightly related males. Likewise both bitches are worthy of mention, particularly Just Coming from whom was bred (through Latto) several coursing winners and runners-up until the early 1930s.

Shortly before the beginning of the 1930s, however, events were afoot which were greatly to accelerate the evolution and refinement of the greyhound. Coursing was by its very nature exclusive, and while the public could applaud the merits of Master McGrath or discuss the prowess of the fabulous Fullerton, few people had much interest in the finer points of coursing, or the relative merits of different greyhounds. Fewer still would have seen their idols of the leash at work, for coursing, while it had changed somewhat from the days when no-one of lesser rank than a baronet could join a certain club, was still an esoteric sport and the greyhound must still have appeared as the emblem of those with wealth and property if not with position and influence. The advent of greyhound racing was to change this image of the dog.

It is inaccurate to state that dog racing began in 1926. Dog racing under fairly strict rules had existed in the Black Country and the Industrial North for more than half a century before the advent of organised greyhound racing. However most record books state that it was in 1926 that Britain literally 'went to the dogs' and few crazes caught on more quickly than that of the Track. Within two years of the official commencement of greyhound racing not only did newspapers carry the dog racing results, but people who, prior to 1926, had never seen a greyhound, were discussing the pedigree of great dogs with the knowledge of a Thornton or a Major Topham. Employers stated openly that the morale of the work-force had been undermined by the sport and blamed industrial unrest and absenteeism on its popularity. Such was the impact that the advent of dog racing made in Britain.

In a sport of such popular appeal, a hero of the track was bound to emerge in a matter of years, a dog to engage public interest, an animal whose progress would be followed with the interest hitherto only afforded to a Hyperion. Such a greyhound was Mick the Miller, one whose fame eclipsed that of Master McGrath, Czarina and Fullerton, and who, to the general public, became the embodiment of the racing greyhound. In 1926 Father Brody took an unknown bitch Na Boc Lei, a daughter of the great and reliable Let 'im Out, to the prepotent sire Glorious Event, a great dog at his craft who became an equally great dog at stud. One of the puppies, a brindled male was to become the rather shapeless Mick the Miller, a medium-sized rather bulky dog who tipped the scales at sixty-seven pounds. Mick was not the fastest dog of his age—there were dogs equally as fast as the Miller in the early days of greyhound racing, but he displayed an unique gift of being what was called at the time 'a craftsman of the track'. He became a master at avoiding trouble on the track, of coming off seemingly inevitable collisions at the first bend when six greyhounds converge at top speed. He could increase or decrease speed to avoid impact with another dog. Edwards Clark states that it was Mick's flexibility of style that made him great 'he would not have been half the greyhound he was had he had a single style of running'. Mick seemingly thought out a race, in the same way as a jockey, rather than a horse, must work out a plan of attack on the course he is to run. Mick seldom ran two races using the same style, he used the rails when it was expedient, but also swinging wide at times, losing time perhaps, but avoiding trouble of collision by doing so.

He was no mere tactician however, possessing only track intelligence as his only attribute—Mick was certainly no slouch. Father Brody brought him from Ireland to compete in a heat of the Greyhound Derby, a heat Mick won in record time; he was then sold to N Wilhans for £800, but before the final £2000, a record sum, was paid for him by R H Kempton. Kempton employed Sid Orton to train and condition the dog and in Orton's hands the dog became the legend of the track. No race in which Mick competed was without excitement. In his first Derby, before he had developed his trouble-avoiding technique, a collision at the always-hazardous first bend brought down all the runners except Patatinus and the stewards declared a 'no race'. In the re-run Mick avoided trouble and after the first bend coasted away to victory. He repeated his Derby win again the next year, making no mistakes, staying well clear of trouble and winning convincingly. Like Jack Dempsey during his championship years, Mick's name had only to appear on a list of competitors to guarantee that this would be no run of the mill event.

On his third Derby once again a re-run was ordered and Mick now a shade past his best was unable to rise to the occasion and although he won convincingly on the first disallowed race, he was phased out during the second. At his 'win' in the first race the spectators went wild with excitement. On the re-run a gloom descended on the crowd as they watched the hero of the dog track fade into the also-rans. Newspapers throughout the world carried the news of his victory and his defeat and tears were a common sight after the dazed spectators left the stadium that night, but Mick's career was far from over.

In 1931 when Mick was five years old and by normal standards over the top as a top class race dog, Orton took the unprecedented step of entering the dog in the gruelling 700 yards St Leger. Mick was no newcomer to Wembley but had never run over this distance before, and the spectators, while they expected Mick to try, did not consider him a serious threat to the winner. He slipped through the heats without any indication that his critics were wrong and to everyone's surprise carried off the St Leger in style.

As a stud Mick was little better than merely mediocre, however, and like Master McGrath and Fullerton was not able to breed stock of the same quality as himself. Clearly when Mick was cast the mould was broken but the same could not be said of The Miller's closest rival, Future Cutlet, who features in the tail line of many stars of the leash.

Times and the quality of both training and blood stock have improved dramatically since 1926 and the times of Mick The Miller, Future Cutlet and the flamboyantly extrovert Wild Worley would not be acceptable on the poorest grade flapping tracks in the country today. The improvement in track dogs has resulted in a corresponding improvement in the coursing field (though many would not agree with this statement) for many stars of the track also appear in the pedigrees of many coursing winners. More recently a dichotomy between the coursing greyhound and the track dog has started to appear. It is predicted that two distinct types of greyhound may well develop if coursing survives into the twenty-first century, which, at the time of writing, seems highly unlikely. Fashions too are changing on the race-track; earlier this century sprint races attracted the most attention from spectators, and it came as some surprise to the punters when Mick The Miller was entered in the greyhound marathon the St Leger. These days, longer races attract attention and canine superheroes seem to be emerging from the ranks of long distance winners rather than from the winners of shorter races. This might be explained by the fact that greyhound racing has been the subject of much TV coverage in recent years and commentators have little chance to indulge in oratory during the shorter races. New track heroes such as Cash For Dan and the wildly unpredictable Scurlogue Champ are emerging, but it appears that the popularity of greyhound racing is waning somewhat. Stadiums seem to be closing down, rather than opening and there is a decided fall in the attendance at the remaining venues. Television has been blamed for this, and to a certain extent this is true, for now spectators and *aficionados* of greyhound racing can watch races, important races, free of charge and from the comfort of their own homes. This however cannot totally explain the fall off of spectators at greyhound tracks. There is an unique atmosphere at such tracks, a flavour which cannot be savoured by someone who views the races from the cosy confines of his own home. To imagine that television, no matter how skilful the direction, can conjure up this aura is ridiculous. Greyhound tracks attract characters who are peculiar to greyhound racing, a band of spectators quite unlike that found at a horse-racing meet. Sadly the reason for the decline of attendance at such tracks is due to the fact that the atmosphere at such places no longer holds the fascination for the general public that once it did. Perhaps man himself is changing, perhaps he is becoming more sophisticated and the raw excitement exuded by the denizens of the greyhound tracks is no longer as appealing as it used to be. If this is so it is a pity for no meeting place is quite as cosmopolitan, no place engenders such excitement, and no place offers better value to the student of canine flesh or the observer of humanity. Long may the greyhound tracks survive and long may they attract their fascinating and varied collection of punters and spectators.

Two types of greyhound track exist, the unlicenced tracks and the more carefully regulated registered tracks with their rules as strict as any imposed by any other form of racing. Unlicenced or 'flapping' tracks are great fun, and should never be avoided because of the obvious chicanery practised by some of the participants at such places. In fact the chicanery is part of the attraction of such places. Owners take their hounds, any hounds in fact, (and some lurchers and longdogs have run quite amazing times at flapping tracks) to the tracks sometimes with the intention of the hounds winning a race but often simply to ensure that the hounds run so badly that they get a better price at the next meeting. To slow up a fast dog even a mere split second is no mean feat, but as times improve year by year a mere microsecond is enough to separate winners from also-rans. A dog gorged before a race puts up a perfomance slower than that which it would put up if run on an empty stomach and a dog given a long drink immediately before a race does not usually put up a very good time. Most of the regular owners of flappers have a series of techniques to slow up a fast dog, yet few are successful at speeding up a slower dog though there are drugs which will give the dog 'half a yard' or so and enable an above average dog to score over an even better one.

Ringing or placing a ringer is one of the most popular methods of fooling both bookmakers and other owners alike. Many good dogs have almost identical but inferior lookalikes and substitution of one for the other is not unknown although regular visitors to flapping tracks—and despite the obviously dubious nature of the participants of the art of flapping, the tracks still attract crowds—can often recognise ringers and bet accordingly. Everyone knows dubious practices take place at such tracks and no-one expects the scrupulous honesty to be found at NGRC tracks, but many flapping tracks still attract crowds despite this reputation or possibly even because of it. Often quite outstanding dogs, dogs of open-race standard are run at such places as are oversized whippet greyhound hybrids, those too large for conventional whippet racing, together with a sprinkling of crossbred longdogs and lurchers.

However all greyhounds need to be trained before being run on any sort of tracks, be they NGRC tracks or the less scrupulous flapping tracks, and the art of preparing a dog for a race is a skill in itself, many books having been written on the subject of schooling and training greyhounds for racing but before proceeding further it may be as well to define both schooling and training. Schooling, as the name implies, is simply educating or preparing a dog to accept its introduction to the track scene so that it finds the rather strange world of the race-track familiar and takes the crowd, the noise, the lights and the presence of other dogs in its stride. Ironically the process of training the dog to travel well to and from the track is of vital importance yet it is seldom mentioned in most books concerning dog racing. Most greyhounds are so phlegmatic as to take a car journey in their stride, but youngsters are often desperately sick within a mile or so of the kennels. There is no instant treatment to prevent car sickness and the chances are that the drugs which are usually administered or advised to alleviate the condition are not exactly an aid to the dog running its best time on the track. A far more effective way of preventing carsickness is to take the sapling on frequent car journeys, even a trip to the local shops assists in getting the dog to accept travelling as normal. Most dogs will eventually get over carsickness, but the few that will not, should be taken to a veterinary surgeon, one who specialises in the treatment of racing dogs rather than a canine GP, and the advice of a specialist sought. There are some chemicals which will help in the treatment of carsickness and also will not cause side effects which will slow down a dog's performance on the track or violate the doping regulations. A specialist vet should be consulted about these drugs, should the dog not respond to ordinary travel sickness prevention measures. However never give travel sickness tablets before getting veterinary advice and above all do not proceed with schooling a dog which, having travelled a distance, is still drooling through the effects of travel sickness. To drive to the training area with a dog which is travel sick, to place it in a trap and release it after a mechanical hare, is bad practice and a process which will sour a dog. Dogs should delight in a training session and look forward to a trip to the training area. Schooling should be a hugely exciting game to the track dog. If the precursor to schooling is an unhappy spell in the car, the dog will obtain little pleasure from the exercise and will certainly not perform well on the track.

Many trainers encourage a dog to chase live quarry before schooling the sapling and this is certainly a good way to make a dog keen. The act of giving the youngster a live rabbit, tame or wild, set down before it is certainly not to be recommended. Even if the rabbit has every chance to escape, the practice falls into one of those shadowy grey areas of the law and although the action may not bring down its wrath, it certainly offends human decency. A tame rabbit placed before a dog is unaware of the danger it finds itself in, and hence will not run in earnest. A wild rabbit released off-territory in front of a dog will invariably panic and simply crouch, refusing to move even when the dog noses it. Neither tame nor captive rabbits should be used to encourage a dog to chase. Likewise, tales of releasing live cats before hounds, tales blown out of proportion by the press, one should add, are not only bad for the image of greyhound racing but often bad for the hound pursuing and catching the cat. Eyes are lost all too easily, for a cat retaliates savagely when hurt or frightened. Advocates of this savagery, and there are those unwise enough to follow the practice, do so under the assumption that feral cats (tame cats running wild or wild-bred tame cats) constitute legal quarry. Frankly the hunting of tame or feral cats is emotive and if practised will bring down the not inconsiderable force of public opinion on the perpetrators of such hunting. Furthermore feral cats live in urban or semi-rural areas and are indistinguishable from tame cats which are beloved pets. Schooling greyhounds on cats of any sort is bad practice and should always be avoided, no matter how efficacious some may consider this method of schooling a hound.

In passing it is perhaps appropriate to debunk a popular myth concerning the schooling of a hound with live quarry. In the Midlands it is frequently believed that a dog encouraged to chase by giving it a live rat is cured of fighting on the track. This is a popular fallacy amongst flappers and at one time the writer was plagued by owners of track fighters wishing to remedy the problems of their wards by putting a live wild rat down before their dogs. This is nonsense for in addition to being a barbaric practice it accomplishes precisely nothing. A track fighter is hostile to the presence of another dog moving in front or alongside it and this hostility is neither lessened nor eradicated by giving the dog a live rat, a practice which is not only ludicrous but dangerous. A rat bite, and rats invariably bite when attacked, can introduce a variety of ills to the dog, ills which incidentally are not covered by the ordinary inoculations given by a veterinary surgeon. The trainer must desist from all cruelty and endeavour to keep the name of greyhound racing free from taint.

Many dogs simply do not need to be 'geed up' by entering them on live quarry and will chase a skin or rag bundle with the enthusiasm that a Waterloo Cup winner displays for a hare, and dogs should always be encouraged to chase a lure before being presented with the problem of running from a conventional trap. A dummy run via a bicycle wheel, as are lures at lurcher and terrier racing, is an excellent way to start a greyhound, and it should be pointed out that whippets, which are little different from greyhounds in their attitude and disposition, are often raced successfully without the dog ever having seen live quarry. Dogs should be held gently as the lure jinks and turns until such time as the dummy has been granted sufficient law to justify the dog running. Then, and only then, should the dog be released. At all times the pursuit of the lure should be treated as a wild exciting game and neither owner nor dog should ever regard the exercise as a chore.

Some dogs simply will not chase a lure, however, and no amount of entering to live quarry will encourage the dog to run the dummy hare. In point of fact allowing the dog to run such quarry often makes for an indifferent chaser of the lure, a dog totally puzzled as to why it should pursue a dummy which is obviously neither a rabbit nor a hare! Some non-chasers will occasionally decide to run the dummy but seldom, if ever will display the enthusiasm that is necessary to produce a good track dog. Many of these saplings are best disposed of; they are seldom likely to become top grade performers even if they decide to chase the lure. Saplings of this disposition are often quite intelligent hounds who would be quite acceptable dogs in the hunting or coursing field. Duggan of Carlisle tells a story about one such dog, a track failure with apparently no instinct to chase. To prevent the destruction of the now unwanted dog, Duggan took the greyhound and almost casually introduced it to hare. It entered on its first field outing and appeared very eager to course. Within its first season with Terry Duggan it began to not only chase and catch, but also to run cunning and retrieve hares to hand. Duggan ran the dog for several seasons and it became as adept as a lurcher at pot filling. Similar tales of track reject dogs are legion and many track dogs branded as failures have entered the competitive coursing scene, where, by dint of their early pace they have frequently achieved some success.

It is often suggested that allowing the sapling to watch other dogs chasing the dummy hare or lure engenders

THE SIGHT HOUND BREEDS

interest in chasing, but there is plenty of evidence to suggest that this may be a futile exercise if the end product is intended to be a track winner. A winning dog must pursue the dummy hare with frenzy, with every fibre of its being, oblivious to onlookers and other attractions, and oblivious to the pain barrier through which it must be prepared to crash. The reluctant chaser, the dog which will not instinctively chase any small animal, real or simulated, will seldom generate such enthusiasm even after seeing other dogs chase, though there have been many exceptions to this rule.

Sooner or later hand-slipping a puppy at the clockwork hare will have to give way to teaching a dog to trap or run from the enclosing structure which houses a dog immediately prior to the race. This is usually best done by holding the dog gently in the trap with the front of it open to prevent the dog becoming distressed by the total confinement of the cage. This can be a testing business, for sight hounds have well-developed hearing and will soon begin to react excitedly at the sound of a bell or a mechanical hare, and a greyhound in this state is very difficult to hold in a trap, particularly as some of the most highly strung dogs make the best athletes.

Two or three attempts at holding a dog in an open trap are usually enough for the hound and certainly enough for the handler! The hound can now be placed inside the trap with the front of the device closed shut and should the dog still be distressed by the experience, a few words to it from the owner while it is enclosed in the trap will usually calm any fears it may have.

The majority of the schooling establishments keep an old-school dog or bitch to run alongside the sapling to get it used to competitive running and to encourage it to run the harder to secure the dummy or lure. Greyhounds are, at the risk of my being considered anthropomorphic, highly competitive animals which respond to the challenge of the presence of another dog and are made keener by competition. To a certain extent this competition should always be encouraged.

Some puppies are over competitive, or competitive in a different way, preferring to warn off competition by aggressive behaviour or fighting. In a hunting hound such an animal is termed a jealous worker and if worked individually such dogs often make fine hunters. When fighting manifests itself in the track dog it is a far from desirable quality and is often the ruination of many otherwise fine athletes. Many methods are advised to stop this nuisance; in fact the majority of trainers have secret methods to prevent a track dog attempting to fight rather than race. The number of prime dogs rejected for attempting to fight which are waiting to be found a home by greyhound kennels, indicates that few of these secret methods work! A fighter invariably stays a fighter and the problem usually worsens rather than improves. Frankly there seems to be little evidence to suggest that any method of training can cure a track fighter and once a dog manifests this peculiarity it should be found a pet home—though just as one swallow does not automatically make a summer so one skirmish should not automatically brand a dog as a fighter. However once a dog is obviously antipathetic to its fellow racers it should be rejected as a racing dog and found a home which does not require a track dog disposition. Schools which take on fighters in order to break the hounds of this unfortunate malady invariably fail to correct it. It should be pointed out that in any batch of puppies only a small percentage of the hounds will make satisfactory top grade track dogs. Hounds which will not chase, track fighters (more common among dogs than bitches), hounds which manifest frequent injuries and inferior athletes (the difference between a top grade performer and a failure is a mere split second or so) are all to be found in the same litter as track legends. Indeed greyhound racing is often referred to as the toughest form of stock breeding in the world. It certainly produces an enormous percentage of wastage, hounds which for some reason or other are unsuitable for racing in good company.

Since the advent of hound racing, and it should be mentioned that the diminutive whippet preceded his larger, more powerful relative, the greyhound, as a track dog by half a century, lures or dummies have improved beyond recognition. The early whippet races where dogs were thrown towards a rag, sack or rolled pelt have now given way to dummy hares governed by electronic wizardry which can be accelerated, retarded or stopped by a touch of a button. Roughly speaking two types of hare are run in Britain, the McGee and the Sumner and there are slight variations on these types in use at the time of writing. Most flapping tracks use the Inside Sumner Hare as the model is fairly cheap to install and maintain. Racing under rules, or rather on tracks, which follow the very strict NGRC rules usually involves the use of the Outside Sumner Hare and so dogs must be accustomed to chasing this type of hare. Sumner hares are attached to an arm and move along parallel to but above the ground and it is argued that such a 'hare' fails to look realistic and inspire a dog to chase. This theory does not really hold water when examined closely, for many dogs have never seen live wild quarry and yet make excellent track dogs.

The McGee hare is set in the ground and runs on a rail and does slightly resemble the appearance of live prey. It is said that many Irish dogs schooled and run on McGee hares—common appliances on Irish tracks—run indifferently when allowed to chase the Inside Sumner Hare. It requires only a little patience and time to accustom dogs to either hare, but this difference twixt types of hare should be borne in mind while schooling a puppy. Most greyhounds simply run for the hell of it, regardless of the type of hare and the excitement of the chase, the infectious atmosphere of a stadium and the presence of other dogs will usually allow a dog to adjust to any type of moving lure. A tale will illustrate the point more exactly. One of the most enthusiastic flapping track buffs in Britain must surely be Bob Berks of Staffordshire who is said to know nearly every dog on the Midland flapping dog circuit and to know almost every pedigree by heart. Berks is a font of flapping track stories and one of his favourite tales is the story of how at one track a strong line up of top class dogs were about to run, dogs of open-race standard despite the sleazy track on which they were running. Half-way round the track the mechanism governing the speed of the hare went awry and the hare slowed to a halt. Not one dog paid the slightest notice to the hare and ran on to finish the race. A rare occurrence no doubt, but one which indicates how easily a race dog will usually adjust to the different types of hare used on certain tracks. Even so, to introduce a dog to a new type of hare 'cold'-running it in competition before it has encountered the hare is certainly not good policy if one wishes to win.

Schooling merely gets a dog accustomed to the task of running a hare on the track, training is yet another matter. Training improves or should improve the dog's performance on the track and the difference between the two terms should be well understood by anyone new to track racing who sends a dog to kennels to be schooled rather than trained. A dog returning from schooling is seldom trained in the true sense of the word.

The art of training a greyhound is a complex and often a very secret art, for few trainers are willing to impart the secrets of their success to laymen or competitors. The art of any training, be it birds and dogs for the pit, hounds and horses for the track or pigeons for racing, lies in regularity and routine. Animals and humans develop an inbuilt clock and respond to regularity of rising, exercising, feeding and bedding down for the night. Equally important is that indefinable quality called stockmanship; some trainers have the knack of watching stock at exercise and rest and knowing instinctively whether to add to or subtract from diet or exercise. It is obviously an acquired skill but it is equally truthful to state that whilst some trainers never seem to acquire the skill, some acquire it quickly. There is a saying amongst pig breeders that no time spent watching pigs is time wasted and the saying is even more true concerning greyhounds.

The day should start early for the professional greyhound trainer and 6.00 am is not too soon. When the tea and toast have been eaten it is time to start cleaning the kennels and to examine the bedding and stools for tell-tale signs that all is not well. Examination of faeces is important as is the stench of kennels first thing in the morning and while the dog is out at exercise in its run or paddock. Sloppy stools or very runny droppings indicate that the dog has digestive upsets and no dyspeptic dog will perform well on the track. Iron-hard stools, faeces bonded together with calcareous concretions are simply an indication that the dog is eating a large quantity of bone in its diet. Worm segments wriggling sickeningly in the stools indicate a dose of proprietary worming medicine is called for, though there is a tendency today to ignore anything other than a severe worm infestation. Hancock of Sutton Coldfield, the world's largest lurcher breeder, relates a conversation with his vet who mentioned that research has shown that mice infected with a mild tapeworm infestation seem to thrive better than mice that are free of tapeworms. Modern thinking seems to be that the tapeworm is not so much a parasite but an indication that a state of symbiosis exists between the tapeworm and the host. It is an opinion not shared by all. Tapeworms are sickening parasites and because of their association with fleas (fleas harbour tapeworm eggs) the presence of tapeworms is symptomatic of bad kennel management.

The stench of urine tells the kennel man much about the condition of the dog. Strong-smelling urine is indicative of nephritis and other allied disorders and the dog should be watched while it drinks. Excessive thirst in conjunction with dark and foetid urine usually indicates all is not well. Furthermore, at this time, vomit amongst the straw should be watched for, although this can be a somewhat temporary problem as some dogs seem to regurgitate and re-eat food with regularity.

Walking the hounds invariably follows the early chores and slightly less than an hour's road work or walking on hard surfaces is advised by most trainers for the morning session, though some dogs will need more and others will be content with far less. Curiously the majority of professional trainers seem of the opinion that quite a few owners of flapping track dogs overdo the amount of walking the greyhound requires and roughly one and a half hours a day—forty-five minutes morning and afternoon—seems to be the right amount of walking required by an average greyhound.

In a sport where a microsecond separates the winner from the also-ran, diet is clearly of the utmost importance. There are no hard and fast rules about feeding, no dietary panaceas, for each dog requires individual treatment to give of its best and each trainer has devised special diets to suit his or her wards, for sexual equality passes unnoticed in the world of greyhound training where many women trainers have achieved phenomenal success. In all competitive sports an aura of secrecy surrounds the subject of nutrition. American cock-fighters are often secretive about their 'keep' rations and *Blackwood's* illustrates the irregular training methods of bare-knuckle pugilists with bizarre parodies. The same may be said of greyhound trainers, or at least the greyhound trainers of pre-complete diet days. These days more and more trainers are adopting the scientifically designed complete diets which are not only balanced but sterile—an important quality when one considers the recent publicity knackers' offal and poultry products have received. Each year new improved complete diets appear on the market—scientifically tested diets, a far cry from Milton Seeley's Wonalancet mix, and hence more and more greyhound owners are forsaking the witch brew mixtures which were common between the world wars, though many still employ secret tonics and legally acceptable additives to supplement the diets.

Die-hard trainers still exist, however, some of whom are still amongst the most successful trainers in Britain. Breakfast for a racing greyhound is usually cereal-based and consists of brown bread (or some other carbohydrate-based food) soaked in meat stock with a vitamin supplement and glucose added. Some trainers also add a spoonful or so of dicalcium phosphate to this mixture, as this not only supplies the bone-making elements, but is said to help cement the faeces and reduce the incidence of debilitating bowel looseness. During the halcyon days of greyhound coursing, eggs were an important part of diets. Today there seems to be some antipathy towards feeding them—particularly the yolks—to racing dogs, as they are said to fatten and to produce bowel disorders.

Meat stripped of all fat as the dog approaches racing peak is still considered to be a 'must' by most trainers, even though the instructions for feeding modern expanded diets state that meat is not necessary. Dogs attack raw meat with great relish and about one to two pounds of meat per day seems to constitute the ideal ration for a racing dog. Beef or mutton are considered the best and pork is usually avoided by trainers as it is said to be fattening and conducive to digestive disorders. Meat is usually carefully boned, for while it is unlikely for greyhounds—some of the most constitutionally sound dogs, one should add—to suffer internal damage through ingesting bones, such is the value of some of the trainers' wards that most feeders seem reluctant to take a chance of allowing bone fragments to be present in the meat fed to such hounds.

Few trainers simply pan out the food to their hounds and then leave the greyhounds to eat in privacy. The majority gain much from watching the hounds feed. Voracious eaters are pleasing to watch, but an excellent trencher, which does not maintain its weight or perform well on the track, no matter how well it feeds should arouse concern. Worms or other minor disorders may be the cause of such behaviour, but if, after worming, the dog continues to lose weight it is well to call for professional advice. Poor eaters, usually referred to as 'picky eaters' in greyhound kennels, are not necessarily ailing, though most greyhounds have ravenous appetites, but some excellent track performers have choosy appetites. If this is the case, trainers should pamper their charges and devise a suitable diet for them. Stockmanship, good stockmanship, does not simply involve the feeding of a monotonous diet to each and every hound. Having said that, however, few dogs are as susceptible to change of diet as a racing greyhound. Hancock of Sutton Coldfield remarks that no matter how he tries to keep to the diet of the original kennels from whence he obtains his greyhounds, there is a drop in their physical condition until they adjust to the slight changes of kennel management.

Little is written on the importance of correct racing weight of racing greyhounds but it is an important aspect of training a dog for the race-track. All athletes have ideal competition weights and at risk of once more comparing the art of boxing with the sport of greyhound racing, Cooper in his biography mentions that a pound below or above his ideal weight indicated he was either sluggish or under strength. Similar considerations apply to a track greyhound; once a greyhound is shown to run its best at a certain weight that weight should be maintained, varying not more than an ounce or so from race to race. A serious trainer weighs his dogs regularly, for weight tells a trainer a great deal about his hounds. Rapid weight losses indicate that the dog's metabolism has changed, be it by design or through illness. Likewise a weight gain suggests that a dog is perhaps feeding too well or exercising too little. It is however nearly impossible to simply run much weight off a fat dog unless the dog's diet is adjusted accordingly. A good policy to reduce the weight on an animal inclined to obesity, no matter how it is exercised, is to decrease the carbohydrate content of the diet and to increase the protein. This diet change should be made gradually and the recipient of such a diet given plentiful quantities of water for the breakdown products of an animal's body fats (oxybutyric acids) have a damaging effect on the kidneys of a dog unless the animal is given quantities of water to wash away these impurities.

On the subject of allowing two dogs or more to exercise at liberty there are mixed views. It is admittedly an easy way of giving hounds exercise as a pair of dogs will achieve more exercise allowed to run free for ten or so minutes than can be given by walking the dogs for half and hour or so. However most trainers seem to frown on this method of exercising, as many claim it produces a hound which is keen to play on the track rather than to race wholeheartedly. On the surface of it such a statement appears illogical since once a hare, real or mechanical, appears, most hounds forget any other activity and chase in earnest. Still many successful trainers prefer to exercise dogs by walking or giving individual exercise rather than simply allowing a pair or more of dogs to romp on a field. One reason for not allowing several dogs to exercise together becomes obvious if one watches greyhounds or large hounds frolic together or worse still if the watcher becomes involved in a collision with a speeding greyhound.

Hounds can and do get damaged while playing around a paddock and injury of any sort, if a hound is racing twice a week or three times a fortnight, is decidedly counter-productive, particularly as very few hounds are kept for less than £1000 per year. The majority of trainers seem to dislike allowing their wards to exercise in number.

Once a hound is racing regularly, it requires only walking to keep it fit and should be exercised on a carefully regulated basis, for just as it is possible for a boxer to leave his form in the gym (to reach physical peak in the gym rather than in the ring), so it is possible for a hound to leave its form on the road—to achieve peak while out exercising and to be stale during its performance on the track. Many flapping track trainers are masters at walking greyhounds, and achieve wonders with an hour a day's exercise. Walks around the same streets, along the same roads each day are said not to be as efficacious as brisk strolls in parks, or along different country lanes each day. It is commonly believed amongst the flapping track fraternity that there is an art in walking greyhounds, and this is almost certainly true. Care must always be taken never to overdo even gentle exercise and thus leave the dog stale. Hounds should be ecstatic at the sight of the lead, delighted at the prospect of a walk.

To the casual observer it must appear that dogs are a much better prospect as track athletes than bitches of the same breeding, for a considerably larger number of dogs than bitches appear in the lists of race winners. This phenomenon is however easily explained. Bitches which are approaching season develop a layer of fat around their hearts, and when bitches are in this condition it is unwise to run them or to exercise them strenuously. Hence it is common to withdraw a bitch from strenuous competition for a period before and after she comes into season, and this practice prevents a bitch from being able to compete for certain periods of a year, while a male greyhound is theoretically able to run for 365 days a year. It has been suggested that a process of selection has altered the oestrous cycle of the greyhound to produce a bitch, which while less fecund is capable of running more races because of the infrequency of her seasons. Some bitches do not come into full season until as late as their fourth year and others 'show colour' as infrequently as once every eighteen months. It has been suggested that this infrequency of seasons amongst greyhound bitches may be due to the somewhat questionable practice of injecting bitches with oestrogenic hormones but there is little to suggest that this is true. Hancock of Sutton Coldfield, who breeds from some fifty greyhound bitches each year, makes the observation that, once a greyhound bitch comes into season, is mated and produces a litter, she invariably comes into season once every six months thereafter. It should also be pointed out that many of the larger sight hounds display a tendency to become sexually mature quite late in their lives and there is no reason to suppress season in these breeds. However the comment that male track legends are more common than female greats is a fairly justifiable one, though track records are frequently broken by bitches.

The racing life of a greyhound is a short albeit a sweet one. By the end of its fourth season a track dog is usually past its best. Rescue societies do great work rehousing some of the ageing hounds, even breaking them of their propensity to chase cats and other livestock, so that the hounds adapt more easily to a life with a human family. Many cannot be found a home however and are painlessly destroyed but the life of a greyhound is a happy one. Greyhounds are superbly fed, housed in the best possible conditions and kept at the peak of physical condition to be required to give performances of less than a minute in duration, perhaps twice a week. Few animals enjoy such treatment for such a small effort.

It would be impossible to conclude this chapter without reference to that baffling enigma the exhibition greyhound. Although the show greyhound shares a common origin with the track and coursing greyhound, to find a licenced track winner in the Big Ring at Crufts is now as unlikely as finding a show greyhound winning on the track or on the third day of the Waterloo Cup. Such is the difference that now exists between the types.

The craze for exhibiting dogs, and craze it most certainly is, began in Newcastle in 1859 where the entries were confined to pointers and setters. By 1862, a mere three years later, Judge, a rather elderly red dog, winner of the Waterloo Cup in 1855, was shown at Islington and despite his age was awarded second prize in a strong class. In 1887 Bit of Fashion, dam of the fabulous Fullerton, was exhibited at Newcastle and won first prize in a very large class of exhibits.

Edwards Clarke believes the differentiation between types began in 1890–1895, some thirty or so years before the supposed advent of organised greyhound racing and from that time onwards it no longer became either fashionable or feasible to exhibit top class coursing dogs. A separate type had begun to evolve, a type more aesthetically pleasing to some, but of a different type from the more muscular, bulky stars of the leash. Edwards Clarke believes that the reason for the schism between the types was money, as in the early days of showing such was the enthusiasm the shows engendered, that really showy greyhounds could be sold for a price far in excess of that of good coursing dogs.

However at the risk of contradicting Edwards Clarke the divergence of type was inevitable as soon as the first greyhound set foot amongst the benches. Coursing dogs, dogs heavily fleshed with hard and bulging muscles, are perhaps not as aesthetically pleasing to the eye of the layman as a more symmetrically muscled dog, less shouldery, less well-endowed in the hind legs and with a soft gentle set of 'curves'. Cornwall produced a large number of these dogs and at one time the exhibition greyhound was referred to as the Cornish greyhound in popular parlance. A bigger hound, often approaching 100 pounds in weight as opposed to 65 pounds which was the average weight of a coursing hound or an early track dog, appeared in the show ring and bright gay pieds became very popular. Briskets resembling those of modern whippets became the order of the day, briskets so deep, one should add, that a genuine coursing dog would be at a disadvantage sporting such a shape. Less shouldery animals of greater symmetry, but less powerfully built, became in vogue with judges and long before the advent of the dog tracks the separation of type was complete and irreversible. There can be no question that the exhibition greyhound is a thing of beauty, that its symmetrical lines are wonderful to behold, and that its grace and elegance puts it a star's flight above other dogs. What must be questioned, however, is how the greatest canine athlete created by man, the most perfectly constructed domesticated animal ever, found its way into the show ring!

D. BRIAN PLUMMER

The Whippet

If the deerhound can be claimed to be the most intelligent of sight hounds—and this is a questionable distinction despite the eulogies of sight hound breed books—then the whippet must certainly be classed as the most versatile. Few species of British quarry outmatch it and tales of rat, rabbit, fox, hare and small deer falling prey to this tiny, seemingly fragile hound are too numerous to mention. As a courser and as a hound used for racing, the whippet is second only to the greyhound, but a close second, a very close second indeed. As a versatile, entertaining, easily kept pet, with few vices other than a tendency to steal food and chase cats, qualities which owners of sight hounds must learn to accept, but attempt to control, few breeds of dog are as suitable as the whippet, and fewer still are as undemanding. Constitutionally the breed belies its fragile shape and apparently placid disposition. Traditionally the dog has been the hound of the working class, sharing hardship with plebeian owners who aged and died prematurely in mills, pits, chain works, cottage industries (a hideous misnomer when one considers the Victorian Black Country) or nail makers. Dainty eaters, poor doers, and carriers of congenital weaknesses have long since been eradicated by back yard breeders who were balanced on the razor edge between stark poverty and penury, and the result of this stringent selection has been the production of a greyhound-shaped dog with a constitution to rival that of the toughest lurcher. Defects, mental or physical, are rare in the modern whippet and if the cloth cap image which accompanies the dog has produced such an admirable creature, long may the breed keep this image.

As to the origin of the type, speculation must suffice, for there is little evidence to support or repudiate theories put forward by cynologists of the last hundred or so years. Victorian doggy books tend to suggest that the breed is the result of either a bred-up Italian greyhound or a bred-down greyhound but in all probability these theories are an over-simplification of the origins of the whippet. What is more likely is that the Italian greyhound, the whippet, the greyhound and the now extinct, or possibly mythical, Scottish greyhound, are simply varying sizes of the same breed. Admittedly dog shows and the production of dogs bred to a standard have widened the differences between the breeds, but physically and mentally the types are remarkably similar. A very similar evolutionary pattern has occurred in the development of the descendants of the now extinct and unstandardised St Hubert Hound which has given rise to the pocket beagle, beagle, harrier, foxhound and staghound, each different sizes of the same breed lines, having similar disposition, appearance and hunting style. Walsh and Lowe in their superbly erudite book, *The English Whippet*, support this theory as to the origin of the type. Indeed they take the theory one stage further and state that judicious selection of a whippet gene pool could produce dogs of identical type to both the greyhound, and the smaller toy Italian greyhound. This theory is lent further credence by the fact that the continental Italian greyhound resembles, almost exactly, a small whippet and is classed as a hound rather than a toy breed.

However, despite the similarity of the greyhound and the whippet, it is curious that, when the Roman Camp Club was formed in 1811 to promote the coursing of greyhounds, anyone holding a social rank lower than that of a baronet was disbarred from membership, the modern whippet had already started to evolve in the Industrial North and the darker than dark satanic mills of the Black Country. A schism had certainly developed in the common stock which gave rise to both the whippet and the greyhound.

The popular tale that the whippet's origins are to be found in the terriers of the North of England—the Manchester, the Bedlington etc—is not without substance for the whippet, in addition to its role as a pot filler for sportsmen of the rapidly growing towns of the post-Industrial Revolution of the North, was also required to take part in the rather barbaric and very testing sport of what is quite inaccurately referred to as 'rabbit coursing'. It is of course quite impossible to course rabbits in the manner in which one might course a hare—indeed the very life-style of the coney prevents this. Such coursing consisted of releasing captured wild conies on a stretch of unfamiliar land, allowing them some meagre law and slipping a pair of dogs at the unfortunate quarry. Sixty yards law was considered sufficient and rarely did a course consist of more than 100 yards. Thirty or so rabbits were usually run during an afternoon and therefore a dog competing in such an event was often required to run roughly between two and three miles. Qualities other than speed come into play when a sight hound is required to run this sort of distance. Muscles tire rapidly after a few courses and each subsequent run becomes a tilt at the pain barrier until finally sheer physical agony, cardiac collapse or lungs as fiery as a furnace's bellows, encourage the dog to quit. Frail and fast small greyhounds, for the type had not yet evolved well enough to be categorised as whippets, might succeed well in the early stages of such a contest, but after a few hard and taxing runs such a dog's stamina might be sorely taxed. It is often said that owners of terriers of the fox terrier type won many such contests, but this is highly unlikely if their fellow contestants ran strong fit whippets. What is likely, however, is that just as Orford saw fit to cross in bulldog blood to increase the stamina, bottom and that curious indefinable quality known as 'thrust' of his greyhounds, so the more plebeian though no less eugenically sound industrial workers of the North added fire to their small greyhoundy dogs via the northern working terrier—a common stock which spawned the Dandie Dinmont, the Border, the Bedlington and, to a certain extent, the Lakeland terrier. A digression is now possibly excusable.

The northern working terrier was a doughty small terrier, often as game as a bull terrier, and ideally suitable to add guts to a sight hound gene pool. Many were kept by itinerants on either side of the Scottish-English border and used not only for badger, otter and fox-hunting, but also for a spot of badger baiting and dogfighting. Rawden Lee, in fact, remarks that when an American terrier fancier wrote to England to buy an utterly game terrier, he was sent a fox terrier and a note that, should the buyer not find the dog game enough, he would need to purchase a Bedlington terrier. The northern working terrier was certainly added to sight hound mixes to produce a dog suitable for rabbit coursing. In fact at the turn of the century the majority of itinerant camps sported lurcher types with the linty coats of Bedlington terriers and early whippet races were often won by slape or broken-coated dogs. Indeed Hubbard records that an almost distinct breed, the rough-coated whippet (a dog resembling a diminutive rough-coated galgo) did exist until the late 1920s, a dog which almost certainly carried the genes of the northern working terrier.

The interchange of genes twixt terrier and sight hound was by no means one sided, however, and certainly precipitated the division between the types later to be known as the Bedlington and the Dandie Dinmont terrier. Whippet blood was almost certainly responsible for producing the dichotomy of types between the low squat, almost dachshundy type terrier known as the Dandie Dinmont, and the taller roached-backed type, later to be known as the Bedlington terrier, though as late as 1870 the Earl of Antrim is said to have achieved some notoriety by winning prizes in both Bedlington and Dandie classes with dogs sired by the same sire out of the same dam. Whippet or small greyhound blood facilitated the emergence of the two separate breeds however.

Rabbit coursing was not confined to the North and was a popular sport in the Black Country even after the 1911 Act had brought about its cessation in the rest of Britain. Seldom was a rough-coated whippet fielded around Walsall however, for here the sight hound was, more often than not, mated to bull terrier blood to produce a dog suitable for the sport. At the turn of the century it was often said that the best pit dogs and the best of the rabbit coursing dogs shared a common origin. Early whippet types bred in the Black Country often had prominent eyes which perhaps indicated their bull terrier ancestry.

The interchange of blood was often two way and a couple of contributors to the *Black Country Bugle*—a magazine concerned with Black Country bygones—have remarked that the pale fawn colour of some of the early Kennel Club registered Staffordshire bull terriers was inherited from whippets which appeared in the ancestry of these dogs. However it should be pointed out that there is absolutely no evidence to substantiate this theory, yet the tale is widely believed.

How much bull terrier blood could be absorbed by sight hounds without slowing down the resultant hybrids is the subject of much speculation. Half-bred sight hound bull terrier hybrids would have been suitable for rabbit coursing perhaps and would have had sufficient substance to win at such events. When whippet racing became popular, hybrids of this type would have lacked initial speed to make a 'showing' in 200 yard races and the bull terrier blood would have needed to be very much diluted before a suitable race dog could be produced. Furthermore as the performances and times of racing whippets improved, further crosses with bull terriers would have been counter-productive to the breeding of racing dogs, further pepping up of such dogs being accomplished then as now, by crossing the whippets with small but game coursing greyhounds.

The Black Country has always been a hotbed of whippet racing. Drabble in his *Of Pedigree Unknown* mentions that it was often the case in his native Bloxwich for dogs to be fed meat while the rest of the family fed on less nutritious food. In point of fact many of the children reared in Walsall seldom ate meat with any regularity until they began to work, since it was considered the food of only those engaged in heavy physical exertion.

To return to the subject of rabbit coursing however. The event must certainly have been somewhat less than sporting. A rabbit taken off country and released in front of dogs will seldom run well, if at all, and prefers to crouch in the hope perhaps that its very immobility will not excite its pursuers. Those that run seldom do so less than blindly and present no test for a sporting dog. The all-embracing 1911 Prevention of Cruelty Act, an act which put an end to the infamous rat pits of London and the Midlands, certainly caused the general public to frown on the quasi sport of rabbit coursing and a single curious and convoluted court case involving a careful definition of the term, 'unnecessary cruelty', probably brought an end to rabbit coursing in Britain.

The cessation of rabbit coursing opened the way to whippet racing under rules, and a faster more finely built type of whippet was developed to run in these 200 yard sprints. Hybrids with terrier blood soon became a thing of the past, though matings with greyhounds (small coursing and race dogs) were not unknown from time to time. The rough-coated whippet now became a rarity, and while it is often said that a wiry-coated dog bred at Maltby won races as late as 1950 there is some indication that this dog was perhaps an Irish terrier/ whippet/whippet hybrid rather than a pure-bred broken-coated whippet.

Kennel Club recognition for the breed came in 1890 and in 1899 the Whippet Club was formed. However, unlike the majority of breed clubs, it did not concentrate on the production of exhibition type dogs to the exclusion of other qualities in the breed, for the exhibition dogs of today will race, will still course and will also put up a good show in the field. Perhaps the antiquity of the breed type—dogs of this shape and type had been coursed since probably before the digging of the foundations of Jericho—has much to do with the lack of deterioration of the sporting qualities of the whippet. Indeed it would probably be quite difficult to eradicate these sporting qualities. However, as Walsh and Lowe in *The English Whippet* point out, few breed clubs organise such wide and varied events for their dogs as do the whippet clubs and they seem to scarcely have an event-free weekend throughout the year (shows, racing, coursing). It would seem that the enthusiasm of the club's supporters, as much as the versatility of the breed, has done much to retain the sporting qualities of this remarkable little dog.

As an all round hunting dog the whippet is hard to better and its worth is probably only exceeded by that of a first class purpose-bred working lurcher. Most whippets will start work early and are usually quite dextrous at dealing with first rabbits (a common characteristic of some of the best strains of lurcher is that they are usually slow to pick up their rabbits and frequently trap their first rabbits with their feet). However, dogs intended for work with rabbits should be worked on skins or road casualty corpses to encourage the dog to seize with its mouth rather than trap with its feet. The breed has a history of puppies seizing a rag or towel from the nest onwards and this quality should be capitalised on as much as possible. Within days of a puppy's arrival the youngster should be worked at a moving pelt—a pelt attached to a string and the string jerked to move the pelt across the floor.

Whippets appreciate socialising more than most breeds of sight hound and unlike greyhounds seldom thrive in kennels. Like the majority of such breeds they are seldom aggressive and live amicably with other dogs. The breed adjusts to kennels all too easily and loses much of its sparkle if not allowed to live with human company. Early training is perhaps best conducted indoors where familiar scents and sounds will not distract a dog. In familiar surroundings the dog soon learns to chase a pelt and while its first encounter with a dried rabbit skin may cause some trepidation and even fear, within days of its introduction to furry objects a whippet will usually chase with an almost frantic enthusiasm. The typical rather cautious and slightly nervous disposition of many whippets is deceptive. Many of the dogs which display such qualities are courageous beyond belief when they need to be and face both quarry and cover without qualm. The most shy and timid dogs are often tremendous workers. Terry Ahern of Tamworth tells of a shy bitch, quiet of temperament and docility itself to kennel. When ratting she absorbed punishment from rats with the silent stoicism of a bull terrier and was seldom deterred by savage bites. Jeffery Burrows of Sheffield tells a more impressive tale still concerning the Poppy-bred whippet that he purchased as a puppy in 1954. The bitch was a nervous and timid creature as a babe and presented this quality to her death. In the fields she came to life and not only became a dynamic courser, but adopted the role of a terrier working both fox and badger, staying to her quarry with the tenacity of a good hunt terrier. Her finding ability below ground became almost a legend and but for her deep chest she could have become as good a worker to ground as a hunt terrier man could wish. She tackled fox in the open with great alacrity, but was seldom strong enough to hold one and while she would latch to roe deer she was often dragged badly when she attempted to pin them. Burrows showed her twice and despite the bitch's aesthetic shape she went unplaced. One comment, passed by a lady judge, has a hint of irony about it in the light of the bitch's performance in the field, 'a nicely presented typey bitch, unfortunately she is far too nervous to be suitable for the work the whippet is intended for' (sic). The next day Burrows's bitch stayed two hours to a pair of bottled-up badgers near Buxton. Appearances are obviously deceptive!

Nevertheless, not every whippet displays terrier like qualities—nor can every whippet be expected to behave in such a manner. Should a young terrier fail to make a showing at rat a few months of ageing will usually correct this failing. Not so a whippet (or any sight hound cross for that matter). Some whippets will simply never take rat, no matter how carefully they are entered, and while they may go on to become formidable coursers, renowned rabbit killers and be game as pebbles to foxes, rats are regarded with trepidation by some dogs. Many lurchers display the same reluctance to catch a rat. Hancock of Sutton Coldfield recalls a tale of two outstanding coursing dogs, Celt and Blue, visiting his poultry farm after a very successful coursing season. Hancock's son, Thomas, had snared a rat in a whip wire and released the hapless brute before the two lurchers. Neither dog made a great effort to try to catch it!

Yet some whippets make outstanding ratters, having nose to seek out the quarry and speed and tenacity to deal with it when it bolts. It must be pointed out that rats in number are formidable and often daunt any dog—a tale will suffice to illustrate the point. Frank Buck of Leyburn once owned an iron-hard black Fell terrier called Davey, a nailer to fox, badger and a terror with cats. A local stream had flooded forming an island of refuse and branches and, into this temporary island, rats had decided to burrow. Buck on returning from his stint as part-time terrier man at a local hunt meet, chanced on the haven, and ever the hunter, waded through the brook with Davey and two of Davey's daughters. For a while they dealt out death and destruction to the marooned rat population on the island and the dogs received many bites and tears for their troubles. After two hours of non-stop rat killing the terriers decided they had had enough. Buck states that his terriers' heads were swollen beyond recognition and he decided to leave the remaining rats until another day. This tale should be borne in mind when a whippet is overfaced by a lengthy rat hunt. A single rat is a doughty foe, many rats are testing quarry indeed.

To match a whippet puppy with a mouth full of deciduous teeth—or worse still a half mouth—at rat is asking too much even if the puppy shows an interest in taking the fight to the rat—and many will! A puppy with such teeth is not designed to face such a hard-biting adversary and will often 'jib' after it has been bitten and, once a sensitive puppy decides to quit ratting, it is the Devil's own job to rekindle any interest in it. It also stands to reason that no puppy should be ratted before it has been inoculated as rats are great carriers of the very dangerous leptospirosis — a lethal type of jaundice.

The natural entering method is perhaps the best way of starting a whippet to rat and throwing a whippet into a barrel with a captive rat, allowing the dog to be bitten by it should be avoided at all costs. More dogs are ruined by such entering methods than by any other. Furthermore captive entering contravenes not only the code of sporting behaviour, but can also fall foul of some of the clauses of the 1911 Cruelty to Animals Act—the first act in fact to afford the rat any protection. Natural entering is often a lengthy process, but a very worthwhile method. Simply walk the whippet puppy in places where rats are known to feed during the twilight or dawn hours, and, if the puppy can be accompanied by a seasoned ratting veteran of any breed, so much the better. Such a puppy will be excited by the squeaks and fleeing forms of the rats and will enter to rat gleefully, but only when it is good and ready to do so. Premature entering—and subsequent jibbing or refusing to tackle rats—is therefore avoided. Whippets trained in such a manner are always the better ratters. Seldom are they overfaced by the largest, hardest biting bucks and, when naturally entered, will never display the last minute hesitation which allows many rats to escape. A whippet entered in the barrel—and this method is advocated in most old books on ratting—is fully aware of the pain of a rat bite and often displays last-minute hesitation when ratting. A split second is often enough to allow a rat to escape and top grade ratters should be willing to face shot and shell to secure a catch.

It is foolish to generalise on any subject, and the subject of hunting is no exception. However at the risk of sounding totally unscientific, whippets have almost an inborn affinity for working with ferrets. Seldom is it difficult to break a whippet to ferret and rarely does the dog become a habitual ferret worrier. It is almost as if they recall racial memories of plebeian cloth cap rat hunts when they encounter ferrets and even seasoned ratting whippets break well to ferret although, as in all cases, it is dangerous to generalise so that when breaking a whippet to ferret it is wise to treat even the most sensitive hound as a potential ferret killer. Secure the whippet, even the youngest puppy with a lead and then introduce it to the ferret, taking care not to excite the hound lest the excitement should indicate that the ferret is a creature that the trainer wishes the whippet to attack. Never break two or more puppies simultaneously to ferret. Puppies are very reliant on that often misunderstood quality called 'pack instinct' and the presence of other whelps causes their courage to multiply tenfold. A ferret dies all to readily from a bite, and whippets, despite their frail appearance and narrow elegant skulls, can administer bites which will kill a ferret instantly.

Should a whelp show a tendency to play with ferrets, a sharp tap from the owner will usually stop this. If it shows antipathy and some are bound to, particularly older dogs and seasoned rat hunters, this too can be curbed by a sharp slap, the word 'No' uttered equally sharply and the lead jerked to reinforce the meaning of the command 'No'. A dozen training sessions will usually see the ferret ignored or viewed with suspicion and only when the dog is really familiar with the sight of a ferret should the pair be worked in conjunction with each other. A mistake while ferreting will invariably result in a dead ferret and a dog well on the way to becoming a dyed-in-the-wool ferret worrier. A whippet can usually be fairly easily prevented from attacking its first ferret, but it cannot easily be prevented from killing a second ferret once it has slain its first. A good test of animosity between whippet and ferret is to place a bowl of milk on the floor and allow both to drink simultaneously. Should the whippet not show the slightest regard for the ferret and should both begin to lap the milk oblivious of the other's presence, it is time to hunt both together. If the trainer should experience the slightest doubt about the relationship between dog and ferret it is best to delay hunting them together. On no account should the trainer attempt to break dog to ferret during a hunt. Once its enthusiasm is aroused and its blood is up, even the most gentle whippet may display a terrier-like interest in killing a ferret. Whippets are so easily broken to ferret that it is a shame to allow a dog to 'riot' on ferret. Once one whippet is completely broken to ferret it can be used to work both rat and rabbit in conjunction with ferrets.

Before leaving the subject of ratting, a well-known sporting authority once commented that during rat hunts whippets are prone to be 'stick shy'. So, for that matter, are all dogs; whippets are not excessively so. No dog should be encouraged to work rats while a band of people also pursue them with sticks. The result is inevitable and utterly predictable for dogs are much more steady to rat than are human beings! The most sane and calm man allowed to wield a stick during a rat hunt behaves like a frenzied psychopath in minutes, partly out of excitement, but largely out of excitement tinged with fear, and it is no uncommon sight to see such a man clubbing madly at a rat which a dog is trying to catch. Terriers are often injured or deterred from further ratting by such a misplaced blow and a whippet is not as strongly built as a terrier. To allow any participant to wield a stick during a rat hunt is ill-advised and while an offended human participant soon forgets a word of warning about his behaviour, an injured whippet has a long memory.

Whippets are tailor-made for rabbit hunting and just as the long stride of a greyhound soon outpaces a whippet which coursing hares, few dogs, pure bred or deliberately created lurchers and longdogs, can hold a candle to a whippet as a rabbit-catching dog. It is often claimed by lurcher enthusiasts that a whippet is a 25-yard dog, a dog only capable of giving its best over a short distance. This is certainly true, for racing whippets are certainly at their best over races of 200 yards or less. However, the rabbit is also a short-distance athlete and, during daylight hours, seldom strays more than 50 yards from its warren. To catch such a creature a 28-inch dog is at a decided disadvantage, for it will need time and space to get into its stride and attain maximum speed. For the task of picking up a sprinting rabbit, of ducking around gorse bushes, of the cut and thrust sport of rabbit catching in bad country, a whippet is the ideal type of dog. True, its build is too frail to weather 30 mph collisions with tree stumps and gateposts, but then it should be pointed out that whippets and salukis often come off collisions of this nature relatively unscathed, while larger more powerfully built dogs are often severely injured by these accidents. To appreciate just how tough and seemingly indestructible a whippet is, one has only to watch a pair working rabbits out of a 'seen better days' crumbling drystone wall, springing like chamois from shaky stone to shaky stone, chasing rabbits amongst the thistles and gorse bushes that grow amidst the rubble such as a distintegrating wall tends to produce. Few dogs match a whippet at this type of hunting. Few dogs can survive the hazards of hunting such a place as well as this diminutive sight hound.

Rabbits seldom choose billiard-table flat country in which to live, for the ideal habitat for most rabbits seems to be the waste ground surrounding cultivated fields. If that wasteland is littered with stones and other detritus cleared from the cultivated fields to use as drainage, so much the better. Weeds, particularly woody plants such as brambles and thorns, also flourish in such spots. The result being that marginal land of this nature is not only a haven for rabbits, but is the very devil to hunt, for it offers sanctuary and makes the capture of rabbits very difficult. On land such as this a strongly built whippet comes into its own and perhaps it is expedient at this point to discuss the viability of that most controversial of animals, the whippet lurcher.

Whippet lurchers are created as a result of a belief that a pure-bred whippet is neither tough enough nor game enough to perform the rough hunting required of a rabbiting dog. As this is a totally false premise, it must also be true that the production of whippet lurchers is a fruitless and pointless venture and it now seems necessary to elaborate still further to justify such a comment. At one time Bedlington terriers were mated to whippets to produce rabbiting dogs as it was argued that not only did the Bedlington terrier add guts and blind determination to the hybrid but also would give it a dense linty coat for it was said that whippets were so fine-coated as to be cover-shy and reluctant to venture into autumn nettles. Neither theory is true, at least not today. The show-bred Bedlington is a travesty of the dog of old with little of its former hunting instinct and even less of its much vaunted courage. Many modern whippets are extremely game and will often take on quarry which would outclass the average show-bred Bedlington. Most modern whippets will work; few Bedlingtons are given the chance to do so.

Many whippets also have quite good noses—possibly because of their somewhat mixed mongrelly ancestry—though this is largely conjecture which cannot be supported by factual evidence. Hence there seems little reason to lurcherise whippets to breed a hybrid with a good nose. Furthermore it is worth examining the process of mating collies with whippets to give the hybrid brainpower. Whippets simply do not have the height or frame to bear a collie cross. The hybrid is invariably too cloddy to perform the nip and tuck task of rabbiting in bad places and as a rule a whippet collie is decidedly unsightly.

That the hybridising of a whippet with a Bedlington or collie engenders the cross-bred with a thicker, rougher coat is patently true, but that this coat encourages the hybrid to face cover more readily is not always the case. Coat is quite a minor factor in the make-up of a dog willing to face cover. If a fine-coated dog has the will to do so, it will face cover as fearlessly as the most thick-coated dogs. True, the thin-coated dogs suffer a shade more from the effects of thorns and particularly nettles, but determination, a fiery determination to get to the quarry is far more important than coat. A game fine-coated dog is more likely to face cover than a thicker coated but rather cowardly dog. Many whippets face cover with great courage and though they may smart from the effects of nettles and thorns after a hunt, and spend hours licking and cleaning minor stings and prickles, such is their enthusiasm that such hurts are overlooked.

Thus it appears that the production of a whippet lurcher (a whippet lurcher as opposed to a whippet longdog) is unnecessary. A pure-bred whippet will perform any of the tasks required of a whippet lurcher and usually performs them more speedily and with greater fire. Crossing a whippet with a Bedlington or a collie may produce a more hirsute, and in the case of the Bedlington hybrid, attractive dog (and the appearance of the hybrid is a good selling point), but the hybrid is usually inferior to the pure-bred whippet as a working dog. The subject of the whippet lurcher now covered it is now necessary to return to the subject of the whippet as a hare-catching dog.

The size of the whippet, or rather the lack of it does not allow the hounds to compete on favourable terms with larger more powerful coursing greyhounds or with reachy, long-legged sight hound-bred longdogs, but make no bones about it, whippets can catch hares, particularly hares hunted up and taken underfoot, a practice at which whippets are incredibly adept because of their rapid reaction rate (25-yard dogs!). Furthermore hares seeking to outrun dogs by weaving in and out of farm machinery often come to grief when using this ploy to evade whippets for no sight hound has the ability to turn on a sixpence to match that of a whippet. It would be ludicrous to match these mites against longdogs in the wild and woolly 'best of three' hares contests run on the Fens, or as Walsh put it so succinctly, at a sport of 'disorganised coursing on Salisbury Plains', but nevertheless whippets can and do catch hares.

Graham Welstead, founder of the ill-fated Ferreting Society tells of one such catch made by his own whippet—a tiny satin-coated fragile bitch, favouring the Italian greyhound in physique more than the greyhound-blooded whippets seen at dog tracks. The bitch, too small for show, let alone to compete on the conventional coursing field, once ran, turned and caught a huge 12 pound hare and was tumbled and dragged several yards before Welstead arrived to despatch the catch. The bitch became extremely adept at hunting up hares and taking them underfoot before they managed to attain full flight—unsporting perhaps, but traditionally the whippet, like the lurcher, was bred to be a pot filler more than as a dog required to run to rules. Many whippets develop the very effective technique of scenting a hare in a form and walking up the hare by slow degrees freezing to immobility when the hare's ears became erect, indicating it is ready to run, and resuming the stalk when the hare drops its ears. Courses following such a stalk seldom last more than a few feet, let alone 25 yards, but to watch such a stalk and see the capture of a hare after such a hunt is equally as exciting as the longest, most taxing course—and from the point of view of pot filling, far more productive.

John Laverack, who farmed in Leicester during the 1960s, tells of one whippet he owned—a pedigree unknown specimen but a trier despite lack of papers. 'When we first farmed here we were "snowed" (overstocked) with hares, and, though I've always liked a hare around the place, we had so many the missus couldn't plant a thing in the garden. Silver (a tall lean dog whippet) came to us when Patterson (a farm labourer from Narborough) couldn't find a home for him. Silver saw off all the cats within weeks which didn't endear him to the missus much, but he could knock down hares well. I've never seen better. He learned to flush 'em out of the cabbages and run to the gate ahead of them, catching them as they passed him. I think he must have nailed 20—it was a long time ago—when we up and lost him just before Stowe Fair. Some didis (travelling folk, gypsies, tinkers etc) had come to take away some old iron and saw Silver. I was stupid I suppose, and boasted of his worth—I suppose I exaggerated his "hares". Anyway next day they were gone and so was Silver. I never had another whippet. We like cats around the farm and another Silver would see them off.'

Walsh, author of *Lurchers and Longdogs*—a masterly piece of work by any standards—owned two fine coursing whippets which knocked down hares quite frequently when hunting with Walsh's bobbery pack of terriers, lurchers and whippets. Walsh, a quite modest man, seldom boasts of the exploits of his whippets (in the light of Laverack's tale perhaps it is for the best) but the haul of hares taken by his whippets is formidable. Walsh courses and hunts pedigree, typey stock which wins at both shows and coursing events, competing favourably with the longdog bred whippet greyhound hybrids run at open races.

Neither are foxes beyond the capabilities of whippets though a fox will often severely injure any dog which is not strong enough to despatch a fox quickly. Walsh's own whippet shown in the book *The English Whippet*, as a very badly bitten and unhappy lady after an encounter with a fox, attests to this, but to sell the courage of a good whippet short is indeed a mistake. Ernie Phillips, an electrician from near Tamworth tells the following tale. 'When the whippet racing started near Tamworth I went to Arblaster (a Walsall whippet racer) to get a bitch puppy. Arblaster sent me to a man called Dunn who was winning quite well locally. Dunn had a lot of pied puppies and I ended up buying a bitch which was a bit bossy and a bit bigger than the others. That was a mistake perhaps, for Bossy as we called her, grew too big to run and finished up at 21 inches—almost big enough to run at Hall Green (the local greyhound track) let alone on Sundays (local whippet races). I made a bad buy I suppose, but once we buy a puppy we keep it.

'She caught some rabbits, but this was in the 1960s and rabbits were scarce because of myxi, and she downed quite a few hares around No Man's Land (a hamlet near Tamworth), but she was a demon with foxes, so much so that when I went out with the Atherstone (the local foxhound pack) I'd get a lot of spiteful jibes from the supporters, particularly if I had Bossy on her lead. Bossy would bowl 'em and kill then and would hunt 'em out of cover like a hound. She went to ground after one once in a big badger set near Fazeley, but she was too big to get close to it and besides I didn't have a spade with me to dig to her. I dug a badger with her and two terriers I bought from Sam Towers who had the Post Office in Polesworth at that time. She took some (sustained a beating) from this badger though. She died about three days before my wife and it was a sad week all round, as I really liked Bossy. I went back to see Dunn, but they had torn down most of the street where Dunn lived, and no-one could tell me where he had gone. I suppose Bossy had some greyhound blood far back—that accounted for her size. Still I had terrific value out of the thirty bob (£1.50) I paid for her. Bad on cats though—not that that was a fault as I kept pigeons at that time and she lived below the loft. She'd let pigeons walk between her legs, but she'd kill a cat in seconds. Still all whippets kill cats, don't they!'

Most Kennel Club-registered whippets, however, are not large or powerful enough to kill a fox without help, or without a particularly bloody battle which does little for the whippet and even less for the reputation of field sports. Should a whippet latch onto a fox while working cover or chance on one half asleep in a hedgerow, the dog will need help in despatching the creature. A drawn out protracted battle may appeal to some, but the results of such a conflict can be very damaging to the dog (see *The English Whippet*, Walsh and Lowe). Courage alone is seldom enough to dispose of foxes. Most are seldom killed by the biting power of a dog, but despatched by a dog lifting the fox from the ground, shaking it and thus dislocating the spine. Even over-sized whippets seldom have the necessary height to kill a fox in this manner and thus what should turn out to be a clean neat kill, degenerates to a messy bloody brawl of the sort beloved only by those who wish to see an end to all hunting.

Foxes do not die readily and need a fairly sharp blow to the head to despatch them. A misplaced blow will certainly despatch the whippet and if there is the slightest likelihood of the dog being damaged, the blow should be withheld and the fox allowed to run free. At no time must the dog be endangered. However, most foxes caught by whippets are caught by accident rather than by design for few serious fox coursers employ whippets in their entourage. Thus, seldom is a piece of suitable equipment to despatch a fox close at hand when a whippet chances on a fox and closes with it.

Drabble, in his *Of Pedigree Unknown*, tells of a whippet breeder, Bert Gripton of Shifnal in Shropshire, who regularly worked a whippet-terrier cross to fox and badger—the dog was worked to ground in the manner of a terrier rather than coursed at fox in the way just described. Gripton bred whippets at that time and had an excellent reputation for coursing them at all quarry. His hybrid lurcher type hunt terrier x whippet was an outstanding worker, but this cross breeding is certainly not recommended for producing a working terrier and its success must be attributed, at least in part, to Gripton's uncanny skill at training any breed of terrier to enter to fox or badger. Gripton's success as a whippet enthusiast was probably also due to the strange ability he has to form relationships with his dogs. The Duke of Beaufort is reputed to have said of Gripton that he was capable of entering any dog to fox or badger—and entering them quickly at that.

There are many who do not agree that a whippet should be allowed to course fox, and consider that a fox severely over-matches a whippet. One, a prominent whippet racer and respected judge who has willingly agreed to an interview, but requested anonymity, stated, 'Whenever I hear club members or whippet owners talking about foxes taken by whippets, I cringe. Don't get me wrong, I've dogs which would certainly tackle fox, most of the dogs bred from Rheingold (a famous racing whippet) certainly would if given a chance, but a whippet just isn't strong enough to kill foxes and usually takes a savage beating when it tackles one. A duel between dog and fox isn't good to watch and is messy. Whippets aren't meant to be scarred like a terrier, and using them to catch foxes always turns out to be a messy battle. I'm a member of the BFSS and I'm not against coursing, provided the contest does not over-run the dog or cause injuries to it. I've never owned a dog which could kill a fox cleanly and I've bred whippets for near on 30 years. I've seen lurchers, big, powerful, rough-coated dogs, make a meal, of killing fox and so what chance has a whippet? The only whippet I've seen to kill fox cleanly was sired by a son of Rheingold out of a track-bred greyhound bitch. One of the puppies grew too big to race and I called it Biggun. I sold it on—a pity as it would race well enough—to a boy called Caldwell from Doncaster, and he used it to catch rabbits that his terriers bolted. Biggun could kill fox, though he was badly gashed after each fox hunt. He's not a good advert for the dogs I breed and the League Against Cruel Sports gets a lot of ammunition from seeing dogs as battered as Biggun. If the boy had said he was going to catch foxes with Biggun I wouldn't have sold him, and I'd have sooner given him away as a pet. I hate cruelty to any of my dogs and I don't think even a large whippet should be made to catch fox.'

It is often said that the whippet is the only breed of dog that can be called in from playing with children or sleeping at the side of a fire, entered in a coursing event and win, and while there are certainly whippets which can claim to have performed this feat from time to time, to suggest that this is the ideal training for a competitive coursing dog of any sort is both ludicrous and inaccurate.

Whippets, possibly because of their light frame and tendency to avoid laying on fat are easily conditioned or perhaps more easily conditioned than the heavier, more muscular greyhound, would be a more accurate statement. However the conditioning of any creature, be it a human athlete, pigeon, horse or dog, is very much an art, and some no matter how hard they try are destined never to master that art. No two animals respond identically to the same conditioning programme, so the programme must be tailored to suit the individual. However some basic rules regarding training can be offered.

Diet has been considered important in the conditioning of sporting dogs since an interest in competitive coursing began, and while it is a general, if rather flexible dictum that it takes roughly six weeks to turn a relatively fit dog into a super-fit, competitive coursing dog, it should be pointed out from the start that there is no method of turning a badly nourished dog into a successful coursing dog, no matter how scientific the conditioning process one uses. Conditioning starts while the puppy is still in an embryonic state, so to speak, for a badly nourished bitch will never produce a suitable whelp for coursing. Puppies intended for competitive coursing must be fed a suitable varied diet and fed ample, but not excessive amounts of food, to allow them to grow properly. There are no short cuts to puppy rearing, no tips to instantly produce a top rate competitor.

General opinion seems to be that some six weeks before a dog is due to compete is the right time to take a hard critical look at the diet of a potential coursing dog. From that time onwards the feeding of such a dog becomes an art. Carbohydrate must be reduced gradually, low protein dog meal giving way to higher protein feed, and starchy food being replaced by meat. It is argued that while carbohydrate is an excellent source of instant energy, the energy released by the destruction of protein molecules is more suitable to fuel a lengthy testing run at a hare. The amount of energy expended during such a course is astounding and greyhounds will often lose a few pounds in weight during a coursing meet. The weight loss in whippets is of course correspondingly much lower, partly due to the difference in physical shape, and partly due to the different styles of coursing adopted by a whippet.

Conditioning any dog for an athletic event should start with cleansing the dog of external and internal parasites, for no animal can achieve its peak of physical fitness while its body is the habitat of worms, fleas, lice and ticks. At the time of writing there is a tendency to regard tapeworms as harmless passengers hanging in the gut of the dog, veterinary research in America having seemingly revealed that mice tend to grow more quickly if they harbour tapeworms. Be that as it may. Few mice are required to run a hare at 30 mph over country somewhat less than ideal. Regardless of current veterinary fashion, dogs intended to start a conditioning programme prior to competitive coursing should be cleansed of parasites some six weeks before serious training commences. A dip in a solution of gamma benzene hexachloride will usually clear all external parasites including mange mites which plague both whippets and greyhounds alike. Likewise an all-round worming treatment should be given to cleanse the hound of tapeworms and roundworms and the treatment repeated two weeks after the initial worming. The dog thus cleansed of parasites is ready to start the lengthy process of conditioning prior to coursing.

Despite the notion that a whippet can be taken up from the fireside and compete successfully on the coursing field, a whippet needs much exercise to enable it to compete successfully. Walsh, who despite his modest demeanour, must be considered one of the authorities on coursing whippets, suggests that the very best form of exercise for conditioning is for the whippet to be exercised with horses, the hound being allowed to walk or canter behind saddle horses for a few miles each day. *Stonehenge* (J H Walsh) suggests marathon 20-mile stints of exercise behind horses for coursing greyhounds approaching physical peak, though this seems excessive for a hound with the frame of a whippet (or for modern greyhounds for that matter). It is possible to over exercise and boxers are often careful about too much road work, as it tends to produce fighters who may 'leave their form in the gym'. There are, however, no hard and fast rules regarding the amount of exercise needed to condition a whippet and a competent trainer will play the subject of exercising entirely 'by ear'.

Road work—exercising a dog on a hard surface, at a walking pace, one must stress, for running a dog over such a surface is a recipe for gashed stops, torn pads and knocked-up toes—is important. Once again just how much road work is necessary is a moot point, for just as a boxer can easily leave his form in the gym, a whippet can be over-walked, over-exercised and thus run 'slack' not give of its best, and run listlessly on the day of the event. What is important, however, is that exercise must be increased gradually, starting out with a leisurely walk around the block, some four or five weeks before the start of the coursing season, gradually increasing the exercise to a brisk two-mile walk along well-surfaced roads as the coursing season starts.

While it is true that whippets, a little like lurchers, rather than longdogs, are easier to keep fit than greyhounds, the peak of fitness required for a dog to put up a good show against a strong hare, running alongside well-matched competition is not easily attained. Once again the reader must be reminded of the athletic prowess of the brown hare. He must disregard, totally disregard the tales of many hares caught by lurcher enthusiasts, the majority of whom seem to be sorely afflicted with chronic Münchausen's syndrome. Hares taken by such people, are 'slipped underfoot', run without law, without sufficient start to allow the hare sufficient momentum to offer a fair course. Others may be young hares killed when scarcely more than nestling leverets, hares with leveret fat—the adipose tissue which will eventually act as a food store for hares living out in hard conditions—bad frost, deep snow etc. Hares, young hares, yearlings at least will usually have reserves of internal fat as winter starts to arrive and the majority of giant hares, around 12 pounds in weight, are usually caught straight after harvest time—a time when hares are not only at their heaviest, but at their 'softest' (most easily taken). Conventional coursing under rules makes allowance for this and hence even early meets are conducted in late autumn when the hares have had a chance to develop wind and limb, to learn the country where they live, to understand every patch of cover, every undulation in the land, every place where they can achieve an advantage over the pursuing dog—every gap in the hedge, every weakness in the drystone walls which abound in Cotswold coursing country where many whippet coursing events are run. These are the hares the whippet courser, coursing under rules, will be required to run and run under pre-ordained laws, not slipped underfoot, hunted up in the manner of a lurcher or catching on the lamp—for often the dog, which would put up a ludicrous show against a hare run under Coursing Club rules, will bring down strong hares while lamping. Reader, close your ears to the absurd boasts heard at lurcher club shows. They are exaggerated tales. A more honest evaluation of such tales is that they are blatant lies. No whippet below peak, let alone below par will put up a show against a hare given fair law, though many are so courageous that they career through the pain barrier damaging heart, diaphragm, lungs and muscles, but seldom spirit, for just as a hare is underrated as nature's greatest mammalian athlete, so is the courage and determination of the diminutive whippet, so often sold short by those who have little knowledge of them.

In a course this courage, this relentless determination, is often the downfall of the tiny whippet. Many of the best coursing dogs will run themselves literally to death. It is often said of collie-bred lurchers, that the hybrid does not 'try'—in other words it will not continue with the course after the agony with the muscles, the fiery burning of the lungs tells it to stop. A whippet rarely, if ever, has this type of criticism levelled at it—at least not by anyone who has owned, or even watched the performance of a good coursing whippet. This quality should always be remembered when the owner of a whippet is invited to a spontaneously organised coursing meet when the dog is unprepared for such courses. A conscientious trainer of professional boxers avoids using any of his fighters as last minute unprepared substitutes, for the results of such ill-matched contests are not only predictable, but unpleasant. Likewise the owner of a coursing whippet should only field his ward at a legitimate coursing meet when it is at its peak and has been prepared for such an arduous and testing event.

A whippet coursing event is often viewed with some amusement by the more pseudo-masculine lurcher owners. Many of the whippet owners are women, and many of the competitive whippets are rugged before and after a course. This is by no means an affectation, nor is it a sign that dog is effete or nesh in any way. A whippet, because of its ability to get into top gear, or full stride, faster than any other breed of dog, sighthound or otherwise, burns up the carbohydrates within its body at a staggering rate and loses a few ounces of weight even during the brief 200-yards dash at a whippet race and also generates much heat. Rugging after a race is essential to prevent chilling, for whippets are not only thin-coated but thin-skinned and thus chill easily.

Rugging before a race or course is often considered excellent practice and frankly is simply good commonsense. An athlete run cold, without previous warming up, is more prone to injury than one previously allowed to limber up. Rugging serves to conserve body heat and facilitates the warming-up process. For this reason sprinters limber up before a race and boxers shadow box minutes before a contest. Whippets, like all other athletes, do not perform well prior to the body being warmed up, and thus rugging a dog before a race or course is conducive to a better performance.

With regard to the fact that many of the contestants at coursing meets are women—and this arouses much mirth among lurcher enthusiasts for some reason or other—it should be pointed out that many of the most successful whippet and greyhound coursers and trainers are also women and thus sexist comments are not only uncalled for and unnecessary, but in the light of whippet coursing results (many of the races are won by dogs trained by women), rather pointless.

So to the actual coursing of whippets under rules. Coursing under rules involving the use of any sight hound, be they whippet, greyhound, deerhound, saluki or even the surprisingly successful events involving the larger more cumbersome Irish wolfhound is roughly similar, though the rules for the coursing meets are adapted to suit the peculiarities of breed and the terrain over which the coursing is to be run. For example the combined saluki/deerhound coursing meets, run at venues near Inverness, are run over peat hag and heather at blue rather than brown hare, for this type of country is the natural terrain of the blue hare. Hence slipping must certainly be adjusted to the terrain and judging the course is the prerogative of a judge who is not mounted, but equipped with binoculars.

Such country would not only be taxing to the frame of the whippet, (though certainly not to the spirit of the dog) but also destructive to a finely built sight hound such as a whippet. Sagar, runner up in the 1979 Grieve Coursing Cup (salukis) remarked that in ordinary circumstances he would not allow his dogs to exercise under such conditions let alone compete. Hence whippet coursing is conducted in more favourable countryside—over preferably flat or undulating plains and the quarry is the brown rather than the blue hare.

A slipper, and most clubs insist that a slipper is not only trained, but given quite an arduous probationary period, so as to be able to conduct himself at all times in a way which is not prejudicial to the good name of the sport, holds two dogs coupled on slips. He or she stands with those dogs in an advantageous position, ready to slip the hounds simultaneously as the hares are driven towards them, or in the case of whippet coursing, the hares are walked up, and once the hare has been given agreed law the hounds are slipped. A hare sprung underfoot is never, or hardly ever coursed, and should it be, this is always a result of accident and the subsequent course frequently declared null and void. Truly the apprenticeship the slipper must endure to become acquainted with the rules, to be able to accurately assess distance (too long a slip is perhaps preferable to slipping underfoot, for the object of coursing under rules is to test the mettle of two coursing dogs rather than to secure a hare, and the law granted a hare under NWCC rules is not less than 35 yards) is a much-needed one. The morality of coursing under rules is often debated and is certainly questionable, as is the hunting of any living creature, but the fairness of such events, and the punctilious adherence to the rules by competitors is beyond both question and reproach.

The catch or kill, and whippets certainly either kill a hare swiftly, or else the creature is certainly quickly despatched by attendant stewards, should the kill be messy or protracted, is not the sole object of the course, nor is the dog that kills the hare necessarily the winner of the event. Points are awarded to the dog which does the most work to secure the capture of the hare, not necessarily to the dog which achieves the catch. Herein, however, 'lies a puzzlement', whippets must vie with deerhounds as the most intelligent of sight hounds and soon realise that it is often expedient to allow the other hound to work hard at turning the hare, and only then to put in, what in lurcher and longdog terms is termed 'the snatch', and thus secure the catch. Such an experienced dog may well be the most excellent of pot fillers (the true purpose of the whippet), but will be of little use at earning points at a meet, coursing under rules. This action of allowing the other dog to do most of the work at turning the hare, and then to benefit from the effort of the other animal, is known in less conventional coursing circles as 'running cunning' and is a quality that is prized above all others amongst owners of longdogs and lurchers. Indeed it is a quality that is deliberately sought and bred in if possible, but it is not a quality desired in any animal coursing under rules. Sadly it is all too easily learned by the coursing whippet, whose only desire is to bring down the hare, for the dog has little knowledge and certainly no appreciation of the rules. Sooner or later all whippets learn to run cunning and possibly do not exert themselves as much as they might during a course, but nevertheless succeed in catching the hare that has been turned by another dog. Therefore an enigma presents itself. Should a dog be allowed to run hares daily as does the longdog which is bred and trained to actually catch hares rather than course them under rules? More to the point, just how much experience of hares should a dog required to course under rules be given? To the uninitiated the statement must seem as ridiculous as for a exponent of the fencing foils to be disqualified as soon as he learns to penetrate his opponent's guard and obtain a 'touch' or for a boxer who becomes no longer suitable for the ring when he learns to perfect the knock-out. However these statements if they do little else confirm the fact that the purpose of coursing under rules is to test the mettle of the hounds, and simply not just to kill hares. It should be pointed out in passing that whippets which have learned to run cunning and are thus no longer of use as competitive coursing dogs (coursing under rules one must emphasise) become the most dextrous of hare-catching dogs, particularly if the hound is allowed to hunt up its hare and take it underfoot—giving it little law. Such conditions are ideal for the experienced coursing whippet with its instant turn of speed, its ability to galvanise into action quickly, and its gift of anticipating the twisting, turning flight of the hare. Brian Vesey Fitzgerald, an astute critic of field sports and the fate of the animals involved in these sports, was once said to have stated, 'A cast (finished or over the top) coursing greyhound becomes in need of a good home—and a track dog seldom able to find one.' The Whippet Coursing Club was formed in 1962, a time when the rabbit was less than numerous because of the ravages of myxomatosis and hares became very numerous to fill the void left by the decreasing rabbit population. A cast coursing whippet, one which had learned to run cunning would have been prized greatly by hare poachers during the lean, rabbitless years of the 1960s, but then the whippet has been accurately described as the most versatile of sight hounds.

Further proof of the versatility of the whippet is the fact that owners of both coursing and show whippets can also race them. After the 1911 Cruelty to Animals Act brought a well-deserved end to rabbit coursing, the popularity of the whippet may have experienced a temporary lull, but there was a rapid revival in whippet keeping after the start of greyhound racing in 1926, when as was said in the music halls, the whole country 'went to the dogs'. Whippet racing, however pre-dated greyhound racing by over 50 years (see Freeman Lloyd, *Whippet and Race Dog*) though for some reason whippet races have never been as well-attended, nor as well-organised as greyhound races. Neither are the prizes for the winning hound as magnificent, nor is the prestige of owning a whippet racing champion as great, which is curious for the whippet races, though of shorter duration than greyhound races, are every bit as spectacular and as exciting.

The Black Country was, and still is, a hotbed of whippet racing and it was said that during the 1930s, a period of depression which was extremely destructive to the leather, chain and nail-making industries of Walsall and the adjacent districts, that 'there was a whippet or a bull terrier in every other house—and even if kids weren't fed right, dogs were'. Quite typey whippets were kept by the racers of the Black Country during these days, dogs which had smooth tight coats (possibly, just possibly, due to bull terrier ancestry, for as has been mentioned, many experts on Black Country culture believe the pale fawn pit dogs derived their colour from whippet ancestry—though is has to be stressed there is absolutely no proof that this is true). Seldom were 'shake' or broken-coated whippets run at the races in the Black Country, though such dogs were by no means uncommon around Sheffield, Doncaster and Newcastle Upon Tyne.

A whippet revival occured in Britain shortly after World War II, and once again there was a renewed interest in whippet racing, running the dogs to the traditional rags shaken by the owners at the end of a 200-yard straight track. Reports in the *Black Country Bugle*—a magazine devoted in part to canine-orientated sports in the country around Walsall—suggests that the early post-war dog racers were dissatisfied with their wards. Perhaps as man grows older the summers are never as hot, nor the winters as white, or perhaps the strains of whippet which survived World War II (and it would make an interesting survey to ascertain how many kennels of all breeds were disbanded during the war) were largely show-bred stock, which showed little inclination to run at the rag with the fire of their pre-war equivalents. Drabble, in his *Of Pedigree Unknown*, believes terriers of certain sizes were added to pep up the mix, and some of the contributors to the *Bugle* have suggested Bedlington terriers were crossed into the strains of show whippet to revitalise them. However, there seems little evidence to indicate that this was done and perhaps less to indicate that this cross would have been efficacious at adding fire to the hybrid whippets. There is, however, considerable evidence to suggest that the Bedlington terrier of the early 1950s was a far cry from the utterly game animal, the death or glory, looks of a lamb, courage of a lion, type terrier, described by Rawden Lee in 1893. Newcombe, breeder of the Rillington strain of Bedlington, notes that by the mid-1950s he had observed that there was a decline in the working instinct of the breed, and Margaret Williamson believes poodle blood had been added to improve the coat of the Bedlington terrier.

What certainly was added to the show strain of whippet was the blood of small racing and coursing greyhounds and at one time it looked as though an utterly separate racing whippet—less roached-backed and lacking typical whippet conformation—was developing—a type quite distinct from that of the benched whippets of the day. Clubs formed to race these 'unregistered whippets' ran their hounds to different rules. Some insisted that only dogs under 20 inches at the shoulder (the same height criterion as applied to coursing whippets running under NWCC rules) should compete. Other clubs allowed any dog to race regardless of its height and appearance if the dog weighed in at less than 30 pounds in weight—and some amazingly tall animals were run at under 30 pounds during the early 1960s. Around Doncaster there was an amazing demand for what were known locally as bred-down grews—greyhound type dogs, reduced in size by mating to show-bred or race-bred whippets. Many of the *Exchange and Mart* advertisements of the early 1960s were for these bred-down grews which found a ready market as hare-coursing longdogs, having the speed of greyhounds and the sharp 'electric' reaction of the whippet. However good these hybrids were at winning Sunday afternoon races, or the larger ones at coursing hares, the loss of shape of typical whippet type caused some concern among whippet enthusiasts.

Thus in 1967 The British Whippet Racing Association, BWRA, was formed to regulate the racing of whippets in Britain and to bring some semblance of conformity to the amazing variation of rules twixt various clubs. The BWRA certainly did not restrict the continued introduction of greyhound blood into the racing whippet stock as many writers have implied, and indeed various whippet racing magazines display pedigrees of winning dogs which translated into layman's terms indicate that the stock is scarcely eligible for Kennel Club-registration.

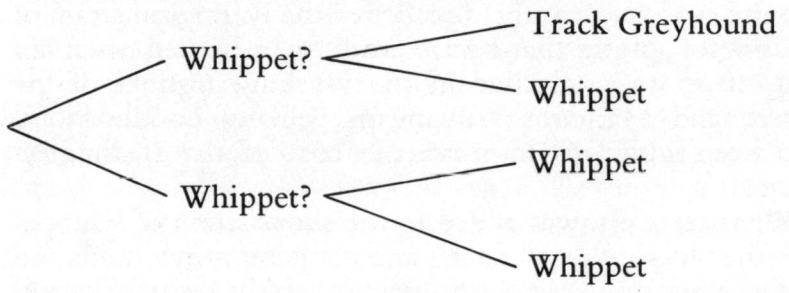

```
                    ┌─── Track Greyhound
        Whippet? ───┤
       ╱            └─── Whippet
      ╱
      ╲
       ╲            ┌─── Whippet
        Whippet? ───┤
                    └─── Whippet
```

The dog so bred is no worse for its somewhat mixed ancestry, far from it in fact, for many are capable of not only winning at conventional BWRA meets, but of competing quite favourably against flapping track greyhounds at sprint races.

However, such crosses are literally ruinous to the type and produce litters which are very variable indeed size-wise. Many litters sired by, and bred out of BWRA champions, have produced the odd puppy or so which grew into an adult quite indistinguishable from a track greyhound. Yet in the same litter were found diminutive mites which would have been easily recognised as whippets.

In 1968 concern amongst the owners of Kennel Club-registered whippets prompted the foundation of the Whippet Club Racing Association, WCRA, to promote and control the racing of pure-bred Kennel Club-registered whippets. The aims of the club were admirable and designed to produce not only a typey, classy bench dog, but also a bench-bred dog which would fulfil the functions for which it was originally created. Had the bench-bred greyhound been evolved through the formation of a similar club, the divisions between show, track and coursing greyhounds would never have occurred. Alas, the members of the greyhound breed club displayed no such admirable foresight and thus each year the gap between racing and show greyhounds widens still further. Sufficient to say that the racing of both pedigree whippets and the 'bred-down grews' is a popular sport today—though never quite as popular as it was in Britain a century ago.

Prior to greyhound racing, whippet racing attracted large crowds. Even though the sport was never as free from chicanery as are modern-day licenced greyhound track events, and the racing was a relatively informal affair, the purses for the winners were often relatively weighty and the sport was taken very seriously. Unlike its larger relative the greyhound, the tiny racing whippet of a century ago was seldom reared in large kennels and most occupied the role as house dog, pet and weekend racer. Few racers fielded large kennels of racing whippets, for the financial reward incurred by winning races was never great enough to merit the upkeep of such kennels, and most of the races were very localised affairs. The late Tom Grundy of Walsall recalled that Black Country whippet racers seldom travelled far to race whippets in the days prior to World War I, as not only was the journey between towns long and tiring by public transport, but a degree of hostility often existed between the whippet racers of various towns. Racers from Walsall ventured with some trepidation into Birmingham to run their dogs, even though only 12 miles separates Walsall and Birmingham.

Puppies were taken from the nest as young as the breeder would allow it—but seldom before the breeder could ascertain which puppy was worth keeping back for himself. Prices of these puppies at the turn of the century varied from the price of a pint—2d, to a guinea paid for a puppy from Star (a famous racing bitch bred in Leamore around 1906–1908)—a bitch so famous that when she retired from racing, a Mr Ross travelled from Chiswick to buy a puppy and paid a guinea for his first choice, a price not far off a week's wages for a Black Country nail maker at the turn of the century.

Training usually began before weaning and the customary Black Country method of starting a whippet's enthusiasm for running the rag, was to allow the children of the family to tease a litter of whippet puppies with an old discarded woollen sock as soon as the whelps developed an inclination to chase (at about five and a half weeks of age a sight hound manifests these interests). Later the sock would have been tied to a piece of string and the puppy encouraged to play 'cat and mouse' with the fleeing sock. A skilled trainer, one who knew exactly when to stop a game before interest began to wane could generate a condition near to hysteria in the pups at the sight of a rag or old sock being shown. It was excellent training indeed, for not only did the practice encourage the chasing instinct of the whelp, but it also socialised the whippet so that it displayed less fear of people and noise when it was eventually called on to race in public—and such races were seldom conducted in silence, silence never having been the rule for any Black Country gathering!

When the litter was separated training began in earnest and the whelp received individual attention. Seldom were more than two of the litter run on, for times were hard, money scarce and the proper rearing of a whelp expensive. Grundy recalls that mutton seemed the most favoured meat for both family and whippet and this across the board nourishment was obtained by boiling a skinned sheep's head until flesh parted from bone and feeding both family and whippet on broth, boiled vegetables and bread soaked in the meat juices. It was once said that the majority of the children of Lower Rushall Street, Walsall—a hard and tough district in which to live, had been reared on a diet of sheep's heads and bread, and that on Saturday night following pay-day, the area near the Arboretum smelled like a crematorium as a result of the burning of sheep's skulls which had been stripped of meat and brain. Whippets and all sight hounds rear well on such a diet—and so perhaps do children, for Walsall has always had the reputation of producing some of the world's best 'heavy industry' workers!

A good rule was to never over-exercise a whelp too young, but to allow heart and lungs to develop before running muscles. Gentle exercising was the rule until the whelp attained maturity. Light exercise was coupled with a high-protein, high-bone diet. When the dog was deemed to be ready, training began in earnest—and in earnest seems to be the correct expression. It was said that a whippet addict—and whippet racing seems to be almost addictive—had little time for any other activity, so time-consuming was the process of getting whippets ready for a race. Free running—allowing the dog to exercise off the leash—was considered counter-productive to the production of a well-conditioned whippet. Exercise was conducted on the leash and the dog allowed to pull, and pull mightily, to develop the propulsion muscles of the hind legs. Whippets approaching racing peak often pulled so hard as to appear to be walking on their hind legs and the muscles of the hind legs often seemed to be bursting through the thin skin. To facilitate this mode of exercise whippets wore a wide collar to prevent asphyxiation and bruising of the throat as the diminutive dogs pulled their owners along during the exercise period. (Such collars called bull collars were once specially made in the leather districts of Walsall and sold to America for the training of pit bull terriers, which were similarly encouraged to pull hard on the leash to develop the 'fighting' hind leg muscles.) These exercise periods, seldom more than an hour in duration, were strenuous to dogs and man alike. A Black Country cartoon of the early 1930s shows a doctor examining a patient who has a right arm developed to Charles Atlas-type proportions while the other seems wasted and withered. The prognosis of the doctor—'Give up whippet training for a week lad, or else change 'ands'.

During this training programme a carefully regulated diet was absolutely essential and once again a high-protein diet was the order of the day. Breasts of mutton, of the cheapest cuts perhaps but substantial nevertheless, were boiled down, the layer of fat stripped off the cooled stock and the liquid added to crusts of brown bread. This high carbohydrate diet was fed late at night and the boiled meat fed during the early morning. Each racer had his own particular system to get, what in Black Country parlance was called 'another yard out of the dog'. Sherry was often advocated as a tonic, but there is scant evidence that Black Country whippet and bull terrier enthusiasts resorted to the use of such expensive fortified wine. Many of the tonic recipes (whether they contributed to the success of the racing whippet is questionable) were kept so secret that the inventors took them with them to the grave. There is a tale that one family of whippet racers in a district called Pleck, Walsall boasted two champion whippet trainers, father and son. When either put together the concoction which was to be used as a whippet tonic, the other was forced to leave the room lest he should see the ingredients used. The tale is probably apocryphal, but is widely believed in the Black Country.

Walsall has a prodigious number of street dogs, as a glance at the papers of the Black Country will attest, but racing whippets were never allowed out of doors unattended lest they scavenged—for whippets are great scavengers—and lost condition. Hence the tales of dogs called in from the streets to compete and win at the races are unlikely to say the least.

The system of handicapping a whippet to ensure that every dog had at least a chance of winning is a curious one, and various clubs had different rules. Some clubs worked on the one pound to the yard handicap—a larger dog was considered faster than a smaller one over the 200–250 yards to be raced. Hence a 23-pound dog started one yard in front of a 24-pound dog. Some clubs handicapped on performance—a 'flash' dog, a dog which had a favourable track record of wins ran from behind, while known laggards were given every chance of winning by allowing them to run from 'out front'. There were no hard and fast rules but members of the clubs were required to obey particular club rules to the letter.

There was little chicanery, but some malpractice was inevitable, particularly in races which involved the use of a 'chucker'. Whippets to be raced were once held by the collar and the base of the tail by an assistant and on the start of the race thrown onto the track to land galloping. Before such a race began owners showed the dog the rag or rabbit skin and set the dogs into a state little short of hysteria at the sight of the object. Many dogs screamed with excitement or barked frenziedly. Hence of course the old poachers' tale of whippets being of little use as poaching dogs as they 'opened up' or 'gave tongue' at the sight of quarry. This is a woefully inaccurate idea though it does have perhaps a grain of truth about it. Whippets are often over-matched by strong hares yet have the courage and desire to chase them. Opening up, or barking as the hare escapes, is usually a cry for help, an indication that the dog is not up to the task in hand, and, when over-matched, nearly every enthusiastic sight hound, lurcher or longdog will in some circumstances give tongue or open up. There is no evidence that whippets are more vociferous than greyhounds prior to the start of a race—a visit to a greyhound flapping track or a lurcher racing club will convince the reader of the truth of such a statement.

It was a popular saying that the 'chucker' often held not only the dog, but also the race in his hands. A chucker could, and did, often decide if the whippet he was throwing would be a winner or an also-ran. By hesitating a split second as the gun was fired, and while the dog he was holding was only handicapped by a microsecond, a race could be won or lost as he decreed. Likewise a whippet could be made to pay attention to the dog running next to it, rather than to the rag shaken by its owner and the dog's chances of winning were then much reduced. A thrower from near Wednesbury once had the nickname of 'Lardhands' because of his rather obvious attempts at throwing a race—having bet on another dog, one supposes. As the shot was fired the chucker threw his dog in the air, rather than onto the track, saying in his defence that the dog slipped out of his grasp. A really adept chucker, on the other hand, could cast a dog so far forward that it would be a quarter of the way up the track before another dog found its feet.

Tales of roguery are common, stories of outrageous trickery legion, but so colourful was the pageant of whippet racing, so intense was the atmosphere the sport engendered that a whippet race attracted huge crowds on Sunday mornings both in the Black Country and in the north of England.

Today both pedigree and non-pedigree events are run much in the same manner as were the early greyhound races of the late 1930s. Dogs are run from traps, chasing after an electrically operated hare on straight, horseshoe or double-curved tracks. Some clubs once employed an unique system of handicapping whereby each time a dog lost a race it gained an extra yard's advantage in the next race. Likewise systems of grading similar to NGRC rules can be used to ensure all the contestants in a race have at least a chance of winning. Top class dogs are thus seldom run against no hopers, and thus no system of handicapping is needed.

The modern races nevertheless lack something of the colour of the early whippet racing meets, traps have replaced throwers, rules are tighter, dogs are infinitely faster and the races better organised, but something is missing. The meets still attract a fairly large crowd, but the spice and piquancy of the races of long ago seem to have gone. Grundy, sexist to the end of his days, attributed it to 'too many women running dogs. Women should not own dogs, just be there to watch'. What is more likely is that the general atmosphere of such events has changed, and the sport of racing this most versatile of sight hounds now attracts a different type of person.

The Scottish Deerhound

In all probability the Scottish deerhound is a slightly smaller version of the great Irish hound which Carson Ritchie, in his book, *The British Dog*, states is extinct. However from the descriptions of early writers and the pen drawings of somewhat later cynologists, a deerhound straight out of the Big Ring at Crufts would blend quite easily into the hounds of Tara's Halls and not be out of place amongst the dogs of Fingal.

It is in fact nearly impossible to distinguish the outline of a Scottish deerhound from the sketch of the Irish greyhound or great Irish hound taken from Taplin's *The Sportsman's Cabinet 1803*. In type and size the breed is still ideally suited to the pursuit of wolf or deer, far more suited, in fact, than its stronger, heavier relative the Irish wolfhound. From a purely pragmatic viewpoint the capture of a deer or wolf is not achieved by bulk and strength alone, but by speed and striking qualities and quite small but speedy hounds have proven to be effective in the taking of heavy quarry, providing these hounds have courage and speed. The more powerful Irish wolfhound is no longer of the shape and size to make it the ideal animal for the securing of heavy quarry such as deer and wolf, but the Scottish deerhound, with some reservations, is.

THE SIGHT HOUND BREEDS

As to description of the shape of the Scottish deerhound, one can do no better than to plagiarise the work of G W Hickman, an authority on slightly exotic dogs of the chase, 'the deerhound is simply the rough greyhound bred to a larger size for the purpose of hunting the larger game, just as the English staghound is simply the foxhound cultivated to a larger size for hunting the stag'. A rough-coated, very large greyhound—what better description of this huge hound, what better description of a hound still capable of pulling down hard, tough and testing quarry?

Of all present-day British mammals, the red deer is the strongest and most testing quarry, standing as it does at 48 in. at the shoulder and coming in at a weight of something slightly less than 250 pounds. Not only is such a beast strong, powerful and swift, but, when at bay a stag, particularly a stag that has some knowledge of being pursued by dogs, is capable of putting up a desperate fight against even the most powerful of hounds. No other British species of deer is so well-armed, no other species of deer is capable of using its antlers to the same deadly effect as the British Red Deer. Sobieski and Stuart in their book *Lays of the Deerforest* give the following description of an ill-fated hunt; 'Two fine young dogs belonging to the late Glengarry (a famous breeder of these hounds) were killed in their first run by a gallant stag which they were driving down the dry channel of a mountain stream and as they sprang at his throat from either side, with a rapid flourish of his head he struck them left and right and laid them dead amongst the stones'. This beast, together with other now extinct doughty quarry, was the game which the deerhound was bred to bring down and it says much that the type has altered little over perhaps two thousand years. A huge rough-coated greyhound, Hickman describes the beast. Long may the description endure and may the type never vary or be prone to the exaggeration that has ruined many other breeds.

Prior to the colonisation of Scotland by the Scots, who were originally an Irish tribe, the land was peopled by a mysterious folk, the Picts, so called because the Roman occupation forces south of the Antonine Wall, believed (quite erroneously as it happened) that the natives painted their faces and bodies eschewing the use of clothes in favour of woad. In point of fact the Pictish people, too, were of Celtic origin, and wore the typical Celtic dress of the Southern Britons. More interesting still is the fact that the stone carvings left by these people indicate that they too possessed fleet greyhound type hunting dogs, possibly little different from the dogs of the Irish tribe, the Scottii. Perhaps social intercourse occurred between the two tribes—both were Celtic and lived similar lifestyles, both had similar passions for the chase and therefore there is a distinct possibility that both kept similar sorts of dogs. However in AD50 or around that date there is a tale that the sons of Uisnech fled from Ulster to Scotland, taking with them 150 hounds, probably of a variety of the great Irish hound. Early colonisation by the Scots occurred some time before AD500 and there is ample reason to believe that these Celtic invaders brought hunting dogs with them when their King Fergus MacMor (Fergus the Great) left his Irish palace at Dunseverick and settled at Dunadd on the west coast of Scotland.

Holingshed, (*Chronicles of Scotland* c. 1577), a somewhat questionable source perhaps, believes that the superiority of the newly imported Scottish hunting dogs over the hounds of the Pictish nobility caused the slaughter of the Picts which in AD288 eventually brought down their empire. Quoting John Mair, a Scottish historian of a century previous, Holingshed states that a band of Pictish nobles were invited to a feast by the Scottish King Crathlint and allowed to hunt with the Scottish nobility. However, once the Pictish hunters saw the hounds of the Scots, they became aware of the inadequacies of their own, for the Scottish hounds were swifter, more beautiful and tougher. Thus they persuaded the Scottish nobles to give them hounds of this type, but, not being content with them, set to and stole a particularly valuable hound belonging to King Crathlint as they left the Kingdom of the Scots. The Scots pursued them and in a Chevy Chase type battle slew a hundred Pictish nobles at a loss of 60 of their own number. The tale, admittedly questionable, gives some idea of the value the newly settled Scots placed on the great Celtic hound and many are the pre-Christian era legends of wars being fought to secure the possession of certain hounds.

In Scotland, divorced from outcross blood lines from Ireland, this type of Celtic hound began to develop along its own lines, but still its essential work, the pursuit of hare, deer, fox and wolf, was the same. As the wolf became rare in Scotland, perhaps a finer type of dog began to develop for the pursuit of deer rather than a dog strong enough to pull down wolf and boar (for boar still roamed wild in Scotland long after the species became a novelty to be kept in enclosed parks in England). Youatt, an enthusiast of all livestock, tends to believe that two distinct types of hound were developing in Scotland during the eighteenth century, a larger, stronger dog with pendulous ears known as the Highland greyhound and the smaller, more neatly constructed greyhound type that Youatt refers to as the Scottish greyhound. Once again it is wise not to pay too much attention to Youatt for he wrote inaccurately about pigs and cattle and his observations concerning dogs which he encountered in Scotland during his brief stays, are hardly likely to be more than speculation. A N Hartley in her book *The Deerhound* (1955) states she believes that Youatt had been shown a cross-bred deerhound and the pendulous ears of the Highland greyhound were the result of the introduction of alien blood into the type.

One can assume with a fair degree of certainty that the Scottish greyhound (later to be known as the deerhound) was perhaps a shade more than partly responsible for the decline and extinction of the wolf. Each and every county in Scotland lays claim to tales of the last wolves in Britain, the majority of which were brought low by a hunter and a team of deerhounds. The tale of the laconic, near idiot, McQueen and his tardiness in attending the last wolf hunt because he held the bloodied head of the last wolf within the folds of his cloak, is well-known. McQueen, so tradition holds, kept a team of deerhounds. Poulsen the Sutherland hunter who supposedly killed the last Sutherland wolf also kept these dogs, while the wolf of Glencoe was reputedly killed in a battle with a single greyhound. However, tales concerning wolves in the Highlands should be treated with some care. Wolves have never been a serious problem in Britain and there is no concrete evidence of a British man-killing wolf. Prior to the Clearances few Highland farms kept sheep (the traditional prey of the wolf) and the Highland cattle kept by clansmen farmers, half-wild, difficult to approach and decidedly truculent with men and dogs would have been difficult prey for the wolf. The extermination of the wolf would have been due more to changes in environment, estate management and farming methods, than to direct assault by deerhounds. It is also doubtful whether wolves existed in sufficient numbers in Scotland to have ever been a real nuisance, but the Scottish hound was sufficiently versatile to be a multi-purpose dog. Foxes, wildcats (though wildcats have never been considered a real nuisance in the Highlands) and all varieties of deer were hunted by these hounds. Most quarry required the use of only one hound to secure it (McQueen supposedly slew his wolf with a single dog but a single hound was frequently over-matched by a fully grown red deer stag).

The coursing and catching of a red deer with one or two dogs was a spectacular affair, and by no means a one-sided contest. Red deer retaliate strenuously when hurt or brought to bay and an unwary or over-courageous dog often came to grief on the antlers of a stag. Roe and fallow deer are fairly easily taken by a good strong lurcher, but a red deer is a very different animal to course. Its sheer bulk as well as the manner in which it moves is a deterrent to all but the most game dogs and the animal's ability to use its antlers makes it a fearsome adversary.

Unless the dog was able to bring down a fleeing deer with a rush to the throat or more frequently by a leg hold (for once a dog becomes aware of the fighting power of a red deer it is often reluctant to chance a head on confrontation) the contest between the antagonists was often bloody. When brought to bay the deer seeks a solid wall of rock to make its stand or when available, a deep pool in which it can stand with water up to its belly and fight off its attackers. When such an animal is coursed even by the strongest hound, the outcome of the course is by no means inevitable and the slaying of a deer at bay can be a very violent and dangerous affair.

By the end of the eighteenth century such were the improvements in the sporting rifle that the sport of deer stalking began to supersede that of deer coursing with large and glamorous hounds. More important to the decline of deer coursing however were the Highland Clearances which began to follow half a century later. Sheep began to replace the scrawny Highland cattle of pre-clearance days and few landowners wished to see a flock of sheep startled by the sight of a raging battle between a hound and a stag.

The cessation of the Napoleonic wars made great differences to the British sporting scene. The war had brought improvements to the military rifle and a precision-built rifle with greater accuracy and longer range had been produced. At the ending of the war these improvements were transferred to the sporting rifle. A lighter, more easily handled sporting gun was being manufactured and British army officers, hot from the campaigns, realised that this improvement would produce a suitable weapon for the newly popular sport of deer stalking. It became profitable for owners of large estates in Scotland to let portions of their estate to the deer stalker. It proved to be almost the death knell for the huge Scottish hound, for now the dog was relegated to the totally unworthy task of tracking down a wounded stag (a stag wounded by gun-shot), bringing the stag to bay and awaiting the arrival of the stalker who with further rifle shot or hunting knife was set to finish the wounded animal. A collie could perform this task as well as the strongest deerhound, a mongrel dog was therefore often as prized as the more valiant and swift hound—more so, in fact, for sight hounds (and the deerhound is typical of the type) by their very definition hunt by sight as much as by sense of smell. A Mr Cupples states that he presented to the Marquis of Breadalbane in 1825, 'a most magnificent brace Glen and Garry, the former nearly 33 inches at the shoulder and the bitch (Garry) 3 inches less, both are rough, lightish grey and though they are perfectly pure would not track a deer but run by sight only'. Such hounds would have been prized during the halcyon days of deer coursing. Now the sporting rifle had made such giant hounds obsolete and their decline became inevitable.

Numbers of the breed plummeted rapidly but, before the type reached the nadir experienced by its Irish counterpart, an interest in reviving it had blossomed, thereby preventing the deerhound falling into extinction, as Carson Ritchie believed the true Irish hound had done. One of the enthusiasts who set to preserve the breed was Captain Graham who is best remembered for his work in resuscitating or recreating the Irish wolfhound. Another was the breeder Mr McNeil, who unlike Captain Graham was more interested in the sporting propensities of the breed than its aesthetic qualities. McNeil's most famous hound was Buscar, a 28-inch dog coming in at 85 pounds in running condition, quite a small dog by deerhound standards of today, but one full of fire, courage and coursing ability. Buscar and his companion dog Bran, pulled down fully grown stags on the island of Jura.

Because of the work of McNeil and fellow breeders, a revival of interest in the breed saved the deerhound from extinction, so that the modern hound is a relatively purebred example of the old Celtic hound—the term relatively pure will be explained shortly. Thus it was that when W R Pape began the trend for dog shows in 1859, or more correctly popularised organised dog shows, the deerhound was in a fairly healthy condition, numerically speaking. Indeed, later in the same year as Pape staged his first show at Newcastle, an exhibition designed to promote Pape's shotguns, (hence only gun-dog breeds, setters and pointers, were represented there) a second show was staged at Birmingham with a more widespread appeal. In 1860 a report of the Birmingham dog show read, 'Colonel Inges' deerhound was a grand winner in a class that was quite unworthy of him and his fair companion Brimstone had the same honour'.

The breed had not been used for its original work of coursing unwounded deer for perhaps a quarter of a century and the work of tracking wounded deer is hardly taxing to a dog capable of making a fair attempt at bringing down a large red deer stag single handed. Henceforth the deerhound was to be bred purely for aesthetic reasons with little regard for, or indeed little chance to test, the original task for which the breed was intended. It is said by many, and sadly it must be endorsed by any thinking person, that the beginning of dog shows brought an end to the breeding of pedigree dogs for practical purposes. Commentators at Crufts must in fact give their commentary tongue in cheek when describing dogs such as Sealyham terriers as dogs 'still capable of handling a badger below ground'. Such dogs have lost most of their physical and mental attributes through many years of breeding exclusively for exhibition. The fault lies partially in the creation of a breed standard which describes a dog totally unsuited for the task for which it was originally intended.

Fortunately the deerhound standard originally drawn up by Messrs Hickman and R Hood Wright in 1892 and the revised standard promulgated at Blackpool in 1948 were carefully tailored so that exhibitors could still breed an animal which was physically, and one must stress the word physically, capable of performing the task for which it was intended. Mentally, these dogs might be incapable of a concerted foray against a red deer stag—for a very special type of animal is required to perform such a feat—but there was no way in which most exhibitors could test the mettle of their dogs in such strenuous courses. Nor, truth be told, would most modern breeders wish their dogs to pursue such quarry for at the time of writing, such are the atrocities committed by deer poachers, and, more to the point, such has been the response of the national press to these outrages, that only the most foolhardy would wish to test their dogs on courses at red deer.

Roe and fallow are relatively easy quarry for a dog of the size of the deerhound, providing the dog has the courage and indeed the desire to tackle these animals. Red deer are seldom encountered except in places where they enjoy partial protection by landowners. Furthermore the pursuit of deer by dogs in Scotland, one of the last refuges of the truly wild red deer, is strictly prohibited by Acts of Parliament.

The standard for the deerhound is quite simply that of a very hairy greyhound, a rather large hairy greyhound, if one might quote G W Hickman, a thoroughly practical breeder and critic of the breed. To illustrate a point one should consult the breed standard drawn up by enthusiasts in 1948—one of the few standards drawn up by breed clubs to produce an animal still capable of doing the work for which it was intended, and reading it one is reminded of the old Gaelic rhyme concerning the appearance of the miol chu, a type of hound (or dog for the Celts made no distinction between hounds and other types of dog) used for the pursuit of large wild animals:

> An eye of sloe with ears not low
> With horses breast with depth of chest
> With breadth of loin and curve of groin
> And nape set far behind the head
> Such were the dogs that Fingal bred

Whilst all traditional Gaelic poetry is automatically suspect since the exposé of Macpherson's supposed translation of *Ossian* and *The World of Tir-Na-Nog*, the poem is not dissimilar to the description of the greyhound type preferred by the Abbess Juliana Berner in her *Book of St Albans*.

The physical qualities of such a doyen of dogdom have been long appreciated by hunters and if the deerhound is no longer found work, legitimate proper work for a dog of its size, then a role has certainly been found for its descendants. Wolf hunters in the South and Central USA used deerhounds to breed the Dakota wolfhounds—literally hounds used to hunt wolves and not to be confused with the borzoi or the Irish wolfhound. Most of these hounds were hybrids between greyhounds and larger hounds such as the deerhound with sometimes a dash of Plott hound to give scent and determination, for timber wolves are large formidable beasts, sometimes weighing in at a few pounds heavier than the pure-bred deerhounds. Such hounds were run as small packs or 'coffles', as Ben Lilly once described them, for a large timber wolf could be a taxing foe for a single very large dog. It must be added that wolf hunters hunted simply for bounty, not for appreciation of the testing nature of the wolf and regardless of the tale by Zane Gray, *The Wolf Tracker*, which appeared in *The Ladies Home Journal* 1924. In this the hero, Brink, an ancient embittered wolf hunter, walks a wolf to exhaustion and strangles it only to reject the $5000 reward since he considers the stand taken by wolves makes the animal more noble than man. Wolves were hunted by packs of large sight hounds or longdogs simply because a pack made short work of a timber wolf, whereas a single dog run at a wolf might, if exceptional, overcome its quarry but would be so badly damaged as to render the dog *hors-de-combat* for weeks after the hunt. Sport played a very small part in the lifestyle of the wolf hunter prior to World War II, though most of them were farmers who must have found the hunting of wolves with packs of hounds more exciting than conventional stock keeping.

Early wolf hunters followed the pack on horseback, assisting in the kill with knife or noose. Since 1945 however a new technique of hunting the fast-depleting stocks of wolves in America has been devised (although between 1935–1955, 20,000 wolves were bounty hunted in British Columbia alone, for where deer hunting is an important source of income in an area, anti-wolf sentiment is strong). Modern hunters tend to favour a more elaborate mode of transport. Station-wagons are now fitted with custom-built springs and remote control back-door releases. When a wolf is spotted in open country the wagon is driven at speed after the wolf and as soon as the time is deemed right the back doors are triggered open to release a small team of wolfhounds (the most popular cross being the ubiquitous deerhound greyhound hybrid) to pursue and sometimes catch the fleeing prey. While the practice might be considered as unsporting by some, perhaps the words of medieval writer Gaston Phoebus should be heeded, for a wolf has a loping effortless gait which 'daunts the pursuing hound sorely'.

Similarly the deerhound is often used in the creation of the kangaroo hound—an unstandardised mix of staghound (a large foxhound type not to be confused with the itinerant coursers' staghound which is usually a deerhound hybrid) deerhound and greyhound. It is assumed that the deerhound gives the hybrid stride and depth of chest, the greyhound a dash of extra speed and the staghound stamina and nose to run the quarry 'cold' or out of sight.

Lest the kangaroo should seem a ridiculous quarry to test the mettle of a pack of large sight hounds, a story might dispel the notion. The success of Antipodean fighter Bob

Fitzsimmons kindled an interest in boxing in Australia at the turn of the century and fights were well-attended. A curious match was staged at Coolgardie, a match which pricked the interest of the British sporting public. Kangaroos were reared by bored gold miners and 'imprinted' so that they lost their fear of man. The feet of the adult kangaroo were then bound or swathed in bandages and encased in boxing gloves and the animal put into a boxing ring with a man. What appeared to be an incongruous match often proved otherwise for the kick of a kangaroo's hind legs carries a devastating 'punch'. Unbound the hind legs would have disembowelled the fighter. A kangaroo 'boxes' or holds with its front paws which are scarcely effective weapons, but the killing blow, a blow which literally tears an attacking dog to pieces, is delivered with the hind leg which is armed with dagger-like claws. Perhaps this technique has been developed since the introduction of the dingo by Aboriginal invaders of Australia, or perhaps the Thylacine or Tasmanian wolf, an indigenous but now extinct marsupial predator also preyed on the kangaroo and such a kicking action was developed to deter the attentions of this marsupial wolf-like hunter.

On the subject of the dingo, the kangaroo hound is not restricted to the hunting of kangaroos but is also used in the pursuit of the dingo. While the dingo is not as ferocious an adversary as the wolf, it is larger than the coyote at which the majority of American 'wolfhounds' are tried. Packs of dogs are run at these dingos (and hybrid dingos, for a mix of German shepherd dog and dingo is the most awesome stock worrier and at one time the importation of German shepherd dogs into Australia received careful scrutiny) and they are captured in much the same way as were wolves by Scottish hunters. Once again sport seems to play little part in dingo hunting, for the dingo is a sheep worrier and considered to be vermin by the Australian stockman.

It is likely that deerhound blood was also absorbed into the lines of bearded collie at some time early in the twentieth century. Logan, writing in *Dog World* mentions that to produce a hill dog with length of leg to allow it to come to terms with sheep on the slopes of rocky valleys, deerhounds were often mated into the unregistered strains of bearded collie. Certainly bearded collies were often 27 inches at the shoulder at the time when Mrs Willison promoted the breed and brought about the formation of the Bearded Collie Club, so it is likely that the deerhound did play a part in the creation of these larger collies. Most working strains of bearded collie are now smaller than this, but large powerful, tall beardies are still to be found in some working strains. Lest it should seem illogical that a shepherd might wish to introduce sight hound blood into a working strain of collie, it is perhaps well to remember that Taplin (admittedly never a reliable cynologist) believed that the lean, mean, herding dogs, for some reason called Smithfield collies by some, that worked the droving trails throughout Britain prior to the introduction of the railway, were hybrids between greyhounds or greyhound type dogs and herding dogs.

There has been a revival of interest in the coursing ability of deerhounds since the World War II and coursing meets testing the mettle of these dogs to brown hare—an elusive and fleet quarry as difficult to take perhaps as an adult red deer stag, are well-attended. The dogs lack the thrust and furious energy of a greyhound, of that there is no question, but their great height and stride makes for a fast if not furious course. From a purist point of view the purpose of the course should be the turning of the hare as much as its capture and, from an aesthetic point of view, a course between two keen and trained deerhounds is a most spectacular affair. Catches or kills are somewhat rarer than at more conventional greyhound coursing events, as the great height of the deerhound makes striking and killing the hare somewhat difficult. The meets are deservedly well-attended and from the point of view of pageantry rather than as hare killing events they must be rated highly.

Solitary hunters using deerhounds to secure a catch, as would a country man using a lurcher, are fairly uncommon but they do exist. Frank Sheardown, the author of *Man of the Field* and *The Working Longdog*, recalls a deerhound bitch he purchased some years ago, bred from nearly pure Ardkinglas lines but which nevertheless grew to only a diminutive 26 inches at the shoulder. According to Sheardown the bitch displayed a sagacity unusual in sight hounds, running hare cunning, and predicting turns and jinks in its course with the skill of a well-bred hunter. During her life-span she took roe and fallow with little difficulty, bowling them so hard they were dead when Sheardown arrived to help her. She ran rabbit by scent, as well as by sight, and worked cover eagerly when needed. She jumped well, synchronising her movements in the manner of a classic jumping lurcher and he describes her as moderately obedient by most standards. He decided to continue her line, but after visiting Crufts he became a little concerned about the leg weaknesses which were manifesting themselves amongst some of the dogs he saw there. Thus he mated the bitch to a greyhound male and kept one of the offspring. The comparison made by Sheardown between the pure-bred sight hound and her half-bred longdog hybrids is interesting. He found not one of the longdogs quite as cunning or as malleable as the dam although faster and more agile.

More recently, Alan Wilkinson of County Durham has worked deerhounds to all types of British quarry. Wilkinson has won well at the competitive coursing events organised by the club and such has been his success, and subsequent involvement with the club that he has taken on the post of official 'slipper' for the Deerhound Club. Wilkinson was first and foremost a lurcher enthusiast, keeping a rather variable collection of running dogs to be run at all available quarry. Thus when he became interested in deerhounds, the sight hounds were forced to slot into the role he expected of his lurchers. Wilkinson's comments were that while deerhounds have to be compared a little unfavourably with lurchers intelligence-wise, they perform extremely well for sight hounds and have considerably more sagacity than typical longdogs (this point was also emphasised by Sheardown, even about the sight hound hybrids bred from his own bitch). Wilkinson's deerhounds take rabbit, but obviously their great height puts them at a disadvantage when it comes to the actual capture of the rabbit. They also take brown hare, though not frequently for few dogs are capable of catching brown hares, given fair law, with any regularity. Blue hares are taken more regularly by Wilkinson as these smaller less powerful rabbit-like hares are less taxing quarry, though when run over cut-out peat hags, and blue hares are wonderfully adept at choosing such terrain in the Highlands, they are doughty adversaries. Foxes are also taken by Wilkinson's deerhounds and once again anyone who has coursed fox will be aware that the fox is no mean quarry, being able to escape seemingly hopeless courses simply by dint of 'slipping the finishing bite' at the very last moment. Foxes invariably seem to find sanctuary in the most unlikely places. Roe and fallow deer are also taken with some panache by Wilkinson's hounds. Wilkinson's comment on the leg weaknesses which Sheardown believes to be widespread in the breed was that in the early days of puppyhood, before it can justify the title sapling, the whelp is prone to leg weaknesses, bone breakages, etc. Whether or not the fault is inherited, and this seems likely, or can be curbed by careful rearing, supplementary feeding and restricted exercise until the dog is stronger, is debatable.

At one time foremost breed expert Anastasia Noble believed that the deerhound was becoming a little too inbred and that the restricted gene pool would eventually produce genetic problems. Thus Miss Noble introduced blood of the best coursing greyhound available. This cross breeding must have been well thought out. Type-wise the deerhound and the greyhound are similar—the deerhound should in fact resemble a large hirsute greyhound, and constitutionally the breed would have benefited by the addition of genes from what must be considered the most physically perfect of all dogs. Miss Noble stresses in her chapter on the deerhound in Standfast Press' *Coursing*, that she brought in the greyhound blood to give a larger gene pool and not to improve the coursing ability of the breed as was thought by some. Nevertheless, the cross would have done just this and in addition to improving type, giving a more sturdy knock-resistant frame, the greyhound blood would have added zest, fire and certainly courage in the coursing field—a place where true courage, not to be confused with aggression or desire to fight an opponent, is all important.

Perhaps someone who would be able to confirm the efficacy of this cross would be Nuttall of Clitheroe. During the mid-sixties and seventies Nuttall was a regular breeder of the deerhound greyhound hybrid, using deerhound males onto good class coursing greyhound bitches. Later he added more deerhound blood until he 'fielded' apparently purebred deerhounds, indistinguishable from top class show stock but one sixteenth greyhound bred. These revived deerhounds had an excellent record as hunting dogs, many boasting noses equal to quite good lurchers and with speed and pluck to spare. Some of the stock bred by Nuttall from this fusion of blood did put up a very creditable show on red deer though in somewhat questionable circumstances and far more questionable legality! Nuttall's stock might have been absorbed into the classically bred deerhound lines with advantage. They certainly performed well at all quarry and more than justified the title deerhound, despite their mixed origins. Why Nuttall ceased to breed these dogs is still a mystery. They were some of the finest coursing hounds available during the 1960–1980 period. Furthermore, few of the offspring manifested leg weakness or brittleness of bones.

Intelligence-wise, the deerhound together with the whippet may lay claim to being the most sagacious of the sight hounds. However despite the eulogies conferred by writers of breed books, the sight hounds are not a very intelligent, nor a very biddable branch of dogdom. No sight hound is unusually bright nor unusually perspicacious but the deerhound is considered by most coursers to represent the upper echelon of sight hound intelligençia.

The Irish Wolfhound

A dog a yard high at the shoulder, as heavy as a welterweight boxer with a regal demeanour more fitting to the Halls of Tara than the Big Ring at Crufts. Such is a fair and accurate description of the Irish wolfhound, a gigantic hirsute greyhound, largest and most powerful of the sight hounds, but such a description, such a glowing eulogy merely scratches the surface of the story of this, the most baffling enigma of dogdom.

The Irish greyhound, or great Irish hound or perhaps the prototype of the dog, first makes its appearance in the pages of history in 273 BC when an upheaval or a series of wars in the southern steppe lands of Europe caused the movement of the Celts, a flamboyant colourful warlike race, much addicted to dogs and even more addicted to hunting. In that year, so Arrian writing 400 years later states, the Celts spread across Europe pillaging Greece, sacking Delphi and then drifting westward to Italy, France and Britain. With the Celtic migration came dogs previously unknown in Graeco-Roman Europe. Prior to the invasion there existed no dog in Europe capable of catching a hare in fair flight. Now a greyhound type entered Europe, a type which could bring down a fleeing hare, given a fair 'law' (previously hares were taken by dint of somewhat slower hounds driving them into trammel nets).

To a reader reared on a diet of Kennel Club regulations and complex breed standards, the term 'greyhound type' must seem puzzling, but the Celtic migration brought with it a variety of greyhound types ranging from the dogs which were to give rise to the giant Irish hound to the smaller vertragus, a more slender, lighter dog, used to pull down hares and probably smaller species of deer. Possibly the vertragus was the ancestor of the modern greyhound (though it must be stressed that there is no concrete proof to justify the speculation that this was so). Certainly the type was a species of sight hound, as Martial describes how one such dog coursed and retrieved a hare live to hand (not an inconsiderable feat as any coursing enthusiast will attest).

The larger greyhound types were probably colossal. A fresco in Tiryns, northern Greece, shows a man (possibly a hunter) accompanied by two horses and a hound, the back of which is level with the man's waist. Dogs of this type were probably multi-purpose rather than animals kept to perform specific tasks. Their very size was probably a deterrent to intruders and their greyhound shape made them capable of coming to terms with wolf, deer and probably the boar which played an important part in early Celtic mythology as well as in the field of hunting.

The origin of these greyhound types, as has already been mentioned, is the subject of much speculation by cynologists for there is little concrete proof as to the origin of the type. It is romantic and not entirely unreasonable to believe that the Celtic chieftains of the southern steppe lands came in contact with traders from Arabia and North Africa and that dogs, closely akin to the present day saluki and the sloughi, were traded with the settlers and after mingling with indigenous Central European hounds produced not only the giant Celtic hounds but also the smaller vertragus. Alternatively, a taller, slender type of animal might have developed quite independently in the steppes of Asia and these may not only have given rise to the Celtic greyhound types but also to the ancestors of the saluki and the sloughi. Certainly there is evidence that the early settlers in northern India also had dogs of a greyhound type and the similarity of language between the early Celtic languages and the Sanskrit type tongues of northern India, suggests contact between the two rather similar cultures. It is in fact extremely unwise to believe that all the greyhound types started off only in Egypt and Arabia if indeed the type originated there at all.

Despite speculation it was only in the fourth century that the rest of Europe adopted the custom of referring to these great hounds as Irish dogs. In AD397 the Christian Consul, Quintus Arrius Symmachus, sent a letter thanking his brother for the gift of seven Scottish dogs—a statement less baffling when one realises that the Scots or Scottii were an Irish tribe who later invaded and conquered the Pictish lands which would eventually be called Scotland. References to the hounds having fought in the arenas of the Roman Empire should also be treated with great caution, for the delicious hyperbole of the fourth and fifth-century poet, Claudian, who describes British dogs which could break a bull's neck with a single bite, refers in all probability to the mastiff or a type of mastiff, rather than the great Irish hound. The hyperbole becomes more excusable when one considers that Claudian may not have seen such 'games', as the blood and sand conflict twixt beasts and men had fallen out of favour half a century before Claudian's birth.

The fact that mastiffs were the traditional dogs of the arena should not disprove the ferocity of the great Irish hound, for Symmachus' letter to his brother mentions that the Scottish dogs were shown at the Circus Maximus and that the people marvelled how dogs of such stature and savage demeanour could have been brought to Rome, except in iron cages like lions and tigers. However once again it should be pointed out that comments such as those of Symmachus may have been used as a way of effusively thanking his brother for such an exotic gift. Such was the impact of the sight of these hounds that during the days just prior to the Gothic invasion of the Empire, an official bearing the title Procurator Cynegii had been appointed to supervise the breeding, collection and export of these Celtic hounds to the provinces of the Roman Empire.

By the time the Roman Empire had accepted the title Scottish or Irish dogs, the type had become inextricably woven into the warp and weft of Celtic legend and history. Shortly before the advent of the Christian era the golden age of Celtic mythology had begun to evolve. Tales of Ossian and his journey to the twilight world of *Tir Na Nog*, a fairy-tale kingdom of perpetual youth, and stories from the latter half of the *Mabinogion* had begun to emerge and their themes and characters had begun to stabilise. These stories of rustic adventurers, a star's flight from the courtly heroes of later Arthurian legends, are littered with stories of monumental hunts of beasts as formidable as Erythmanthian boars and the participants in the chases are invariably hounds of epic proportion, beasts renowned for their sagacity and fidelity. Later illustrations by authors of the Angevin period invariably depict these animals as types intermediate between the foxhound and the larger more powerful staghound, but in all probability these legends refer to dogs which were types of Celtic hounds similar to the modern deerhound.

One of the tales purporting to relate to the great Celtic hounds, is the legend of Cuchulain. A child is born to a mortal woman and a type of Celtic sprite or demi-god, a denizen of a nether world. The boy called Setanta is small and dark as a result of his fey ancestry but, unlike the more robust blonde youngsters of the tribe, is possessed by such a single-mindedness and energy that youths of his age are unable to prevail against him in sports of any sort. Such is his fervour that the King notices him playing a game of hurly and invites him to a feast at the hut of Cullen the Smith, a strange and almost mystical character who believes his life to be threatened by numerous enemies. The lad declines the offer until he has finished the game, leaving the King to journey to the heavily guarded hut of the paranoid Cullen.

Cullen the Smith (in Celtic and Germanic mythology the art of working in iron was heavily shrouded in magic possibly because the making of steel, a combination of iron plus carbon was not understood and the alloy only produced by chance) was a gloomy man who lived in a hut surrounded by a high stockade, the gateway of which is closed by dragging thorns across the entrance each night. Attacks on his life are frequent and once he has allowed the King and his retinue inside his stockaded hut and drawn the thorn branches across the entrance, he turns loose his final deterrent, a huge dog of fearsome appearance and ferocious disposition. The King suddenly remembers he has invited the youth Setanta to Cullen's house, but darkness has fallen and Cullen warns that no man, himself included, is safe venturing out, because of the wrath of the hound, during the hours of darkness. Thus the King is forced to await the fate of the lad with stoical resignation.

Setanta, because of this fey ancestry, is the stuff of which superheroes are fashioned and on arriving at the gateway of the stockade and finding it blocked with its barrier of thorns, he sets to climb the wall to keep his appointment with the King. The King and Cullen listen sorrowfully to the cacophony as the hound attacks the boy and the King and Cullen await the inevitable outcome. However the door is flung open and the bloodied and badly bitten boy throws down the body of the dead hound, exclaiming apologetically, 'He would have killed me, so I slew him'.

The jubilation of the King, who is not only delighted to see the boy alive but is aware he has met a champion of Ireland, is not shared by the paranoid Cullen who exclaims that the boy may just as well have slain him, for now deprived of his guardian hound he is naked to the blade of the assassin. The youth Setanta promptly offers to lie across the doorway of Cullen's hut until a similar dog can be procured and trained, whereupon Setanta becomes rechristened Cuhullain or the hound of Cullen and accepts the *geise* or taboo that he will not eat dog flesh. Carson I A Ritchie, in his *The British Dog Its History From Earliest Times*, states that this may be an indication that the Irish (if not the Celts generally) ate dogs, as do many South east Asian tribes today, but a *geise* placed on a superhero was likely to be a most unlikely happening which would ensure the immortality of the hero (see the fate of Llew Llaw Gyffis, *The Mabinogion*). Like all superheroes Cuhullain is tricked into breaking the taboo and accepts the flesh of a dog from some crones who are roasting a dog on a spit. The *geise* now broken, Cuhullain's fate is inevitable and he meets with the hideous Dianic cult death expected of a hero who has broken a personal taboo.

Despite the fact that all books concerned with the great Irish hound faithfully record that the dog encountered by the youth Setanta was an early type of wolfhound, at the risk of seeming an iconoclast, one can find no evidence to suggest that this is so. The Gaels unlike the modern hunting fraternity made no distinction between hounds and lesser dogs, so the name Cu or Ci is applied to any breed of domesticated canine. Perhaps a mastiff—the Celts also bred and exported these dogs—would have been a more likely opponent for Setanta, but likewise it should be pointed out that, despite the views of the uninitiated, any large dog is more than a match for a man. Nevertheless the tale is a good one and essential reading for any potential cynologist.

More of an enigma is the somewhat fraudulent tale of the great hound, Gelert. Many historians believe that during the late twelfth century the constant preoccupation of the hunting, warring classes with the crusades meant that there was an increase in the number of large and fierce predators in Britain. King John declared war on wolves, collecting taxes in the form of wolf skins from some districts to ensure that the numbers of the beasts were kept in control. There is some scanty evidence that John encouraged the breeding of the great Irish hound to hunt wolves (and also other larger quarry). There is a tale that John gave a leash or sometimes a single hound to fellow kings and vassals, made a gift of one such hound, supposedly called Gelert, to the vassal King Llewellyn the Great, a son-in-law of his, who had a rude hunting lodge in Snowdonia. Legend has it that Llewellyn set out to hunt one day but Gelert, his favourite hound, refused to follow him, preferring to stay at the hunting lodge with the king's infant son. Llewellyn accepts the hound's reluctance to hunt and returns at evening to find the house in confusion, the walls daubed with blood, his infant child's cradle overturned and the child missing. Gelert bounds to his master, mouth dripping gore, and Llewellyn, believing the dog has killed and eaten the child plunges his sword into the beast which dies with a look of sadness and bewilderment on its face. In true Grand Guignol fashion the death howl of the beast awakens the child sleeping safely behind the shattered furniture and Llewellyn on exploring the hut discovers not only the child, but the huge blood-bespattered cadaver of a wolf which has been killed by the great hound.

Overcome with grief and guilt Llewellyn buries the body of his sagacious but misunderstood hound on the roadside near his hunting lodge, erecting a pile of stones over the body, and to this day the place near the cairn is known as Beddgelert or the place of Gelert. It is a spot beloved by pilgrims who flock there each year to see and photograph the grave of the world's most famous Irish wolfhound.

The tale, pretty as it is, does not stand up to close scrutiny. Perhaps John did make Llewellyn the gift of a hound and perhaps the hound was called Gelert. Perhaps, although the tale has an unlikely ring about it, the story of Llewellyn's mistake and the death of the great hound is also true. One thing is certain, however, the body residing under the cairn at Beddgelert is not that of the hound nor is it the skeleton of any wolfhound for that matter. In 1793, David Pritchard was landlord of the Royal Goat in the village of Beth Kelert (Kelert was a Welsh saint—there are many Welsh saints!). Pritchard was an amateur student of Welsh tradition and had heard of the tale of the great hound and its demise at the hands of Llewellyn and gave the hound the name of Gelert. He then took the trouble to bury the body of a collie-sized dog under the cairn (the cairn was later excavated to investigate the myth) and thus brought many tourists to the area and trade to the Royal Goat Inn.

However, like most legends the tale has a basis. A similar story is recorded by Cadog the Wise, a saint who predated Llewellyn by some six centuries, and there is a Welsh proverb which states, 'I am as sick at heart as the man who killed his greyhound'. Actually the tale of an animal being badly rewarded for its loyalty in defending its owner's children, is as old as the Indo-European group of peoples itself. *Brewer's Dictionary of Phrase and Fable* states that the tale may be traced back to a Sanskrit legend, the wolf of the tale being replaced by a black, venomous snake and the part of Gelert being played by an ichneumon, a species of mongoose.

The tale of the duel between the great Irish hound and the murderer Macaire, while it is less credible, may be factual. In 1371 a French noble and owner of a great Irish hound, Aubie de Montdidier was out hunting with his friend, Macaire, when he was murdered and his body buried under a tree. The hound later found the spot and like Greyfriars Bobby lay on the grave, refusing food, and began to pine away. Unlike Bobby, however, the hound later made its way to the house of a friend of Montdidier and, taking the man by the sleeve, led him back to the grave of its murdered master. The body was exhumed, identified as Montdidier and the friend adopted the hound, taking him to the court of the French king.

While at court the hound encountered Macaire and attacked him violently, having to be pulled off the man before it killed him. Subsequently, the dog attacked him on sight and, so untypical of the behaviour of the hound was the unprovoked attack, that tales of a quarrel between Montdidier and Macaire reached the ears of Charles VI who brought both antagonists before him, whereupon the hound attacked the man Macaire with fury. The King, curious or perhaps simply amused by the hound's insane hatred of Macaire, ordered a trial of Ordeal by Battle, an outmoded custom by that time, but it was considered that the hound could not be expected to give evidence in a more conventional court of law. Macaire was given a club with which to defend himself, while the Irish hound was allowed to retreat into a barrel to seek sanctuary when hard pressed. The hound prevailed, during a long and savage combat, and Macaire, his throat between the jaws of the hound, screamed admission of his guilt to the King who had the hound pulled off the lacerated man. The reprieve was short lived, however, for the King, now convinced of Macaire's guilt, ordered the knight to be hanged.

Once again it must be added that there is no historical evidence to corroborate the tale though the story of the curious combat is widely believed. It is fairly certain that a trial of this nature, an Ordeal by Battle, between a man and an animal would have been so unusual in the late fourteenth century as to attract interest, interest so great, in fact, that lack of documentary evidence concerning the encounter must certainly make a serious researcher suspicious as to the authenticity of the story of Macaire and the great hound.

Evidence of the fighting ability of the hound is legion however, and in 1670 John Evelyn, the diarist and author, describes an epic battle between an Irish wolfhound and a mastiff, in which the hound 'acquitted himself honourably', whatever that may mean. However some 600 years before the encounter described by Evelyn there is evidence that a large and powerful hound was sent as a guard dog from Ireland to Iceland. The *Saga of Burnt Njal* records that King Myrkjaten once sent one such hound to the warrior Gunnar Jarl, a Norwegian settler in the turbulent Iceland of AD1000, an Iceland poised on the uncertainty wrought by the coming of the disruptive force of Christianity to the land. The hound 'equal to two men in battle' with 'the virtue of a stout warrior' becomes the idolising slave of the warrior Gunnar and then, just as abruptly as it appears, disappears from the text of the saga. Frans Bengtsson's masterly book *The Long Ships* borrows heavily from the text of the sagas and gives Orm Tostesson the hero of the tale, two such hounds, more fierce guards than hunters perhaps, but an indication that the Norse people, once they had laid claim to parts of Ireland, took back hounds of this type and probably distributed them throughout the Viking Empire, which included Russia, where it is feasible they entered into the pedigree of other types of wolfhound. It is certainly reasonable to hypothesise that the great height of some of the strains of borzoi could not have been inherited from southern sight hounds such as the saluki and the Afghan hound. Moreover, it is wrong to underestimate the trade and social intercourse which took place between Britain and central Europe, as a glance at the genealogy of some of the Hungarian noble families would reveal. It is equally likely that adventurers of the sort who brought about the Bathory family could have brought giant hunting hounds with them on their travels. Gifts of Celtic hounds—the dogs of Scotland rather than Ireland but undoubtedly derived from the same root stock—were sent by James VI of Scotland (later to become James I of England) to the King of Denmark and descriptions of Norwegian wolfhounds published by Conrad Heresbach in Cologne in 1570, indicate the Celtic type hound was perhaps well established in Europe, though Heresbach's names for these rough-coated hounds, leporarius (hare hounds), emissairius and vertragus might indicate the dogs may have been hounds of a lurcher type rather than the giant Celtic hounds. Heresbach makes mention that the hounds were more famed for their speed than sagacity—the Celtic hound in fact seldom receives acclaim for its intelligence amongst critical writers.

So far the writer has deliberately omitted a description of these huge Celtic hounds which would in time result in the Scottish deerhound as well as the Irish wolfhound. Few skeletons of these beasts have been unearthed, Ritchie mentions that perhaps the dogs were killed and buried with their owners, their remains being interred under huge Celtic burial mounds rather than being committed to the midden pile—the lot of most dogs. Ritchie describes the hounds as being as large as a calf, and one skull recovered from a bog in Ireland (peat has remarkable preservative qualities) was 17 inches long, a quarter as big again as the skulls of modern Irish wolfhounds. Large modern specimens may be nearly 40 inches high—the owner of the peat bog skull may thus have stood perhaps 48 inches at the shoulder. The majority of these early dogs, were according to legend and somewhat scant historical evidence, yellow or sandy-brown or dun-red in colour, and Ritchie believes that the steel-grey colour seen in modern hounds is proof of the impurity of the modern stock.

Thus the reader might be excused for asking what actually did become of the giant Celtic hound. Ritchie believes the breed became extinct and the modern Irish wolfhound is at the best a very second-rate replica of the great hound of Tara's Halls, the monstrous hounds of Ossian's pages. The decline of the breed must have coincided with the extinction of the wolf and the deer from Ireland during the late Middle Ages and the breed or type denied its rightful functions became firstly, simply, an ornament or status symbol and later extinct. Taplin, unfortunately never the reliable observer he is purported to be, writing in 1803, describes the dog as midway between a greyhound and a mastiff in shape and a mere 30 inches at the shoulder.

Captain Graham began his work of reviving the breed in 1862—but Ritchie believes that long before this time, the bonafide great Irish hound was extinct. Graham managed to gather together a few of what he considered to be typical specimens of the breed, although by today's standards the specimens were small, rather weedy and untypical. He bought stock from the Earl of Caledon and possibly came by dogs of a Major Granier, both of whom had used Great Dane blood to aid the very small gene pool of surviving hounds. To this mix Graham added Scottish deerhound blood, dogs of a very similar type to the old Celtic hound, smaller and lighter of frame perhaps, but true descendants of the old breed. Later according to Starbuck, he used just one cross of Tibetan wolfdog—perhaps a mastiff type animal to give substance to his new type and add a little bulk to his rather lean and deerhoundy dogs. However the Tibetan wolfdog of Graham's breeding programme remains a shadowy creature, maybe a large nondescript beast given an exotic name for the sake of convenience. Starbuck argues that despite tales to the contrary Graham never used a Great Dane outcross in his recreation or revival of the Irish wolfhound. However, by the time Graham had begun his work, the initial stock he purchased had already been heavily adulterated with Great Dane blood.

Sufficient to say that the dog of long ago is not the dog of today. In the last two decades a schism has occurred amongst breed fanciers, and while some are in favour of the heavy, powerful, hirsute Great Dane type winning at the shows of the present day, a few breeders are of the opinion that the standard has produced a type of dog widely dissimilar from the original wolfhound. The evidence is that the modern standard tends to produce an animal that is too bulky to have stamina enough to come to terms with its original adversary, the European wolf, and now a digression is necessary to justify the statement the writer has just made.

Wolves lope rather than run and, while the loping stride is deceptively fast because of the seemingly effortless gait, the wolf is a stamina runner, an animal that is capable of outrunning most scent hounds in a war of attrition type hunt. Lopez, in his book *Wolves and Men*, tells a story to illustrate this incredible stamina of the wolf. An Inuit seeking to kill a wolf for bounty and being out of ammunition decided to run the animal to exhaustion with his mechanical snowmobile. The wolf ran for 12 miles at speeds of 15 to 30 mph before slowing to a trot which he kept up for four miles, after which he walked for another four miles before collapsing. This then is the traditional quarry of the wolfhound and it requires a somewhat exceptional type of dog to catch it in fair course.

Photographs of North Dakota wolf hunters in 1904, the end of the golden era of bounty hunting, show a typical pack used for commercial wolf coursing. The majority are simply cold-blooded greyhounds (greyhounds plus a dash of some other breed to produce an all-round hunting dog, having both pace and stamina). A dog of the stature of the modern Irish wolfhound would be singularly out of place in such a pack, despite its impressive size and demeanour. Custer, the ill-fated victim of the Little Bighorn disaster, also kept a similar pack of 'wolfhounds', most of which were simply greyhounds or greyhound hybrids, yet there was considerable interest in importing exotica from Europe at that time.

Yet there is abundant evidence to suggest that coursing instinct is still strong in the Irish wolfhound, for such the breed must be called, as it is a star's flight from the great Irish hound which was certainly at least one of its ancestors, however distant the relationship may be. Coursing events have been organised for these great hounds and, while the dogs lack the vivacity and coursing enthusiasm of the greyhound or the whippet, they perform tolerably well behind a hare and display an unexpected enthusiasm for the exercise. However, the breed turns badly and seldom comes to terms with a strong January hare. The very height of these dogs also makes striking and the picking up of the hare more than a little difficult. Dawson, author of the once popular *Finn the Irish Wolfhound*, a very popular between-the-wars dog novel, describes quite well the dog's rather incongruous first attempts at catching a rabbit, but goes on to relate how the great hound excels as a catcher of larger game in the outback of Australia.

At larger quarry the dog may well be of use. Conventional hunting aside, during the Lambourn Lurcher Show in 1980 a pair of 'deerhounds' were offered for sale. Deerhounds they were by use, if not by conventional nomenclature, for the pair were Irish wolfhounds which had been used to bring down deer in South Wales. Neither of the pair experienced any difficulty in pulling down and holding the strongest fallow, and both had, according to the vendor, put up a creditable, if questionably legal, show at the larger, more tenacious red deer. Amazingly the vendor experienced some difficulty in selling the pair, despite the fact that the price was reasonable, and a guarantee as to the working ability of the pair offered.

Clearly, if the dog's working ability is to be exploited to the full then the hunter must seek larger quarry to test the quality of his hounds. Britain simply no longer offers scope to hunt these dogs—nor for that matter does the continent of Europe which no longer boasts the incredible variety of game it once did, and, one hastens to add, protects the remaining game from the ravages which could be inflicted by indiscriminate 'coursing' with sight hounds and allied breeds with a set of often curious statutes, sometimes seemingly designed to bring an end to the pursuit of game with dogs.

Australia offers more scope for hounds of this size with quarry ranging from that enigma, the dingo, to larger unprotected marsupials such as kangaroos. In more recent years feral pig, as ferocious, or perhaps nearly as taxing a quarry as the Prussian boar, buffalo and wild cattle, which like the rabbit are creatures imported by well-intentioned settlers and allowed to 'run feral', all constitute ideal hunting for hounds of the proportions of the Irish wolfhound. Dawson's *Finn the Irish Wolfhound* makes exciting reading as one follows the exploits of the hound when the great dog casts off the fetters of civilisation in the Australian bush. While the book is credited with being one of the great dog tales, one should remember that the work is essentially a novel and is anthropomorphic in the extreme. Finn easily handles the giant kangaroo that has kicked a kangaroo hound bitch savagely, nearly disembowelling her, and he slays without too much trouble the now extinct Thylacine or Tasmanian wolf, a marsupial replica of our own European *Canis lupus*. However, while the breed is readily available in Australia and suitable feral quarry increasing rather than diminishing in number, few serious hunters consider using the Irish wolfhound. Despite Dawson's relegation of the kangaroo hound to second place behind Finn, the type is still used by professional hunters in preference to the Irish wolfhound or other pure-bred hounds. Boar, feral pig derived from escapee Tamworth type pigs, which revert to wild colouring and disposition within a very short time, would seem an ideal, if very testing, quarry for the dog. In point of fact, the hounds are seldom used to hunt this quarry, this being carried out by a mixture of collie or cattle dog mated to Staffordshire and English bull terriers, which are apparently better at coming to terms with feral pig and of giving an excellent account of themselves. In passing, it should be noted by all hunters that the pig, wild, tame or feral, must represent the bravest and most intelligent of quarry. It possesses a hide almost impervious to all but the most powerful bite, a bulk capable of throwing off even leech-like antagonists, and when hurt, upset or angered, a courage quite unexpected of a farmyard animal. It is perhaps mute evidence regarding the constitution and qualities of the Irish wolfhound that few Australian hunters use these hounds in the pursuit of feral pig!

The Americas offer an incredible variety of suitable quarry for the hound, ranging from the jaguar—almost an endangered species, now that the habitat of the beast is being reduced, to the jack-rabbit, a testing and very fleet species of American hare. Starbuck, in her comprehensive tome, *The Irish Wolfhound*, relates the tale of a course on one such jack-rabbit. One hound, a ten-month-old bitch, ran a jack-rabbit two miles, caught it and brought it to hand. The same kennels kept braces of greyhounds also testing them to hare (jack-rabbit) and comparing greyhounds with the Irish wolfhound, the owner remarked that while greyhounds have more initial thrust and early speed, the more powerful wolfhounds come into their own when the protracted course becomes longer than three miles.

With reference to the account of a Mr McAleenan who erected a tablet over the grave of his hound, which had killed a grizzly bear, the reader must draw his own conclusions! Sufficient to say that a bear nine feet in height and topping half a ton in weight is the world's most powerful predator. Many despatch fully grown bulls with an almost contemptuous ease and create mayhem on whole packs of Plott hounds, bred specifically for the purpose of hunting big game. Such a beast, unwounded, fit and well, is a match for any breed of dog and would find the contest scarcely taxing!

Likewise the tale related by Bob Becker in his very popular column 'Dog Notes' in the *Chicago Tribune*, stretches credibility a trifle. Becker states that Tom Lawler, a student at Beloit College was charged by an enraged bull and his Irish wolfhound, a puppy of some eighteen months old, set about the 1100-pound animal and killed it. It should be added that bulls baited by dogs prior to 1837, the year which saw Britain's last bull bait, were not over-matched by 10 or so mastiffs and bulldogs bred specifically for such a bait and that many contests lasted for several hours and saw the demise of many large dogs.

More credible is the account of Ronald K Munroe in Starbuck's book. Munroe, an Australian enthusiast, ran his hound on rabbit, lamping the dog by use of car headlights, progressing to foxes, wallabies and dingo, and eventually pulling down a huge kangaroo with the dog, though he was badly ripped by his adversary. Later still the hound pulled down large sambhur deer (a deer with a Kipling flavour, famed for its speed and strength, imported from

India, and allowed to run wild in the mountainous northern coastal forests).

Breed books tend to eulogise on the breed in question, giving glowing accounts of the dog's qualities but omitting any failings, however obvious. Few breed books concerned with the wolfhound are prepared to mention that the dog is seldom famed for its intelligence and that while some obedience champions have been trained in America, the breed is not easy to train. Delightful inaccuracies such as 'the dog was too smart to be trained' are all too frequently related by proud, but unthinking owners of these dogs.

The truth is few sight hounds are particularly gifted IQ-wise and Irish wolfhounds are no exception to this rule. Obedience training is never easy with any sight hound and if the type once had some inbuilt sagacity of the kind displayed by Montdidier's dog, then such innate intelligence has long since been lost. The breed is perhaps easier to break to livestock than other sight hound types though it must be stressed that, should a dog fail to respond to livestock training, carnage is sure to result.

The very size and weight of the dog has produced problems, problems which may never have been encountered in the original more streamlined Irish hounds. Sore hocks caused by the excessive weight of the hounds are all too evident in the elderly dogs and despite the fact that Starbuck makes reference to hounds of 12 and 15 years of age, the dog is seldom long-lived. A 12-year-old hound is in fact quite an old dog and many appear positively geriatric long before this age. Increased weight also tends to produce a tendency to hip disorders, though it is fair to point out all giant breeds, St Bernards, Newfoundlands, mastiffs etc, all have hip dysplasia schemes to try to breed out the incidence of this abnormality in the breeds. In fact, wolfhounds show less of a tendency to this unpleasant malady than other giant breeds.

Heart problems, gut disorders and other irregularities frequently encountered in the giant breeds are not unknown in the Irish wolfhound, though the rigorous selection of its sight hound ancestors has made for a fairly athletic type of animal. The breed is probably subject to less heart disorders than any other giant breed (deerhounds excepted) but as the breed becomes heavier, bulkier, taller, less typical of the original Irish hound, perhaps it is likely that the incidence of physical abnormalities will increase.

The rearing of any bulky giant breed is never straightforward, and the type of diet which is admirable for the rearing of a smaller breed is unsuitable for bringing up a giant hound. Additives such as vitamins, essential minerals, etc, are needed if a perfectly formed hound is to be reared and exercise must be careful and restricted during the early life of a sapling to prevent bone abnormalities. A person contemplating the purchase of a puppy to run on for any purpose, should consult a recognised and successful breeder and heed his advice to the letter.

The Saluki

The saluki has been described by many as the most beautiful dog in the world. While it is obvious that beauty is in the eye of the beholder, and many would describe the most hideous canine anathema with the same eulogy, no student of symmetry could deny the beauty of these dogs of the desert.

The saluki type exists from Afghanistan and northern India to Spanish Morocco, becoming more glabrous or hirsute as the climate dictates. In colder regions the type develops a longer protective coat, while the saluki of the hotter, drier areas tends to be less well-feathered and more sparsely coated. The classic saluki, the type the general public associates with the breed, is a native of Arabia and possibly the Levant, but each nomadic race, subdued by the irrepressible force of Islam, seems to produce desert greyhounds similar in type to the saluki. The Berber hunting dog, the sloughi is certainly a saluki type, even the name is similar, while the Tuareg, the veiled men, the Guaramante of Strabo, keep a similar dog, a little more broken-coated perhaps, but nevertheless a type of desert greyhound or saluki.

Which type was the ancestor of the others will always perhaps be debated, but there is no evidence to suggest that the type originated in pre-Hyksos Egypt as many breed books suggest. That tombs were decorated with drawings of greyhound type dogs—or more often dogs resembling hybrids twixt the Niam Niam type or basenji and the greyhound (often having a tendency to an odd spitz-like tail carriage) is indisputable but this is no more conclusive a proof of the origin of the type than that the ornate, elegant borzois, paraded by 1920s socialites, were natives of Knightsbridge. That one such lady requested she be buried with her Pomeranian does not mean that the Pomeranian was a native of Britain. Likewise, the fact that narrow-skulled dogs of a greyhound type have been exhumed from tombs dating from predynastic times circa 3000 BC to Middle Dynasty Egypt is not conclusive proof that the saluki or greyhound type was indigenous to Egypt. In fact, as Zeuner points out in *The History of Domesticated Animals* the greyhound type may have its origins anywhere in the Old World, from the steppes to the Atlas mountains, or the type may have developed independently in several districts. If this were so, the British greyhound may well be unrelated or only distantly related to the saluki, the borzoi and the Afghan hound, though the breeds manifest a very similar appearance. Zeuner indeed suggests that selective breeding of native dogs in any part of the world to produce a fleet type of dog more dependent on visual rather than olfactory senses could have produced dogs of the greyhound type.

Arabia seems an obvious choice for the distribution centre of the saluki type, but only perhaps because Arabia is the birthplace of Islam and, wherever Islamic culture seems to have spread, dogs of the saluki type are to be found. After the death of Mohammed, the conquering Omayyads spread perhaps both faith and saluki type dogs west as far as Tours in southern France where the Moslem armies were turned back by Charles Martel, grandfather of Charlemagne, to northern India where Rajput princes slowed down further Islamic expansion. Thus saluki types, or possible saluki or greyhound types are found in Spain; the smooth-coated galgo of the Chalo-speaking Spanish gypsy is often nearly identical to some types of Berber sloughi, and the Rhampur hound of northern India and Afghanistan might also pass unnoticed in gypsy encampments in the Meseta.

Yet another theory concerning the origin of the saluki or desert greyhound type is that the dog was created by domesticating certain types of Arabian wolf which have narrower, more fragile skulls than the more powerful Palaearctic wolf of northern Europe and Asia. Once again this theory does not bear up to examination under a strong light. The long lean head of the typical sight hound, the narrow cranium and the well-developed carnassial teeth present a skull only vaguely similar to the Arabian wolf. It is also worth noting that Zeuner mentions that the most important changes wrought by domesticators of animals are exhibited by the skull of the domesticate and that the facial parts of the skull tend to be shortened, relative to the cranial parts rather than lengthened—though this probably proves little or nothing as to the origin of the type for there are notable exceptions to Zeuner's rule.

Whatever the origin and distribution point of the saluki, the dog can be considered as the Arab greyhound, or more exactly the greyhound type of the Arab world. Some variation must be expected in its native lands, quite simply because the dog is bred according to personal preference and its type not regulated by Kennel Club type standards. For example, Upton, *The Saluki of the Desert* in Standfast Press's *Coursing* states that two distinct types exist: the dark, smooth-coated dogs favoured by the more easterly tribes such as the Mutair, dogs with fine coats dark fawn, red or black in colour totally unlike that of the modern greyhound and the lighter-coloured silky-coated dogs of the Howeitat. This is a deliberate over-simplification of type, perhaps, for in recent years white and cream smooth-coated salukis have been imported from Saudi Arabia and these in fact have proven extremely useful in the coursing field.

Salukis have acted as the hunting dogs of the nomadic tribes since pre-Biblical times. The greyhound of the song of Solomon is probably a reference to a type of hound more of the calibre of the saluki than the modern track or coursing greyhound, though the breed type probably existed long before Abraham, let alone his descendant Solomon. At risk of appearing an iconoclast, salukis must be regarded as the lurchers of the nomadic tribes, acting as pot fillers, pulling down hare, gazelle and the great bustard or houbara, a large turkey-like bird which will run a considerable distance before taking flight thereby affording a somewhat untesting course before capture.

Breed books always tend to eulogise and indulge in hyperbole concerning the saluki, stating that the nomadic Arab tribes refer to it as El Hor, the noble one as opposed to camp curs which are regarded as Naq or unclean, but this too is an over-simplification of fact and circumstance. The nomadic tribes were slow to embrace Islam and reluctant to forget old gods and even more ancient customs. Thus the laws of the Koran, similar to, if not based on, the much older Mosiac codes of the Torah were of necessity more tolerant and more flexible than the laws of Moses. The Arabian tribes had kept salukis for several thousand years before Allah dictated the Koranic scripts to Mohammed, and hence the rules regarding the rejection of the dog because of its unclean habits were probably bent a little by the more tolerant Muslims to allow hound-loving Bedouins to embrace Islam.

Camp curs are still regarded as unclean, as, like all pariah types, they eat waste and human filth. Salukis are usually more carefully kept, seldom allowed to scavenge and are thus regarded as less unclean or perhaps even a different species from the more omnivorous camp dogs. Tales however of women suckling orphaned saluki puppies should be regarded with suspicion. Tolerant the Bedouin may be, but there are depths to which few people will sink, particularly in nomadic encampments where goats' milk would be readily available.

The saluki is simply a nomad's lurcher, a provider, a pot filler and it would be wholly wrong to think that such dogs were kept only by oil-rich sheiks. Prior to the overthrow of the Turks during the 1914–1918 war, few sheiks were much richer than the rest of their tribe and ate the same food, following the same lifestyle as did the average tribesman. This is the light in which the traditional owners of the saluki should be regarded and if there are tales that no Arab would part with his dog, so neither would the caring western lurcher owner, or the dog-dependant Norfolk poacher of last century be willing to sell his best and most beloved lurcher. Much mystique surrounds the saluki, but it is likely that such mystique has been invented by western owners of the dog rather than by the type's original nomadic breeders. Tales of the prowess of certain dogs are legion and repeated with monotonous regularity in most books concerning the breed, but such tales are simply Middle Eastern editions of lurcher tales repeated in public houses throughout Britain and probably subject to the same degree of exaggeration. If the saluki is regarded as an aristocrat it is the western world which has created this image. That oil-rich sheiks now own the very best salukis is probably true. They also own the very best British greyhounds and racehorses, but before it was embraced by the Kennel Club the saluki was the hound of the nomadic Arab, not just the Arab potentate.

A variety of middle-eastern quarry is still pursued and brought down by the saluki in its native land, and hounds certainly respond best if entered gradually. Puppies and saplings are seldom slipped on gazelle or the fleet desert hare, but are first run at long-legged jerboas, a type of kangaroo-like desert rodent which will run to ground like a rabbit when pursued. Later the dogs are entered to the desert hare, a lagomorph supposedly as swift and elusive as our British brown hare. When the hound is more mature some salukis will take jackal, but as with all sight hounds, the catching of an adversary, which will retaliate, depends much on the disposition of the dog, although probably more on the mode of entering. Jackal, which are midway in size between the fox and the wolf, will retaliate furiously if brought to bay. Few dogs are thus run singly at jackal and the best results are usually obtained if a youngster is entered alongside a seasoned veteran. A young saluki so entered is carried into the battle by the enthusiasm of the older dog and is heated, rather than deterred, by the retaliatory bites of the prey. A youngster entered singly, and bitten during its first encounter with a jackal, may become totally wed to the quarry and become ecstatic at the sight of a jackal. Equally likely, once badly bitten, when run singly at jackal, the saluki will refuse to tackle the quarry ever again.

The most testing quarry for the saluki, or any hound for that matter, is the fleetfooted desert gazelle, the few related species of which are balanced on the slender arete of extinction at the time of writing. This type of gazelle is not only capable of sudden and blindingly fast acceleration but also possesses incredible stamina. Shortly after the importance of crude oil made the Arab rulers rich, it is said that cheetahs, reputedly the world's fastest mammal, were brought over from Africa to be trained to run these gazelle. Even when properly conditioned, cheetahs which run at such a speed that during their 70-mph sprint they neither inhale nor exhale, made little impact on these gazelle. Herbivores of this type, naturally fleet of foot, are made more alert still by perpetual harassment from predators. Hence few will allow a hunter to achieve the short slip essential to cheetahs. Long slips are clearly impractical for them, for an animal which achieves this phenomenal rate of acceleration is unlikely to be able to stay with its quarry for more than a few hundred yards. For this reason the brown hare or its desert counterpart is able to outrun a cheetah if the prey is given fair and reasonable law. For the same reason the desert gazelle must be regarded as the most testing of quarry for any hound of either scent or sight hunting type.

As in the case of the nineteenth-century Scottish deerhounds attempting the capture of a red deer stag, the majority of salukis are run as a brace in order to catch a gazelle—although single-handed gazelle catchers are greatly prized by the Bedouin and it is said that a nomad will journey several hundred miles to mate a bitch to such a dog. An unique combination of qualities is required for a single dog to bring down a gazelle. The hound must have speed to exceed that of the gazelle as well as stamina, for few gazelle will allow a short slip. The hound must have timing to bring about a catch at 30 mph, and strength to hold down the gazelle. If one quality is missing, the dog becomes less than first rate. If the dog lacks two of these essential qualities, its value as a catch dog becomes greatly diminished.

So difficult is the capture of this desert gazelle that a strange alliance has been devised to secure it. The combination, involving salukis and hawks (either the saker falcon, a peregrine-like species, nesting from Hungary to the equator, or the shabbaz, a large, powerful, but rather untidy species of goshawk obtained largely from northern India, though the shabbaz is usually flown at an Indian species of gazelle, the Abu Dashri), is a delicately balanced one and involves not only a hunting symbiosis, but also a mutual respect between hawks and dogs. To enable a saluki to come to terms with the gazelle a hawk is used to slow down or baffle the beast so that the saluki is able to come up on, catch and hold the quarry.

The training of the hawk would delight both Pavlov and Frederick Stupor Mundi. A nestling hawk, never a wild-caught haggard, is allowed to feed only upon the head of a stuffed gazelle and meat is hung between the horns of the preserved creature. As the hawk begins to be able to fly, it is encouraged to jump to the head to be fed. Later the head of the gazelle is towed behind a horse and the bird is encouraged to fly to the moving head in order that it may be fed. At no time is the bird fed anywhere other than on the stuffed gazelle's head so that it considers the head as its sole feeding place, the only place in fact where food is to be found.

When the bird is considered ready for use, its weight is reduced greatly. European falconers usually consider that a falcon is ready for flying when it has lost roughly a tenth of its body weight—a peregrine weighting two and a half pounds on capture must lose four ounces of its body weight before it is biddable enough to train. A saker falcon or a large goshawk to be used for the taking of gazelle, a sport which is called chirk hawking, must be reduced much lower, and flown so hungry that its droppings usually become bright emerald green, an indication that the bird has begun to reduce all its body's food reserves. A delicate balance must be struck, a balance wherein the body weight of the hawk is reduced enough to make the bird keen to fly this large and unnatural quarry, yet remain strong enough to be able to fulfil the task.

A hunting party now takes both salukis and falcons in pursuit of the gazelle and, once the beast is sighted, should the slip be too long for the saluki to make a catch, the hawk is allowed to fly free. On seeing the quarry, it believes that meat is to be found between the horns of the creature and flies at its head in the belief that it will be fed. The gazelle, baffled by this aerial attack, races hither and thither to throw of its attacker, heedless perhaps of the fact that the saluki has been slipped and is gaining on it. Dogs that are regularly used for the capture of deer, and deer-like creatures, usually forego the full-blooded throat hold which brings dog and deer crashing over, rendering both dog and deer injured, and as a rule grab the deer by the hind leg, holding it while the hawk or falcon flutters around the horns. The gazelle is quickly despatched and the still-warm heart or liver fed to both the falcon and the hound. Chirk hawking is the ultimate form of hunting symbiosis, but so rare has the desert gazelle become and so uncommon are the falconers who can condition a bird to act antagonistically towards the gazelle, that chirk hawking is seldom seen these days. The gazelle is afforded some protection in many Arab states and now the desert hare is the principal quarry of the coursing saluki of the Bedouin.

The practice of chirk hawking must seem abhorrent to some and savagely cruel, but it does nevertheless represent the most difficult training programme any hunter is ever likely to attempt. Sadly, the skill required to train such a combination of dog and bird is as much of an anachronism as the world of T E Lawrence and it is unlikely that chirk hawking will survive the twentieth century. Upton, whose article on the saluki in Standfast Press's classic book, *Coursing*, lends an exotic atmosphere to the book, suggests that only one sheik is still practising chirk hawking, although the interior of Arabia, a largely unknown country, may well still conceal experts in this archaic art.

The pursuit of the desert hare—supposedly a more fleet species than even our own British brown hare (though this is almost unbelievable) and the equally elusive desert gazelle has resulted in the evolution of sight hounds with unusual characteristics. A hound suitable for the pursuit and capture of long distance athletes such as the hare, the gazelle, and to a certain extent the golden jackal, needs speed to come up on its quarry, but speed should be coupled with great stamina, for the pursuit of these animals is often a lengthy one. The blindingly fast sprint that characterises the running style of the English greyhound, the fastest of dogs, would hardly be suitable for the pursuit of desert quarry, many of which are afforded great law by the nature of the countryside, and amongst dune and desert scrub a gazelle or a hare is unlikely to be taken 'underfoot' by any dog. Hence, a hound with an unusual combination of speed, coupled with stamina, is needed to course and catch hare and gazelle, and, as no dog is able to sustain the powerful running style of the greyhound for any length of time, the saluki has developed a loping style of propulsion which enables it to stay with its quarry for a great distance. Despite the loping style the saluki is deceptively fast and is seldom outrun by any quarry. *Aficionados* of coursing are quick to condemn the breed as a dog which does not try, a dog which does not favour the power-house burst of speed of the greyhound, but there are constitutional and mental differences between salukis and greyhounds, and any coursing enthusiast must recognise this before the purchase of a saluki for coursing.

To digress slightly, however, since the arrival of the saluki in Britain, the breed has been used to good effect by longdog enthusiasts who are concerned with producing the single-handed hare-catching dogs which either run hare with fair law or slip at a pre-arranged distance. Such lengthy slips in open country are destructive to even the gamest of greyhounds, for greyhounds, even the very best English coursing dogs, are seldom geared to fare well in such competitions. Thus longdogs are bred deliberately, reducing the speed of the greyhound an iota—no more, lest the dog be too slow—with the blood of other sight hound types. At one time the deerhound greyhound hybrid swept all before it, but with the increasing popularity of the saluki, longdogs of saluki breeding are now the most successful competitors at the best of three hare catching contests beloved by longdog enthusiasts. The saluki hybrid is tailor-made for such a contest, for while it retains some of the speed of its greyhound parent, some of the hybrids (not all it should be mentioned) will inherit the stamina imparted by the seemingly effortless running technique of the saluki. Too much saluki blood is not considered advantageous however, for the saluki-saturated hybrid seldom makes a showing at a strong hare. Most top class longdogs today have saluki blood—indeed the deerhound greyhound longdogs of the 1960s and early 1970s are seldom seen except perhaps at shows. The majority of longdog breeders tend to prefer a dog with roughly a quarter saluki breeding, as the hybrid has greyhound thrust coupled with some of the saluki stamina. At the time of writing (1989) the most famous longdogs are all saluki bred—Dee, Merlin and Southerd's Lady all carry roughly 25 per cent saluki in their pedigrees.

To return to the saluki in its pure, rather than its adulterated, state. Despite the fact that the majority of the salukis kept in Britain have never seen a hare, there is a marked enthusiasm for maintaining the coursing qualities of the breed amongst the members of the Saluki Club, and a number of coursing meets are staged, the slippers for which receive the same training and guidance as do the slippers for the greyhound coursing clubs. Sportsmanship rather than a large bag of hares is the objective of such clubs, though the salukis coursing under rules before Christmas usually take an incredible number of hares. Courses are usually quite long and most exceed even the lengthy second day Waterloo Cup courses at Lydiate where a course of 90 seconds duration is the order of the day. Salukis take longer to come up on their hares than coursing greyhounds or longdogs, but once on to them, are seldom run to a standstill as are many coursing greyhounds.

Some saluki meets are run in conjunction with the Deerhound Club and it is astonishing how well deerhounds fare against the smaller, more fluidly moving salukis. In the New Year, meets are run around Inverness and the quarry is the blue or white hare, rather than the larger, more athletic lowland brown hare. The terrain, however, compensates for the somewhat lesser athletic ability of the blue hare, for rocks, peat hags (the most feared of obstacles for the longdog enthusiast must be the precipitous peat cuts which often terrace the Highland landscape) make the course difficult and the capture of hares not as easy as the coursing man may at first believe. Blue hares run in natural conditions, conditions not ameliorated by forestry and such operations as moss clearance are not easy quarry. Blue hares will spring from stone to stone in cairns over which a man has difficulty in walking—and where a man cannot walk, a dog, even a saluki, can seldom run. Hares of this type will seemingly float over deep and fairly compact heather, and the dogs pursuing these hares must crash through this plant growth, frequently damaging feet and leg muscles. When hard pressed, blue hares will seek sanctuary in cracks, crevices and even rabbit holes far more readily than the brown hare, and these qualities make it a hard and testing quarry. So uneven is the ground coursed during these Highland meets that the judge must forego the use of a horse and do his best to follow the course with the aid of binoculars. Such courses must wreak havoc on the feet of the dog following the hare, and it is all the more amazing that deerhounds, scarcely the most agile of dogs, perform quite well at these meets. To watch such a course over such a lunar landscape a coursing supporter must be prepared to see spills and thrills which, while they are certainly exciting to see, can damage even the most agile of dogs. Yet amazingly few salukis suffer damage from these courses. The evolution of the type and an unintentional process of selection, when the breed has been run for millennia over desert scrub, bashan and foot-destroying *zeugen* and *yardang* rock-scape, has produced a type of dog with exceedingly tough, if rather untidy-looking feet, which are almost injury proof. Thus, while these Highland meets are seemingly unsuitable for conventional coursing under rules, they often present the saluki with a terrain which, while wetter, boggier and colder, is not entirely dissimilar from the land which has seen its evolution. The smooth, fine-grained sandy bashans or crescentic dunes seldom produce enough herbage to feed even the desert hare—a species rarely known to drink and capable of extracting water from the woody xerophytic desert plants, but the shattered rock surfaces, the *zeugen* or *yardang* deserts, will often support the salt-tolerant scrub on which hares feed. Thus the saluki, while its exotic, oriental appearance must make it look a little out of place coursing blue hare over rock scree, peat hag and heather, is far more suitable for these assault course type athletics than the English greyhound. To watch such courses is to see the saluki at its best and to be able to appreciate the wonderful process of selection that has produced this rugged athlete.

The seemingly frail appearance of the saluki is deceptive. Pattison, writing on lurchers in *Coursing* (Standfast Press), states that the type is far from suitable for enduring the bumps and spills of the English countryside, bumps which the more robust lurcher will often take in its stride. Pattison is woefully wrong in his appraisal of the breed. Salukis do in fact survive the tumbles which would incapacitate or kill a greyhound or a lurcher. The peculiar loping gait often enables the dog to come off high speed collisions with tree stumps—the kiss of death for most coursing dogs. Dr Philip Maxwell who once coursed dogs from a show-bred strain of saluki, running them in single-dog slips to brown hare from Hampshire to Northumberland has this to say on the subject: 'My dogs often give the impression they are indestructible and have survived bumps the like of which I find too frightening to watch. In 1967 (or thereabouts) I ran old pastures with two of my hounds and they took the problems of collisions with tree roots in their stride. Sheyda, my best bitch, once hit such a stump set on the downhill portion of a field and somersaulted maybe 10 feet down the slope. I closed my eyes not to witness the almost inevitable bone-shattering crash when she landed, and winced as I prepared for the scream of pain, but on opening my eyes I saw Sheyda still running, a little shakily perhaps, but still on her hare. The smaller lighter salukis would be my bet for coursing hares over such country, though I have owned large dogs which will certainly take punishing courses. Berkut, a pale red dog I once owned, ran a hare into a stone quarry filled with ancient farm machinery and discarded household appliances (old cookers, washing machines, etc) and succeeded in coming out of the tangle without a scratch.' Hares will often seek out such places and use them to good effect to evade and bring a dog to grief. Barbed-wire rolls, rusted until they are in a state of disintegration, often act like magnets to a hard-pressed hare and many will almost deliberately seek out such a tangle to confuse a dog or bring it down by darting in and out of the piles of farm rubbish. Injuries amongst coursing dogs running in country where such rubbish is encountered are far from rare. Contrary to Pattison, salukis do remarkably well in such places and are seldom damaged as much as a longdog or lurcher might be.

Surprisingly, but perhaps not so on reflection, the saluki fares well when it chances on a hare and runs it over frosted ground that has puckered to form sharp ridges. A Mrs Ellen Parkes writes: 'Winter time in Minnesota is far from clement. When the snow isn't too deep to prevent coursing, the land is hard frozen and tough running. Elsa, a white fawn bitch I bought out of a pair of English imports, comes into her own on hard going where the land is frozen tight. She has taken jacks (an American species of hare) after a two mile course over frozen fields and seldom so much as knocked up a toe. A friend has a cold-blood dog (a greyhound type longdog, more often than not deerhound blooded) which often comes to grief and will not hunt jacks when the temperature goes below $-10°$ Elsa seldom comes to grief under such conditions and has taken more jacks than any dog here about.'

Ideally, however, the wide open fields of the fens and similar country is the best running country for both salukis and hares. Here courses are not shortened by what is known in coursing parlance as 'short field running' where a hare is captured as it turns back into the field having encountered an unfamiliar stretch of hedge. Small field running usually gives a tyro-coursing enthusiast a false impression of the dogs in his care and geese invariably metamorphose into swans under such conditions. In small fields, hares are often brought down by inferior dogs of all breeds. In open fen country, land devoid of hedges, but criss-crossed with deep and wide water-filled dykes, the brown hare comes into its own and in such country a middle-distance runner such as the saluki can be seen at its best whilst the tight-bred longdog—a dog with a high proportion of greyhound to other sight hound blood—is seldom at an advantage, for whereas such a dog usually comes on its hare quickly, few hares are brought down after the first turn in open fenland. Here the relentless loping stride of the saluki is ideal in a coursing dog, for the courses given by strong fen hares at the turn of the year are often long and exhausting to the dog. A pair of salukis run to rules will often produce a course long enough to reduce the very best greyhound to a walking pace. Southerd once said that he wagered heavily on a particularly good, smooth-coated saluki against any longdog in such conditions, for in such places a saluki will often perform extremely well. Indeed this is the country to see salukis perform at their best.

Sagar, a slipper for the Saluki Club, is of the opinion that the saluki is perhaps the most suitable pure-bred dog for bringing about the capture of hares, and one of the only pure breeds of dog that makes a consistent single-handed hare-killing dog. Certainly his success with his white, smooth-coated Boutflower bred bitch has been little short of phenomenal. This bitch bred from a first generation import to an imported bitch has competed favourably both in coursing under rules when it was 'pipped' at the final of the Greve Cup by its stronger litter brother and against top-grade longdogs running singly at 100 and 200 yard slips. In late 1988, Sagar won a 2–0 victory over Southerd's best quarter-bred saluki longdogs, Southerd comments: 'It is no disgrace to be beaten by such an animal.' It should be pointed out that Southerd had enjoyed an exceptional three-year stint with his strain of longdog and had, apart from one split decision, beaten all comers. Thus Sagar's success against this longdog becomes all the more creditable.

Sagar has some interesting tried and tested theories concerning salukis. He gravitated to the breed from conventional lurchers of mixed and dubious origins so his theories cannot be said to be coloured by what is often called breed blindness—a malaise endemic amongst writers of breed books who fail to see the faults and foibles of their beloved breeds. Sagar's approach to the training of his salukis is both unusual and unconventional. His dogs, a smooth and a feathered bitch, have worked rabbits with ferrets, and Sagar reports that they display a fairly high attention span (attention span is an essential quality in a ferreting dog and is not related to intelligence. Many sight hounds have an attention span that equals that of a collie-bred lurcher) run the beam for rabbits and hares and have hunted up quarry. Running 'singles' against longdogs and besting all competition is hardly conducive to the production of a successful dog for the sport of coursing under rules. Dogs used as hare-catching dogs, as opposed to hare-coursing dogs, develop a quality known as 'running cunning'. Dogs which have learned to run cunning seldom put in the maximum effort to come up to and turn the hare, but hang back a little, anticipating the turn of the hare in its erratic jinking flight. Such a dog, while it makes a satisfactory hare-catching dog, is unlikely to pile on points in a coursing under-rules event. Yet Sagar has succeeded at both types of hare coursing, and succeeded against the best salukis and longdogs.

This versatility is not unique, however. Michael Lyne, coursing artist and saluki enthusiast, remarks that one of the saluki coursing 'greats' was Mrs Baker's Knightellington Esmail. The dog was greatly over-coursed by Captain Rodney Baker who ran hares regularly on Salisbury Plains, and never learned to run cunning in the manner of the hare-catching lurcher or longdog, yet was a persistent winner coursing under rules. Lyne states that Esmail produced a spate of winning offspring—winners in the field if not the show ring, for the field, not the show bench, is the rightful place of the saluki.

Sagar, however, is something of a heretic amongst the saluki fraternity, and believes that salukis are not as recalcitrant and difficult to train as they are reputed to be. He believes that salukis mature more slowly than other breeds and are ready for obedience and discipline only after their third year. After that time the most difficult of them will respond to command more quickly and become a responsible hunting dog. Longdog enthusiasts are frequently of the opinion that saluki blood can often introduce a tendency to nervousness in the breed (Southerd once produced a saluki hybrid which was so sensitive as to not perform in public) but is due to an absence of socialising at the puppy stage. Two American psychologists, Scott and Fuller, in 1962, produced a table which indicated that at certain times of a puppy's development, socialising—close contact with human beings—was more vital than at other times. Sagar believes that the saluki needs far more contact with human beings and this socialising could prevent or at least reduce the incidence of nervousness in salukis. In short salukis need far more human companionship than other breeds and if denied this contact with human beings become not only more nervous but also decidedly recalcitrant.

While enthusiasts such as Lyne and Sagar may eulogise on the speed, stamina and elegance of the breed—and there is no denying that the saluki has all those qualities there are many who do not sing the praises of the breed with such enthusiasm. A glance at a paper selling dogs will illustrate the point fairly vividly. A great many saplings and older dogs are invariably offered for sale often free to good homes and the Saluki Rescue Society is always fully occupied finding homes for unwanted salukis, salukis which are untrainable, destructive, sheep worriers, stock killers and above all sociopathic dogs, displaying nervous dispositions and the other qualities which go hand in hand with these problems. Clearly the saluki is not a suitable dog for everyone. Caring breeders will often vet buyers before selling them a saluki puppy. Other breeders are less careful and seem only too keen to part with their wards, and the incredible beauty and exotic nature of the dog attracts hosts of unsuitable buyers, most of whom realise that the dog is an unacceptable pet shortly after purchase. Matters worsen quickly and if early socialising and basic training is omitted or neglected, the saluki becomes a 'difficult' animal all too easily.

Salukis are not an easy breed of dog to train. No sight hound is, for that matter and hence sight hound rescue services are certainly needed. More exotic sight hound puppies (Ibizan hounds, Afghan hounds and salukis) are bred than breeders can find the right sort of homes for, hence the dogs often fall into the hands of the wrong buyers. It has been suggested that those who breed salukis should advise and supervise purchasers about the training of puppies, but a great many saluki breeders also have little idea of how to train their wards other than to lead break them to be paraded around a show ring. Obedience classes for buyers of saluki puppies are an excellent idea, but once again the slow response of sight hound puppies may daunt a tyro dog owner, particularly if the trainer starts to compare the progress of his hound with that of a collie or German shepherd dog puppy of the same age. Breed books which enthuse about the intelligence of sight hounds are not only written inaccurately, but do the breed a disservice. Most first-time dog owners treat these breed books as bibles and are bitterly disappointed when their dogs turn out not to be the canine Mensa candidates which these books have suggested they are. Comments such as 'these hounds are too intelligent to want to do a mere human's bidding' are misleading and downright inaccurate. New buyers should be informed of the limitations of sight hounds, be advised that the hounds are difficult to train, slow to respond, and prone to be stock worriers if they are allowed too much freedom. Obviously unsuitable clients should be discouraged from buying a puppy. That a person requires a dog as an image maker is not necessarily a reason for not selling a person a puppy—most dogs are kept as image makers anyway, but an obviously unsuitable client should not be sold a whelp. Furthermore, every buyer of a saluki puppy should be advised to attend obedience classes with their new purchase.

A saluki is a specialist dog, a dog bred for generations to run hare and gazelle in desert conditions. It was never produced as an all rounder, a family pet type dog with the inbuilt obedience of a Border collie. It is difficult to assess canine intelligence, indeed it is difficult to even define the word intelligence, but while it is not totally scientifically accurate, canine intelligence should be equated with tractability. A breed should be regarded as intelligent if it can be trained to a high level of proficiency. Salukis are not biddable and are difficult to train and this point should be borne in mind and considered before attempting to teach a saluki puppy simple obedience. They respond to commands with a maddening slowness, a slowness which makes one think that they hear the command, translate the sound to something meaningful, debate the validity of the order and finally decide that the command was not really worth obeying. Such an attitude, if attitude is the correct word, is disconcerting to the professional trainer and soul destroying to the beginner. Many first dog owners met at shows with salukis on slip state that they are unable to get the dog to return to hand once it has been allowed to run free, and tales of hunts to return a dog to the lead are so usual as to be unfunny. Sagar, who has worked his dogs to quarry in the manner of a lurcher as much as that of a pure-bred sight hound, comments on similar tales he has heard, but adds that because of what he believes to be the somewhat slower rate of maturity of the saluki, one should be tolerant with them until three years have elapsed, after which they become more receptive to training and less recalcitrant. Sagar's success with working salukis would indicate that he is probably correct. He has worked his hounds with considerable success, both the feathered-eared type of saluki and the less popular smooth-coated dogs, salukis recently imported to Britain and proving somewhat superior in the coursing field. Both types, he assures us, can be trained and the fact that his dogs return to hand fairly readily after a course is verified by many longdog enthusiasts, many of whom have sought to use these unusual smooth-coated salukis in their bloodlines. Southerd comments on the type thus: 'Whenever I have been beaten by any dog (sic) I seek to use it. It is the only way I can improve the type and performance of my own dogs. I was bested by Sagar's bitch, she was one of the only pure-bred salukis that I have known to beat me, so that is the saluki blood I shall try to bring into my own strain.' Sagar, however, comments that he is prepared to tolerate the aloof and remote attitude of his breed because of their athletic prowess: 'They are to my mind the only breed, the only pure breed of dog that will regularly catch, rather than just course, hares.'

Longdog owners frequently remark that one of the virtues of the saluki as a hare catcher is that it is relatively easy to condition. Few longdog enthusiasts will accept a heavily wagered challenge unless they are given time to prepare the dog for the event. Thus tales of longdogs, of top class longdogs with success in the field, being bested by an itinerant's bull terrier/greyhound released from his chain at the scrap yard and run without conditioning, should be ignored. A dog needs careful conditioning before being slipped on a hare that is given fair law. The average longdog trainer estimates that to catch a winter hare, again with fair law and not killed underfoot, requires a six week programme of careful conditioning. Single dog hare coursers usually believe a saluki requires somewhat less of a conditioning programme to produce the finished article.

While it is obvious that the saluki's frame is unlikely to house the internal fat of a rested greyhound—and greyhounds gain fat rapidly if allowed to rest up and are fed ad lib.,—what is interesting is the saluki's laid back attitude. Many take to training with the boredom of a Max Baer preparing for a fight. It has been said that while anthropomorphism is unscientific, the saluki is one of the only breeds of dog that can actually tell its owner it feels bored. Many simply languish around the owner's house, draped like ornate fur rugs over chairs and dog baskets disdaining road work and only coming to life when they are taken into the field. This does not mean that the saluki can simply be taken from its cushion and run against all comers with success. Road work to ensure good feet is still essential as is free running exercise to condition muscles, for an unconditioned dog that chances on a hare will usually return to the owner in great pain, as a hard run sorely tests the muscles of a dog. Salukis are like any other breed of dog and need to be fielded physically fit if they are to course or catch hares, but the conditioning programme needed to produce this super-fit condition is shorter, usually less taxing, and needs if anything to be a more varied and interesting session of conditioning than the programme needed to field a greyhound or tight-bred longdog.

Conditioning dogs by running a lure, or worse still treadmills of the type used to condition a bull terrier, will usually result in boredom when the method is used to condition a saluki. At the lurcher races which are common at country shows where lurchers and longdogs become literally frantic to chase a fur-covered line, salukis can often be seen around the course displaying some interest in a passing lure until they realise the lure is simply a dummy, after which only a mild enthusiasm is manifested by them. Salukis have been run from traps in the manner of greyhounds and whippets, but they run a lure with less enthusiasm than do their occidental counterparts. Thus while it can be said that salukis are more easily conditioned than most sight hounds or longdogs, they are not easy dogs to get fit and to 'field on form'.

Exercise behind a horse along bridle-paths seems to be favoured more than trotting these dogs behind a car, a method used by longdog trainers, perhaps because the sight of a pair of salukis running behind a car is less picturesque, or maybe because the saluki has closer contact with the owner mounted on a horse than it would have if he drove on ahead in a car.

A pair of salukis will usually exercise well and gain more in condition from a ten minute exercise period than a single dog may gain in an hour. Muscle, or running muscle, can only be encouraged by hard strenuous exercise. Indeed the weight trainers' adage 'there is no gain without pain' may well be true and there is no substitute for hard taxing running to create muscles suitable for coursing. Exercise periods should begin gently and be of short duration. They should never over-tax or strain a dog—strain will often put the dog in sick bay rather than condition it—and exercise periods should stop as soon as the trainer sees that the saluki is becoming bored, or out of love, with the exercise session. Once the owner/trainer notes that a dog is becoming pained, bored or unwilling during any training exercise, the programme should be stopped for the day. To continue when the dog is obviously not enjoying the training period is counter-productive.

As training becomes progressively more rigorous, and the operative word is 'progressively' not simply 'rigorous', diet should be adjusted accordingly. Salukis are some of the greatest omnivores of the dog kingdom and, alongside their Arab owners, have endured feast followed by fast for generations. Many will exist and seemingly hold condition on an almost totally vegetable diet. Indeed there are tales that salukis and Arabs can often exist for indefinite periods of time, their only sustenance being 'the black ones'—dates and water. However, this diet, while it may sustain the body condition of a saluki, is certainly not the best diet to condition a coursing hound. A good rule, one used to condition boxers, runners, and racing pigeons (and pigeon flyers often have conditioning down to a fine art) is that, once strenuous exercise commences, the diet should be one of reduced carbohydrate and increased protein. Pigeon racers simply step up the feeding of high-grade pulses and reduce the ration of low-grade protein food, such as wheat, barley and maize. Saluki coursers should simply reduce the quantity of biscuit and increase the quantity of flesh fed. As a coursing event nears, the dog should be feeding on a very low biscuit diet and a high meat diet. Many longdog trainers fielding saluki crosses take the preparation of the meat for their dogs a little too seriously. Some, particularly those who advocate feeding mutton, strip all fat from the meat, cook the meat, allow the broth to cool and then skim off the thin layer of fat on top of the cooled broth. This is not only unnecessary it is also a bit undesirable. Fat is part and parcel of the flesh, and some fat is needed in the diet of a dog about to run its hare. A better policy would be to strip off unwanted fat and feed a mineral/vitamin supplement as well as the meat, for red meat alone is lacking in calcium; in fact puppies reared on a red meat diet alone will often develop rickets. A mineral and vitamin supplement as well as the flesh diet—either a proprietory brand of supplement or a bone meal/calcium phosphate mixture—will ensure that the bones of the dog remain sound during the course.

Feeding prior to a big day's coursing or a competitive event is critical, however. No dog will run properly if it is weakened by a long fast before a course. Likewise no dog will perform well when it is bloated with food. No heavy meal should be fed for 24 hours before an event with perhaps an egg in milk fed the night before the course. A dog should run on an empty stomach, not because it will run the better to secure a meal—this is a popular misconception amongst the travelling fraternity—but simply because a full stomach may well inhibit the proper functioning of the dog's heart and lungs during a course. Stockmanship determines the way a dog should be prepared for there are no hard and fast rules and each dog will respond best to a different method of conditioning. Commonsense, observation and sound, clean feed is far more important than any magical 'keep' before a coursing meet.

Care of the dog after a day's sport is crucial. A dog which has run a hard and taxing course may well pant madly and seek to drink, but to allow a heated dog to drink before it has had time to cool is not good practice. A good half hour after a taxing run should elapse before a dog should be given water—and then the quantity of water given should be regulated. Likewise the rugging of a dog after coursing is certainly not an effete affectation. Salukis are thin coated—even the feathered variety, let alone the smooth-coated types—and will chill badly on a cold day after running an arduous course. Rugging a dog after such exercise is no more effete than handing Mike Tyson his dressing gown after a hard 15-round battle, and serves the same purpose. Above all, commonsense must prevail during a day's coursing, be the event coursing under rules, or simply a day's single dog coursing with friends. Once a dog displays a lack-lustre attitude after a course or takes an inordinate length of time to recover from an exercise, it is time to stop, and stop for the day. A lunch break will not revive such a dog and a short rest before the next course simply will not suffice. It is lunacy to run a somewhat jaded dog on what must be the world's most taxing quarry. Once a dog looks a shade below par, stop coursing it, rug it up, and let it rest for the day. Nothing will be gained from over-running a dog. All might well be lost!

Nothing is gained from being a purist where a breed of dog is concerned. A saluki is perhaps not one of the most versatile breeds, but what versatility it has should be exploited. Salukis can certainly be taught to lamp, and while few perform the task as well as a collie lurcher which is almost designed for the task, salukis will certainly run a beam of light and catch well in that beam. Few salukis are famous for their olfactory senses, though some will hunt up as well as a lurcher, but this absence of nose is an advantage to anyone who is solely a lamper and not interested in daytime hunting up work. A dog which does not use its nose is unlikely to pursue scents after it has caught or missed its quarry on the lamp. It is unlikely to run deaf—to pursue quarry by scent, oblivious to the commands of the trainer. A saluki will certainly lamp well enough, though equally obviously salukis never become as proficient at the task as do lurchers which are bred for lamping.

There is absolutely no mystique about lamping, so the saluki owner should shut his ears to the image-seeking lurcher keepers who seek to tell him otherwise. It is child's play to attach a lamp to a battery, shine a beam of light down a field, illuminate a rabbit or hare and slip a dog at the quarry, and while the salukis are not specifically bred for the task, they will make reasonably competent lampers. Nevertheless, there are reservations. Lamping requires a dog which not only responds to commands as instantly as a collie, but also retrieves the catch to hand. Failure to respond to commands instantly will put every rabbit for miles back to ground, as will repeated entreaties on the part of the owner for the dog to return to the slip. This action will not only infuriate the trainer but also alert the rabbits to the motives of the hunter. Likewise a dog which simply makes the catch and then stands over its quarry—most pure-bred sight hounds tend to favour this approach to hunting—will certainly exhaust the patience of the lamper and the stamina of a marathon runner, for each catch must be fetched to hand by the lamper or the lamper's assistant. Retrieving is essential and obedience to commands more so.

Salukis, however, are not famed for their instant response nor are they particularly obedient—a delightful understatement! Furthermore the saluki tends to favour the typical sight hound technique of catching and standing over the prey rather than retrieving it to hand. Some will retrieve—all can, and should be taught to—yet a saluki makes an intermittent retriever and once the dog refuses to retrieve it is very difficult to rekindle its interest. A non-retrieving dog does not make for a high catch rate. A dog will often retrieve a rabbit to hand, through a batch of sitting rabbits without disturbing them. Not so a man walking towards a dog standing over a 'downed' rabbit or hare, for the movements of the man with beam in hand will, unless the night is both very dark and windy, return every rabbit to ground. Salukis will certainly work the beam, but it would be a very strange person indeed who would buy a saluki puppy simply to use as a lamp dog. Salukis were meant to be pot fillers for the nomadic tribes of the Middle East, but they are not as efficient a pot filler in Britain as the humble lurcher.

However, it is good policy to train a saluki to lamp, for nothing produces top class condition for coursing under rules or single dog coursing as much as a hard night's lamping but once again the 'hard night' should not be given to an unfit or scarcely fit dog. It was Jack Dempsey, heavy weight champion of the world after Willard and before Tunney, who once remarked that the best training for a fight was a fight. Likewise the best training for a hard days coursing is a night's lamping and by now the reader must be aware how similar the conditioning of a fighter for a 15-round contest is to the training and conditioning of a saluki or sight hound hybrid for a hard day's coursing. It would be clearly suicidal for a fighter to embark on such a project unless he was fit and well-trained, and an unfit dog will certainly fare badly against the January hare with fair law, run in open country. However, the fighter is allowed to quit cold in such a contest, the saluki will often go on until it is injured.

At the time of writing the saluki is being woefully overbred and unwanted dogs are now as much a stock in trade of the unscrupulous dog dealer as the lurcher and longdog. This is indeed a great tragedy, for whereas the phlegmatic disposition of the saluki seems to make the dog appear relatively unharmed by the chop and change world of the dog dealer, all is certainly not well. Most dog dealers who traffic in unwanted, uncared for, sight hounds will allow a dog on trial, and as most of the clients of dog dealers are people who have neither skill nor aptitude to train a dog, a saluki purchased by one of these people is invariably taken straight out of kennels and tried on a hare without conditioning and without any preparation for the course. Salukis are seldom short on courage and may well try extremely hard, but an unfit dog has little chance of a catch and the wretch will usually be returned to the dealer by the dissatisfied client to await the attentions of yet another 'instant' coursing enthusiast. Many salukis will know a dozen homes in a month, all will be tried and sorely tested, run unfit and in bad condition. The saluki is a great courser, a grand if unpredictable athlete, and it deserves better than treatment of this kind. The Saluki Club is a wonderful organisation and has done much to ensure the breed does not gravitate to the status of a benched dog, suitable only for exhibition. Would it not be possible for the club to stop this loathsome trade in salukis, or at least disuade breeders from producing surplus puppies which will end up in uncaring dog dealers' kennels?

Long may the breed flourish, long may the breeders improve the type and performance of the hound, but some regulation of the number of salukis bred is called for, lest the breed degenerates to the rank of the lurcher and the longdog, many of whom are truly 'despised, rejected and sorely acquainted with grief'.

The Borzoi

The hallmark of the aloof aristocrat, a dog as Russian as vodka, the insignia of a long-forgotten class of boyars, questionably the most beautiful dog in the world. These are the descriptions of the borzoi, a word derived from the Russian word meaning swift, but the animal itself, its history, its character and its uses, is yet another baffling enigma.

Russia is an immense land, a country of opposites, partly Asiatic, partly European, stretching from the Carpathian mountains to the port of Vladivostock, from the Arctic Ocean to the mountainous region of Afghanistan. Its people once ranged from the deliberately effete boyars, speaking French instead of Russian to enhance their sophistication, to the Mongoloid Chukchi and Goldi people, who resisted the spread of the Russian language and rejected the settled ways demanded by the newly emerging USSR. It is a land whose plains and mountains have seen conquests by a dozen races. Swedes 'a-viking', travelled down its rivers on route for Micklegarth (Constantinople) stayed to found a country the name of which derived from their trade—Rus—a raider. Half a millennium later an explosion in Central Asia brought the Mongols into Russia pillaging, burning, looting, destroying sacred and profane alike, so that Rusudan Queen of Georgia called them Tartars (from Tartarus—Hell). Wave after wave of conquerors swept west then east, rupturing cultures, bringing new languages, creating new ways, destroying the records of the times. Thus evidence regarding the origins of the borzoi or Russian wolfhound has long since been hopelessly lost

THE SIGHT HOUND BREEDS

and forgotten. To write of the origin of these Russian dogs is speculation and guesswork and scarcely educated speculation and guesswork at that.

One theory as to the origin of the breed or type is that the borzoi is simply a descendant of saluki type dogs brought north into Russia by traders and crossed into the boarhounds or herding dog types of Russia. Groshans, in her *Complete Borzoi*, suggests that Mongols may have brought in the greyhoundy types from Iran or even North Africa and introduced them when they invaded Russia in the 1300s. However contact twixt Russia and the Arab world had already been well established by the ninth century when trade in mammoth tusks at Bolgari was recorded. There is some record of hare coursing at Novgarod in 1260 although neither the type of dog nor the manner of coursing has been mentioned. As the greyhound or greyhound type is the only breed of dog capable of taking the hare in fair chase it has been assumed that the dogs mentioned were some type of greyhound or greyhound-like dog.

The change in coat length and type between the silky-coated saluki and the more profuse-coated borzoi is subject to much speculation, most of which is questionable to say the least. One theory is that the more glabrous saluki type dogs were unable to stand the cold of the Russian winters and hence developed the long flowing coats of the borzoi to withstand the biting cold of Russia. Several generations of breeding from saluki-coated dogs in adverse conditions therefore produced the borzoi!

Yet another theory to suggest the origin of the coat of the borzoi is that saluki type dogs were mated with wolves. Firstly the coat of the wolf does not resemble the borzoi's jacket and secondly no evidence suggests that wolf-like features appear in the borzoi. A cross with any species of wolf would have done almost irreparable harm to the development of any sight hound. Wolf crosses (and the cross-breed is produced not without difficulty) are invariably shy and nervous—ill at ease in the company of humans. Furthermore there is an incredibly high incidence of dog/wolf hybrids which make attacks on their owners. Indeed, Lopez considers that any account of a wolf attacking a man found in European and Asiatic records is in reality an account of a wolf/dog hybrid rather than a pure-bred wolf. Wolf blood would lend nothing of advantage to a sight hound either in speed, stamina or disposition.

A further hypothesis which may well be considered is that of independent development. This assumes that a hunting community which relied on the speed of the hunting dogs to secure quarry would develop a type of dog which resembled a sight hound, simply by a process of judicious selection of readily available native dogs. Hence the borzoi could possibly not be related to the saluki or other southern greyhound types and may have developed independently on the steppes of Asia. Zeuner (*History of Domestication*) puts forward this extremely plausible theory although most cynologists seem to overlook such notions.

Another possibility is that the greyhound type originated in the steppe lands of Asia—an ideal country for the development of a greyhound/sight hound type, and that the type dispersed throughout the rest of the Old World. Evidence of greyhound types in Egyptian and Persian archaeological finds proves nothing as to the origin of the types. Neither does the absence of such evidence in central Asia. Nomadic tribes, the traditional denizens of the steppes, leave little evidence of their passing and erect no permanent memorials to their cultures. Indeed they are invariably secretive about even the location of their burial grounds. The presence of abundant American literature on the Siberian husky and the existence of the statue of Balto in New York does not prove the breed originated in Manhattan rather than around the Anadyr river where there is no such literature and no such statues.

In all probability the borzoi is a composite of many breeds. Saluki/Afghan hound types probably feature quite strongly in the ancestry of the dog, but it would be by no means unreasonable to assume that so did the great Celtic hound which may have contributed the great height to the borzoi, as well as a more profuse coat. Social intercourse between Celtic lands and Russia was not unknown. Norse men colonised both Russia and Ireland, and furthermore gifts of huge hounds were frequently made to Polish dignitaries by Scottish kings, social intercourse between Russia and Poland obviously being practised. It is customary to regard the borzoi as an entirely different type from the Scottish deerhound and allied types of Celtic hound, but it is entirely possible the types are closely related.

Little, however, was known of the Russian wolfhound until the mid-seventeenth century although there is documentary evidence to suggest that in 1516 an Austrian diplomat, Heberstein, failed to negotiate peace between Russia and Poland but was presented with a pair of Muscovite-bred wolfhounds. There is no evidence that these were borzoi types, but the term wolfhound implies that the dogs must have been large greyhoundy sight hounds. It is indeed a mistake to assume that every wolf-hunting hound exported from Russia was a classically bred borzoi. It is also well to remember that prior to the advent of dog shows, dogs were bred and kept for use rather than for aesthetic appeal. True, many did appreciate a beautiful hound—a hunter, or rather courser, called Artem Boldacroff once remarked that he would not keep a hound that was not good to look at but then borzois were shown in Russia as early as 1824.

It is a mistake to imagine that the borzoi was owned by the aristocrat alone, however, and it is likely that the breed had many plebeian owners. In all probability, despite its noble demeanour, the chances are the dog was used in the same manner as the lurcher is today—although as to the manner of its use, whether the dog was slipped or allowed to hunt up its quarry is in doubt. Hares were coursed with these hounds, as were rabbits, though the rabbit is not numerous except in parts of southern Russia where the climate is a little more like that of the Iberian peninsula which is the home of the rabbit. Foxes and sables (mustelids, similar in type to large martens) were coursed and taken by borzois. Furriers generally prefer pelts of animals which have met with sudden deaths, as would be the fate of any small animal captured by a large sight hound, to pelts from beasts which have been shot or trapped or snared, for such skins are disfigured more than that of an animal which has died from a breakage of the neck.

Two types of borzoi once existed—and two very distinct types at that. The Siberian variety was thick coated and gay pied in colour, white predominating but with black or black and tan, and lemon or brindle markings. The Circassian variety was frequently black and tan and often had markings similar in type to the markings displayed by northern Iranian salukis and Afghan hounds (—perhaps this is the reason for the belief that the saluki or rather the saluki type (saluki, Baluchi hound, Ramphur hound or Afghan hound) was the ancestor of the type of dog which would eventually become the borzoi. Furthermore the Circassian hound had the same coat texture and feathered tail of the northern saluki types. At one time during the early stages of the development of the borzoi as a show dog, black, and black and tan specimens were barred from competition because they were considered untypical, as were the curly-coated dogs, it being considered that a curly-coated borzoi contained the blood of the Courland greyhound, a rather deerhoundy type dog found in Courland province, an area bordering the Baltic Sea. The Courland greyhound, now an extinct sub-type, was kept by fur hunters as an all purpose hunting dog, coursing all quarry from boar to sable. Like many other sub-types the breed fell into decline when its more glamorous, striking-looking relative became popular. In all probability the Courland greyhound was hunted as a modern-day lurcher, but the same may be said of the more glamorous borzoi.

Towards the middle of the nineteenth century the borzoi ceased to be the dog of the fur hunter and the artisan and became the insignia of the aristocrat, the boyar, and many estates kept fairly extensive kennels of these hounds (later the breed was to pay quite dearly for its aristocratic associations). The Imperial Kennels, the property of the Czar, were usually well patronised but not every Russian ruler was an enthusiastic hunter or follower of wolfhounds, and many of the nineteenth-century Russian philosophers considered the pursuit of game with borzois an extravagance and a mark of boyar decadence. Extravagance it must have been, albeit a glittering and colourful extravagance, but labour was cheap and plentiful and a post at the Czar's kennel was considered prestigious. However, unlike the more plebeian owners of the hound, who used the borzoi to secure the capture of practically all types of Russian quarry, from deer to hare, the nobility seemed to run the borzoi almost exclusively at wolf.

The wolf hunts—hence the borzoi became known as the Russian wolfhound—of the aristocracy were spectacular affairs, as much pageant and an opportunity of meeting influential aristocrats as the pursuit of wolves. It is argued that the borzoi was bred to keep the population of Russian wolves in check, but this is blatantly untrue. The hunting of wolves was as much a prerogative of the aristocracy as the pursuit of deer by the Norman and Angevin kings of England. Wolves were fierce harmers of flocks, killing animals the size of fully-grown bulls, but despite the tales of troika-borne travellers attacked by packs of wolves, the wolf has never been a danger to man. If troikas were attacked, and there is no evidence to suggest they were, it was to kill and eat the horses rather than the occupants of the coach. The wolf hunt served no really useful purpose and many wolves, once captured, were released back into the forests from whence they were driven. Regardless of tales to the contrary, hunting wolves with hounds is seldom as successful a method of wolf control as the use of traps or better still poison. The carcass of a sheep or pig liberally laced with strychnine will kill off 30 wolves, a tally which even the famed Perchino Kennels would have been pushed to equal in a month. The wolf hunt, no matter how superlative the borzoi proved as a coursing animal, was simply a spectacle staged for the amusement of a lively aristocracy.

Tolstoy's *War and Peace* gives an oft-quoted account of a typical wolf hunt, a colourful pageant of an affair, but the tally of the prey could scarcely justify the expense and effort to stage it. Here over 100 dogs and 20 horsemen take part in a hunt for wolf. A trapper equipped with monkshood, strychnine or traps would have secured a greater haul, no doubt, but the purpose of the hunt was to provide entertainment. The actual killing of wolves was secondary.

Such was the expense of keeping a large kennel of borzois that numerically the breed began to diminish for few of the aristocracy were as wealthy as they may have appeared in a country engaged in conflict internally as well as internationally. However, in 1887, the Grand Duke Nikolai Nikolaivitch began to take an active interest in the development of the breed. It is said that the borzoi was so highly prized that its aristocratic owners never sold a puppy or an adult but condescended to give them as presents to visiting diplomats and aristocrats. This too is clearly incorrect as the advertisement must illustrate, for the Perchino Kennels of the Grand Duke not only bred the finest borzois in the world but also sold them, sometimes for incredibly high prices.

The Imperial Kennel started in 1613 was a splendid affair, the kennel management of which was conducted by Prince Galitzin at the time of the founding of the Perchino Kennels, and boasted 40 couples of borzoi, 20 couples of foxhound, eight couples of bearhounds (an unidentified type possibly similar to mastiffs or Great Danes) and 100 horses. It was however overshadowed by the establishment kept at Perchino.

Nikolai Nikolaivitch was a colourful character, a horseman fit to put Mazeppa to shame, a swordsman of some repute and a military adviser. He was in fact the very model of a Russian aristocrat—although the demise of that aristocracy was already at hand. His early interest in borzois had been kindled by the present of a hound called Udar and subsequently he became addicted to the breed, its ethos and the spectacle of the well-organised wolf course. The Grand Duke's kennel of borzois at Peterhof was disbanded in 1884 when he left to take command of the Imperial Hussars in which he served flamboyantly, though without distinction, for a blasé apathy had begun to appear in the army, an apathy to be revealed in the forthcoming campaign against Japan. Nikolaivitch tired of his military career and retired to found a kennel at Perchino in Tula Russia, a kennel which was an extravagance in itself and he spared no expense in stocking it. Nikolaivitch was in fact a shrewd businessman despite his extravagant stocking of his kennel. The kennel had by 1908 exported many champion borzois and had won every award for borzois available in Russia. Three hundred hounds, the best kennel of borzois ever gathered together, constituted the breeding stock of his kennel and superb coursing hounds were always available for export.

These hounds found a ready market in America, though not from the rank and file wolf hunters of Dakota who fielded a rough and ready pack of 'cold-blooded hounds' to wolf and coyote. A growing band of hunters from Europe had travelled to the Americas for some 30 years by the time the Perchino stud had reached its peak and whereas 'wolf bounty hunters' did exist, American big game was being hunted by European aristocrats, eager to see spectacular hunts and pageants as much as to appreciate the quality of the quarry. Louis L'Amour, the western writer, describes such hunts in his book *Shalako*. The borzoi found a ready market amongst entrepreneurs of sporting ventures catering for the European sportsman.

As to the efficacy of these sporting hounds when compared to other sight hounds available to the American sportsmen, it should be pointed out that nothing causes decline of sporting instincts in a dog more than the lack of use of those qualities. Hence it is foolish to expect a Sealyham, bred for generations simply to parade around a show ring, to put up even a creditable show at a badger dig, even though it was once a great badger-digging terrier. Similarly a fell terrier kept only for work, and bred only for work, will usually display qualities such as courage, nose and sense, when faced with a hunted fox. Hence the Perchino stud, while it could not possibly have entered all its 300 dogs and bitches to wolf, did at least try some of them, and while the Grand Duke certainly did have an eye for the aesthetically appealing animal, he also displayed a passion for the traditional wolf hunt. That his dogs became show champions wherever they were exported is true, but they were bred essentially to satisfy the coursing requirements of hunters. The capability of other sight hounds at the time is a little more questionable. Not since the Napoleonic wars had the deerhound seen legitimate work at large quarry and the Irish wolfhound, revived, resuscitated, recreated, call it what you will, was being bred exclusively for aesthetic reasons in its native Britain. Greyhounds, which are still coursed, seldom see quarry much larger than a fox to test their mettle, but the Perchino stud did offer hounds, which, even as late as 1908, had been entered to wolf. The very price demanded by the Grand Duke prevented or deterred professional American wolf hunters from including borzois in their mixed packs, however. At the time of the Perchino stud, borzois would have still been capable of catching and holding wolves equally as well as the mongrel 'wolfhounds' of the Dakota wolf hunters.

As to the method of entering hounds to wolf, the custom of running hounds in pairs or trios did much to help entering a young hound. Lurchers and sight hounds alike when run singly at a fox (a much less taxing quarry than a wolf) often fail to put their heart into the capture of the animal, but display great enthusiasm for the chase. When run in pairs with an older or more experienced dog that has been 'wed' to fox, entering usually is a great deal easier. It should be noted though, that there is no natural emnity between dog and fox or between dog and wolf (except that wolves usually consider domesticated dogs as prey) and some hounds never learn to tackle either, no matter how they are entered. Furthermore, such were the stocks of wolves around Tula province at the time of the Perchino stud that a wolf enjoyed a certain degree of protection. They were regularly coursed and often captured, but seldom if ever killed, and when captured, trussed, bound and returned to the forests from whence they had been driven in order that they might be coursed at some later date. It is of note that the ideal size for a coursing borzoi at this time was considered to be 30 inches at the shoulder.

In passing it is of interest that at one time the German shepherd dog was suspected of having lupine genes and Herr Strebel, in a celebrated piece of writing, *Die Deutschen Hunde*, tells the tale of how at a show at Dresden the German shepherd dog, Phylax Von Eulau, had engendered terrible fury in a pair of Perchino bred hounds. Supposedly the hounds smelled the 'wolf blood' in Phylax! No doubt the same fury would have been generated had a pointer or retriever passed the bench, for there is no natural enmity between dogs and wolves, though pairs of any sight hounds will often run and kill other smaller dogs.

The Perchino stud did not enjoy its heyday for long. The conflict between Russia and Germany was fast growing, and would be resolved in Bismarckian style blood and iron conflicts some six years later at Tannenburg and the

Masurian lakes and the days of the effete French-speaking boyar, like the Russian wolfhound were numbered. In 1917 a tempestuous though muddled revolution swept away the nobility and all objects associated with them. In particular the Romanoff family were attacked and destroyed without mercy. The borzoi, unaware of its aristocratic connections no doubt, was nevertheless slaughtered indiscriminately, although such were the hardships after the revolution that other dogs with totally plebeian connections were also slaughtered and perhaps eaten. Ivan Nazhivin, a minor writer of the early twentieth century, a personal friend of Tolstoy, in his book *The Dogs* does, however, relate tales of the fury of soldiers slaughtering the pet dogs of the aristocracy, but lest one should attribute this insane ferocity as being an exclusively Russian passion, it should be pointed out that the breeders of German shepherd dogs were quick to change the name of the breed to Alsatian (the dog of Alsace—the breed has little connection with this province) to allow the breed to escape hostile attentions from a very anti-German British public during the 1914–1918 war.

Neither the Russian-bred borzoi in its pure form nor the Perchino stud seemed to have survived the 1917 uprising in the USSR, but due to the auspices of various Russian kennels, the stock had been fairly widely distributed throughout the world by the time of the Revolution and while the lack of available quarry meant that throughout most of Europe while the hound was kept as a companion dog and for exhibition, dogs which found homes in America and other countries where large game still existed fared somewhat better. In passing it is wise not to equate the fragile, seemingly wispy shape of the dog with a delicate disposition. Neil Davidson, who kept a large mixed kennels at Penybryn Hall, North Wales, remarked that the borzoi will still course well, and would survive accidents incurred during coursing almost as well as a lurcher.

Borzois have been coursed with some regularity at quarry in South Africa—jackal and Cape hunting dogs being the most usual animals to be hunted, although the borzoi is capable of putting up a favourable attempt at coursing certain types of very fleet antelope. Cape hunting dogs make formidable quarry for any team of hounds and despite Van

Lawick's appealing books concerning the species, they are savagely destructive to all forms of domesticated livestock. As a long distance runner, the Emil Zatopek of the animal world as it was once called, the Cape hunting dog is possibly one of the fastest animals in the world, running down its prey with a relentless, easy stride which is deceptively fast. The species for all its canine appearance is not a true dog and once a hound is introduced to this quarry and is not too damaged by the encounter, it enters to coursing them with great enthusiasm. Slips must of course be favourable, as the Cape hunting dog is easily capable of outstaying a foxhound, let alone a sight hound over a long course. It is considered that a single large sight hound of the size of a bitch borzoi is capable of bringing down one of these creatures, but the use of a pair of hounds is more efficacious at the capture and killing of a Cape hunting dog.

Jackals—midway between a fox and a wolf in size—are skulking runners rather than athletes and use cover, lairs and uneven country to good advantage when pursued. A single borzoi is not over-matched in a pitched battle with a jackal and once a jackal is lifted from the ground by a large borzoi its fate is seldom in doubt. The jackal is not a testing quarry for this hound although its ability to find a place of refuge, where apparently none existed, is phenomenal. The use of a shooting brake with remote controlled rear doors had been used by jackal hunters with some success, but in recent years when the animals have become urbanised, scavenging into the very hearts of large cities, this method of hunting obviously cannot be practised.

Ironically, the use of the borzoi in America has been slightly neglected in favour of deerhound and cold-blood greyhounds (longdogs bred from greyhounds), but early in the present century a breeder exhibitor, Joseph Thomas of the Valley Farm kennels in Connecticut, imported several good coursing hounds from Russia. Connecticut is hardly the country to test such hounds (nor was it at the time that Thomas imported the hounds), for the country had long been denuded of big game and large predators, but Thomas endeavoured to sell hounds to wolf hunters further west, hunters who worked country more akin to the steppes, over which the hounds were originally

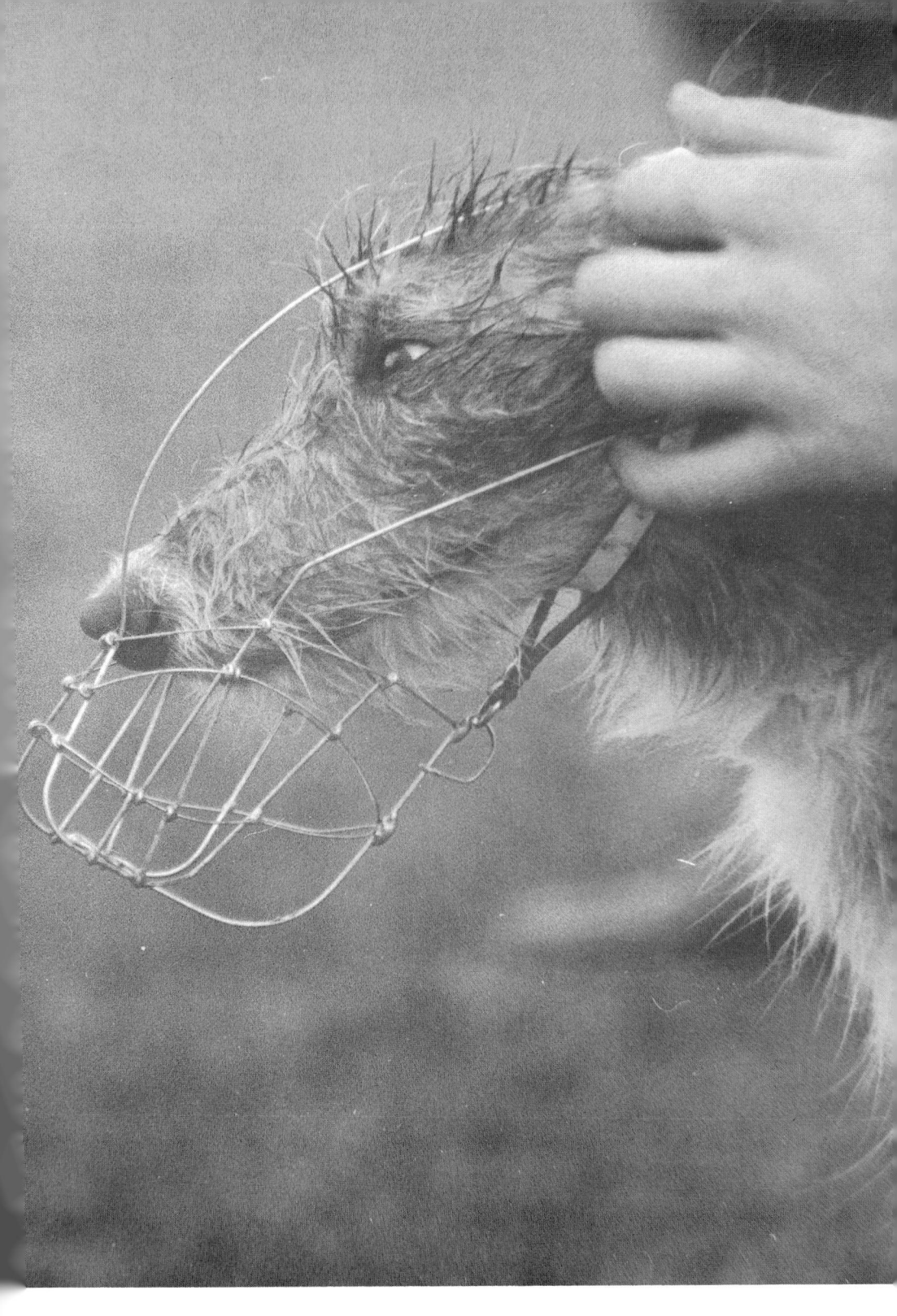

Preparing for racing. *(Photo: Lal Hardy)*

An 800-yard track greyhound — stamina, speed, grace and beauty in one creature. *(Photo: David Hancock)*

1. Head study of a saluki, the hunting dog of the nomadic tribes since pre-Biblical times. *(Photo: Lal Hardy)*
2. Afghan hound. Modern Afghan hounds are far too long in the coat to be of much use in the coursing field.
3. Pharoah Hound, a native of Malta where it is used for night-time rabbit hunting.

1. Scottish deerhounds, the descendants of the old Celtic hound and essentially huge, rough-coated greyhounds. *(Photos: Mark Wilson)*
2. *The Stag at Bay* by the Victorian painter Edwin Landseer. During the nineteenth century, deerhounds were principally used to track deer wounded by inaccurate marksmanship.

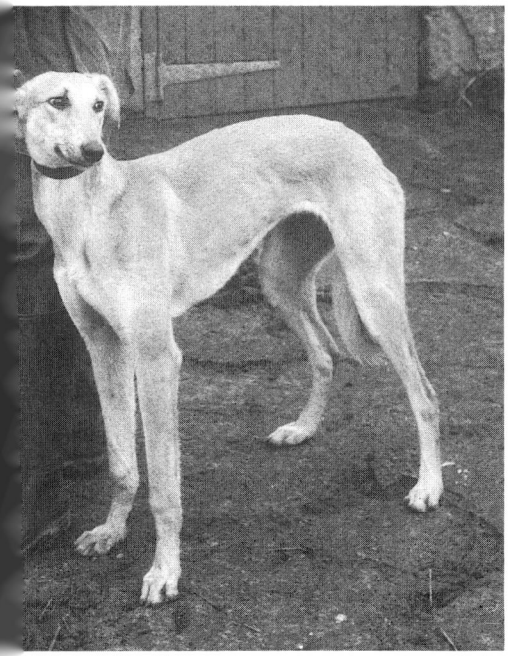

1. The rough and the smooth — longdog and whippet. As a versatile, entertaining, easily-kept pet few breeds of dog are as suitable as the whippet. *(Photo: Lal Hardy)*

2. A classic longdog, a saluki/greyhound cross, combining the speed of the greyhound and the effortless stamina of the saluki. *(Photo: David Hancock)*

3. Ibizan hound. Seemingly the ideal, dual-purpose sight and scent-hunting hounds, the Ibizan is harder to train than most lurchers. *(Photo: Lal Hardy)*

1. Norfolk-type lurcher. *(Photo: David Hancock)*
2. Smithfield collie-type lurcher. *(Photo: David Hancock)*
3. A superb rough-coated three-quarter bred collie/greyhound lurcher. *(Photo: David Hancock)*

1. Deerhound/collie/greyhound lurcher. *(Photo: David Hancock)*
2. Collie/greyhound lurcher. *(Photo: David Hancock)*

David Hancock, the world's biggest lurcher breeder, with a litter of well-reared whelps. Young puppies need socialising if they are to train well later on. (Photo: David Hancock)

1. All sight hounds should be trained to jump. *(Photo: David Hancock)*
2. If a sight hound is used for hunting, it must retrieve or be relegated to the rank of a second-rate hunting dog. *(Photo: David Hancock)*

Hard mouth — the curse of the pot-filling lurcher. *(Photo: David Hancock)*

Unchanged. (Top). Painting by Thomas Gainsborough of hounds taking a fox from the eighteenth century, and (bottom), the same scene today.
(Photo: Lal Hardy)

1. Lamping should only ever be carried out with one dog at a time.
2. Lamping kit.
3. Familiarity breeds contempt. Allowing the ferret and dog to drink from the same bowl helps the dog accept the presence of the ferret at all times.

Coursing the hare with the fair law is the ultimate test of a dog's speed and stamina. *(Photo: Lal Hardy)*

1. A hound must have nose to be able to mark an inhabited earth. *(Photo: Denise Adam)*
2. Setting a purse net. A dog easily learns not to snatch at a rabbit tangled in a net. *(Photo: Denise Adams)*

1. Picking up the ferret, between forefinger and thumb. *(Photo: Denise Adams)*
2. One that escaped the net. *(Photo: Denise Adams)*

Sight hound shows and races should be fun. *(Photo: Lal Hardy)*

bred to hunt. Coyote, wolf and even feral razor-backed swine—pigs descended from primitive English breeds of pig such as the Tamworth, and allowed to run wild or simply escapees from farms run feral—were the most common quarry of Thomas' hounds. The breed never really caught on or became popular amongst hunters in America. Possibly its aristocratic background deterred the dyed-in-the-wool predator hunter, but the pure-bred hound certainly did not become popular as a coyote hunter and its place was soon occupied by mongrel deerhound/greyhound hybrids. Davidson, a keen sportsman stated that he found this amazing as the breed has a great deal of fire and would pursue a fight even when quite badly bitten.

In Britain the borzoi has somewhat limited uses as the wolf became extinct long before 1800. At one time the Borzoi Club used to run coursing trials each year conducted at one of the saluki coursing meets, but the enthusiasm of the members for such an event was never great and the trials have now been discontinued. An excellent account of fox hunting with borzois occurs in Standfast Press *Coursing* and is concerned with T Landsman-Gorrie's hound, Reyas Rodniki. The writer makes a point that the hound ran fox instinctively, killing it, quickly and silently, by the neck-breaking action and becoming totally wed to the quarry once the fox had bitten the hound. The author makes the point that while the hound could be restrained from cat chasing by a word of command, when pursuing fox the dog ran with furious enthusiasm, oblivious to any commands. As a courser of rabbits, the hound displayed what the author described as 'a cold indifference', but then few experienced sight hounds will attempt to course quarry at which they are unlikely to succeed.

It should be noted that, in common with all sight hounds the borzoi is scarcely noted for its intelligence, but in recent years the breed is becoming involved in obedience testing. Training any sight hound for the precision task of competing in these events is never easy and much praise must be given to anyone who succeeds at training a borzoi to these tasks.

On a happier note Pralle (Standfast Press *Coursing*) mentions that despite the fury displayed by the revolutionary troops towards the borzoi, the attitude in Russia towards surviving hounds is very different today. Kennels where borzois are being bred are now common—although not on the grand scale of the Perchino Kennels—the world will probably never again see such a majestic kennel. State-controlled kennels are usually smaller but no less successfully managed and while these hounds are seldom used for the pursuit of the dwindling population of wolves, Pralle states that half the number of fox pelts sold in Russia are the result of catches by borzois.

Despite improvements to type, coat, tail carriage etc wrought by breeders of exhibition hounds, the basic physical type of the breed, its bone structure and musculature has changed little since the golden era of the hound—a time when the breed pursued deer, wolf, fox and possibly boar. Long may the breeders of these hounds seek to keep the shape of these dogs as it should be. Whether or not the borzoi's instincts have been dulled by almost four decades of inactivity in the field is debatable, although it is fair to point out that the borzoi's coursing prowess has certainly not been improved by breeding exclusively for aesthetic appeal and exhibition qualities.

2. Rare Breeds

The Pharaoh Hound

There is little doubt that the Pharaoh hound is closely related to the Ibizan hound and may well have developed from the same root stock. It is similar in type, uses the same style of hunting to secure its prey and is quite simply a Mediterranean lurcher type, though with dogs roughly 23–25 inches in height, and bitches perhaps an inch or so less, it is a smaller dog than the Ibizan hound. In its native Malta, the story has it that the dog is used for night-time rabbit hunting and drives the rabbits into the drystone walls which crisscross the island giving it a patchwork quilt-like appearance when viewed from the air. Once the rabbits are put into the walls the dog begins to bark frantically to alert the owner who then nets the wall with an elaborate net which resembles a hybrid version of a long net and a purse net. The rabbits are ferreted out of the wall to be entrapped by the net. A dog which gives tongue when it locates a rabbit, is hardly an asset to a British ferreting *aficionado*, but such is the manner of the dog's method of hunting rabbits in Malta!

When the breed became popular in Britain—although the word popular is questionable, for the breed has no great following in the United Kingdom—various lurcher enthusiasts bought specimens to use in the same way as whippets and small lurchers were employed in Britain. Many crossed these small Maltese hounds with whippets and greyhounds to produce longdogs. In recent years the lurcher enthusiast has begun to favour the exotic, and various foreign breeds have been absorbed into the gene pool of lurchers and longdogs, often with highly questionable results, one should add. It must be added that the use of exotics is a relatively modern practice amongst lurcher breeders. In the 1920s the saluki longdog—now the most common of the longdog types—was held in suspicion by the sporting fraternity because of its foreign origin, but during the late 1950s a search began to produce the superior lurcher or longdog and many exotic types were tried, tested and frankly found wanting by the British coursing enthusiasts.

The method of hunting adopted by the dog in its native country caused some suspicion amongst the lurcher fraternity where a vocal dog is seldom wanted, for not only does such a dog alert the game to its presence, but many lurcher owners prefer a silent dog for somewhat more sinister reasons. Some of the pure-bred stock displayed some tendency to give voice while hunting, but others were found to be no more vociferous than the whippet or greyhound. Longdog *aficionados* report that the breed, admixed with other sight hound blood, is said to produce longdogs with much better than average noses and pure-bred hounds do hunt well by scent as well as sight. Giving tongue is, in fact, more often than not the manifestation of frustration in any sight hound—it is unable to come to terms with the quarry either because it is outpaced or because the would-be prey has sought refuge in an inaccessible place—a lair, a burrow, a drystone wall etc. Often barking at the mouth of a temporary, rather than a permanent, refuge of a rabbit does effectively bolt the creature, so giving tongue, opening up, or call it what you will, is not always totally counter-productive.

Not even the most devoted breed enthusiasts could claim that the Pharaoh hound was one of the more tractable of dogs, though in the USA it is becoming a popular practice to work particularly intractable breeds, sight hounds, Siberian huskies, Malemutes, etc at obedience shows. Hence in the USA there is no shortage of Pharaoh hounds, Ibizans, salukis and Afghans with a CD qualification. However once again it must be pointed out that, while it is one matter to demonstrate the obedience of a dog in the restricted settings of a show ring, when the dog encounters quarry under natural conditions, matters often go awry and here again one must mention the problem of training a dog with a strongly developed olfactory sense and a typical sight hound disposition.

Unless any dog of this type (Ibizan, Pharaoh etc) is given intensive obedience training before it is fielded at quarry, these hounds are incredibly difficult to control and any attempt at in-field training is doomed from the very onset.

Pharaoh hounds must be totally under control before introducing them to either quarry or domesticated livestock. Likewise retrieving training must be given and reinforced by reward during the early training sessions. The breed seems to have a natural propensity to carry, but qualities which manifest themselves naturally often disappear and it is nearly impossible to re-start such a dog retrieving once it has decided it no longer wishes to carry. This retrieving should be reinforced while the dog is still a puppy.

More important still is recall training, for nothing is more infuriating than seeing a dog running head down on a scent, refusing to come to hand and obviously deaf to any recall or execration heaped on it. A badly trained lurcher with a good scenting ability is all too prone to manifest this disobedience, but Ibizans and Pharaoh hounds are more so. Training in an enclosed space—a yard free from the scent of game or other dogs—is essential before the dog is introduced to legitimate game, for once such a hound learns the pleasures of hunting it will simply run deaf to commands, entreaties or curses. Frankly, this is not the ideal first dog for the amateur trainer, though sadly such people seem to be attracted to difficult exotics rather than more easily trained but more common British breeds. Hence Breed Rescue Societies involved with exotic sight hound types are usually far too well-stocked.

Rabbit is of course the principal quarry of this Maltese hound though hare can be taken if the dog is allowed to hunt up its quarry rather than the owner simply slipping the dog at the escaping hare in the manner of a match-running longdog. A Pharaoh hound is certainly unable to outpace a whippet, though it has a fair reputation for having a higher degree of stamina than either a whippet or a greyhound. Some will give a reasonable show at small deer up to the size of roe and there are tales of foxes being run, caught and even killed by these hounds. It is however a breed which all too quickly degenerates into a difficult dog if in the hands of the wrong owner.

The Ibizan Hound

There seems to be no half measure where this strange-looking hound is concerned, for people who have seen or owned such dogs are either totally wed to the dog, forsaking all others, or are decidedly antipathetic to the Ibizan hound, its curious temperament and even more curious appearance.

In type the Ibizan hound resembles the hounds that appear on paintings on the tombs of pre-Christian burial chambers in Egypt, and the standard of excellence adopted by the various governing bodies concerned with the exhibition of this hound have probably served to accentuate this similarity. However the mystique of such an exotic origin aside, there seems to be scant evidence to suggest that the Ibizan hound is descended from the dogs of the Pharaohs.

The hound is a native of Ibiza, an island in the Mediterranean Sea, and while it is admitted that Phoenicians visited the islands perhaps even before the establishment of the Phoenician settlement of Carthage, there is not the slightest indication that the Phoenicians were responsible for introducing this particular hound or even the greyhound type into the Mediterranean. The tale that Hannibal crossed the Alps bringing Ibizan hounds atop of his elephants is unlikely to say the least, despite the fact that Brearly states that Hannibal, the last of the Barsids, was born in Ibiza. The Phoenicians, in common with some other Semitic races, abhorred the dog and its carrion-eating ways, and there is no evidence that any dog of any sort was shipped out with these intrepid early explorers.

What is equally likely is that Hannibal's contact with the Gauls, a Celtic tribe renowned for their sight hounds, may well have introduced the hound to the Mediterranean and that the Ibizan hound may have, at the most, a somewhat tenuous connection with the dogs depicted in the tombs of the later Pharaohs. In all probability the Ibizan hound originated as a lurcher type derivative of the Celtic greyhound and was brought to the island by settlers journeying south from Europe, rather than immigrants travelling north and west. The possibility of greyhound types arising independently in various parts of the world has been dealt with earlier in this book and it is not deemed necessary to repeat the theory. Sufficient to say that the Ibizan hound is a native of Ibiza, an island in the Mediterranean.

The hound occupies the place of the British lurcher in Ibiza and is predominantly considered as a pot filler. As the dog is clearly of a greyhound type it is fleet, nimble and capable of catching rabbits with no more difficulty than would the more mundane British lurcher or longdog. Indeed it is one of the few sight hounds which has a well-developed sense of smell and, once allowed to hunt in the manner it wishes, will display all the attributes of a typical lurcher. Most adopt sight hunting for preference, scanning fields as would a whippet or a greyhound, but, once the quarry has run out of sight, the hound easily adopts hunting by scent to find its quarry. The flowing action displayed while the hound courses is similar to that of the effortless motion of the saluki, rather than the power running style of the whippet and greyhound, and this has led *aficionados* of the breed to believe it is descended from north African hounds rather than from Celtic greyhounds.

The appearance of the dog is not to everyone's liking—a putty nose is regarded by many as unsightly and its red, lion-coloured, or pinto markings make it, if not attractive, at least a striking-looking dog. Size-wise it is roughly the same as a typical British lurcher, approximately $23\frac{1}{2}$–27 inches at the shoulder and around 50 pounds in weight.

Rabbits are the traditional quarry of this hound although its loping action seems hardly the right one to deal with the quicksilver dash of a rabbit running to ground. Many will put up a favourable show at a hare run underfoot rather than with law one should add, for such a course requires a very special and specifically bred dog. The Ibizan, as suggested, occupies the same role as the more plebeian lurcher and some cope quite well with feathered game as well as fur. There are reports of the hound coping well with foxes—and quite small hounds have the zest to tackle fox, so it appears—and in America bobcat and raccoon have also been bagged by these hounds.

Seemingly the hound has all the capabilities of a lurcher, and in both America and Britain has competed in obedience tests with some success, a degree of success, one should add, which is attained by few pure-bred sight hounds and longdogs. To all intents and purposes the dog must appear the ideal all-round hunting dog, the ideal dual-purpose sight and scent-hunting hound which apparently seems set to oust the lurcher as the countryman's ferreting, rabbiting and companion dog. However this is not exactly a true and accurate picture of the hound.

A sight hound, a pure-bred sight hound or an amalgam of sight hounds such as a longdog, is scarcely famed for its tractability and often displays an infuriating slowness to command. They return to hand slowly as a rule, as if to display a reluctance to heed a command. For this reason collie blood was blended with greyhounds to produce the all-purpose hunting dog—the lurcher. Ibizan hounds are true sight hounds and respond with characteristic sight hound slowness. Add to this recalcitrant behaviour a finely developed scenting ability and the end product is not only a reluctantly obedient dog, but a dog which is very likely to run 'deaf' (reluctant or unwilling to come off an interesting scent when commanded) when interested in fresh scenting conditions. All in all the breed is not the easiest to train or discipline in the field and is therefore streets behind a tractable lurcher as an all-round hunting dog.

Such comments are likely to arouse wrath and indignation amongst the more enthusiastic supporters of the Ibizan hound, but the facts bear out the truth of the statement all too well. The exotic origin or rather the supposed exotic origin of the dog attracts unsuitable owners, owners who have no previous experience of dog training in general, and sight hound training in particular. Such owners seem to expect a dog to emerge ready trained with little expenditure of effort on the part of the trainer and this simply is not realistic. A dog such as an Ibizan needs a great deal of socialising, a great deal of preliminary training and to have learned absolute obedience to command long before it is allowed to see a field likely to harbour quarry of any sort. Sadly the majority of owners fail to appreciate this fact and as most breeders are also simply not interested or 'au fait' with the sporting qualities of the hounds they keep, would-be buyers are seldom advised about the peculiarities of the Ibizan hound.

The contact between a tyro dog enthusiast and a dog with a finely developed olfactory sense and a typical sight hound disposition is often catastrophic. Dog trainers who specialise in the training of damaged dogs, dogs which have been ruined or badly mentally scarred by bad training, find numbers of Ibizan hounds in their custody—numbers one should add, far out of proportion to the ratio of Ibizan hounds to other breeds. At one time the author specialised in the training of recalcitrant sight hounds and Ibizan hounds were by far the most frequent visitors to his kennels.

Breeders should select the would-be owners of puppies with more care and should always advise:

(a) the dog be trained at obedience classes under the instruction of competent handlers, who are au fait with sight hound disposition;
(b) under no circumstances should the dog be introduced to quarry before it is competently trained, and no dog should even be allowed off the leash until it is completely trustworthy with cats, sheep, fowl and other livestock. There is considerable evidence to suggest that any Ibizan hound should not be taken into rural settings before it is completely trained and trustworthy. To allow the dog to self-enter at quarry at an early age is madness, a recipe for disaster, and a training malpractice which is difficult, if not impossible to correct.

There are of course obedient, well-trained Ibizan hounds, dogs which are a delight to own, but trainers capable of producing such dogs are in short supply. Sadly the sense of exotica is strong amongst breeders and there is, according to Brearly, a move afoot to popularise the breed in Egypt—its supposed country of origin! Such enthusiasm for a breed is admirable but misplaced. Breeders would be better employed in forgetting often spurious genealogy, telling buyers ludicrous stories about the breed's antiquity, and acquainting would-be clients on the problems of training a dog which has a sight hound disposition and a highly developed olfactory sense.

The Sloughi

This is a dog of similar type to that other Middle-Eastern sight hound the saluki, indeed the sloughi closely resembles the smooth-coated saluki in type and coat though many specimens are slightly heavier and more strongly muscled. Curiously this breed has never become popular in Britain, either on the show bench or more importantly on the coursing field. Few breeders have sought to perpetuate the type in Britain and only one breeder, Miss Jacqui Saunders of Poulton Engine near Bristol, can lay claim to be an authority on the type.

The sloughi is quite simply a Berber hunting dog of the sight hound type, and perhaps deserves more recognition as a hunting dog than has actually been given to it. In its native North Africa it is trained and used to bring down quarry the size of a gazelle, and a pair are more than a match for a jackal. Hounds are apparently entered on jerboa, a rat-like desert animal. Later the sapling hounds are entered at desert hare, then to the larger, more taxing gazelle. However it seems to be in the pursuit of the strong, powerful jackal that the sloughi excels, as it tends to give of its best against tough and aggressive quarry. This is curious, as in Britain the breed has a reputation for being timid.

Miss Saunders, at an interview conducted in 1984, remarked that because of the breed's, reputation for nervousness, she chooses the buyers of her puppies with care and attempts to socialise her puppies to alleviate this tendency to nervous behaviour. Sagar, a saluki coursing *aficionado*, believes that the majority of the Middle-Eastern sight hound types need far more socialising than the Celtic greyhound types and that the reputation that besets salukis—capricious behaviour, nervousness on the field and in the show ring—is entirely due to problems in socialising or rather the lack of socialising. John Bromily, kennel man to the coursing greyhound expert Sant, once obtained a pair of sloughis from Miss Saunders with a view to entering them to British quarry, for the physical type of these hounds would render them unnoticed in a batch of good-quality competitive match dogs. Bromily failed to train either sloughi and finally returned them to Miss Saunders who remarked that many of her buyers experience similar problems with these hounds. She added that puppies reared amongst children are easier to train and enter, though she admits she is no coursing enthusiast and is interested in the sloughi for itself rather than for its performance in the field.

Most of Miss Saunders' hounds are pale cream or fawn but brindle-coloured sloughis are not uncommon on the continent. There is a theory that because of the sensitive disposition of the sloughi, breeders have mated sloughis to sound track greyhounds to improve temperament, and this has introduced the brindle coloration to the breed. Continental breeders often deny this, stating that many of the native berber dogs are brindle in colour.

It is a pity the type has not been tested on the coursing fields of Britain. In shape and size it resembles a heavily built saluki and is ideally formed to be a successful single-handed hare catcher. Its speed is reputed to be almost equal to that of a good saluki and the flowing gait indicates that, like the saluki, it is a stamina runner rather than a powerhouse type athlete. As such, its promise as a potential match dog should at least be exploited.

A few sloughi greyhound hybrids have been bred, and according to Miss Saunders in her article in Standfast Press epic book *Coursing*, they have proved quite excellent—'one almost unbeatable'. Miss Saunders, however, discourages hybridising with both greyhounds and whippets (though whippet sloughi hybrids are reputed to have been bred) for she believes the innate nervousness of the sloughi could create longdogs, which unless properly socialised could be particularly wild and unmanagable. Thus the hybrid is seldom bred and almost never advertised.

As to whether or not the entire breed is of a nervous disposition, or whether the strain imported to Britain is a nervy one, may be disputed. Certainly there is a very small sloughi gene pool in Britain and it is probable that inbreeding is inevitable. Should the initial stock imported into Britain carry qualities which produce nervousness, inbreeding to that line will only accentuate the problem. A similar inbreeding programme amongst the very small number of Inuit dogs (Greenland huskies) imported into Britain produced such a spate of epileptic dogs that breeders discontinued the line. This does not indicate that the world's Inuit dogs are carriers of epilepsy, merely that the lines imported into Britain were so. Similarly perhaps a rather nervous strain of sloughi entered Europe and inbreeding to that particular line has accentuated the problem. Certainly puppies reared in households of parents of several children are usually far less nervous than puppies reared in kennels. Sagar believes that no Middle-Eastern type sight hound thrives in kennels, and that all desperately need human company if they are to develop properly. He is probably right!

The potential of this interesting breed in the field has yet to be realised, but one has the feeling that with the right strain, the right training, the correct physical and mental conditioning, the sloughi may well be the ideal pure-bred 'match dog' and prove a shade too testing for the conventional longdogs.

3. LONGDOGS

To the owner or breeder of pure-bred sight hounds of any breed, the deliberate creation of longdogs brought about by the crossing of such hounds, must seem a baffling enigma. Certainly, the hybrids which are invariably derived in part at least from greyhounds, are not as fast as pure-bred greyhounds and deerhound derivatives are seldom as glamorous as their pure-bred parent. Likewise, saluki hybrids, at the time of writing seemingly the most popular type of longdog, are rarely as graceful, elegant or as attractive as salukis, yet the longdog has a great market among coursing enthusiasts and the creation of good top quality longdogs is both an art and a highly scientific breeding project.

So having defined the term 'longdog', it is now expedient to explain the difference between a longdog and a lurcher. A longdog is a hybrid between two sight hounds, between two dogs of similar type, both bred essentially for speed but also specifically 'tailored' for a particular task. For example, both the whippet and the greyhound are extraordinary fast dogs but a whippet was bred for the hunting and catching of rabbits, whereas a greyhound was essentially a dog bred for coursing hares. Lurchers were bred as all-purpose hunting dogs and are the result of ameliorating pure-bred sight hounds with the blood of other breeds, breeds other than sight hounds, that is—namely collies, Bedlington terriers, and occasionally, gun dog breeds. Such alien blood is added to the pure sight hound stock to give qualities which in the sight hound are conspicuous by their absence. Sight hounds are not amongst the intelligentsia of the canine world, no matter what authors of manuals of specific sight hound breeds write or perhaps even believe. Neither are most sight hounds particularly gifted with olfactory senses, though it must be stressed some have abnormally well-developed senses of smell. Above all few sight hounds are famed for being very biddable—there may (though it is by no means certain) be a connection between tractability and intelligence. Hence to correct these defects, blood of other breeds other than sight hounds are added to the pure-bred sight hound lines, and the resulting offspring are then termed as lurchers.

However accurate the above-mentioned definitions are, they must exacerbate rather than clarify the reasons why longdogs are deliberately created. So perhaps it is time to elaborate on the purpose for which a longdog is bred. Conventional coursing, the principles of which are basically the same, though there may be slight differences in the rules drawn up by certain breed clubs, is the pursuit of hares by two dogs. Points are awarded for the hound which contributes most to the capture of the hare, if indeed the hare is captured, for the quarry is so adept at evading its pursuers that it frequently escapes. However, this is not the only type of coursing (the ill-conceived letter by Sandy Mackenzie, *Shooting Times* 1981, must have brought that point home) and dogs are deliberately run as singles at hares, the test being the actual capture of the hare with no system of points being awarded for the speed of the dog and the turning of its hare. The contest is simply the running of a hare with a single dog or a competition involving several dogs, each running singly, against a hare. Rules for such contests, the affording of the quarry the correct law, and the method of slipping the single dog may be as stringent or as lax as the group competing at the meet decide. One point however should never be overlooked. The taking of a hare with a single dog, the hare being allowed fair law, is a very taxing exercise and it is also a task which is beyond the capabilities of various sight hounds or lurchers to perform with any regularity. It is the pursuit and capture of these hares by a single dog that is the forte of the longdog. It is at this sport that this type of hybrid excels.

The development of superlative longdogs, specifically bred hybrids with much thought given to the disposition of either parent, is a relatively recent occurrence however, and when examined in the light of the available quarry, it is easy to see why this is so. Prior to 1953 there were few serious longdog (or for that matter lurcher) breeders and the lurcher was the dog of the warrener, the artisan hunter, and the poacher. The lurcher of the time, usually a ragged, ill-conceived mixture of breeds with greyhound predominating, was fast enough to take the odd hare or so providing the hare did not gain sufficient law to put up a fair course, but the principal quarry of the lurcher was, and still is, the rabbit. Some types of lurcher, or perhaps particular specimens were antipathetic towards taking feathered game and so hunted rabbits exclusively with the odd hare or so for bonus. Lurcher coursing events of the 1930s were nearly all cloth cap affairs and seldom very effective or for that matter taken seriously. Brian Vesey Fitzgerald, who attended many of these meets, mentioned in an interview in 1977 that, 'The event was incidental, the capture of the hare even less so, but the bonhommie engendered by these meets all important'. Many of the contestants at these meets were simply warreners who kept useful and possibly fairly fast lurchers, but the type of dog required to work with a warrener's ferrets and nets, and to capture an escapee rabbit is seldom the sort of dog which puts up a credible display at a fair law course at a hare. A rabbit-hunting dog with instant take-off speed, ability to sense when a rabbit was about to slip a net and act accordingly was treasured. A hare-catching dog was, and is, a specialist athlete, and besides, hares were not easy to sell and certainly not to everyone's taste. Longdog hybrids, particularly deerhound crosses were bred from time to time and were bred primarily for the pursuit of hares, but the lurcher of the time was essentially either a fur and feather dog of the poacher, or basically a rabbit-hunting dog.

In 1953 a deliberately introduced rabbit disease called myxamatosis began to infect the European rabbit (and only the rabbit, despite hosts of articles and radio programmes to the contrary) and by 1956 Sheial estimates that 95 per cent of the population of the rabbits in Europe had been wiped out. The changes that accompanied this ecological disaster were many. The rabbit had, in the 900 years since its introduction to Europe, carved itself a very secure niche in the ecology of the British countryside and its eradication or its partial eradication caused serious changes. Buzzards, stoats, foxes and feral cats teetered precariously on the tightrope of extinction and the role of the warrener, or trapper as he is known in Scotland became superfluous. A spate of trained lurchers were advertised in *Exchange and Mart*, at that time the only really practical way in which to sell a lurcher, and few litters of lurchers were advertised anywhere in early 1957.

Hares, however, are not affected by the disease, possibly because of their different lifestyle, and many naturalists believe that since the hare became free of competition for food from the rabbit, its numbers increased accordingly. To catch these hares, a somewhat faster dog was required, faster than the traditional warrener's lurcher, and while a system of eugenic improvement could possibly have brought about the production of the required article, an easier method was to simply mate sight hounds into the strain and to add more and more sight hound blood to produce superlative hare coursers with great speed. Vesey Fitzgerald was of the opinion that by the end of the 1960s the true lurcher, the pot filling lurcher of the poacher, the subsistence level farm labourer and the warrener was extinct, or the blood so diluted by the addition of that of sight hounds, as to be simply longdogs.

During the late 1960s the most popular sight hound cross-bred was undoubtedly the deerhound/greyhound or the second cross, the deerhound/greyhound/greyhound, known to itinerants as the staghound though such is the way with most itinerants that staghound was applied to any rough-coated lurcher or longdog even though the rough coat may well have come from a bearded collie or Bedlington terrier. Staghound to greyhound advertisements abounded in *Exchange and Mart* during these years despite the fact that the true staghound was a type of very large foxhound and not related to any of the sight hounds.

Genuine breeders of the real article were rare, but one of them, arguably the greatest breeder of longdogs ever, was Nuttall of Clitheroe whose *Exchange and Mart* advertisement invariably started 'Sports men . . .', followed by an evaluation of the stock Nuttall had for sale. Nuttall's breeding pattern was interesting, if predictable, for he used a purebred deerhound male onto cast track or coursing greyhound bitches. The stock produced by Nuttall was almost legendary and during the early 1970s few of the top class hare-coursing longdogs in the field did not originate from Nuttall's kennels. In addition to hare, deer and fox were regularly taken by these hybrids, and while a few of these males produced by Nuttall were a little too large to be serviceable as all-round coursing dogs, bitches from this kennel, after training and entering by specialist coursers, changed hands for what at that time were regarded as absurd prices. These longdogs were truly magnificent animals and the winners of many of the classes during the early days of Lambourn, certainly hailed from Lancashire. Leg weakness, a common fault in deerhounds and in first-cross deerhound hybrids was practically unknown in these kennels, partly due to the judicious selection of both sire and dam by Nuttall and partly due to careful feeding of the whelps at his kennels.

How many longdogs were actually produced at Nuttall's kennels will probably never be known, but the value of these dogs was certainly appreciated by itinerants. At one time, so distinctive were dogs of Nuttall's breeding that it was possible to instantly identify them on itinerant sites. In addition to the more common blue-blacks seen in most litters of this cross-bred, good fawn tans were also bred from time to time, as were dark and impressive-looking brindles. One of these brindles, a bitch weighing perhaps 60 pounds in running condition, changed hands for £850 at Grantham in 1974—a record for a longdog hybrid at that time, though a trivial sum by modern reckoning.

A further infusion of greyhound produced the even more serviceable deerhound/greyhound/greyhound, another hybrid which was, and to a certain extent, still is popular in the coursing field. Drabble in his estimable *Pedigree Unknown* did much to popularise this hybrid. His bitch, Gypsy, was, according to the author, one of the best dogs he had ever owned, though a photograph of her shows a far from typey animal. The popularity of the second cross can best be explained by the fact that while the first cross deerhound/greyhound hybrids often produced 30 inch dogs—too large for most purposes except perhaps as takers of deer, a task which is well suited to this type of dog—the second cross produced a smaller, more neatly built hybrid, which fared well on the coursing field. Few giants occured in litters of this breeding, though it is argued by some that the deerhound/greyhound/greyhound hybrid is no better than a coursing greyhound.

In the 1960s saluki hybrids were rarely advertised in the pages of the *Exchange and Mart*, the lurcher bible of the time, and there were many critics of the hybrid. Drabble records that he has no love for the saluki longdog as their famed stamina was simply an indication that the hybrid 'never tried'—or in layman's terms, never ran itself to the best of its ability behind a hare. Pattison in *Coursing* (Standfast Press) describes the saluki as too fragile for the English countryside and implies that it is likely to come to grief in a landscape full of hollows, fence posts and obstacles. More to the point, the saluki lurcher or longdog has a reputation of being recalcitrant, difficult to manage, even more difficult to run fit and, above all, capricious in its desires to run its quarry. Despite this condemnation, this longdog hybrid is one of the most popular longdogs amongst the so-called owners of gambling dogs—although such a title needs debunking fairly quickly.

One of the other great *aficionados* of the saluki greyhound hybrid is Don Southerd of Burton on Trent. Southerd's strain of longdog, and the word strain is probably applicable, began rather curiously as a springer spaniel/greyhound hybrid. One of Southerd's spaniel/greyhounds was described in E G Walsh's *Lurchers and Longdogs* none too glowingly, but Southerd has progressed considerably since those times. His initial bitch was biddable (despite the account of the £5 fine in *Lurchers and Longdogs*) but not gifted with great speed. However, her qualities, her ability to hunt, work well and retrieve to hand made Southerd believe that this bitch was a suitable foundation for his line. By dint of judicious crosses with salukis, saluki greyhound hybrids and best quality greyhound blood, Southerd has produced some sterling coursing animals which still bring to hand, a legacy, so Southerd believes, of the springer spaniel ancestry. Drabble says that an excellent proof of the value of coursing dogs is their proneness to being stolen (the sire of Drabble's Gypsy, a blue/grey deerhound/greyhound was stolen), if this is so, Southerd's stock must be priceless. Some years ago, when Southerd's longdogs were beginning to make a name for themselves, a daring and annoying theft took place at his kennels. Southerd had arrived home from work that day and had turned loose his dogs for exercise. While eating his tea he saw a van pull up in his yard, and a man snaffle up Southerd's best dog and disappear, never to be seen again. The honesty of the longdog fraternity must surely be questioned at all times.

Southerd, himself a physical fitness buff, is of the opinion that perhaps breeding is responsible for only 50 per cent of his success as a courser, and that judicious carefully regulated exercise must be given to his wards. Southerd normally allows a good six weeks for his dogs to ready themselves for a competitive coursing meet. Like *Stonehenge*, J H Walsh (who had the dubious distinction of being the judge at Britain's first ever dog show in 1859), Southerd believes in slow conditioning, walking his wards gently at first (*Stonehenge* advised up to 20 miles a day behind a horse for greyhounds) and finally a gruelling 15mph for five miles behind a truck—backs like beams, the Abbess Juliana considered desirable in her hounds, and Southerd's dogs are built just so.

It is perhaps time to debunk the gambling dog image. The majority of advertisements concerned with the selling of saluki longdogs state 'suitable as gambling dogs' as an evaluation of the merit of their stock. Gambling meets—places where a fortune is wagered on the outcome of a single dog taking two out of three, or five out of six hares—are seemingly highly romantic events. More to the point, most tales about them are highly romantic fiction. Just now and again, people believe they have longdogs which are capable of beating any hare, and even less frequently, they are prepared to wager money to substantiate their faith in the dogs. The wagering of huge sums of money on dogs in the coursing field running singly and under somewhat unorthodox rules is rarer than hen's teeth, however. Firstly, the killing of five out of six hares running against seasoned January hares (the witless, the inferior, the young and the foolish September hares are a different matter) is a feat likely to put the majority of dogs to shame, particularly if the hare is afforded proper law, and when coursing enthusiasts are asked to show their dogs at work, let alone wager a good sum on the outcome of the event, they will usually offer a reason for not appearing at a suggested meet. Some such meets do take place but they are rare, for while talk is incredibly cheap, actions are often a little more costly.

No-one is able to prove the reality of these statements more than Southerd. Southerd can justify his desire to wager great sums of money on his dogs easily enough. He is of temperate disposition, a non-smoker, a bachelor with few interests other than his dogs. In 1985 he published a challenge of £1,000 against any dog in a carefully regulated, best-out-of-three, hare contest, the January hares being allowed 100 yards law and slips to be umpired by a farmer on whose land the courses were to be run. It was no catchpenny event and scrupulous fairness would have prevailed. Southerd had cards printed to this effect and published his challenge in all sporting papers against any breed of dog, sight hound, longdog or lurcher. He had but one taker—the owner of the saluki hybrid, Anna, and Southerd ran against this bitch twice, losing one contest, and winning one. The number of gambling dogs, supposedly common amongst coursing enthusiasts, evaporated like the dew in the morning. It is said that actions speak louder than words, and there was a great silence after Southerd's challenge.

Straight saluki greyhound hybrids are favoured by some longdog enthusiasts, but Southerd believes that a first cross seldom has edge enough to be a successful competitive courser. A dash of saluki, rather than a full-blooded, fifty per cent portion is Southerd's choice and indeed the majority of serious coursers will plump for a three-quarter breed saluki/greyhound rather than a half-bred. Greyhound blood should predominate and the quarter portion of saluki blood added to give the stamina for which this hound is famous, although whether or not this supposed stamina is due to generations of testing at durable quarry such as gazelle and desert hare or simply because (as Drabble believes) the saluki does not try, is questionable. The majority of successful single-handed coursing longdogs are, in fact, three-quarter bred and many are the claims on behalf of this hybrid. Longdogs of this breeding are currently in vogue amongst itinerants and quite high prices are paid for a dog capable of 'doing the job'. Conversely the three-quarter bred hybrid is reputed to have a very short working life, starting at the age of two perhaps, and being burned out long before its sixth birthday. However they do have a reputation of being mighty coursers in the intervening four years of active life.

Saluki whippets are questionable performers at the best-out-of-three hare contests. Salukis vary in size considerably and while a 28-inch dog is not unknown, neither is a 20-inch bitch. Incredibly variable results occur when crossing salukis with whippets, with a view to producing a longdog. Most schools of thought consider that the addition of whippet blood in a sight hound mix may work well for one generation but owing to the fact that the hybrids may throw variable offspring, the line is best discontinued after the first cross. In 1979 there was a spate of whippet/saluki longdog hybrids for sale. Now they are seldom encountered and seldom included in the pedigrees of successful coursing dogs. One of the age old adages of lurcher breeding is never mix greyhound and whippet blood in a family, as the offspring of otherwise good lurchers becomes decidedly variable in type. Perhaps the same applies to the breeding of longdogs.

However, at one time one of the most popular all-round coursing dogs was the whippet/greyhound and during the late 1960s any litters of this breeding were invariably snapped up by coursing enthusiasts. Most of these hybrids had been bred to pep up, or revitalise, whippets which were a little reluctant to chase the rag and hence a dash of good greyhound blood was usually added. Alan Watkins of Doncaster once fielded a black bitch called Carrie, which had a phenomenally successful season in 1964, but was retired through leg injury at the end of that year. She appears in many pedigrees of racing whippets, but her sire was an elderly son of Crazy Parachute, a track greyhound, while her dam was a show-breed whippet which displayed only a moderate enthusiasm for coursing rabbits and would not pursue a rag. At that time any greyhound dog under 30 pounds in weight was entitled to run in the whippet races and two small bitches from this greyhound/whippet union qualified for them. Watkins originally bought Carrie to race and once at Malby she did, in fact, come in at slightly under 30 pounds. However, she gained both muscle and weight and had to be excluded from competing in 'whippet' races.

In 1963 she began coursing at Fenland meets, informal affairs, loose of rule and regulation, but hard taxing meets, as indeed are most Fenland meets, and acquitted herself well; she ran as a 'greyhound' at the local flapping tracks, winning one short distance race at Rotherham late that year. In 1964 she literally swept the boards against all comers in informal coursing meets, running singly against a variety of dogs all of which exceeded Carrie in weight, height and experience. During the 1964 season she competed weekly and never failed to beat her opposition. Later that year she pulled a shoulder and Watkins retired her to breed. She appears in many top class racing whippet pedigrees and while she is described as a whippet she came in at her best at 40 pounds in weight and she measured 20 inches at the shoulder. Carrie was an illustrious bitch by any standards, though no looker. She resembled a small greyhound and displayed none of the conformation expected of a whippet.

Another illustrious coursing longdog was the famous Sabre, a whippet/greyhound hybrid owned by John Mason of Lechlade. There is little known of Sabre's breeding, but his record as a coursing dog was little short of incredible. A strongly built dog despite his fragile whippet sire, Sabre's ability as a catch dog lay not so much in his stamina, but in his incredible take-off speed and ability to snap up opportunities whenever they presented themselves. He is reputed to have entered the pedigree of many families of lurchers, although it is said that, such was his fame, he sired litters two years after his death! Sabre never competed in competitive coursing under rules, but was a wondrous catch dog in any country in which Mason worked him.

Longdogs which are composites of several sight hound breeds are not uncommon, the most popular mix being a blend of deerhound, greyhound and saluki. This blend is usually bred to have greyhound pace, saluki stamina, and deerhound depth of chest. This type has its critics, as indeed has every type of lurcher and longdog and many believe the blend to be apathetic about chasing quarry unless the sire or dam of the blend is a pure-bred greyhound. If the greyhound appears far back in the pedigree, i.e. if a deerhound/greyhound is mated to a saluki the offspring have the reputation of lacking fire and courage to be really successful coursers. This blend is more popular amongst all-round hunters, lampers and deerhunters, than it is amongst coursing enthusiasts who tend to favour single dog coursing competitions.

Exotic crosses involving borzois, Afghan hounds, etc are conspicuous by their absence as a rule. The fact that few people breed these hybrids says much for the ability of longdogs bred from these crosses.

Few *aficionados* of longdogs claim that their hounds are particularly perspicacious. Retrieving should be taught young, if a longdog is meant to return its quarry to hand and constant refresher courses should always be maintained. Perhaps the best advice concerning the training of longdogs is not to expect too much, but do not accept too little.

4. LURCHERS

Prior to 1973 the lurcher enjoyed a curious reputation. The dog was the hallmark of the disreputable, a sign that its owner was a person not to be trusted, a poacher, a ne'er-do-well, the sort of man it would be unwise to employ. Gypsies were said to own these dogs, as were skulkers after dark, people who were as dishonest as the very dog itself. Nowadays the dog is paraded by fashionably dressed ladies and occupies the same role as the elegant borzoi once did. Plushly upholstered Range Rovers now sport a lurcher on the back seat, as much a part of the decor as the seat covers, as socially acceptable as the vehicle itself. The lurcher has undergone a curious metamorphosis, both in genealogy and in its social acceptability.

There is little historical data concerned with the lurcher—it was the dog of the social pariah, the rural misfit and as few historians ever concerned themselves with the social life of the lower echelons of the rural *hoi poloi*, reference to the dogs kept by these low livers is scant and scarce. Stories of medieval poachers and their greyhounds (the notorious black greyhound Collying springs instantly to mind) are often exaggerated, but judging from his exploits, and the value his rowdy ne'er-do-well owners placed on him, he was a lurcher not a greyhound, a bastardised sight hound rather than of blue blood.

Lurchers were designed to be the all-round hunting dog and while the expression pot-filler trips all too readily off the tongue, no other term defines the purpose for which the dog was bred quite as well. Sight hounds of all breeds are swift, quick of movement, and sharp of response, but only the most kennel-blind of owners would credit a sight hound with being supremely tractable, or possessing a sagacity to place it high on the list of canine intelligentsia. Thus a more biddable, a more intelligent dog was required to blend with the sight hound to produce an all-round hunter or, once more, to use that most familiar of clichés, a pot-filler.

The chances are that long extinct herding dogs were used to bring about this amelioration of the greyhound type—there were few other breeds of dog available while Britain was a very insular conservative land. However the reader should dismiss the notion that herding dogs were a homogenous type or simply rather primitive border collies. Herding dogs were simply dogs that herded, no more no less, and were unstandardised and probably seldom the result of planned deliberate matings.

There is a wealth of literature concerned with these primitive herding and droving dogs, some of which are referred to as Smithfield collies. According to Taplin (1803) these were lean leggy collie-like curs used to drive flocks twixt countryside and town, but the type was unstandardised and in all probability a host of different types of cur would have resided under the umbrella title 'Smithfield collie'. Coats would have been variable, ranging from smooth to very hairy, and little importance would have been placed on the height of the herding dog if the type did the work required of it. Indeed the importance of breed purity is a notion that has arisen only in the nineteenth and twentieth century, a notion that has come about only since the exhibiting of dogs, and the subsequent development of breed standards has placed a high value on conformity of type for conformity of type's sake.

Whatever the breeds which were used in the creation of the early lurcher, a lithe greyhoundy animal of variable coat and of a height slightly less than that of a greyhound resulted, but it was not until the nineteenth century that literature regarding the lurcher began to appear.

Shortly before the middle of the nineteenth century a series of what can only be described as land reform acts were begotten and these acts, coupled with the improvement of sporting guns and the subsequent popularity of game shooting, produced a division amongst the population as distinct as any schism produced by the repressive Forest Laws of some 900 years before. Such is the disposition of the European and particularly the British that, should laws be passed, there are people ever ready to question if not break these laws. The modern poacher, a man who simply contravenes those game laws simply for the sake of doing so, made his appearance shortly after the mid-nineteenth century. Romantic literature concerning the poacher abounds, but most of this is simply ill-researched fiction or the writings of authors out to glamorise rural Robin Hood-type characters.

Few poachers poached simply to feed a wife and starving children. A well-managed garden or a pig in a sty produced more nutritious food than a foray into the pheasant coverts. Cobbett hinted lightly at this in his *Rural Rides*, but failed to develop the theme of how to alleviate malnutrition amongst farmworkers of this time. Poaching was, and indeed still is, a way in which certain people wish to express their opinions about the have and have not world. Social privation never made a poacher, although once a poacher became well known for his actions, social privation was likely to follow, for employment was often denied the man with a tendency to flout laws and 'kick against the pricks'. Poachers, so Jeffries believed, could be identified on sight by their very demeanour. Often the insignia of their trade, their badge of office so to speak, was a lurcher.

The sagacity of the lurcher was perhaps overrated by mid-nineteenth and twentieth century country writers. The seemingly innate suspicion and the wily artful disposition of the lurcher may well have been a manifestation of nervousness, a nervousness either inbred or induced by the often unscientific methods of training practised by poachers. Superstition abounds amongst the field sport enthusiasts, and is never stronger than amongst the lurcher fraternity. The insularity of the owners of these dogs made the lurchers equally remote, and the mistrust afforded lurchers by the rest of the rural community must have enhanced the dogs' natural suspicion of people. This remoteness, this suspicion of strangers, in all probability produced an impression that the dogs were a lot more sagacious, a lot more intelligent and astute than the lurchers actually were.

Brian Vesey Fitzgerald was one of the first country authors to write at any length about the lurcher, but his assumptions are far from accurate observations. Fitzgerald travelled widely amongst itinerant people finally writing his masterly *Gypsies in Britain* as a culmination of his adventures. He believed the lurcher was a blend between the Bedlington terrier and a greyhound and perhaps even questions its collie ancestry. In his book *It's My Delight* he evaluates the intelligence of the breeds of dogs that he has encountered and places the lurcher's intelligence above that of the collie. His contact with the lurcher-owning fraternity was a trifle limited, however. While he gleaned much information from James Arigho a Romany tinker (Didikai) of the Welsh Marches (he dedicated *Gypsies in Britain* to Arigho) much of his contact with dog-owning itinerants was with what he describes as the Blackface people, itinerants north of the Border, families such as the McPhee's (the name is derived from the Gaelic word Dubhi, blackfaced), the Williamson's and the Stewarts, itinerant families who had lived in Britain long before the invasion of the Romany during the fifteenth and sixteenth century. These people kept many lurchers and had an affection for the 'stag' (the deerhound hybrid) and in all probability the blue-black coats of the northern itinerant lurchers may have been derived from deerhound as much as Bedlington terrier blood. Certainly there was a rise in popularity of the Bedlington/greyhound lurcher between the time Fitzgerald put pen to paper on the subject of lurchers (1948) and in 1973, a date which must rank in the watershed in the history of the lurcher.

The dilution of lurcher blood with further additions of sight hound stock to produce what in effect were simply longdogs, has been discussed in the chapter 'Longdogs' so it has been well covered, but the early winners at Lambourn in 1973 were so infused with sight hound blood as to be longdogs rather than lurchers. Lambourn contributed much to the resurrection of interest in the lurcher and the advent of the show was followed by a spate of lurcher literature. Breeders and lurcher enthusiasts became more aware of the types of lurcher available to them and a number of experimental crosses were attempted in a bid to resurrect the old type of lurcher. Greyhounds were mated to border collies (for old herding strains had long since vanished) although Patterson in *Coursing* suggests the old Dartmoor collie, which was supposedly leggier, taller and bolder than the border collie, is the best type of herding dog to create the desired type of lurcher. Later, experiments involving bearded collies were attempted and some laid claim to own the probably extinct Smithfield collie. The majority of collie crosses produced were scarcely attractive types and certainly did not compete well with the more elegant deerhound hybrids of the shows, for since Lambourn, country shows frequently stage lurcher classes. Lambourn lurcher shows ceased to exist after 1982, when a band of disreputables and half-wits caused so many problems that the natives of Lambourn village requested the show organisers to seek another venue. It was a great loss and for a well-organised, friendly show at a superb venue to be finished because of a relatively small number of louts, is indeed a shame.

Lambourn did, however, slow down the experiments conducted to produce a Prester John type superdog, experiments which did almost irreparable damage to the lurcher gene pool. Amazing dogs were mated together in an effort to add certain qualities to the resulting 'lurchers'. Borzois, Dobermans, American pit bull terriers were all mated to greyhounds as was every conceivable breed of terrier. The lurcher shows did at least allow enthusiasts to see a good selection of stock in order to further blood lines and the very damaging experiments with a view to producing lurcher crosses have slowed up if not ceased.

The majority of lurchers offered for sale with spurious pedigrees must be legion. Few of the dogs are what they are supposed to be breeding-wise, and genealogies and pedigrees are lost in the mists of wild surmise. Pedigrees are invented on the spur of the moment and a litter, supposedly collie/greyhound/greyhound one week, will be offered for sale as deerhound/collie/whippet/greyhound the next, if the original advertisement has not succeeded in producing the correct response from buyers. Few long term lurcher breeders can relate the pedigrees or genealogies of their stock

LURCHERS

accurately, but it should be stressed that the lurchers are no worse for their fictitious pedigrees.

Legitimate breeders, producing stock with authentic pedigrees, do of course exist. Perhaps the world's biggest breeder of the collie lurcher is David Hancock of Sutton Coldfield. Hancock began his successful lurcher breeding venture by a curious quirk of fate. In the late 1970s a rise in the price of maize and fish meal made the production of eggs and table poultry a risky and often quite unprofitable business. Hancock sensed the 'ripple' in the market but was at that time farming broilers, ducks and battery hens in such a big way that pulling out of the business was out of the question. Quite soon, debts began to pile up and so Hancock declared himself bankrupt in the early 1980s.

He was left with a maze of poultry sheds and little else to show for his lifetime with poultry. However being of an inventive mind, he set to acquire good quality cast greyhounds, mating them to collies and half-bred collie greyhounds to produce lurchers of good quality. After a very shaky start he produced dogs of very fine quality indeed, using a bearded collie/border collie hybrid (blue merle with a rough coat) on some good quality greyhound bitches, keeping a blue merle half-bred stud and mating the dog to other greyhound bitches. Hancock breeds two prime crosses, half-bred collie greyhounds and three-quarter bred stock. Half-bred collies find a market amongst lampers and fox catching enthusiasts while the more versatile three-quarter breds, faster and having more greyhound blood, are sold to hunters with an interest in securing hares, as well as rabbits.

Hancock's views are fairly straightforward. Hare coursing is a pastime best left to sight hounds and longdogs and general all-round work dogs are what Hancock has decided to breed. His three-quarter bred lurchers (collie/greyhound/greyhound) often win well against the more classically bred saluki greyhounds or saluki/greyhound/greyhound hybrids although Hancock states that, should he require a dog exclusively for hare coursing, he would buy and train a longdog. More recently his experiments in back crosses of collie/greyhound/collie have produced a more collie-like type of dog, easily trained and still fast enough to perform the task of rabbit catching and lamping.

Hancock has sold many puppies abroad and at American meets where cold-blood greyhounds (cross-bred sight hounds—either lurchers or longdogs carry this title in America) are allowed to enter an event, his stock has often swept the board. American huntress, Teddy Moritz, fields one of his three-quarter breds and has produced a first rate hunting dog by this male. Hancock's stock has fared well in most countries and few countries throughout the world do not have 'Hancock' lurchers.

Despite the popularity of the type, the Bedlington/ greyhound lurcher has few serious breeders. Most of the first-cross hybrids are very typey and finish up as blue-black 23 inch males with bitches a shade smaller. Good ones will knock down hares, though not with the regularity of a good three-quarter bred collie or a classically bred longdog from a good strain. Bedlington lurchers are essentially workhorses, however, and are usually very versatile. They invariably excel at working rabbit, lamping and put up quite a fair show at coursing foxes, though much depends on the way the hybrid has been entered, for while the cross-bred is obviously terrier blooded, it is often sensitive, slightly shy as a puppy and 'put off' if over-matched and hurt by any encounter. A good living certainly awaits anyone who regularly produces good class Bedlington/greyhound hybrids in any number and manages to breed out the copper toxicosis that is destroying the Bedlington terrier.

As to the much-vaunted, much-publicised Bedlington/ whippet hybrid, Walsh, author of *Lurchers and Longdogs* believes the cross is a little unnecessary, as is the lurcherising of any sort of whippet. Small lurchers can do nothing that cannot be brought about by a pure-bred whippet. The courage of the pure-bred whippet is underrated. Despite their thin satin-like coats, many face cover quite fearlessly, and often enter with such enthusiasm to fox, that they have been known to follow one to ground and bay it. A Bedlington/whippet hybrid can, or will do no more, so perhaps the advice to all small lurcher enthusiasts is to buy a whippet rather than create under-sized lurchers that are not as fast as a whippet, and no more versatile.

Interest in bull terrier lurchers bred by mating an English bull terrier, a Staffordshire bull terrier, or more lately, an American pit bull terrier to a greyhound is growing. While on first impressions, the cross appears incongruous, it is far from a senseless hybridising experiment. In the 1700s Lord Orford became disenchanted with the performance of his greyhounds and hence introduced the blood of top grade bulldogs, thereby adding a dash of courage to the progeny. Though Orford's first hybrids were a trifle unsightly, the three-quarter bred stock bred by the addition of more greyhound blood, performed with more courage than most greyhounds of the time. The mating of bull terriers to greyhounds is therefore a way of replicating Orford's work. However, it might be argued that the greyhound is already courageous enough and what a lurcher needs is brain and nose—neither of which are imparted by the addition of bull terrier genes.

A rough coat does not make a dog a lurcher. Neither does an aesthetic frame. Speed alone is not an all important factor, for, if speed was all important, would not a greyhound, the fastest of dogs, be superior? A lurcher is first and foremost an all-round hunting dog, and at the risk of once again using a very hackneyed old cliché—a pot-filler. Lurcher shows should be fun, and the creation of an attractive dog satisfying, but if the dog is not an instinctive hunter, when it is given a chance, and many are not, if the dog is not capable of catching suitable quarry, then no matter what the breeding, no matter how beautiful the animal is, it is not a true lurcher.

5. SIGHT HOUNDS, LONGDOGS AND LURCHERS —A SUMMARY

Thus the breeds of sight hounds and their derivative types have been outlined and it is the reader's choice as to which breed or type to select. However, before buying any type of dog, potential buyers must ask themselves their reasons for the purchase of a particular breed. Obviously if the reader is eager to have a dog with a racy elegant shape, a flowing movement and is a devotee of a dog with a turn of graceful speed, then one of the sight hounds is the obvious choice of pet. Once again it should be pointed out that the ownership of a dog, any dog, and more particularly any sight hound, is seldom trouble free and that all breeds of dog have their peculiarities, their idiosyncracies and their disadvantages.

Few breed books, books which deal only with specific types of dogs, are free from exaggerated eulogy, simply because the writer of that particular breed book is quite definitely a breed enthusiast who is unlikely to relate the all too obvious shortcomings of a much-beloved breed. Indeed, so partisan are some of the writers of breed books, that they may well be unaware of these shortcomings. No enthusiast of this calibre is likely to decry any quality which their much-beloved breed may possess. To illustrate this point more fully, no breed book on the northern spitz type sled or sled-cum-herding dog is likely to mention that the Siberian huskies, the malemutes, the ostiaks and the Inuit dogs are resistant to formal training, desperately difficult to persuade to return to hand and perfectly horrific in the presence of sheep, poultry and cats. No book on the Boston terrier or the modern bulldog types seems to relate that the breeders are producing monstrosities, canine anathema, that have to be helped into the world by means of Caesarian operation and assisted through life by veterinary surgeons because ill-advised breed enthusiasts have produced biological abnormalities in order to create animals to conform to breed standards. Few books on GSDs are prepared to admit that epilepsy, hip dysplasia and hyperactivity of the sort that makes life hell on earth for the luckless owner of an animal possessed of these abnormalities, is present in the breed. Yet these peculiarities do exist, these difficulties will almost certainly be encountered, once a person obtains a specimen of a peculiar breed.

Sight hounds are remarkably free from physical peculiarity. The type (or types if Zeuner's hypothesis, that sight hound types have developed independently in the old world) have evolved over an extremely long period of time and genetic abnormalities, deformities and weakness have long since been bred out by the most stringent of methods of selection—the coursing field. Sickly, inefficient, slow and physically abnormal animals have simply not been used to continue the bloodlines and hence it is scarcely hyperbole or exaggeration, in any form, to state that the sight hound group is perhaps the most physically perfect of all types of dog, and while abnormalities are present, and indeed are bound to exist amongst the giant types, because no legitimate method of coursing suitable quarry still remains in a world with a rapidly diminishing number of animal species, sight hounds generally are usually physically peerless animals, tough, hardy, strong and singularly free from parturition problems.

Yet the type is not problem free, and potential buyers must be aware of these problems before even considering the actual purchase of a puppy. Sight hounds are seldom very intelligent and are not capable of learning either a great deal or very quickly. They have been bred for their physical qualities and mental aptitudes have usually been neglected in the development of this type of dog. Sight hounds simply are not designed to cope with elaborate training methods, which would not so much as tax the brain of a retriever, a collie or a German shepherd dog. Thus the reader must decide to ignore the type of stupidity and breed blindness manifested by many breed-book writers who suggest that a particular sight hound is too intelligent to heed man's stupid demands during training. To all intents and purposes, intelligence and tractability are synonymous in all domesticated canids and the sight hounds are certainly not particularly tractable, biddable or particularly eager to please an owner. For this reason lurchers (as opposed to longdogs, one should add) have been created by ameliorating pure sight hound with the blood of more intelligent, more tractable breeds such as collies.

It is, however, often argued that in America at least, most sight hound breeds have performed frequently, if not well, in obedience tests, and this cannot be denied. It can also be argued that obedience tests are carried out under synthetic conditions within enclosed halls or rings surrounded by spectators and free from the distractions which are likely to beset any sight hound during a typical day's exercise. The desire, will or instinct to chase, far exceeds the type's will to please its owners and, once free of the restrictions imposed by the lead, the sight hound, unless very carefully trained or rigorously disciplined will all too frequently run amok. The desire to chase has long been indelibly imprinted into every fibre of the sight hound's body, and its structure has been adapted to facilitate that desire. Hence, the presence of livestock, which trigger off that desire to chase, will often result not only in carnage but in extremely expensive carnage. Unless taught that such quarry is absolutely forbidden greyhounds, whippets, salukis and Afghan hounds often find cats are irresistible and pursue them with anything but friendship in mind. Tales of salukis hurtling through window panes to catch and kill cats are all too common. Restraint and steadiness to stock should be taught early, and taught thoroughly, or the sight hound never allowed to see any creature which could precipitate a reaction. The purchase of adult animals from breed rescue centres should be carefully considered, as the animals found in these breed kennels are usually recalcitrant ones which have seldom had the necessary preliminary training to make them socially acceptable.

Such animals are usually very difficult to train or break to stock and, frankly, often become liabilities to their new owners. Many rescued adult sight hounds, and this fact must be told, are never really safe enough to be allowed off a lead, and while it is true that many of these unfortunates do become rehabilitated enough to lead normal lives, they are usually, because of the absence of early training, or perhaps because of the poor quality of this, very difficult to stock break or obedience train.

The traditional quarry of most sight hounds, whippets and Pharaoh hounds aside is deer (the hare was originally a secondary and what was considered to be a rather undeserving and inferior sort of quarry for the larger sight hounds) and the outline of a deer usually produces an amazing reaction in even the most suburban and civilised sight hound. Most show-bred hounds, sight hounds whose very remote ancestors were the last of the lineage ever to course a deer, galvanise into action at the sight of one, as if it conjures up some long forgotten archetypical desire in the dog.

The owner of a sight hound is very unlikely to encounter deer under ordinary conditions (although such is the deeply ingrained desire to do so that sight hounds of any type, including whippets, need little encouragement to pursue them). The silhouette of a sheep is very similar to that of a deer, and often provokes the same reaction in sight hounds. All such dogs and their derivatives must therefore be absolutely steady with sheep and such stock-steadiness can usually only be achieved by introducing the dog to a sheep while the hound is still a very young puppy. Sight hound puppies of all types are usually quite effete as youngsters and are seldom as precocious or aggressive as a terrier puppy. If a sight hound is to be broken to sheep, and frankly all dogs should be, then it must be broken while still in puppyhood and long before the instinct to chase has properly developed. Tales of Afghan hounds, greyhounds and salukis creating red and bloody murder while still puppies and long before the instinct to chase has properly developed, are all too common and, not surprisingly, stories of lurchers creating mayhem are legion. It is easy to understand why lurchers are deemed prime culprits in the destruction of flocks. Since 1973 the lurcher has enjoyed, if enjoyed be the right word, a tremendous popularity, indeed it may well be Britain's most popular dog, though the absence of any form of registration would make this statement impossible to prove. However, since the advent of Lambourn Lurcher Show the lurcher has become a symbol of the 'real countryman' and is very numerous in rural areas. While many lurchers are, by analysis of their supposed breeding, longdogs (a combination of sight hound breeds to the exclusion of pastoral breeds or other types of dog) there has been a revival of interest in the true lurcher—a mix of sheep dog and sight hound. The resulting hybrid, properly trained, is superb. Ill-trained, the dog is an unholy terror. A sight hound's desire to pursue quarry is well known and the instinctive ability of a collie to be able to handle sheep, to herd, to cut out certain members of the flock is also well-understood. The combination of qualities of the two breeds produces an animal which is tailor-made to be a sheep worrier and collie lurchers left untrained, untutored and not stock-broken, become unparalleled sheep worriers. In the early 1980s a spate of notorious sheep worrying in the Scottish Highlands was attributed to a collie whippet hybrid brought in from England, reared in an urban home, purchased by an enthusiast who became less enthusiastic after the purchase of the dog, and allowed to run riot. The result was predictable and unpleasant. It also cost Highland farms thousands of pounds and created an even stronger antipathy to lurchers and sight hound types than had existed previously.

Despite nineteenth-century tales of lurchers and greyhounds running loose all day poaching, but not causing problems amongst domesticated livestock, it is sheer lunacy to allow a sight hound or one of their derivatives the liberty afforded to a farm collie in either rural or urban conditions. Training, stock-breaking, even the most stringent and careful methods of conditioning, creates but a thin, easily ruptured degree of steadiness on the sight hound, and it is almost inevitable that, sooner or later, the unrestrained dog will slip the fetters wrought by training and revert to its natural instincts to become a diabolical stock worrier. Nor is the sighthound a suitable dog to be allowed to run the streets of a town, for once again cats and even small dogs become prey and accidents brought about by wandering dogs fleeing in front of cars are all too numerous. More dangerous still is the 'composite pack' a mixture of dogs of various breeds, each contributing some quality to the capture of a prey, the sight hound lending speed to assist the capture and other breeds also supplying some attribute to bring about the demise of the quarry. It is a popular saying amongst stock keepers that a sight hound plus another dog of any breed constitutes a pack, and the havoc caused by unruly packs is well-recorded in Britain and abroad. At no time should a sight hound, or any other hunting dog for that matter, be allowed to wander at liberty.

These then are the problems that are likely to beset an owner of sight hounds and such are the canine frailties of these dogs of the chase. Disadvantages of this nature, peculiarities of breed or type, are seldom mentioned in books about specific sight hounds but must always be borne in mind and never ever ignored. A sight hound, however aesthetic its appearance, however graceful and flowing an accoutrement it may be, is first and foremost a hunting dog, bred, designed and mentally programmed to be a dog designed to pursue, and if possible, kill quarry. Training may ameliorate its instincts, or even partially sublimate its desire to kill its prey (greyhounds chase dummy hares) but the veneer of control is all too easily lost.

6. Choosing a Puppy

There is no hard and fast rule which enables even a sight hound expert to go to a nest of puppies, reach down and choose a whelp which will develop into a show champion or a successful coursing winner—although quite obviously it must be considerably easier to select a puppy on only its aesthetic qualities rather than on its coursing potential. Much of the dog's eventual appearance and even its possibilities on the field are determined at conception and while good kennel management will allow this to develop to the full, no amount of feeding, however careful, and no amount of love and care will produce the silk purse from a sow's ear, although good stockmanship does improve a dog's physical performance in the field.

There are, however, certain hard and fast rules regarding the selection of healthy whelps and these should be adhered to fairly rigidly. Firstly, a sterile, swish kennel with all mod. cons. is no guarantee that the whelp one is purchasing, is superior to another, obtained from less salubrious kennels, though such spick and span chromium-plated efficiency gives one a rough idea that the pup will cost quite a bit more than is usual. Conversely, the evil-smelling, filthy, badly managed kennel (which should be a *rara avis* since the 1973 Dog Breeders' Act, but isn't by a long way) is not automatically the home of badly reared, unhealthy whelps, though it should be fairly apparent that such conditions are scarcely conducive to the rearing of disease-free puppies. However it should be pointed out that quite a few greyhounds which have become Derby winners, or Waterloo Cup successes, grew up on farms in Ireland, romping in garbage and the excreta of herbivorous animals, eating (in addition to their normal diet) a quantity of extraneous substances, the nature of which would disgust a vulture, let alone a canine nutritionist. Somewhere there is a happy medium between the totally sterile (and frankly quite dangerous) environment, and the horrendous squalor sometimes found, even in licenced kennels, for the 1973 Dog Breeders' Act has produced fairly dubious results.

Sight hounds, and particularly sight hound derivatives such as lurchers and longdogs, seem to attract the dog dealer like a magnet, and it is fairly easy to understand why. Sight hounds change hands easily. To be more precise, they are remarkably tolerant of new owners, or a variety of new owners, and display little of the neurosis which would be manifested, should collies or German shepherd dogs be subjected to such treatment. Whether or not a sight hound suffers because of such chop-and-change merchants, is perhaps another story, but they display few of the peculiarities which beset other breeds which have been subjected to similar treatment. Sight hounds are naturally robust, hardy, tough of frame and tissue, and if traded (a word with grim connotations) in fairly good condition, they take some time to deteriorate seriously, even if subjected to the most barbarous treatment. Lurchers and longdogs are the most common occupants of such dealers' kennels, failed, dispirited dogs, often desperate for care and affection, and recipients of mistraining and mismanagement by, perhaps, a score of owners. Of late, salukis are commonplace in these establishments, but Afghans, because their heavy coats necessitate grooming, are seldom found in such places. Irish wolfhounds and, particularly Scottish deerhounds, a popular base for longdog breeding, breeds so dignified as to appear out of place in such surroundings, were once not unknown in dealers' kennels, but happily, restricted breeding, and perhaps some careful choice of clients by breeders of the majestic hounds has largely removed such breeds from the barter lists of dealers.

Dealers too, are subject to scrutiny by the Department of

the Environment, and should possess a pet dealer's licence, but such kennels rarely receive the correct attention from the authorities and pass unnoticed until flagrant cruelty, often of an unbelievable nature, attracts the attention of the RSPCA and results in a prosecution and a temporary closure of the premises. So light are the fines for the violation of both the Act and of human decency that most dealers simply move on and start afresh in pastures which are newer, if not greener.

These kennels are certainly not the places to buy a puppy of any breed—although there are usually litters aplenty in such places. The death rate amongst puppies, bought and sold there, must be staggering. Normally, a puppy will come into the hands of a dealer at roughly eight weeks of age (sometimes at a very much younger age than this, actually) and by this age, the whelp will be losing some of the maternal immunity that has been conferred by its dam's colostrum. The change in environment, the change of food, the separation from its dam, all accelerate this process and leave the puppy wide open to infection.

The very nature of a dog dealer's trade, necessitates many different dogs passing through the kennels, and each dog has a distinctive intestinal flora and fauna which its faeces will contribute to the bacteria and viruses of the kennel. Some of these bacteria will be harmless, or relatively so, others will be less than harmless. All will infect puppies with mixed results. Such kennels are the lairs of parvo viruses and others of the distemper complex, and few puppies pass through these places without receiving some infection from the micro-organisms found there. Add to this the type of dog which is likely to find its way into a kennel of this sort, or more to the point, the nature of the previous owner of such a dog. Few of them will have been cared for, and even fewer will have been inoculated for the deadly ills which can beset puppies. Most of these dogs will have been neglected to some extent, prior to their departure to the dealer for the disenchantment of an owner will usually be accompanied by a lack of interest in the welfare of his animal.

All manner of ills will beset a puppy from such a menagerie of misery and frankly while the Department of the Environment officers are usually fairly prompt at

CHOOSING A PUPPY

bringing actions to bear on breeders who have failed to register with the correct authorities (1973 Dog Breeders' Act), they are frequently very remiss about acting against an unregistered dog dealer. Some places often defy belief. Some are suitable material for a TV animal/horror documentary. Most are operated illegally and many should be subject to very close scrutiny by Local Government Officers. Few are subject to this scrutiny and pass unnoticed until a prosecution for some unbelievable cruelty arises. An unlicenced dog dealer's kennel is, frankly, no place for a thinking, caring dog owner to buy a puppy, or to visit, for that matter.

A far from swish house, and many dog breeders' houses are reduced to this condition by their wards, is often not a bad place to buy a puppy, however, particularly if such a place is the home of fairly well-controlled children. Often the bitches used for breeding, are not only broods, but family pets, and allow the examination of their puppies by the children of the household, together with their friends. Thus the puppies reared in such houses are seldom remote and difficult to train, but socialised and frequently bold and biddable even before their departure to new homes. Providing the puppies are in good health, in good condition, and fair specimens of the breed, then the 'home-reared' litter is usually a far better purchase than similar stock reared in a large antiseptic, but impersonal kennel. Dogs, particularly sight hounds, have enjoyed a symbiotic relationship with mankind for perhaps as much as half a million years. A certain intertwinable bond between man and dog must surely be woven between them. A kennel-reared whelp denied a lot of human contact, as frankly, most kennel-reared whelps usually are, must certainly be classed as a deprived animal, no matter how clean and hygienic its surroundings may be.

A newcomer to the breed wishing to purchase a showable animal with above average aesthetic qualities is in something of a dilemma. Most show enthusiasts start their interests in a particular breed by purchasing a pet animal and progressing to better quality stock as soon as interest in the breed develops. A newcomer wishing to purchase a show-bred typey puppy should therefore not only read up on the standard, but take a person well-versed in the showing and breeding of this particular breed to assist in the choosing of a puppy, but having said that, it is also well to say that no expert is infallible, and no right-thinking expert would wish to be considered as infallible, when it comes to the selection of a future champion in the nest. A veterinary surgeon is the very last person to assist in the selection of a show puppy unless he is an expert in that particular breed of dog. Few have any specific knowledge of the breed in question, few are au fait with the breed's standard and most will simply select a robust, healthy puppy from the nest, no matter how typical of the breed the whelps may be. Any novice wishing to select a puppy from a nest of whelps must certainly take an expert to view the litter and respect the choice of that expert.

Regardless of the breed type or hybrid, a nervous puppy, one which cringes or moves away from the would-be purchaser, should be avoided at all cost, no matter what attractive qualities the animal may otherwise possess. An animal which lives indoors rather than exists in a kennel, left to its own devices until the day of the show, should blend into its owner's lifestyle, rather than have that owner's life tailored to the needs or requirements of the dog. A nervous dog seldom adjusts totally to the way of life of a normal family and nervousness in a puppy should suggest that something is seriously amiss in the make-up of the whelp. A well-reared puppy of any breed, even a reserved type of dog such as a German shepherd should be sycophantically friendly and should fawn and grovel and display all the qualitites of a typical epsilon member of a dog pack. A reserved, nervous whelp, one which shrinks away from the hands of the would-be purchaser should be avoided. The majority of dogs which tend to bite humans, and fortunately aggression of this sort is not typical of the sight hounds, are invariably nervous dogs who are basically afraid of the person they have attacked, but the attack of a shy biter is none the less serious because of the reasons for the attack. Avoid any nervous puppies. Sight hound puppies should be wildly ebullient, absurdly friendly. A puppy which fails to behave in this way, is not typical and should never be purchased.

CHOOSING A PUPPY

Healthy puppies should have healthy dams and for a breeder to excuse the condition of a bitch by the statement that the puppies have done so well as to have reduced the dam to a state that is skeletal is ridiculous and untrue. No bitch which has just reared even a giant litter should look skeletal or emaciated. An emaciated dam has not only not been fed well enough to ensure her own health, she has not been fed well enough to nourish her whelps properly. A thin-ribbed, decidedly emaciated bitch particularly, should she manifest mange symptoms, as do many greyhound bitches if allowed to rear a litter on an inadequate diet, is not a suitable dam of the puppy the buyer wishes to purchase. A caring breeder, a thoughtful stockman will increase the quality and quality of a bitch's food if he notices even a slight drop in her physical condition, and will treat mange from its first onset, not allowing it to run riot to infect the puppies. No bitch, not even an elderly bitch which has reared a large litter should be in bad health. If she is, the chances are the puppies are not satisfactorily reared. Once again this should act as a warning to a potential buyer, and, frankly, the potential buyer of a whelp from a badly conditioned dam would be well-advised to avoid the purchase.

It is often said that the general smell of a kennel is an indication of the health of the kennel occupants. This may have been true at one time but, since balanced dog meals and non-meat feeds, it is not so. Meal-fed dogs usually produce stools which have a somewhat sour smell while meat-fed dogs in normal health generally produce faeces which are practically odourless, particularly if a large quantity of bone is fed in addition to animal flesh. Dogs fed primarily on a diet of sheep's heads usually pass white cement-like stools with practically no odour.

However, the faeces passed by a puppy are an excellent indication of its general state of health. Avoid purchasing puppies which pass loose, ill-smelling stools, while puppies which produce blood-stained faeces should be instantly rejected. The blood-stained stools may well be the result of minor digestive upsets, mild and very ephemeral enteritis, or far more serious still, parvo virus which can render a puppy dead within a matter of hours, and more sinister still, may damage the heart muscles so badly that in later life various cardiac disorders will manifest themselves when a dog exerts itself violently. As it is a sight hound's disposition to run at great speed, no puppy with a history of parvo virus—or no uninoculated puppy—should ever be countenanced. Lurchers and longdogs are usually worked quite hard when adults and, if affected with parvo virus as puppies, frequently collapse and die when subjected to a strenuous period of coursing. Blood-stained faeces and a limp dehydrated body are usually symptoms that all is not well and the puppy best left with the breeder.

A thin patchy coat on a puppy is usually symptomatic of neglect and bad rearing and scarcely a recommendation for a client to purchase a whelp. Likewise this condition can easily be brought about by the presence of a large number of roundworms in the gut, though a more obvious symptom of this infestation is a pot-bellied puppy. Buying an unwormed puppy, or a puppy which has been damaged by roundworm infestation is seldom good policy, for roundworms are highly injurious to the intestinal tracts and unless they are eradicated early in life, can do a great deal of damage. So easy is the process of ridding a puppy of worms, using modern anthelmintics such as piperazine, that there is really no excuse for an unwormed puppy above six weeks of age, and the presence of such an animal should be an indication not only that worming has been omitted, but also that the stockmanship of the breeder is slightly questionable. Admittedly, it can be argued that sometimes a whelp may vomit its medicine and thereby continue to be worm infested. Likewise, it must be pointed out that a stockman, even a mediocre stockman, will soon notice a puppy which is obviously a bad doer and act accordingly. Frankly, there is no excuse for a vendor trying to sell an unwormed puppy, for worms are indicative of neglect and poor kennel management.

The importance of a pedigree to the potential buyer of a puppy has long been a subject of much debate. The presence of red-lettered champions in a pedigree does give an indication that the puppy may be a fair to presentable specimen of its type. Likewise, the presence of such star-studded names in a pedigree does not automatically ensure that the whelp will grow into an animal which will be

CHOOSING A PUPPY

healthy (physically and mentally—though the sight hounds are not noted for mental instability). Frankly, pedigrees are usually regarded as status symbols—slips of paper taken out to show visitors—but having no significance other than that. Research into such pedigree and publication of this research—as recommended and practised by Dr Willis of the German Shepherd Dog Club—is essential if a pedigree is to be at all meaningful. Most pedigrees are anything but meaningful, however.

Pedigrees are important to the buyer who has set out to purchase a show specimen although the standard eugenic cliché, like produces like, is not always proof that a star-studded pedigree gives rise to a star-studded litter. Not all champions produce good stock, let alone further champions, and, quite often, sires and dams which are good but not superb specimens, become producers of stock which is far superior to either parent. Pedigrees are however, proof of the purity of the breed, proof that the puppy bought will grow up to be a typical (though perhaps not particularly good) specimen of the breed which, of course, brings the reader quite neatly to the subject of the pedigrees of longdogs and lurchers.

It is often said that verbal pedigrees, like verbal contracts, are not worth the paper on which they are written, a ludicrous piece of logic which, when held up to a strong light, is perhaps a shade more enigmatic than logical. Both longdogs and lurchers are deliberate cross-breds—though perhaps some are rather obviously less deliberate than others—and, as such, pedigrees are seldom authenticated by Kennel Club registrations. However, a pedigree by definition, is simply a list of ancestors or more often, in the case of lurchers and longdogs, a list of breeds which have been included in the make-up of the particular hybrid, e.g.:

lurcher—greyhound × collie × deerhound
or
longdog—greyhound × saluki × greyhound

Few pedigrees of either lurchers or longdogs are authentic. Many, though not all, are bred by dabblers who are seeking, none too wisely perhaps, to produce a first class hunting dog with good qualitites derived from all the ancestors in the pedigree. Most are owners of animals of dubious ancestry and the pedigrees are therefore fictitious and made up on the spur of the moment for sales purposes. All lurchers should, so the public believes, be a known mixture of breeds, so advertisements which simply read 'lurchers for sale, good working stock', will seldom attract a buyer. This less honest approach, advertising the stock as deerhound x greyhound x collie whippet x Bedlington (an anathema of a mix by any standards) is likely to produce a more enthusiastic response from the pedigree-orientated, but very gullible public. Frankly, pedigrees of this nature are not worth heeding, and are best disregarded. A better policy than simply the examination of supposed pedigrees, is to visit the vendor, see the parents, and then, if the parents are what the would-be buyer wishes to own, buy a puppy. Lurcher litters are common and well advertised by the vendors, as a rule, so the buyer has great choice. Likewise, the buyer should exercise that choice and disregard most pedigrees.

To dally a while on the subject of lurcher pedigrees however, some breeders specialise in certain hybrids to the exclusion of other types. Nuttall of Clitheroe specialised in deerhound x greyhound hybrids, Hancock in collie x greyhound crosses. Thus, if pedigree is taken as the foremost consideration in the purchase of a puppy, then these specialist breeders are obviously the people from whom one should buy a puppy. However, it must also be pointed out, that many excellent strains of both lurcher and longdog have extremely dubious ancestors, and are certainly none the worse for their questionable pedigrees. A pedigree, or rather a list of breeds comprising the make-up of a lurcher or a longdog, does not automatically produce a good specimen, though that *rara avis*, an authentic lurcher pedigree, does give some indication of the physical type into which the puppy may grow.

Quite clearly, the purchase of a lurcher is thwart with risk, and while the quote of the once famous James Arigho, 'Any mixture of greyhound will in the right hands turn into a reasonable hunting dog' is perhaps true, an ill-advised purchase can result in a score of years of regret, for sight hound hybrids are very long lived. The absence of

CHOOSING A PUPPY

authentic pedigrees (and the relative cheapness of hybrid lurchers and longdogs) does much to account for the reason why these sight hound derivatives are the chop and change stock in trade of the dog dealer—though the inability of many trainers to fulfil the potential of their purchases (lurcher owners are among the worst dog trainers) is also an important factor in the trade of the dog dealer.

The choosing of a puppy is difficult in the case of the purchase of a pure-bred sight hound, bought to fulfil a specific purpose—i.e. exhibition or coursing. In the case of the choice of a longdog or lurcher puppy, much is in the lap of the gods (unless a reputable regular breeder is consulted). The beginner, purchasing a sight hound or a hybrid for the first time, should consider taking an expert with him to help make the choice. However, once again it should be mentioned that in the matter of selecting any livestock, no expert should be considered as infallible.

7. Rearing a Puppy

One of the most popular epigrams concerning the sight hound family is an aphorism concerning the greyhound—a greyhound is like any other breed, only more so—and it is now essential to explain this seemingly enigmatic statement. The very nature of the shape and disposition of the sight hound ensures that it literally propels itself through life at a somewhat more tumultuous pace than other breeds of dog. The type is far from injury prone, but the very nature of its work, the velocity of its movement, makes it quite susceptible to often furious damage. Such is the physique of these incredible dogs however, and such are the recuperative powers of the type, that they sustain and recover from injuries which would render other breeds dead from shock. Some of the injuries from which a greyhound type recovers are past belief and their resistance to shock is such that veterinary surgeons are often amazed at the recuperative properties of the type. However, to attain this state of near physical perfection, to grow into an animal capable of surviving normal coursing injuries, a puppy must be reared properly, fed on a good healthy diet and given adequate and plentiful suitable food.

Basically, an all-purpose dog food can be used to rear any type of sight hound from the diminutive and deceptively tough whippet to the enormous Irish wolfhounds—though additions to the diet in the form of extra mineral and vitamin supplements are advised. The frequency of leg bone breakages in deerhounds, at the time of writing, (and most coursing deerhound owners seem prepared to admit that this peculiarity does exist) may well be due to excessive exercise of the animals as puppies, coupled with a diet which is perhaps deficient in minerals, or bone-assimilation vitamins. Diets which are suitable for rearing breeds with a more sedentary disposition, may not be entirely suitable for the rearing of sight hounds, particularly the larger breeds such as the Irish wolfhound, the borzoi or the Scottish deerhound.

The reader must now reject the tales of Victorian poachers who reared lurchers on diets deficient in protein and minerals alike, producing animals which were superb in condition and intelligence. Most of these tales are exaggerated for no animal, not even the traditional poacher's lurcher grows to its full potential if not properly fed. Such legends may be explained by the tales that these lurchers were allowed to supplement their diets by foraging and self-hunting, but once again it must be stressed that between the ages of six weeks and six months old, the most critical time in the development of any puppy, and certainly the time when young animals need the very best of feeding, a whelp has certainly not developed well enough mentally, or physically to fend for itself and to exist on its own 'catches'. Tales of Victorian poachers, their methods, their dog training techniques and their lurchers, are seldom accurate and, frankly, should be disregarded.

Dogs are by nature carnivorous, that is their metabolism is geared to the intake of relatively small quantities of high grade protein rich food. The natural food of dogs is meat and no amount of domestication, no amount of genetic manipulation, can alter a process which has taken several million years to evolve. In recent years an entirely vegetable dog food has been created, substituting soya bean meal for animal protein, and it speaks highly of the animal nutritionists involved in the creation of such meals that dogs thrive on the product. On the debit side, such foods of this kind are inordinately expensive if one considers the nature of their constituents. Nutritionists argue, quite plausibly, as it happens, that the protein found in conventional dog meals is usually derived, in part at least, from fallen animals which have been victims of certain diseases before their demise and subsequent conversion to dog meal, and that chemical changes are often wrought in the carcasses of fallen beasts producing harmful substances despite the fact that the flesh is subject to scrupulous sterilising before inclusion in stock feed. Conversely, soya meal is not subject to such possible hazards.

Ordinarily, meat should be the main component of any dog food, be it sterilised and treated or red raw, bloody, and straight from the abattoir. However, meat alone is simply not enough to rear a sight hound and should be augmented with a calcium-rich supplement, a cereal for preference. Puppies reared on a red meat diet to the exclusion of all alternative foods and denied access to grassland, frequently develop conditions akin to rickets. A red meat diet is fine, providing a suitable calcium-rich supplement is also fed.

The back to nature cult which emerged in the early 1950s and advocated the whole-carcass diet still has its adherents. It was noted by the founders of this cult that wolves and other large predators immediately after despatching their victim, set to work on the bowels of the herbivore and ate the red meat of the carcass only when replete with the bowels. The evidence is that perhaps the bowels of the victim were the most easily masticated parts of the beast and hence were the first parts to be devoured by the predators. Whole-carcass feeding adherents claim that the needs of the predator for vitamin and mineral-rich feed dictate which portions the beasts eat. However, this should not concern the reader. The feeding of whole carcasses of fallen beasts is forbidden under a 1936 Act—though the sight of a litter of sapling greyhounds stripping the carcass of a fallen calf is no uncommon sight on certain farms in Ireland (farms which incidentally have justly deserved reputations for rearing healthy greyhounds). The practice of feeding fallen beasts is thwart with danger however, for the disease which saw off the herbivore may also be injurious to the dog, added to which, the chemicals used to treat the sick beast prior to its demise may also cause upset in the hound. The practice of letting cattle, sheep and pigs—though pig meat is seldom favoured as a dog food—hang for a week in foxhound kennel storage rooms may well reduce the incidence of stomach upset in hounds, but unless one is included in the list of kennels allowed to feed fallen beasts—foxhound, staghound, beagle and harrier kennels—and has adequate provisions to keep skin, clean gut and boil the meat and entrails, the feeding of fallen stock is best avoided. Furthermore, the broth obtained by the boiling of the meat should be fed back to the whelps. This broth is an excellent source of minerals.

Perhaps the best diet for rearing puppies lies somewhere between the cereal and meat diet, thereby incorporating the virtues of both animal and cereal foods. Hancock of Sutton Coldfield, the most successful lurcher breeder in the world, uses what he calls a happy medium feeding plan, which he insists has been brought about by necessity because of the somewhat capricious supply of butcher's meat in the Midlands. Hancock boils sheep's heads and other butcher's waste in a huge copper boiler, letting the meat cool in its own juices. To the broth, obtained by the boiling, he adds flaked maize or a cheap low-grade, all-purpose dog meal. Hancock then adds a quantity of dicalcium phosphate and limestone—a far cheaper source of calcium and phosphate than bone meal—to the mix, and a sprinkling of vitamin supplement for good measure. Further to the mix, he adds a liberal dressing of fish meal substitute (a blood and bone mix) if he considers the porridge he has created is of a lower than usual protein content. He is of the opinion that such a diet, unpleasant to see perhaps, but nutritious, is suitable for an across the board feed for dry, lactating, pregnant bitches, stud dogs and puppies alike. It must be pointed out that Hancock rears perhaps 300 whelps a year on such a diet and bone weakness or malnutrition is unknown in his kennels. Alan Wilkinson, an official slipper of the Deerhound Club, believes that a correct diet may well reduce the incidence of leg breakages in young deerhounds, and despite the protestations of breed enthusiasts, these breakages are far too common in the breed.

However, a commercial kennel, finding a niche in the market for their particular breed, may well have to experiment a little before arriving at the correct diet for rearing whelps. There is no fixed diet, though there is a general rule of thumb. Different breeders should adopt the most suitable of diets for their kennels and may choose to feed pregnant and lactating bitches a protein-rich diet while a dry bitch is fed a somewhat poorer mix. Furthermore, a large scale breeder must operate according to the availability of flesh in a particular locality and must adjust the rest of the diet accordingly.

Mineral supplements are certainly a 'must' if one is attempting to rear sight hound whelps, particularly the very large breeds of sight hound such as the deerhound, the borzoi and, of course, the Irish wolfhound. These mineral supplements can be, (a) proprietary brands compounded by canine nutritionists and based largely on bone meal, (b) steamed bone flour—specially treated, finely ground bones of herbivorous animals—and, (c) mineral phosphates, basically the same elements as are found in bone meal, bone flour, etc, but considerably cheaper. Whether or not these mineral phosphates are as readily absorbed as powdered bone flour, is questionable. They cost a fraction of the price of bone flour, or bone meal, however, and keep indefinitely.

Sight hounds have quite small stomachs—their very shape indicates this fact. Hence puppies need regular small feeds rather than one large feed which puts pressure on the diaphragm and causes discomfort. Four meals a day are recommended for most breeds of dog, but because of the stomach size of the typical sight hound, five meals are not too many. Despite their fragile shape, and whippet puppies often look positively ethereal because of their outline, sight hounds are usually excellent doers and attack food with gusto if they are in good health. A puppy which is not a voracious doer is in fact suspect and should be watched carefully for symptoms of other ailments, the precursor to which is a capricious or poor appetite. Food should be literally wolfed down without courtesy or preliminaries and a clean dish is a good indication of the state of health of the puppy. There are no hard and fast rules as to how much food a particular sight hound puppy should eat and to invent such rules is surely courting disaster. No puppy will follow such a rule and invariably suffers if it is practised. A puppy running at liberty will eat more than a puppy confined to a house. Likewise, the presence of another dog (in a litter might spring to mind) will spur on a puppy to eat voraciously.

REARING A PUPPY

Hancock makes a note of this and states that the puppies he sells rarely do as well in the six weeks following purchase, as do the puppies he retains. The answer lies, not so much in the fact that a puppy's growth is checked by the change of home or by inferior kennel management, but simply because the competition of fellow youngsters spurs the whelp in kennels to eat more and with more gusto, whereas a solitary puppy sold to a buyer has no such competition and attacks his food with less enthusiasm (and possibly eats less). It is an old adage that no farmer should buy and rear a solitary piglet, as two do better simply because a pig's natural greed causes it to eat with enthusiasm when in company. Likewise, sight hound puppies which, despite their aristocratic demeanour and their elegant appearance, gulp food with the voraciousness of a piglet.

At the time of writing, there are different opinions as to the value of feeding cows milk to puppies. It is an important source of calcium and as the Milk Marketing Board is always emphasising, has essential vitamins and minerals. However, there is some evidence to suggest that it is a very dilute form of food and scarcely worth buying for feeding to puppies. If milk is available, then by all means feed it. It is unnecessary to feed cows' milk to a dog living on a well-balanced diet however, and too much can cause some looseness of the bowels.

Likewise, eggs which were, at one time, considered the ideal food for puppies; now it is realised that the various components of eggs actually dissolve certain vitamins and allow them to pass out of the body undigested, thereby defeating the idea of feeding eggs as a source of vitamins. Furthermore, feeding a puppy regularly on a diet of eggs, makes the animal a little less than desirable as a house dog for the stench emitted by an egg-fed puppy is unpleasant, to say the least.

As to the various meat products fed to puppies, bones are a remarkably good source of protein—green bones, bones uncooked and untreated, have roughly the same protein content as beef, but the protein is largely unobtainable to the young puppy who, equipped with small deciduous teeth is unable to crush, and thereby digest the protein within the bones, hence bones are of questionable value to a puppy.

Tales of splintered bones damaging the intestinal tracts of a dog are legion but constitutionally vigorous dogs, and sight hounds certainly qualify for this title, are seldom damaged by ingesting particles of bones. Raw green bones are seldom dangerous to the sight hound, even the quite small rib bones of mutton.

Tripes are good cheap food for any breed of dog. The tripe is one of the cow's stomachs, called the rumen by anatomists, and is composed of white muscle tissue encased in quite a lot of fat. Fed green, with particles of grass adhering to it, dogs enjoy it greatly, some even eat the partly digested grass shed by the tripe before eating the stomach itself. Tripe is quite low in minerals and some of the vitamins found in red meat. It is a good source of energy however, and despite its nauseous appearance, dogs tend to enjoy it. Abattoirs sell tripes at extremely reasonable prices for the market in bleached tripes (tripes cleaned of grass and treated to produce the white tripe seen in butcher's shops) is a little variable. It is false economy to feed bleached, cooked tripe to dogs, for dogs enjoy the raw green tripe more.

Liver is an excellent source of both vitamins and minerals. If obtained direct from abattoirs, it can be bought quite cheaply, and is a valuable source of protein. In its raw state, it is slightly laxative, but when cooked, is astringent. Dogs enjoy liver, but a puppy fed exclusively on liver would not flourish as well as a puppy fed a more mixed, varied diet. A monotonous diet is not only boring, it can also be quite an injurious and unnatural one. Liver should be fed in small quantities, mixed with other types of flesh and cereal.

Lights, the lungs and tracheae (known in abattoirs as throttles) are of dubious value. Few dogs enjoy the spongy tissue raw and some will not even countenance eating uncooked lights, although most enjoy the unnutritious, but more interesting cartilaginous throttles or tracheae. Lung tissue, even when cooked, is poor quality meat and contains quite a lot of indigestible vascular tissue. Fed to the exclusion of other meats, lights tend to cause scouring and the passing of black faeces. Fed cooked in small quantities, or fed as a change from other flesh, lights do no harm, but are not a good food for a growing puppy. Still, lights are cheap and easily obtained, but if they are the only source of meat available for feeding a puppy, supplementary feeding in the form of good quality complete dog meal or regular mineral and vitamin supplements is essential.

Raw beef or horse flesh is expensive and lacking in calcium. Horse flesh has a reputation of being extremely laxative and hunt servants usually allow a dead horse to hang a full fortnight before feeding it to hounds. Fed to the exclusion of other flesh it needs vitamin supplement and mineral additives, particularly calcium salts, to be considered ideal. Beef, unless condemned and therefore sterilised by cooking, is too expensive to feed as a rule, but adds variety to a meat and meal diet.

Good cheap food can be obtained from sheep's heads which may be fed raw (there is supposedly a slight risk of tapeworm infestation if heads are fed raw) or cooked. Dogs really enjoy tearing the flesh from the skulls of sheep, and adult sight hounds leave only the teeth and jaws of the heads. Puppies will find great pleasure, stripping sheep's heads of meat and may well ingest some of the bone to good advantage. A recent Act of Parliament has made the sale of unskinned sheep's heads illegal in England and Wales (the Act does not concern Scotland) and this tends to push up the price of sheep's heads considerably, for the skinning of these heads is a skilled and tedious job, seldom enjoyed by butchers.

Fish, fed in moderation, is an excellent food, rich in minerals and protein. Fish heads, boiled and minced (bone, flesh and brain) are much appreciated. Sight hound enthusiasts living near the sea would do well to contact local traders to secure dogfish—for usually the lesser-spotted dogfish is impossible to sell and is caught, killed and thrown back. During late May to September, many tons of dogfish are thus wasted, and can be obtained cheaply from the trawlers. The meat of the lesser-spotted dogfish is bland and almost odourless. It is also cartilaginous and therefore free of bones which could be dangerous if ingested. Dogs fed on a monotonous meat diet will often wolf down raw dogfish, even dogfish still in its harsh sandpaper-like skin. When cooked, dogfish is seldom rejected even by a dog which is 'off colour'. Fed to excess, fish is said to cause eczema. However, fish (even fish waste) is usually so expensive as to be seldom fed to excess!

Cereal feeds may include flaked maize, a cornflake-like cereal made by crushing and cooking maize grains. Most cheap complete dog foods contain large quantities of flaked maize. Fed to excess, it causes foul-smelling faeces and is slightly laxative. As with all cereals, flaked maize is best fed as part of a complete commercial dog feed, but to get the best of the low grade cheap dog feeds, which are usually less than 20 per cent crude protein, they should be fed in conjunction with high protein feed such as meat or fish.

The secret of rearing a healthy, strong and lively sight hound is to feed a variety of foods but to exercise discretion at all times. A puppy introduced to a new food will often scour badly and so it is best introduced gradually. It is well to remember that no single feed item in a diet, meat, fish, meal, etc, is a complete dog food in itself. A variety of foods ensures that a puppy gets adequate supplies of vitamins and minerals, but supplements, both mineral and vitamin, are often used to ensure the diet fed to a puppy is adequate.

Continue feeding five times a day, until a puppy is six months old, then reduce its meals to three. At a year old a sight hound puppy should be able to cope with two feeds. Never allow stale food to remain on a plate. Such food becomes putrid all too quickly and will cause stomach upsets.

8. Rudimentary Training

A good rule to adopt when training a sight hound is not to expect too much, but do not accept too little. Sight hounds are not the Mensa candidates of the dog world, no matter what the breed books say, but sight hounds can and should be trained to at least a standard which ensures basic obedience. Likewise, if the hound is to be coursed or worked on any living quarry, it is absolutely imperative that it receives some level of training and absorbs some basic obedience before it enters the coursing field. Furthermore, it is essential to remember that as soon as the hound sees quarry, its level of obedience is tested to its utmost. Nothing, but nothing, is more unpleasant to watch than an unruly sight hound hotly in pursuit of forbidden quarry and few events are so financially hazardous as a course of this nature. A sight hound is, in fact, first and foremost a hunting dog, and despite its acquired exhibition qualities and lack of opportunity to exploit its inbred skills and instincts at the first sign of potential prey, a sight hound will seek to pursue and attempt to kill it. It is therefore the duty of every owner of sight hounds to ensure that they are not only stock-broken, but obedient.

Dog training manuals of the nineteenth century usually state that, in common with all dogs, sight hounds should be left entirely alone until they are six months of age and should not receive any formal training whatsoever until that age. Why they looked on the age of six months as the time to start training is a mystery. In all probability it is the earliest time when a bitch of a small breed comes into season (though the majority of bitches seldom show any sign of sexuality until their ninth month). A more logical explanation as to why trainers of working dogs believed training should be delayed until the sixth month is the fact that by that age most dogs have completed most of their growth (though some of the larger breeds do not finish growing until the end of their second year) and that the puppy has developed permanent teeth by the end of its sixth month. It is decidedly illogical and unscientific to credit dogs with human qualities or to assume that there is a parallel between canine and human development. Human wisdom teeth are usually cut at the age when a human is deemed to have learned enough discretion to be classed as an adult, though recent research tends to favour Rousseau's theory that human adolescence lasts until a person is twenty-five years of age (there is some slight evidence to suggest that female canids and hominids develop earlier than males). Likewise, the theory that one year of a dog's life is equivalent to seven years of a man's life should be subject to scrutiny. A bitch becomes sexually mature at roughly nine months of age (earlier in a small breed, later in a large breed). Whereas no young girls are sexually mature at the age of five. Likewise, young males of small breeds are often vigorous studs by the age of six months, but boys of three and a half show no interest in sexuality of any sort. There are in fact few biological similarities between dogs and human beings.

In fact, in the case of sight hounds, it is essential to train a puppy from the nest. A dog left to spend its days in kennels until it is six months of age may still be trainable, well to a certain extent at least, but will never really develop its full potential. Should the buyer be interested in working or training his wards to a higher level the purchase of a sapling of six months or more is seldom a good policy, as few breeders who are trying to sell a sapling of this age will have put in the necessary training that a six month old whelp will have needed. The purchase of a lurcher or longdog puppy at this age is almost certainly a mistake, for lurchers should be given a great deal of training if they are to realise their full potential and much of this training, or at least much of the preliminary training, must be given to the puppy before the age of six months. One of the most common questions asked by disenchanted lurcher keepers is, 'How do I teach an adult lurcher to retrieve?' It is in fact, very difficult to get any adult sight hound to retrieve unless the dog has had some preliminary training as a puppy. When then should training begin? The answer should be, of course, from the nest onwards and the first task a trainer of sight hounds should attempt must be to get the puppy to come to call. Puppies, at least normal healthy well-socialised puppies, should be naturally effusive and should attempt to rush over to a visitor as soon as he appears. Far from being an action to discourage, this effusive fawning, this racing to the owner or visitor as soon as the said owner or visitor appears, must be harnessed to produce the coming to command reaction. As soon as the excited display starts, the owner should reciprocate by stroking the puppy and uttering the whelp's name in an excited manner as the puppy is 'petted'. The puppy's name should be repeated and the owner should drop to a crouch as soon as it approaches, making a display of affection as soon as it comes to hand. Food can be offered, together with affection, when it comes to call and it should also experience a sensation of pleasure when its name is uttered. The dropping to a crouch gesture, made by the owner is interesting and often has the effect of bringing in a rather reluctant puppy instantly. Utter its name and crouch, and most puppies will race to hand. Perhaps it is baffled by the owner's change of shape, perhaps the gesture is one which it has come to associate with some archaic pack response, or perhaps the proximity of the owner's face to it causes this interest in returning to investigate the trainer's change of shape. Whatever the reason, the movement has the effect of bringing most puppies to hand fairly quickly.

On the subject of plurality, i.e. the word 'puppies', no puppy should be trained while another, even an older more reserved dog is present. The presence of another whelp certainly isn't conducive to training and usually produces a chaotic play reaction between the puppies, rather than the response desired by the trainer. The training situation should ideally involve one person and one dog, and situations involving other members of the family or other dogs should be avoided. Training classes, classes with other people and their dogs, are fine once the puppy comes to call and is over the silly behaviour associated with extreme puppyhood, but it is very difficult to get a young whelp to do this when there are the distractions which are inevitable in any training class. If the whelp is to perform in competition then obviously it must be accustomed to training classes and their accompanying distractions, but early training, very basic come-to-call training, is best taught on the one person, one dog basis.

Puppies which are reluctant to come to call in the home, sometimes experience a change of heart when on unfamiliar ground, always providing no other dog is present. The owner should try taking a puppy to strange surroundings, preferably quiet peaceful surroundings, and attempt the recall (dropping to the crouch as the puppy is called), feigning a ridiculous excessive degree of pleasure when the puppy comes to hand. A word of caution regarding this method of training 'off campus'. Should the response not succeed and the puppy not come to command, then the owner can be in a predicament. The very structure of a sight hound makes the whelp impossible to catch and the presence of livestock will exacerbate the situation considerably. Thus the art of training for recall should always be performed on territory which, while it may be unfamiliar to the puppy, should be very familiar to the owner/trainer. Any livestock, particularly small livestock, hens, ducks, sheep, all too easily become quarry to the sight hound puppy, and once wed to this quarry, once it has made a kill, or inflicted hurt on any particular species, it is very difficult to get the animal on amicable terms with such livestock again. Cats, which seemingly materialise out of thin air, are problems, particularly as their very shape and movements seem to trigger off the chase reaction in a sight hound puppy. The larger, more phlegmatic hounds, the Irish wolfhound, the Scottish deerhound and the borzoi, are, strangely enough, easier to control in the presence of cats, whereas greyhound whelps and quite tiny fragile whippet puppies are often devils. Thus any 'off campus' training area should be free from human interference (young children are

RUDIMENTARY TRAINING

particularly distracting to young puppies of all breeds), dogs and chasable livestock.

Breaking to the lead or leash training, is absolutely essential, for the countryside, let alone the town, has few places where a dog can be allowed to roam at will. Lead training is usually less strenuous a venture to the owner and dog and less traumatic if the whelp is taught young. A collar or choke chain should be fastened around its neck and the whelp allowed to run around in familiar surroundings. Next, the lead should be attached to the collar or choke chain and it should be walked around the house, yard or garden. A display of bucking, rearing and often screaming, is frequently manifested but this should be only a temporary reaction. Most pups trained from the nest take to gentle (and gentle should be the operative word) lead training very quickly. However, make sure it is well accustomed to the lead in familiar surroundings before taking it to country which it may find frightening or hostile,—a busy road amongst cattle, a crowded street, etc. Lead training is absolutely essential and so the trainer must persist and lead train the whelp regularly to accustom it to the restrictions imposed by the leash. Further training, retrieving excluded perhaps, involves considerable use of restraint brought about by the leash, so lead training must be thorough and continuous.

Once lead training has been accomplished, it is imperative to stock-break sight hound puppies. Though it may sound repetitious it is essential that the owner realises that sight hounds, regardless of the reason for their acquisition by the owner, and regardless of the owner's attitude towards field sports, and the morality of such, are essentially hunters and the veneer of restraint is very thin indeed when the sight hound encounters living creatures. To prevent a puppy chasing and destroying livestock is very simple, to repair the damage wrought to its training, once it has worried stock, is extraordinarily difficult. Cat chasing can be as addictive as an opiate and hence cats are the first animals to which a person should introduce a sight hound puppy. Take it near to a cat, and should it show untoward interest or an inclination to chase, jerk the lead violently and, using a harsh and scolding tone, shout 'No'. Repeat, until the puppy seems stock steady and then continue the exercise daily. Cats are amongst the most common rural and urban livestock and should always be regarded as 'verboten' by the sight hound. Never, not even in fun, encourage a sight hound to chase a cat. The habit is usually impossible to break once it is established, and a cat, despite its reputation of having nine lives, uses up those lives all too quickly in the jaws of even the most diminutive sight hound. Feline shape, movement, their very disposition, encourages a hound to chase them and cats are very skilful at bringing a hound to grief in traffic or taking out the eyes of a dog with their claws. Prevent cat chasing at all costs. Field sport activities, particularly coursing, are very much under fire at the time of writing, and the cessation of coursing seems a little closer than merely on the horizon. The end of coursing can easily be precipitated by a spate of stock worrying by dogs which have been specifically bred for coursing. Cats, or rather the agonising death of cats, certainly makes excellent press, and rightly so, as it happens the public has become antipathetic to cat killing and cat-killing dogs.

Breaking to poultry and sheep must follow in the puppy's education, even though it may mean travelling many miles to do this. Historically, the wealth of this country has depended on sheep and their products. The Lord Chancellor sits on the Woolsack, a symbol of wealth, and hence the offence of worrying sheep is a heinous crime indeed. Sooner or later any dog, whether or not intended as a hunting dog, will encounter sheep and unless the dog is broken to them, disaster is certain to follow. At the time of writing, there seems to be a natural mistrust of lurchers amongst farmers. The fault, dear Brutus, is alas not with the lurcher, but with the mindless fools who do not bother to break a lurcher to sheep and thus allow their dogs to cause carnage. All dogs can be stopped from worrying sheep and though, incidentally, no certain method has been devised to prevent Siberian huskies from becoming stock worriers, sight hounds of any sort are prone to be almost as bad and so great care should be exercised in breaking any sight hound, or sight hound derivative, to sheep.

Basic obedience training is essential. An ill-disciplined recalcitrant dog gives its owner little pleasure and much

RUDIMENTARY TRAINING

grief, but dog training is so simple that there is no excuse for the owning of a wild and unbiddable animal. Sight hounds, as a rule, are not capable of performing elaborate PD or TD tests, either through disinclination, or more than likely due to their sheer lack of intelligence, but it is the duty of every owner to ensure that his ward is at least moderately obedient. Most running dogs, particularly large hirsute lurchers, are bought as image makers, but that image is sadly shattered when a dog becomes obviously out of control. Therefore every sight hound, or sight hound derivative, should receive something more than just recall training. When the owner of a sight hound states that his excuse for the recalcitrance of his dog is that he has no desire for a trained animal, what he is actually saying is that he has no aptitude to train the dog for while there are few naturally 'wayward' dogs, there are many inadequate owners.

Many trainers, including police-dog handlers, question the value of teaching a dog to sit. The position does not have the prohibitive fixing quality that the lie position seems to command, and for a dog to sit while its owner is ferreting a rabbit warren is fairly counter-productive as, should the rabbit bolt and the dog be required to pursue it, this involves two movements from sit position, but a single movement from the 'freeze' advocated by many ferreters. Clearly, the dog's chances of catching a rabbit are diminished if it has to perform two movements to be in pursuit, rather than a single movement. However, the sit position is frequently the prelude to the lie position and the lie is part and parcel of teaching 'the stay'.

The sit is one of the most easily taught exercises and is so readily learned that it can be taught with the puppy 'off leash'. It is more easily taught if the puppy is restrained with a lead, however, for then the training can continue even if the puppy decides otherwise. To teach the sit position, keep the puppy on a fairly tight lead, press down the hindquarters and utter, 'Sit', as the pressure on the rump increases. When the puppy has been pushed, pressured, in the language of police-dog trainers, to the sit position, the puppy should receive praise and made to feel pleasure at its accomplishment. The lead should then be flicked, bringing the puppy out of the sit and into the stand position, and a few seconds later, the sit procedure repeated. A bright and fairly sensitive puppy may learn to sit in a matter of a dozen or so repetitions of the exercise, but it is bad practice to continue with the training, should the puppy show displeasure. Effusive praise by the owner does much to alleviate boredom during any form of training, but should the puppy show the slightest dislike of any training exercise, the owner should desist at once and engage the puppy in a wild, exciting game of some sort so that the training session finishes on a pleasant note. Never finish a training session on a failure, and if a puppy fails at a task, let it perform some other task it enjoys, or engage it in a lively and exciting game.

The lie position usually follows on from the sit training, but the automatic following on of these positions, first sit and then lie, is not without its problems, for dogs placed in a sit position often then opt to lie even before the command lie is uttered. Few large hounds enjoy sitting, and all too easily revert to the 'lie'. To teach the 'lie' movement, the dog should be at a sit position, and its shoulders pressed downwards rendering the dog in a supine position while uttering the word 'down' or 'lie' or whatever word the trainer cares to use. Both the sit and the lie positions are simplicity itself to teach.

The lie/down position is as easily taught as the 'sit'. The dog is first dropped to the 'sit' position, and then pressure is applied to its shoulders while the command 'down' or 'lie' is uttered. The lie/down position is invariably a follow on from the 'sit' and hereby slight confusion may be encountered.

Avoid at all costs the method of teaching the 'lie' or 'down' position suggested by the German military dog trainer Konrad Most. Most took on recalcitrant German shepherd, Dobermanns and later Rottweilers and broke them in just a few weeks to be instantly biddable. His methods would be unsuitable for the training of sight hounds though, no doubt, they are still used by police forces and guard-dog trainers the world over. Lie, was taught by a process which can only be described as savage Pavlovian conditioning. The word 'down' was uttered and a twitch brought sharply across the dog's back with stinging force. Within days of this sort of training, a dog drops instantly to avoid the cutting slash of the twitch. The method is used to teach instant response and to ensure the dog drops to the down position immediately. This rapidity of response is obviously necessary when a dog is attack-trained, for a dog which has been encouraged to attack at a moment's notice, must also be able to be restrained just as quickly. This method of training would devastate a sight hound puppy and reduce it to a cringing wreck of a dog, for despite the fact that sight hounds are not particularly intelligent, they are extremely sensitive and easily damaged by savage treatment. Mostian methods, of the type described, should have no place in the training of sight hounds and allied types. To use methods of this sort is to guarantee the production of a half-crazed, terrified and useless sight hound.

The teaching of a dog to stay (to remain at the down position for an indefinite length of time) is a slightly more difficult process and takes quite a lot longer. Sight hounds puppies of a very young age can learn to stay for a considerable length of time, even with the trainer out of sight, but puppies are often disturbed by this task and, should distress be noticed, the exercise should be discontinued immediately. The down/stay position, with the trainer out of sight is a fairly traumatic experience for a young sight hound puppy, but it can be taught to a very young whelp. Bearing the aforementioned problems in mind, on how to continue with the down/stay position training, command the puppy to the down position and back away from the supine dog, the trainer 'fixing' the puppy with his eyes. The slightest movement should be greeted with 'down/stay', while the trainer backs away to perhaps three yards from the puppy, but not more for the first training session, nor should the puppy be kept prostrate for longer than perhaps half a minute. Return to it and pet it effusively, but do not begin a further session of down/stay training until the puppy has calmed down and become less exuberant, for it is difficult to persuade an excited puppy to stay. Return to the lesson and repeat no more than two or three times, longer sessions, more frequent exercises in the down/stay training, tends to daunt a young puppy and in extreme cases may cause the puppy to break, run and possibly refuse to return to hand for some time. Such an event can be rather a severe setback in the training schedule and should indicate to the trainer that there is absolutely no point in continuing with the down/stay training for another day or so. When the puppy has decided to return to hand, and most forget an experience of the type just described fairly quickly, indulge in a wild excited game with it, petting it effusively and encouraging it to forget the unpleasant events of a few minutes previous. No training session ever runs quite smoothly and few according to plan. A trainer should therefore make allowances for his own mistakes, his own misjudgements, as well as the foibles of the animals he trains. Skinner, an American behaviourist, states that animals can be taught quite extraordinary tasks, providing the task is broken down to a series of very small 'learning parts' and providing the animal continues to display an interest in learning the task. Always finish training sessions with a wild uninhibited romp, no matter how foolish the trainer may appear to the passer-by.

If the first down/stay training exercise has met with success then continue the next day with a further session, this time backing away to a distance of perhaps six yards, fixing the puppy with one's eyes, uttering the down/stay command fairly sharply (but not aggressively) as the puppy attempts to stand and follow. Repeat the training session as before, always returning to the prone puppy to pet and praise, never calling the puppy and then praising it, for such praise tends to reward the recall, rather than the success of the down/stay training exercise. A puppy is not a human being, and has a limited understanding of why it is being praised.

On the subject of recall training, and here a digression is surely permissible, continue with recall training during walks, exercise periods and other activities. Call the puppy to hand frequently during a day's training or even casual exercise, and praise effusively every time the puppy does return. Much can be ascertained from the behaviour of the puppy when called to hand. A quiet, self-disciplined puppy will respond with a wag of the tail, a more sycophantic one will roll on its back and sometimes wet itself with excitement when called and praised. Never sell such a sycophantic puppy short. The grovelling gesture, accepting its role as the epsilon member of the pack, is usually an excellent indication the puppy will literally go out of its way to please its owner. Such a whelp is usually easy to train, far easier in fact than the more reserved puppy, which may appear more sensible, but will surely not train as well as the more exuberant, but sycophantic one. A dog which is defiant, resistant to learning or obedience training, recalcitrant in every way, may present a challenge to the professional trainer. To an amateur, training his first sight hound, such a dog is not to be desired. The groveller, the placating sycophant is certainly the ideal animal for the beginner to train. An expert may experience some pleasure training a difficult dog, but a lay trainer should find the more malleable animal more to his liking. Both types of puppies will 'train' and will train well, but the puppy which accepts its low-ranking position within the pack and indicates this by a grovelling manner, is far more rewarding to train. Lorenz in his masterly *Man Meets Dog* compares the aloof attitude of the typical spitz dog (the chow chow) with that of his wife's German shepherd, an epsilon category male, and considered the more reserved chow chow more to his liking. Fine, but it must be pointed out that Lorenz probably never achieved a high standard of training with his chow chows or German shepherd dogs.

To return to the down/stay training. When the puppy has mastered the concept, and above all is at ease with the down/stay, its trainer fixing it with the eye and retreating perhaps 20 feet in reverse, the time has come for him to turn his back on the puppy and still expect it to stay in the 'down' position. Eye control amongst animals, or between humans and animals, and even between humans, is possibly an underrated quality and certainly not fully understood. Staring is a prelude to attack in the animal kingdom and hence eye-to-eye contact acts as a type of warning of possible punishment to the inferior participant. A dog will fix sheep by a similar staring. Once such contact is removed, however, once the trainer attempts to walk away from the puppy, it is almost inevitable that the puppy will move from the down/stay position and attempt to follow him. This can be counteracted by the command 'down/stay' as the trainer turns and walks away, a command which is usually necessary for it is a racing certainty that the puppy will rise and attempt to follow. One handbook concerned with dog training, published in Europe, advises the use of a mirror to ascertain if the whelp has arisen and is following the trainer. A mirror has its uses perhaps, but it is a shade superfluous. The puppy will almost always break the down/stay position and slink after the trainer. The down/stay command should be repeated as the trainer walks away from the puppy, but the trainer should remember not to walk too far or to keep his back to the whelp too long in the early stages of this part of the training exercise. Once the puppy has accomplished the required results the trainer should return, praise the puppy effusively and indulge in a romp, returning to the training only when the puppy's excitement has subsided.

The notion of breaking the training session into several small sections, punctuating the sessions with wild and exciting praise and games, is not favoured by most full-time dog trainers perhaps, but it should also be remembered that most full-time dog trainers seldom deal with sight hounds. Most sight hounds have quite limited attention spans as puppies and are also rather sensitive in the early stages of their development. The majority cannot take the sustained training sessions which would be commonplace in the training of a retrieving breed of gun dog or collie or German shepherd dog. It is said that the essential difference between play and work lies not in the nature of the activity itself, but in the attitude of the participant towards it. It seems unlikely, however, that the down/stay session can be made exciting to the dog as it is simply a restriction of what the dog wishes to do. A wild game between training sessions is therefore essential to make the whole training session, rather than the specific exercise, pleasurable. Once again it must be added that once a training session or a particular exercise is becoming bland, boring or distasteful to either puppy or trainer, the activity should cease immediately and the training session should end in a wild game which is both exciting and pleasurable to the dog—and possibly the trainer! Training sessions which proceed to a state of exhaustion, boredom or pain are totally counter-productive. An animal is essentially a hedonist, deliberately seeking pleasure and avoiding pain. Values such as honesty, integrity and diligence are entirely foreign to the nature of the dog, and no thinking trainer must credit a beast with the possession of such values.

Once the puppy will stay for a fairly lengthy period out of eye contact, with the trainer's back to it, training can proceed further. A further stage in the down/stay exercise is to keep the dog at this position while the owner is out of sight. This is usually a fairly difficult procedure in the training of a young sight hound, for sight hounds, despite their aristocratic and indifferent appearance, are seldom the most confident of dogs. The training session should take place in a spot where a concealed position is available within a matter of 20 or so yards from the puppy, so that the additional trauma of the owner slowly walking away into the distance before disappearing out of sight can be avoided. As the trainer walks away he should repeat the down/stay command and this must be repeated as he disappears out of sight. Further commands need to be uttered as the owner stays behind some object, and if the puppy believes that once he has slipped out of its vision and is simply waiting behind the object which conceals him, so much the better. As the training continues, the frequency of commands may diminish until the trainer can walk away and slip out of sight in silence. Remember however, that dogs are essentially pack animals and detest solitude unless mating, or in a state of parturition. So the sight of the owner or trainer disappearing from view seldom constitutes an attractive training session for a puppy.

The validity of such an elaborate training session is questioned by some. True, if the dog is required as an image maker, and many dogs are simply this, then the elaborate training recommended is futile. If the dog is required for exhibition purposes alone, then once again the training recommended is superfluous and can be omitted, and it must be accepted that the majority of sight hounds and derivatives are kept solely for exhibition and little else. However, if the owner wishes to compete in the now-popular obedience tests at country shows, or if he wishes to use the dog as a hunting dog/companion, then such training sessions are essential. A hunting dog will always need to be restrained, and restrained quickly, when an entirely new situation presents itself, and a dog which cannot be easily trained is not only an embarrassment, but an annoyance and a danger. The training of sight hounds to a good standard is never easy and there are many who will mock the trainer's efforts. Lurcher shows frequently stage obedience tests which are seldom of a high standard but excellent entertainment for both those taking part and spectators. Some audiences will have a fairly heavy sprinkling of those who scoff at the efforts of the competitors and pass comments that such feats are not required of a hunting dog. Without exception, these people are totally unable to train a dog to the standards required in even the most simple of obedience tests. Their comments are strongly indicative of sour grapes. The skills demanded by a typical obedience test exactly replicates the skills demanded during a day's hunting. For a scoffing spectator to say otherwise is ludicrous, but the handler must accept that such spectators do exist. Training, particularly advanced work, develops a special link between the dog and the trainer, a link which most trainers are reluctant to break, by selling the dog. Most of the critics of the obedience tests at lurcher and longdog shows have never developed these links, and subsequently buy and sell lurchers like used cars, finally relinquishing their interest in dogs for another temporary passion. A trained dog is a pleasure to own and the more a dog is trained, the more pleasure its owner gets from it.

Retrieving is a very controversial subject, though it should not be. Sight hounds left untrained, are usually very reluctant retrievers, preferring to stand over a kill, rather than return it to hand. Some sight hounds show a natural aptitude to retrieve, however, and it is not uncommon to see a hare caught by coursing greyhounds, returned to hand. All sight hounds used for hunting should retrieve however, and be enthusiastic retrievers of the quarry they have caught. A hound which runs and kills a hare, simply standing over it until its interest in the 'kill' has waned, often makes the recovery of the catch difficult. Also, a hound which simply returns after a chase and is a known non-retriever, leaves the owner in doubt as to whether the hound has caught its prey. Furthermore, a hound which retrieves its prey to hand as soon as it is caught, is less likely to cause mischief than a hound which kills, and stands over its prey until attention has waned, then seeking further quarry. If a sight hound is used for hunting, it must retrieve or be relegated to the rank of a second-rate hunting dog. The trainer should ignore the comments of those who state that they can easily fetch the kill themselves and hence that they have no need for a retrieving hound. By stating this, they have relegated not only the dog to second-rate status, but also themselves to the rank of incompetent trainers.

It is child's play to teach a young, playful sight hound whelp, in good health and reasonably biddable, to retrieve, but it is very difficult to teach an older dog, which refuses to retrieve, to bring its catch to hand. Another peculiarity of sight hounds is that while they may not chase a dummy and bring it back, they will be enthusiastic retrievers of game they have run, caught and killed. The persistent bleat of lurcher enthusiasts is that the adult dog, which they have just purchased, will not retrieve. It should be stated that once a sight hound or a sight hound derivative, has decided not to co-operate, it is extremely difficult to get the dog to mend its ways and become a competent retriever. Yet it is necessary to reiterate that a dog that will catch well, yet not retrieve, must be regarded as second rate. So every effort must be made to ensure the whelp one has purchased will retrieve, and the training of a playful puppy to do so is ridiculously easy.

Unlike the sit/stay/down training which is never really enjoyable to a young sight hound puppy (or an old one for that matter), retrieving can, and should be very pleasurable to both trainer and hound. Indeed, retrieving should not be taught in conjunction with wild exciting games. Retrieving itself, if it is to be taught satisfactorily, should be such a game for both the whelp and the trainer. For this reason, a grown dog, a more serious animal than a young puppy, may well refuse to be taught to retrieve by conventional methods.

Puppies literally beg to be taught retrieving, and sight hounds, perhaps more than most breeds. Sight hounds pursue a fleeing quarry or prey. It is their very nature to do so, and this is an added bonus when teaching a sight hound puppy. A simple experiment will illustrate this point more successfully than a thousand words. Take a sheet of ordinary writing paper, crinkle it into a ball, show it to the puppy and throw it perhaps three yards (few very young puppies can see much further than this, even sight hounds which are the 'far sighters' of the canines). As the ball of paper falls, it makes a rustling sound, and it is a very strange puppy which does not run to investigate the sound and sight of the object. Some, very few actually, will return without it, others will pick it up and seek some place in which to lie and chew the paper, while others, for some reason best known to themselves, will return it either to hand or very near to hand. Teaching retrieving is as simple as this if one purchases a young puppy and attempts to train it. It is certainly not easy to teach a non-retrieving adult the same task. Once a puppy will pursue and pick up an object, any object, the process of retrieving is half taught, and nothing could be more simple.

All puppies will race to investigate a rolling ball of paper, for both sight and hearing tells them the ball is moving away from them and therefore is a type of quarry. Some however, will at first, refuse to pick it up and simply return to hand to be petted. Fine, and by all means pet them. Then pick up the ball, offer it to them, snatch it away from the puppy, offer it again and perhaps make a deliberately fumbling attempt to hide it. Generate excitement in the whelp, enthusiasm for the chasing game, a desire to possess the paper ball which has now become a coveted object. When the trainer has provoked enough excitement the ball should be thrown and the puppy will invariably race after it. If the puppy picks it up and even if it fails to return it to hand and skulks, chewing the paper in an out of way place, the training is well on its way. Take the ball, engender the same excitement and throw it, and the chances are the whelp will pick it up and return it, if not to hand, at least close to hand.

When a puppy carries the paper ball out of reach, and spends its time chewing it or simply playing with it, pushing it with paw and nose, encouraging it to 'run and be chased', watch these qualities carefully. They tell you much about the sight hound, far more in fact than a book concerned with its exhibition qualities. Later in the puppy's life, the trainer may well see this 'cat playing with mouse' gesture manifest itself again. Some sight hounds are extremely reluctant to pick up a crouched rabbit until it moves and some will prod a rabbit with nose and feet until it does move. Likewise, in the case of myxomatosis-infected rabbits many owners believe that their lurchers will not pick up a myxomatosised rabbit, but it is the absence of conventional movement, not the presence of a virus, which prevents the dog paying attention to the coney. Some hounds prod a rabbit into movement, and then catch it as it runs away. A running rabbit, even an infected rabbit, will cause considerable interest in a sight hound, or any sight hound derivative but it takes an experienced lurcher to pick up a rabbit which refuses to move. The puppy prodding the paper ball is encouraging it to move, to become quarry to be coursed.

Progression from a puppy chasing and picking up a ball of paper, to quite complex retrieving is relatively simple, and usually straightforward. The training of any animal, or human for that matter, seldom proceeds without the odd hiccough or so however, but once a puppy becomes used to mouthing an object thrown away from it, training can proceed. Should the puppy refuse to return the paper ball to hand, the game can proceed in a passageway devoid of any furniture under which the puppy can hide and chew the ball of paper, and once the retrieve to hand is conducted properly, praise should be effusive which in turn generates further interest in retrieving. Praise should always be given and rewards of favourite food do not come amiss, despite obedience-training guides comments to the contrary. Never ever throw the paper ball more than perhaps three times, lest the puppy loses interest in the game. Retrieving is easily started, but the puppy will soon become bored and refuse to fetch the ball again. It is far more difficult to regenerate interest in retrieving than to simply kindle the same interest.

Should the puppy fail to pick up the paper ball, even when it has displayed a frenzied interest in the object before it is thrown, all is certainly not lost. A sight hound, even a sight hound puppy, is bred to be geared to the chase, and while only a few are instinctive retrievers, few can resist chasing a fleeing object. Harness this instinct fully. Fold a piece of writing paper lengthways and tie a length of twine to the paper fold, making what in America is called a 'kitty tease' for obvious reasons, for cats go wild when such toys are jerked and made to look animate. Toys of this nature, suspended from a makeshift frame, are said to prevent, or at least reduce claw damage in a house, and some have been patented by certain companies. A toy like this may not prevent a puppy from chewing up a home, but it is an irresistible aid to the teaching of retrieving. Place the paper fold (attached to the twine) in front of the puppy, and jerk it sharply. The folded paper will leap as though alive and any lively puppy will seek to chase it. Encourage this chasing, but for a moment do not allow the puppy to catch the fold, merely jerking it out of its way at the moment when the puppy considers that the capture of the paper is inevitable. Once again, harness the chasing instinct, and allow it to seize the lure. Jerk it out of the puppy's jaws quite gently, for milk teeth break easily at this age and cause permanent teeth to come through irregularly. Thus, when the puppy is deprived of its quarry its interest in the piece of paper increases (a dog which drops a retrieved rabbit and sees it run off unharmed, pursues it with extra vigour). When excitement is at its greatest, fling both the folded paper plus the string attachment and let the puppy run to it. The whelp will almost certainly pick it up, if it doesn't, repeat the game but only while interest in the paper lasts. If interest even looks like waning, stop the game and indulge in wild excited play of some sort. Interest in the jerked piece of paper is unlikely to evaporate, however, particularly after the puppy has been allowed to 'catch' the prey.

Once the puppy is prepared to carry a dummy, the trainer may consider that the retrieving session is progressing well. It now behoves the trainer to ensure the puppy carries the dummy back to him. This is easily accomplished simply by crouching and calling the dog in an excited voice. It may possibly drop the dummy before retrieving to hand, but this is unlikely as the whelp has only recently acquired the coveted object and will be reluctant to leave it. Should the puppy return to the trainer with it, the trainer should gently ease the paper from the puppy's mouth, while making a tremendous display of excitement about the retrieve. Should the puppy drop the dummy, repeat the entire performance but generate a little more excitement about the puppy's capture of the dummy. This time, the puppy should return to hand with the paper. Beware, if the puppy doesn't display enthusiasm for the string and dummy, do not persist. Wait until another day, though a four-and-a-half week old sight hound puppy will usually chase a dummy on a string.

Retrieving is not a particularly addictive habit among sight hounds, though some lurchers with collie, retriever or German shepherd blood will continue doing it until exhausted, and sooner or later the sight hound puppy will tire of retrieving the paper dummy. It is now time to replace it and a very suitable object is the cardboard stiffener within a toilet or kitchen roll. The cardboard stiffener will not only roll, but also roll noisily, thereby making it attractive to the puppy. Watch at all times for disenchantment with the object the puppy is sent to retrieve. As soon as lack of interest in the object is apparent, use an entirely different dummy, an object of perhaps a different shape or a different texture. Throughout the training period, or rather initial training period (for a sight hound should live in a state of perpetual training from weaning until death) a variety of dummy types may be used, starting with the all-convenient ball of paper and finishing with a rabbit or hare carcass.

A point of interest is well worth mentioning here. The transition between the dog retrieving a dummy or a stuffed rabbit skin, and a real bona fide rabbit carcass, is often puzzling and to the uninitiated, a bit disheartening. Very often puppies will retrieve a rabbit-fur dummy with great enthusiasm and pleasure, but immediately a rabbit carcass is substituted for the dummy, the sapling may appear as if afraid, or at least bewildered, by the carcass. For pity's sake do not sell the puppy or part with it in the belief that its apprehension regarding a carcass is an indication that the dog will show no enthusiasm for the pursuit of the quarry, for this simply is not true. The rabbit carcass is a new and bewildering object, probably a little frightening, for sight hounds, both whelps and saplings are seldom the most bold of puppies. Never be disappointed by the sight of a puppy refusing to approach a carcass or a puppy staring apprehensively at a glassy-eyed rabbit cadaver. Allow the puppy to investigate the body, and when the examination is seemingly complete, give the hind legs of the rabbit a gentle tug, (not a violent one) to give the appearance that the carcass is alive. Should this movement attract only slight interest, revert to the principle of harnessing the chasing instinct, which is so strong in every sight hound. Place the carcass on the end of a length of string and drag the rabbit around in front of the puppy, first very gently and then more quickly and violently as the game progresses. Eventually throw the carcass and watch for the enthusiasm engendered by the exercise. However, should the puppy refuse to retrieve the carcass to hand, repeat the exercise from stage one once more, but never despair, for eventually most sight hound puppies will retrieve a carcass, and from the carcass it is only a relatively short step (magnificent meiosis perhaps) to the retrieving of a catch.

It would be entirely wrong for the trainer to object to the amount of time given to the teaching of retrieving. It is essential to have any sight hound or sight hound derivative (particularly a lurcher, for by definition a lurcher is meant to be a pot-hunting dog) learn the techniques of retrieving. A non-retrieving sight hound makes the trainer of the dog look like a crass amateur no matter whatever else he thinks of his own ability, for a sight hound to fail to retrieve a kill looks bad. There is nothing that sells a field sportsman's reputation so short, as his being accompanied by a badly trained dog, and nothing reflects a person's inability to train a sight hound properly, more than the fact that the hound does not retrieve the catch to hand.

A carcass presents a whole new world to a sight hound—a little like a canine Keats first opening Chapman's *Homer* perhaps—and it is the task of the trainer to engender interest in the carcass, and in its retrieval. The sight of an adult human being dragging a carcass of a rabbit around the garden on the end of a length of twine, may be a little disconcerting to the neighbours, and more than a little embarrassing for the trainer. The trainer involved in such a display may certainly worry that the neighbours may consider him to be a certifiable lunatic, but it should also be pointed out that the ownership of a sight hound, the training of it, and the capture of rabbits with it, is to the

RUDIMENTARY TRAINING

ordinary man an indication that the hunter is a shade more than just a little eccentric anyway.

Therefore, to summarise the art of the teaching of retrieving:

(a) harness a sight hound's every instinct in the task of teaching the puppy to retrieve;

(b) make the act of retrieving a game, a wild enthusiastic game;

(c) vary the game as much as possible, vary the dummy used, the way it is propelled, and the training ground on which retrieving takes place. Teach retrieving in the house and garden first, where familiar smells and familiar sights do not distract the puppy as much as the scents of an unfamiliar training ground;

(d) never continue a training programme to the point where the puppy's interest is waning let alone having arrived at the stage when it may have ceased. Terminate each session while the puppy is still eager to continue. A puppy should experience exuberant excitement at the appearance of a dummy;

(e) never teach retrieving with another dog present. Despite the fact that the dog is a pack animal, jealousy plays an important part in the make-up of any dog. A dummy which might be snatched by another dog, will seldom be retrieved to the owner/trainer again. The most certain way of stopping a dog retrieving is to work it with another dog present. A catch will not be returned to the trainer if there is the slightest danger that it will be taken by another dog;

(f) a non-retrieving, hunting, coursing sight hound is the trademark of a meddler and an inefficient trainer. A person who states that he is not bothered by the fact that he owns a non-retrieving sight hound, or doesn't need a dog to retrieve its catch, is really stating that he doesn't have the ability to teach the hound the skill of retrieving;

(g) a non-retrieving adult, one who refuses to retrieve, will usually be untrainable as a retriever. The time

to teach retrieving is while the puppy is young, when enthusiasm and energy is high. It is usually very difficult to teach an untrained adult sight hound to retrieve;

(h) the trainer may appear undignified when he teaches his hound to retrieve. The exuberance which must be engendered in a puppy by a trainer during a training session will always appear a little foolish, and more than a little eccentric to the uninitiated bystander. The trainer must accept this, or if he cannot, stop training dogs;

(i) at the time of writing, lurcher and longdog enthusiasts tend to treat obedience-test competitors as second-rate hunters who teach hounds to sit, lie and stay. This is ridiculous, but while obedience in the ring is not the same as obedience in the hunting field with its numerous distractions, an obedience-trained dog, given a chance, will out-perform an untrained dog in the task of pot hunting, and furthermore, will be a pleasure to own. (Competitors in the obedience ring must take spiteful remarks in their stride and credit them to (1) sour grapes, (2) the embittered remarks of crass amateurs and (3) a rather silly attempt by the critic to appear masculine. Obedience tests always involve retrieving, and long may they do so. Retrieving is an integral part of hunting, and a sight hound which will retrieve in a show ring amongst many other dogs, will almost certainly retrieve in the hunting field when performing by itself. A successful hunting dog is an obedient hunting dog.

9 Breaking to Livestock

Sight hounds are natural hunters and will, left to their own devices, pursue any quarry that moves or even looks like moving. A greyhound or whippet puppy, scarcely out of the nest, will race across a field to investigate the movements of a plastic sack. A saluki or an Afghan hound, the result of many years of breeding solely for aesthetic qualities, whose sole contact with wide open spaces has been the Big Ring at Crufts, will galvanise into action at the sight of a cat moving across a TV screen. Natural hunters are, unless checked, natural stock worriers, for a dog, any dog, particularly a sight hound regards all moving livestock as suitable prey and must be taught to differentiate between legitimate quarry and animals which are 'verboten'.

To begin at the beginning however, and the beginning has a somewhat unsavoury defeatist note about it, make sure your house insurance covers damage done by one's dogs—damage to motor vehicles, accidents caused by dogs straying on roads, damage to livestock and, above all, damage to humans. Sight hounds are relatively neurosis free (there are exceptions) and were perhaps, even in the time of Arrian the most gentle of dogs in the company of people, seldom boisterous, let alone aggressive. They are however, justly famous stock worriers, and one's insurance policy should cover any damage done by them. Sometimes the damage wrought by an escaped sight hound which has wandered out of suburbia into pastures green, is literally staggering, but also financially ruinous. Also, it is as well to check one's insurance policy for an exclusion clause, for such is the fame of renegade stock-worrying sight hounds, that insurance policies exclude sight hounds from their coverage. If one's house is not insured, then if one owns sight hounds or sight hound derivatives, it is well to get independent third-party insurance. The cost is negligible if compared with the compensation likely to be sought by an irate farmer or pet-owning householder, for any damage wrought by a dog.

As has already been mentioned, sight hounds should be broken to livestock while they are still puppies. At eight weeks old it will invariably be over-matched by an aggressive cock or a broody hen, or put to flight by an angry back-arching cat. The same puppy allowed to grow unstock-broken will, at eight months of age, reduce such foes to a bloody pulp in seconds. An untrained adult hound is usually prone to sheep worrying, a puppy is a little apprehensive in the company of even a half-grown ewe. Furthermore, once blooded, once allowed a kill, an exciting chase or a 'hold', a sight hound is difficult to break to stock and likely to worsen rather than to improve. The Greyhound Rehabilitation Society which takes retired track dogs and breaks them to livestock before allowing a caring person to own them, is to be congratulated. Flapping track greyhounds (it is hoped licenced trainers do not indulge in such barbarous practices) are often 'geed up' by allowing them to kill all sorts of livestock ranging from tame rabbits to cats, and despite protestations to the contrary, any owner of a ferret can earn a fair sum of money providing live rabbits for the training of flapping track greyhounds. Ironically, the act of allowing greyhounds or other dogs to chase released rabbits, or 'bagged quarry', to use a euphemism, is not strictly illegal and represents one of the grey areas of the 1911 Act through which the various societies seeking to outlaw field sports, will eventually creep and bring an end to all hunting.

Cats are never fair game, and should not be regarded as such. The present trend of magistrates, who simply treat cat killing by sight hounds as little more than a joke, is to be deplored. Most farmers are by tradition pro-cat—the time when cats were considered as the best farm vermin controllers is not long past—so permission on land to course, is usually withdrawn if one's dogs set about and kill, the farm cat. Furthermore, the sight of a dog madly chasing a terrified cat, oblivious to the shouts and entreaties of the owner, is hardly likely to inspire confidence in the landowner. The use of a check lead and a puppy yanked nearly off its feet when it shows enthusiasm for cat chasing, may seem a cruel measure, but it is well to break dogs to cats as soon as possible. The sight of a hound killing a cat does not make the owner of the hound appear in any way masculine or enhance his prestige—it is the sight of a pitiful inadequate, who should be prevented from owning a dog which has the qualities of a sight hound. Punish cat chasing severely, and deliberately take the hound to an area which cats are known to frequent to break it of the habit of chasing them. It is well to remember that, once a dog has killed a cat, it is very difficult to break them of the habit of chasing them.

Poultry, running on free range, are now seldom seen, as it is almost impossible to make a profit, keeping poultry under these conditions, but every coursing dog will encounter poultry at some time in its life. Chickens are fairly easy to accustom a dog to their presence. Ducks which are always slightly paranoid, are less so, for their noisy fluttering ways seem to drive dogs wild. Nevertheless, a dog must not kill stock, so a puppy must be taken amongst poultry and chastised for chasing or showing an unhealthy interest in them. It may be tedious to continually walk a dog amongst these creatures but it is a lot more trouble to pay for the damage done to poultry by a dog. Ducks literally go off lay, and into moult, if merely startled, and while poultry survive amazing damage, they are seldom worth keeping after a bad mauling. Don't allow a hound to create misery for the owner and the farmer/stock-keeper alike. Sight hounds must be broken to poultry.

Sheep are the coursing man's nightmare, for sheep invariably live in the same country as hares. Furthermore, for some reason, perhaps merely coincidence, hares will seem to deliberately run straight into a flock of sheep to escape capture by hounds. Coupled with this fact, sheep are perhaps justly paranoid, and ewes are invariably pregnant when the coursing season is at its height. Obviously, a sight hound must be totally and utterly steady with sheep, ignoring them at all times, even as they scatter wildly when a hare pursued by a dog flashes through them. Attempt sheep breaking while the whelp is young—a dyed-in-the-wool sheep worrier is virtually impossible to break of the habit, and the anguish such a dog will certainly cause makes it hardly worth keeping. The courser should give frequent refresher courses in sheep steadiness to his hounds, and if possible, bring the dog into contact with old angry rams. A black-faced tup can be fearsome and will put the most savage greyhound to flight if it is brought to bay. A bad fright from sheep—some sheep with lambs are outrageously aggressive with any dog—works wonders with a hound puppy. Never ever allow a puppy out with another dog which is not stock steady. The sight of any dog pursuing quarry awakens baser instincts in a sight hound, and recidivism is common even amongst stock-steady dogs. A sight hound is never really totally trustworthy, no matter what the owner may believe, thus no dog should be allowed to roam in sheep country.

Dogs should be stock steady to both cattle and ponies, but for somewhat different reasons. Some dogs will admittedly chase cattle and horses, but this habit is often self-correcting after a bad kick has been received. What is more likely, however, is that cows will deliberately seek out a coursing party and follow behind, terrifying the dogs and even chasing them. A horse will often deliberately make a bee-line for a sight hound and not stop pestering the dog until it leaves the field. Horses seem to materialise from nowhere when a lamping party appears, perhaps they are attracted by the light, or perhaps by the curious ritual of hunting with a spotlight or beam. Sight hounds should be broken to cope with eventualities of this nature, as much as being taught not to worry sheep or other livestock. A cow or a horse appearing suddenly in a field will usually cause a great deal of concern and fright in the puppy or sapling, and the youngster may panic, and if not on a leash, seek to run away. Numerous lurchers are found by keepers after abortive lamping forays, on certain estates, and the presence of these dogs can usually be attributed to the fact that they have panicked and run away after being frightened by cattle or horses. A puppy should be taught to 'come in' and 'stay close' or accept being put on the lead for horses and cows are seldom antipathetic towards human beings, even after dark.

To summarise:

- *(a)* insure any sight hound—insurance is an essential safety net—an accident can be indeed unfortunate, if a dog is not insured;
- *(b)* check whatever damage done by sight hounds is excluded from one's insurance policy and, if so, try to insure elsewhere; though many companies are reluctant to insure sight hounds;
- *(c)* break puppies to stock when the sight hounds are still young. To break an adult hound requires a great deal of physical and mental effort;
- *(d)* cows and horses can panic a puppy—act accordingly.

Never, under any circumstances, try to break more than one puppy at a time to stock. The courage engendered by the presence of another dog is likely to be an invitation to disaster.

10. Jumping

The statement that sight hounds are not the most intelligent of breeds may be disputed by some, and considered as a magnificent understatement by others who have tried and failed to train a sight hound. One opinion must receive unanimous agreement by all, however. The sight hounds are some of the greatest athletes of the animal kingdom, and not only does their athletic prowess inspire admiration in spectators, but the same physical movement delights the dog which is performing. Thus, it is patently obvious that there is no excuse for the ownership of a sight hound which does not jump, or more to the point, does not exult in the action of jumping.

Yet surprisingly, many sight hounds—and more surprisingly still, many lurchers—do not jump and the fault is clearly in the training of these dogs, rather than in the hound's disinclination to jump. Hurdling, the simplest and least exacting of a test of a dog's jumping ability was once a competition staged at many country lurcher shows. Now, few shows stage these events, simply because few dogs jump well enough to put up any sort of spectacle and hence racing on the flat, an event which only taxes the speed of the dog and requires little or no training, has replaced the more exciting, more interesting hurdling. It is also a sad indication that the high jumping events staged at lurcher shows (there is seldom enough interest in the activity at sight hound shows to stage them) are often badly attended. More amazing still, is the fact that many of the spectators, who decline to enter their dogs in the jumping competition, allege that they keep dogs as hunters and coursers, for no non-jumper is successful in the hunting field.

Britain is a somewhat crowded country, and prairie-like fields of the sort found in Canada and the USA are noticeable only by their absence in the UK. The landscape of Britain is criss-crossed by hedges, stone walls and horror of horror, barbed-wire fences. Hares, rabbits, foxes and deer learn all too quickly how to use such obstacles to their advantage, and slip between, over and under these divisions, to avoid capture. Thus a sight hound which will not jump (and 'will not' must certainly replace the term 'cannot', for all sight hounds can jump) is at a terrific disadvantage. In fact, a sight hound, or more particularly a sight hound derivative such as a lurcher or longdog which does not jump has limited its value as a coursing dog, and must be relegated to the role of the second-rate. In fact, in the case of most hare hunting (as opposed to traditional hare coursing) the expression 'no jump—no catch' is all too patently obvious. In the development of a good all-round hunting, coursing sight hound, the teaching of jumping is essential.

In view of all the non-jumping sight hounds and coursing hybrids whose owners claim to own otherwise first class hunting dogs, it is amazing to realise how easy it is to teach a sight hound or any dog to jump, and more amazing still to see the great pleasure a well-trained dog gains from the exercise. Many dogs, which have been so taught, will leap to and fro over an obstacle as if delighted by their own physical prowess, exulted as 'a strong man to run a race.'

The act of jumping, however, must be learned and is seldom acquired by day to day unintentional training. A dog not so taught, will often run up and down a pitifully low fence, whining to be with its owner, looking dejected and causing great embarrassment to him. Jumping is seldom self-taught, one should add, and even if it is, like every similar skill acquired by a dog, is also easily abandoned by the animal once it has found the task less than conducive or has met with an accident, either in the process of jumping, or in landing. Many self-taught jumpers will in fact quit, and quit for good, when they have encountered difficulty or have been hurt in negotiating a barbed-wire fence, or become tangled in sheep netting. Furthermore, a self-taught jumper may well clear an object through which it cannot see—a boarded division, etc, but may balk and run up and down a fence through which it can see and will seek to find an opening rather than jump the fence. Hence, jumping must be taught, and even if a dog has displayed a natural propensity to jump, it must be subjected to proper and controlled training. Always bear in mind, a self-taught skill is all too easily lost in a sight hound.

Jumping training, like retrieving training should also be fun, always exciting and never a bore or a chore. Praise and affection must always be forthcoming, not only when the dog succeeds in accomplishing a task, but, more important still, if the dog incurs a slight hurt or fright while actually jumping. Once a dog's confidence has failed, it is extremely difficult to get it to attempt a particularly difficult jump again. As I have previously mentioned, dogs are hedonists—they seek out pleasure and avoid pain, boredom or discomfort. This should be borne in mind when training any breed of dog for any task whatsoever.

Jumping training may be accomplished in two ways:

(a) calling-on jumping—during which a person goes to the other side of an obstacle and calls the dog to him. This type of training is fine if one intends a dog to work only in the field and not to compete in obedience tests;
(b) running-up training—this involves running the dog up to and over an object one intends it to jump. This is not only suitable for teaching a dog to jump while out hunting, but it is also the way to train a dog which is to be used in competitive jumping.

Both methods have their advocates and both can be used to produce top grade hunting dogs. Both methods simply encourage a dog to acquire the physical skill of putting feet and body in such accord as to lift the weight of the frame over an object and, once accomplished, will make the act of jumping not only easy but a pleasure to the dog.

JUMPING

Whatever the method used to teach this, and whatever the variation of these methods used, it should be taught by what psychologists call Skinnerian methods, and what ordinary mortals refer to as 'gradually', never over-matching the dog, and never allowing it to experience discomfort.

Calling-on training can start at the earliest age, at the time when puppies can focus their eyes properly and heed the commands issued by a human voice. The 'nest' is not too soon, was once a slogan of whippet racers when accustoming the whelps to 'seizing' (a prelude to chasing) the rag. Likewise, the same slogan should be applied to preliminary training for jumping, although in the case of large breeds with much bone and muscle growth to make, care should be exercised at this early age lest irreversible damage be done to the whelp. Lesser breeds, smaller, lighter-framed dogs such as whippets, salukis, lurchers and longdogs should certainly start training in the nest, however, and the actual training is, of course, simplicity itself. A board, some six inches high, should be placed between the spot where the puppies sleep and where they feed, and the whelps called to their meals. Sight hounds are notoriously good trenchers, so that food is a wonderful encouragement and reward and the puppies readily scamper over the board to be fed. Increase the height of the jumping board to a foot, and then perhaps to as much as two feet by the time the whelps are six to eight weeks, but a two-feet board is an ample training aid. The action is easily learned at this age when the puppy has neither weight, height or bulk to hinder it. Pigs, yes, even pigs, can be taught to jump and scale obstacles if taught at this age, so the action is almost second nature to the more streamlined, naturally athletic sight hound! Two feet is an optimum height for a nestling to scrabble or jump, though much higher scrabbles can be accomplished. There are authenticated accounts of ten-week-old lurcher puppies scaling six feet high-wire fencing to get to the feed, but whether or not such precocious behaviour precedes any damage to the dog is questionable. The physical effort of scaling this height is probably not detrimental. The landing after a six-feet fall is certainly bruising to developing bone.

Calling-on, can be continued, increasing the height of the obstacle and uttering the words, 'over', or 'up', as the puppy lifts its body upwards. Once again, avoid over-stretching the ability of the dog, particularly a dog intended primarily for exhibition, for few dogs which have been over-jumped as puppies, are perfectly sound in the pasterns or leg joints. Sight hound saplings should be taught to jump/touch (or at least the action of jumping) which is the way most sight hounds prefer to do it, gently touching the topmost bar of the gate with their hind legs (even barbed-wire strands are negotiated thus) before their first birthday. Even whippets, the smallest of the truly workable sight hounds are phenomenal jumpers and in fact, for two years, the lurcher high jump champion of Britain was a twenty-one inch mixed breeding dog, scarcely bigger than a whippet. Few dogs need to be able to clear more than the height of a five-bar gate, over which a trainer can scramble and call-on his hound. Higher obstacles usually require a different technique and a different type of training to teach the sight hound the necessary skills. However, before considering the training of a sight hound for advanced jumping, a word of advice to the beginner with his first hound. Dogs are frequently reluctant to jump and scale an obstruction through which they can see—a wire fence, a slatted gate—and will usually try to push their way through, or crawl under such a barrier. Training is therefore far more easily accomplished if the object to be negotiated is solid, though it is wise to ensure that the puppy has a rough idea of what is behind it before jumping it.

Competitive jumping is a different matter, for here the sight hound has to scale the object on command, and not simply to reach the other side because it wishes to. Hence, the process of running-up jumping needs a slightly different method of training, more suitable for the teaching of a competitive dog, though the whole process, the co-ordination between limb and body movement is essentially the same. That some top-winning dogs, from time to time, have been trained by the follow-on method has to be admitted, although the majority of top grade competitive jumpers are not trained by the follow-on technique.

Running-up jumping—there are various names, for this type of training—obviously has to start somewhat later than the follow-on method, because it involves the use of the lead to guide and encourage the hound. Therefore, until the whelp is lead broken, it is not possible to start proper training. Once the puppy is lead broken, and one should add, happy with the wearing of the lead and not before, training can begin. The puppy should be walked up to an obstacle, preferably a board of say six or eight inches in height, and the trainer, while stepping over the board, gives the lead a slight jerk and utters, 'up, over', or equally appropriate words and encourages the puppy to step over the board. The first stages of training, that is, the act of encouraging a puppy to step over the board, a mere six inches in height, must on first impressions seem a ludicrous and rather pointless exercise for an animal as athletic as the sight hound. In point of fact, the early stages of this particular type of jumping training are the most important, for once the puppy has developed the skills of jumping, of actually lifting its feet and body over an object, the rest of the training is quite simply a progression.

Progression should be gradual, and should a puppy 'jib', be hesitant or unhappy about going over a certain height, then the trainer must reduce the height of the scaling boards and allow the puppy to forget the upset it has experienced. If a puppy (or indeed a grown dog) meets with an accident while jumping, the trainer must abandon training for a few days until it has had time to forget the injury or fright. Never allow a dog to jump a rickety or unsteady frame during training, and indeed during competitive jumping. Always insist on a rock steady frame for a dog to surmount. Nothing makes a dog more unhappy and reluctant to perform, than an unsteady jumping frame, and the damage wrought by the collapse of an obstacle of this nature may be much more injurious to the confidence of the hound than a tyro trainer may be aware.

Gradual progression, increasing the height of the frame by an inch or so a week, is the best method of training, and a dog should only be trained if it is fit and well. An unhappy dog, one slightly under par, a shade off colour, should be given a rest. The act of jumping, particularly when the scaling requires an incredible bound to clamber the object, is an extremely physically taxing exercise for a dog, and hence they should be trained only when in peak condition. Jumping an unfit animal may mean a mistimed jump, an awkward fall, and either physical damage or loss of confidence.

Sight hounds and allied cross-breds are phenomenal athletes. Shortly after World War II, the German shepherd dog, Crumstone Danko, scrambled a frame 16 feet 4 inches in height, a staggering jump by any standards, but a sight hound is a considerably better athlete than the best German shepherd dog, and so is capable of greater feats of athletic prowess, and certainly possesses the ability to scale greater heights. True, most types of sight hound are not as biddable as German shepherd dogs, but with suitable training, more persistent, more careful training perhaps, sight hounds can easily beat German shepherd dogs' records regarding jumping at least. Quite short training sessions can produce greyhounds, longdogs and lurchers capable of leaping cars, minibuses and goal posts, and it is likely that better training could produce phenomenal jumping dogs.

To summarise:

> *(a)* two methods of jumping are successful, calling-on and running-up. Both methods are successful in producing suitable coursing and working dogs. The latter technique is probably the most common way of producing dogs for competitive jumping;
> *(b)* jumping can be taught from the nest, but with some reservations, as puppies can be bruised or spiritually damaged if pushed too hard too soon;
> *(c)* avoid training on shaky frames and with rickety apparatus. A dog damaged or frightened will certainly result from the use of inferior equipment;
> *(d)* the sight hounds are the canine world's greatest athletes—this ability should be exploited to the full.

A word of warning concerning jumping a sight hound. Hideous accidents can, and do, occur in the hunting field. Tractors, harrows and ploughs are often left on the unploughed headland around the field, land close to the hedges

JUMPING

and invisible from its other side. The hunter must know the land over which the dog is to course, and if there is any doubt concerning a dog's safety, it is inadvisable to go on that land. Coursing dogs run at great speed and collisions of any sort often result in injuries and damage almost too ghastly to comprehend. There are few second chances if a sight hound jumps onto tangles of machinery or rubbish.

11. Entering to Quarry

The process of entering a sight hound to quarry is extremely easy, due to the sight hound's natural tendency to chase. This enables the hound to be the supreme natural hunter of the dog world. Sight hounds usually need restraint, rather than encouragement, to start them hunting. It is therefore totally bewildering that the most persistent bleat of the tyro lurcher owner, is that he finds it impossible to get a lurcher or longdog to 'catch' or to pick up. There certainly are sight hounds and sight hound derivatives which are disinclined to chase, but these must be in the minority and are not typical of the type. Likewise, certain of them will pursue the quarry madly, with obvious malice aforethought, only to pass over, run past and simply refuse to pick up the quarry. Perhaps there are sight hounds which will never learn to catch, no matter how they are taught, and no matter how they are trained. These are clearly in the minority, and the majority of failures are simply the result of bad training, bad entering, or perhaps, more commonly, downright impatience on the part of the owner. Lurchers and longdogs seem to attract flash-in-the-pan enthusiasts, people with a limited attention span who are only too willing to buy second-rate, flaw-ridden entered dogs trained by someone else or to purchase puppies, which are then passed on to dog dealers, when the puppy fails to catch on its first venture. Fortunately, most of these enthusiasts soon lose interest and develop other passions, forgetting the somewhat complex process of training and entering sight hounds. Such is the ease with which sight hounds take to coursing, and such is their deeply ingrained instinct, that dogs with a minute proportion of sight hound blood, will often pursue game with the fervour of a greyhound. Hancock of Sutton Coldfield records that puppies bred by crossing collie with greyhound and with a further dash of collie blood, to further dilute the amount of greyhound blood in the hybrid, are usually dedicated coursing dogs, while a misalliance between one of Hancock's dogs and a springer spaniel (a puppy one-sixteenth greyhound) earned a terrific reputation as a working lurcher. When presented with some of these facts, the reader must be able to understand why a sight hound, either pure bred or adulterated with other blood as is the lurcher, will, given time, invariably course and catch quarry. Having mentioned this, it is expedient to cover oneself with the statement that, while most sight hounds become great catch dogs, some will not chase, and others are disinclined to catch. Such dogs are rare, exceedingly rare, and the majority of failures are due to human error in their training and entering.

From the start, however, it is well to explain that some quarry will over-tax even good sight hounds, and even some first-rate sight hounds. A red deer stag, fully antlered in good condition, coming into the lists at 15 stone or more, running in country of its own choosing, will be more than a match for all but the most incredibly powerful sight hound or sight hound hybrid. Few single hounds are fast enough to pursue and hold such a creature. A single deerhound may run well enough over broken ground to bring such a stag to bay, but few are strong enough to hold one. An Irish wolfhound may hold such a creature sometimes (but only sometimes) although it will seldom be fast enough to come to terms with a mountain-bred red deer. Sight hound hybrids, both lurchers and longdogs, are usually able to bring one of these animals to bay, but lack strength to achieve a kill in all but the most exceptional cases.

Despite the much-vaunted claims of lurcher enthusiasts, hares are desperately difficult quarry to bring down, for a dog which is to catch hare should be fast enough to come to terms with the quarry, adept enough at interpreting the movements of the beast, and able to strike and secure the hare which is the most amazing animal athlete on the face of the earth. A hare run in January is as fit, fast and strong a creature as can be found, and will over-match the majority of dogs. Dogs which catch hare with any regularity are, either:

> (a) dogs which catch quarry after dark, running it with the aid of a lamp;
> (b) dogs which run young foolish hares, after the corn is cut and before the first frost;
> (c) dogs which are exceptional athletes—and there are very few good, consistent catchers of strong winter hares.

Hares are certainly not the best of quarry on which to start a dog, for few adult dogs can take hares which have been given fair law. Puppies are pitifully outclassed by a good strong January hare.

Thus the ideal quarry on which to start one's lurcher, longdog or sight hound is the rabbit, but to assume that rabbits are easy meat for a dog to catch is to make a fairly serious error. It is suspected that the reason so many young lurchers are offered for sale is that the young tyros amongst lurcher trainers have greatly underestimated the rabbit as a quarry. Rabbit should be considered as the starting point of entering a sight hound, however, and it is now necessary to describe the various types of quarry available to such a dog or one of its hybrids.

The Rabbit

The rabbit comes into the lists at $2\frac{1}{2}$–$3\frac{1}{2}$ pounds and perhaps, in some localities, a shade heavier. If a much larger specimen does occur, one should suspect a hutch escapee, or maybe a first generation escapee/wild rabbit hybrid, but despite its small size the rabbit is no mean quarry, fast, nimble and above all, an opportunist using every obstacle, every fence, every gap and crevice to escape capture. When a rabbit seems almost certain to be caught, he invariably just manages to scamper down a burrow out of harm's way. The rabbit is both persecuted and plentiful simply because he is quite an athlete, a Harold Abrahams perhaps, rather than an Emil Zatopek, but quite an athlete nevertheless. Owners of sight hounds listening to hunters' tales (more furry and even more exaggerated than fishermen's tales perhaps) of dogs which never fail to catch every rabbit they pursue, should listen tongue in cheek, for the teller is a stranger to the truth or else a sufferer from Munchausen syndrome. Make no mistake about it, without the help of ferrets and lamping devices, the sight hound has a tough time catching rabbits during daylight hours. Rabbits run quickly, about 24 mph as their top speed, but like super fast, high-powered cars, they reach their top speed in seconds. Run in daylight hours they dodge and duck well enough to put a hare to shame and seldom feed far from home. Rabbits are never easy catches.

It is generally considered that the rabbit was introduced into Britain by the Normans, not as a sporting animal, but rather as a delicacy which could be kept in walled enclosures, allowed to burrow into mounds of fine earth and twigs, and when required as food, flushed from the earth with ferrets and entrapped in nets. The walled enclosures were two-fold in purpose. Firstly, to prevent rabbits escaping into the countryside and, secondly, to restrict the ravages of poachers and predators.

Poaching rabbits in the traditional sense of the word, is a relatively modern practise, and prior to the early 1800s, there were few references to it, as applied to rabbits. This can be explained by the fact that before that date, rabbits seemed to have remained within the confines of their enclosures, and those which got out, and of course there must have been many, must have failed to establish themselves outside the warrens. After 1800, runaways seem to have been more successful for there is evidence that not only were rabbits far more successful at living outside the warrens, but that they must have been quite a problem on the farms surrounding certain warrens during the nineteenth century.

Patches of uncultivated woodland, where loose soil and twigs could produce very serviceable warrens (some of the more successful rabbit colonies still live in waste piles of a similar nature), were often utilised as such while the rabbits could be restrained and kept within the confines of the fences and walls. When allowed to establish themselves on arable land however, they became something less than desirable to the agriculturalists. The tale of a landowner, committing suicide because of financial ruin brought about by rabbits, saying, 'Rabbits have killed me', has a slightly jocular note about it, but once the rabbit had taken the leap from semi-domestication, and become a truly wild animal, the havoc wrought by it was incredible.

The flora of the countryside changed rapidly, for the constant grazing of leguminous plants and succulent grasses, allowed the less edible grasses and less nutritious plants to replace the more desirable stock fodder. Furthermore, constant defecation (rabbits produce a staggering 360 pellets a day) and the production of urine made the soil acidic and not conducive to the growth of edible plants. Spurry and sorrel dock, inedible to most grazing animals, replaces vetch and clover in a rabbit-infested area and the soil develops a sour and barren nature.

Proof of the damage wrought by a super abundance of rabbits was manifest in Strathy, a small village in Sutherland, in 1987. Strathy was famous for its rabbit population, and scarcely a square yard of its seafront did not boast a rabbit warren. Ferreting, constant hunting by trappers and itinerant tinkers did little to curb the ravages of the creatures and the land was covered with low grasses, grazed flat as a badly kept lawn, by rabbits. Spurry, encouraged by rabbit urine, flourished. Erosion must have been at a fairly high level, as there was little plant cover to prevent it and in places the land had a pH factor so high that legumes would not grow. Sheep did badly on the hills, competing with the omnipresent rabbit for any available herbage. In 1987, a particularly virulent myxomatosis virus swept the area and carcasses of rabbits dotted the dunes and surrounding landscape. Scarcely a rabbit survived the attack, but the result of the rabbit clearance was spectacular. Vetches and clover experienced a new lease of life, and succulent grasses too flourished on the once acidic land, once rain had flushed the soil of its urine residues.

To return to the subject of rabbit escapees however, no literature exists on why the rabbit suddenly became successful at this in the 1800s. Perhaps a drop in the number of predators was responsible. Pheasant rearing had certainly caused a decline in the number of British stoats, weasels, polecats and martens, for huge numbers of these mustelids were trapped in the early 1800s when an improvement in firearms meant that more successful game shooting was possible. Perhaps the warrens experienced a temporary loss in profitability and were not as well fenced and walled as they may have been. There is even a remote possibility that new vigorous, cold-resistant types of rabbit had developed in the warrens at that time (this seems to be a little unlikely, although rabbits are natives of warmer, less inclement southern Spain and do not appreciate severe winters). Whatever the reason, rabbits ceased to become cosseted dwellers of the warrens and became serious agricultural pests well before the middle of the nineteenth century.

'Breeding like rabbits', is a common and now not totally accurate modern expression, but prior to the myxomatosis outbreak of 1953 the breeding potential of a colony of rabbits was prodigious. Does reach sexual maturity at five months of age, mating and producing young—up to eight seems to be a fair average, though questionable reports of litters of sixteen are not unknown (there is a distinct possibility that two does have kindled in the same nest to produce this quantity of young). Immediately after parturition, does are at their most fertile, and hence mate again, producing young some 28–31 days later. The cessation of frosts usually marks the start of the breeding cycle and the advent of cold weather usually stops further breeding in winter. In mild years, as many as eight litters can be produced, although this seems a shade excessive, but a single pair of rabbits can produce large colonies in a single season if the land around the warren is relatively predator free, but disease has always been an important controlling factor in the spread of the animal, even before the advent of myxomatosis. When rabbits became too numerous, an outbreak of coccidiosis—a disease indicated by the presence of white specks on the rabbit's liver—usually controlled the number in a warren, though since the advent of the far more serious myxomatosis, the presence of diseased livers in wild rabbits is a rarity.

Prior to 1953, coccidiosis must have been the principal controlling factor of the rabbit population in Great Britain, but in that year a French doctor, Armand Delille, upset the ecology of Europe by introducing a South American rabbit disease called myxomatosis to his rabbit-plagued estate in France. There was no way of controlling the disease, and by the end of the year it was estimated that at least 95 per cent of the rabbit population of Europe had been wiped out by the ravages of the virus. Thus, while it was suggested that, because of the fecundity of the rabbit, the species would be immune to the disease in a matter of a few years, no such complete immunity has appeared to date.

Myxomatosis manifests itself as a series of swellings around the anus, ears and particularly the eyes of the rabbit, swellings which may be so severe as to obscure the rabbit's vision. Rabbits infected with the disease usually display a curious lethargy, an indifference to danger, or death itself, finally becoming so weak, listless and lack-lustre as to allow themselves to be picked up by humans and other predators. Despite opinions to the contrary, the meat of a myxomatosis rabbit is still edible and certainly not harmful to humans or dogs and cats. The virus is specific—only capable of infecting rabbits and some Eastern European species of hare—but the sight of an infected rabbit is usually so revolting that few find they have an appetite for infected rabbit carcasses.

It is sometimes noticed that dogs display a reluctance to pick up a rabbit infected with myxomatosis, but this is not due to any revulsion felt by the dog because of the nature of the infection. Dogs are creatures of habit and possibly because dogs behave in a totally predictable manner they expect other animals to also behave as expected. Thus, a dog expects a rabbit to make a very strenuous dash for home when it is chased. A rabbit which does not, or one which fails to struggle strenuously when caught, is untypical and puzzling to a dog. There is no evidence to suggest that a rabbit infected with myxomatosis smells or tastes any different from a healthy rabbit. Dogs do sometimes pursue and catch an infected rabbit but display a puzzled attitude at the obvious indifference of the rabbit to escape capture.

Myxomatosised rabbits are, however, despite their irregular behaviour and flight patterns, quite ideal for starting a young dog at the activity of rabbit catching. The flight of a myxomatosised rabbit is both slow and irregular. The infected rabbit often lies in the sun and, when frightened, fails to run for home. Some, suffering from an advanced stage of the infection, make almost suicidal dashes away from the warren or cover, thereby providing an easy chase for the puppy or sapling. A myxomatosised rabbit is often quite easily caught and as the dictum 'nothing succeeds like success' is as true to dogs as it is to humans, then a sight hound so entered will need very few such catches before it becomes very enthusiastic about catching normal healthy conies. Dogs dislike failure, as much as any creature, and constant fruitless runs, near misses, but misses nevertheless, produce dispirited puppies and owners alike. The owner of the puppy just about ready to start to work must close his ears to the boasts of seemingly established hunters who state that they own dogs which invariably catch the first rabbit they ever see. Such claims are totally false unless, that is, the puppy or young dog is worked to the lamp or spotlight.

Training a dog to hunt rabbit by the use of the lamp is a far easier task than trying to get a puppy to catch a healthy rabbit during daylight hours. Lamping, the basic principles and fine points of which will be explained at a later stage, is an interesting sport, but it is not difficult to get an indifferent puppy to catch after dark, if it is trained to look down the beam of light and is aware that rabbits will appear in that beam from time to time. Rabbits do not freeze in the beam, terrified and afraid to move, as is commonly believed by the uninitiated, but bolt for home at a rate which is just as fast as their daytime velocity. Rabbits feed further from the warrens during night-time hours however, and this extra distance from home gives a puppy a sporting chance to catch them. The subject will be dealt with fully at a later stage in the book.

Ferreted rabbits are usually a fairly good quarry at which to start a puppy, although even a ferreted rabbit is far from easy quarry for a puppy. The subject of ferreting will also be dealt with at a later stage. Rabbits can be flushed from their burrows by ferrets and, between leaving the burrow and the time they find refuge in another hole, crevice or cover, they provide a chance, just a chance, no more, for a sight hound puppy to catch them. Despite the apparently panic-stricken bolt of a ferreted rabbit however, the rabbit usually has a fairly shrewd idea of its next port of call and will attempt to get there as quickly as possible. A puppy placed strategically over a hole, or rather near the hole, adjacent to the rabbit run, has a sporting chance of catching the fleeing rabbit, but once again it must be stressed, the operative term is a 'sporting chance', no more, no less. Running a dog on a ferreted rabbit is not a sure-fire method of guaranteeing a catch, unless of course, the rabbit is netted and then taken a fair distance from the warren and released. Despite the fact that releasing a live, undamaged, unfrightened (and hereby lies the problem) rabbit before a dog is not strictly illegal, it is nevertheless an action which is fairly certain to cause offence to the general public, and the chances are, bring about an investigation by police and RSPCA alike. In fact, the pursuit of a previously captured and then released rabbit is likely to cause considerable interest in all those who are antipathetic to field sports and allied pursuits—and such interest should never be invited.

The owner of a sight hound puppy with neither lamp nor ferrets to assist in the capture of a rabbit, is faced with a far more difficult process of entering his puppy to quarry. At the best, he must be up at dawn and run the spot where rabbits are enjoying the last gambols of the night, and then be at the same spots, placing himself and the hound strategically, one should add, at dusk when rabbits still hungry for the night's feed, will be tempted to emerge from the warrens. Rabbits know the paths to and from the warrens like the backs of their paws and waste no time retracing their steps when they are startled. A puppy will experience many a daunting run and many an abject failure before he manages to catch his rabbit, though regular visits to the feeding ground, and acute observations of the runs and warrens by the trainer, may shorten the odds and possibly secure a capture. This method involves patience and a great deal of patience at that, but it does tend to teach both dog and man a great deal of bushcraft and perhaps in the long run makes for a better trainer and a better hunting dog.

Perhaps it is time to discuss the sight hound/terrier combination which is advocated by many lurcher and longdog enthusiasts. The partnership has little to commend it, unless it be the bolting of fox for the hound to course. As a method of catching rabbits—the terrier drives out the rabbit from the hedge for the hound to course—the use of such a partnership is little short of disastrous. Both terriers and sight hounds are jealous hunters. Neither is prepared to relinquish the prey it has caught. For a while the team may appear to work well or moderately well, but the use of two dogs to secure a rabbit has little or nothing to commend it. Sooner or later the terrier will pursue the rabbit out of the brush or hedge as the hound catches the rabbit. Neither hound nor terrier will be satisfied with the situation, and either the terrier will latch onto the captive rabbit, or the hound will race off, away from the terrier (and trainer) and be reluctant to retrieve its catch to hand. Such a method of hunting will bring about the ruin of a retrieving lurcher, no matter how carefully the retrieving process has been taught. Perhaps, just perhaps, a spaniel will work a thicket and obey commands not to follow the rabbit as it bolts but to demand obedience of this nature from the average working terrier is asking a little too much. Terriers are not of the same disposition as spaniels and are certainly not as biddable. Rabbits caught by terrier/lurcher combinations are usually damaged and fit only for dog or ferret food, but worse may follow. Enmity between sight hound and terrier is almost inevitable and bad fights often ensue. A terrier, no matter how valiant, is no match for even a medium sight hound, and terriers once lifted clear of the ground and shaken by an angry hound seldom survive. Thus a terrier, kept to work with a sight hound, should be used exclusively for bolting foxes. The rabbiting sight hound/terrier team is not recommended.

A rabbit is not easy prey and it is a good policy to remember Aesop's tale of a hare out-running a greyhound—the greyhound was running for its supper, the hare for its life! Thus, at such an appropriate time it is appropriate to deal with the second species of quarry, the hare—and no tougher type of quarry ever existed to test the sight hound.

The Hare

Before embarking on a description of the hare, its habits and suggestions for catching the hare, it is necessary to make the following statement. The majority of sight hounds, lurchers and longdogs, are over-matched by a strong winter brown hare, given fair law and unhindered by the lamp. Stories, such as, 'This dog will take five out of six hares, anywhere' are ridiculous, and beginners to field sports would do well to ignore the teller of such tales, and all further rubbish he may utter, should also lose credibility. Few dogs can catch hares with any regularity in winter, and boasts to the contrary are clearly lies. Top grade greyhounds, invincible lurchers, and five out of five longdogs, are put to shame by the prowess of a January hare in good form, and on country of its own choosing. A September hare, a leveret of the year, foolish and baffled by the disappearing corn and crops, may not be sterling quarry. A November hare, more wise, stronger of limb, will not give of its best, for its best is yet to come, but a hare run in January, a survivor of nature's most savage culling, fully developed in wind and limb, its mind free of thoughts of coupling with its own kind, its senses honed to razor sharpness, its knowledge of every inch of its territory, developed to the full, is almost invincible. Few dogs look at ease with such a prey, fewer still look like catching such a creature, and fewer yet can bring such a creature down. Tales such as I have mentioned of, 'This dog will catch five out of six hares' in such condition, evaporate like marsh miasma when put to the test against such a creature, and the teller of such stories is reduced to his true status of liar, when confronted with the strong winter hare. Such a hare has lived long enough to perpetuate its own species, a species harassed and thinned since the dawn of time, a creature rigorously culled, for all hands are seemingly turned against it, a beast whose pedigree has been written in speed, agility, stamina and survival. Tales of dogs which make light of the capture of such an animal should be treated with disdain, for they are quite simply lies, and the teller of such tales a buffoon.

There are two types of hare living in the British Isles—three, if one counts the Irish hare which is simply a subspecies of the blue hare. Blue hares are smaller, more drab creatures, fleshed like a rabbit, and coming into the weights at about five pounds, halfway in size twixt the rabbit and the brown hare. Blue hares once inhabited land above 2,000 feet in height, but there are pockets of blue hares found in the midst of brown hare country. Watten, in Caithness, has overlapping populations of brown and blue hare, but there seems to be little association between the species and no hybridising. Blue hares are not the athletes brown hares can claim to be, for the heart of the blue hare is small and the flesh ill-supplied with blood (in contrast to the dark bloody meat of the brown hare). This type of hare is clearly not designed for a hard, gruelling course, but it would be a mistake to consider it a slouch. Blue hares use every inch of the terrain to their advantage, to shake off a dog, and seem to skim over heather through which a dog must plough and crash to keep pace with its quarry. Peat hags, places where deep troughs filled with dark peaty water and banked by rough and jagged 'cuts' of peat, are used to terrific advantage and few dogs can cope with a hare of either species, leaping from block pile to block pile, like a chamois, to escape a pursuing dog.

Blue hares turn white in winter, not the clear spotless white of an albino meat rabbit, but a dirty white, the white hair follicles interspersed with brown-grey outer guard hairs. Like most sub-arctic creatures, the ears and topmost part of the tail retain some of their natural colouring at such times. The pelts, even in a hard winter, are seldom very attractive or worth keeping except for novelty value and the carcass is not easy to sell for it has little flavour as compared with the gamey, blood-filled taste of its brown relative. Blue hares are seldom allowed to hang for more than a few days and unless the temperature of the room where they must hang is critical, they develop a less than agreeable taste.

The Isle of Man, or rather the centre of the island, has an incredible population of blue hares, a seemingly inordinate number if one compares the number of brown hares which might be expected on a similar area. Braemar and the land between Braemar and Tomintoul is also a haven for hares, and in November, a night trip over the mountains to Inverness, will illuminate literally hundreds of blue hares on the road and verges of the highway.

Brown hares are a different species and if the blue hare is classed as an upland dweller then the brown hare is a denizen of the lowlands. However, just as there is evidence that there is an overlap of blue and brown hares in certain districts of Scotland, likewise there are places, the altitude of which is seemingly more suited to the habit of the blue hare, that harbour numerous brown hares. The Peak District (Buxton is a town that springs most readily to mind) is a haven for brown hares, while Northumberland has some of the world's best beagling country. Few districts in Britain can match the traditional flatlands of Lincolnshire, Cambridge and Norfolk for hares however, and it is here the record-breaking 13-pound hares are sometimes, though not often, seen. Natural selection, Darwinian selection of the first order, has produced the 7–8 pound hare, the hare of optimum size, capable of phenomenal athletic feats and of eluding the most athletic predators.

There are accounts of hares staying in front of cars travelling at 35 mph and of hares running at this speed for a mile or so—a feat probably beyond the very best and most fleet of sight hounds—but it is not speed alone that makes the brown hare the most difficult sporting quarry in the world. A hare is capable of racing at top speed, stopping suddenly, and then almost miraculously side-stepping the dog, jumping at right angles and continuing at the same speed as though no process of gentle acceleration is needed to propel the creature into full flight. Its ability to duck and dodge, to evade the fatal strike of a dog, is legendary, its stamina seemingly endless. The muscle fibres of its body are bathed in oxygen-giving blood to facilitate the process of flight and to ensure that that speed will not cause irreparable damage to the muscle fibres. A hare bled will yield a large amount of blood for its size, but the muscle tissue is still bloody, long after the veins and arteries are emptied of their contents. The meat of the hare is dark and strong to the taste simply because the fibres of the muscle seem reluctant to give up the vast amount of blood the hare seems to produce. The heart, five times the size of the heart of a rabbit (though the hare is perhaps only twice the weight of a large rabbit) is no mere accident. It is one of the most efficient hearts of the mammalian kingdom, capable of sending blood coursing (a curiously apt word) around the body to supply tissues with ample oxygen during the hardest flight and the lungs, again seemingly too large for the size of the creature, are capable of trapping a large quantity of oxygen even during the most arduous courses. It has been said, perhaps unwisely, that man represents the pinnacle of mammalian intellectual development. It is seldom disputed that the hare represents the most physically perfect artifact ever created by God. Cheetahs capable of bursts of speed up to 70 mph are soon winded by the stamina of the brown hare they are pursuing, and should the cheetah fail to catch at the first turn of the hare, the course is lost, for no creature, not even a cheetah, can generate such velocity a second time—except perhaps the brown hare!

Hares nest above ground producing leverets in spring, summer and sometimes a further crop of young in a mild autumn. They establish territory and know every foot of the land, every wire enveloped by tufts of grass, every protruding tree root capable of bringing down a pursuing predator. Every gap in every hedge or fence is known to them, and dykes, ditches, ragged rough patches of land treacherous to the dog, is friendly terrain to the hare. Lagomorphs—the family to which hares belong—are not credited with intelligence, or much of it, yet a hare pressed by dogs, in danger of being captured, will head, instinctively perhaps, for the most dangerous environment, and dozens or perhaps thousands of dogs have been brought to grief, others have been crippled or have sustained damage to heart and diaphragm, as a reward for pursuing this 7-pound athlete. Most dogs are over-matched by the hare, and more are made to look pitiful and awkward in the pursuit of such a creature.

This, then, is the quarry, and no dog will treat it lightly, regardless of the boasts of the owners of those dogs. Flowing eulogies concerning the hare's speed, its agility and guile, are inadequate testimonials. Hares taken easily, are hares taken off guard, for once a hare has gained its full stride, once it has had time to gather speed and assess its situation, few dogs are capable of staying with it. It must now surely be realised how spurious are the boasts of hunters who claim to be able to kill six out of seven hares in any condition, in any place, and treat the advertisements for puppies, bred from these paragons, with disdain. One of the most popular ways of exploiting coursing and the stupidity of owners of such wonder dogs to one's advantage, is to offer £50 for each hare killed, providing the owner gives £10 for each hare lost. Few owners of coursing dogs, few owners with experience that is, will accept the snare offered. Those who will, are not only inexperienced, but are soon to be fleeced of their cash.

A true coursing enthusiast groans aloud at the sight of hare shoots or lines of shotgun carrying hunters walking across fields, while hares, appearing before them are ruthlessly mown down by gunfire. Yet the truth is, that to control the hare population by legitimate fair law coursing would be a futile gesture and the numbers of hares surviving to plunder fields—and hare damage is considerable in some districts—would be staggering. The fact is that coursing is a very poor way of controlling an out-of-hand hare problem—a sporting method and spectacular without a doubt, but certainly not an efficient method. True, some of the coursing enthusiasts with lurchers and longdogs, aslip or otherwise, are less than desirable people to invite on one's land, but even meets involving sensible folk, held regularly and run efficiently, would not control a population of strong hares.

Yet the fecundity of the hare does not rival that of the rabbit. Hares are born fully furred and sighted, and within hours of birth, are able to run. Few exercise this option, however, preferring to sit in a form—a rough grass nest—in the hopes of passing unnoticed. Once the bitter-smelling foetal fluid has been cleaned from a leveret by the rasp-like tongue of the doe, the leveret, for some reason, is practically without scent, and is able to escape capture simply by freezing to immobility. A hare cleans the belly of its young perhaps four times a day, passing from leveret to leveret to feed them, eating the excreta of the leveret as it is passed from the anus, so that this waste does not attract predators to the presence of the young hare.

Adult doe and buck rabbits are reputed to kill leverets in their forms, biting and stamping them to death, hence hare country is seldom good rabbit country, and vice versa. Foxes, cats, badgers, rats, owls and buzzards thin out the population still further, and stoats and weasels, with the delicate noses of carnivorous gourmets, certainly kill leverets in the nest. However, at a month old, a young hare is capable of outrunning most foxes, and of outwitting wandering predatory cats.

The majority of hares killed by lurchers and longdogs are taken with the aid of a lamp, for the capture of hares by lamping or spotlighting, is not as difficult (the word 'easy' is not an accurate one to apply to the capture of a hare at any time) as the catching of a hare during daylight hours. An indifferent dog, one not capable of putting up a good run by day, will pull down a hare that is baffled and running a circuitous route within the lamp's beam. The pursuit of a hare with dog and lamp seems perhaps unsporting or even a little unfair when one considers the effort required to bring down such a quarry during daylight hours, but if a large hare population is to be controlled by dogs and dogs alone, then lamping of the hares, running the hare at night with a spotlamp and dog, is perhaps the only feasible method. Hares certainly cannot be controlled by daytime coursing. Sight hound enthusiasts who claim to have brought down large numbers of hares in a season, undoubtedly run these hares by night—an exciting pursuit perhaps, but scarcely as sporting as daytime coursing, and certainly an inferior dog is capable of catching a prodigious number of hares, if aided by a lamp.

The entering of a sapling hound, lurcher or longdog, to hare, is a testing experience. Eighteen months is perhaps the right age for a dog to be tried at this type of quarry, and while it can be said that the average lurcher enthusiast will almost invariably claim that his dog has brought down a huge number of hares before the dog's first birthday, it is amazing to note how many lurchers of this type are offered for sale before the age of eighteen months. Dogs are easily strained if tested too soon, and heart, diaphragm and lungs, once damaged, are not easily repaired. Dogs will often run themselves to a state of exhaustion at a hare—hardly a commendable quality in a dog, but strangely the less intelligent members of the lurcher fraternity seem to prize a dog that will damage itself at a course—though they will quite often sell such a dog for a song. A young hound should not be over-matched, and certainly not over-tested, and a hare over-matches and over-tests most young dogs. Thus, a puppy should not be run too young at a hare, but this is easier said than done if a whelp is exercised off leash in country where hares abound. The deliberate seeking out of hares on which to run a young puppy should be avoided, however, and will invariably result in the creation of a damaged, dispirited and disenchanted young dog.

A puppy or sapling, having reached perhaps its eighteenth month, and being strong in wind and limb, should be ready for its first joust with a hare. The trainer must now, for a while at least, forget notions of 'law and fair play' (law being a fair slip of a hundred yards or so) and seek out a hare, which preferably will be a little too young to be classed as a strong hare (though the coursing of a young rabbit-sized leveret is both foolish and unsporting) and denying the hare the right degree of law, slip the dog when the hare is at its most vulnerable. A strong January hare ridiculously outclasses a puppy unless, of course, the puppy is slipped at one which has already been coursed, tried and winded by another dog. Unsporting—well perhaps—but the puppy or sapling outclassed by a hare, made to look ridiculous, and to feel ridiculous by the efforts of the hare, loses much of its confidence and does not give of its best against later hares.

Likewise, a puppy can be started on the lamp or spotlight—though the hound must certainly be used to chasing and catching rabbits by night before being tested on this more taxing pursuit. A hare is never an easy quarry, not even if the dog is assisted by a beam of light. Therefore, bearing this fact in mind, the trainer of the young hound should not expect immediate success. Few dogs are successful at catching a hare on their first encounters and may even seem a little mystified by the sheer velocity of the quarry. No hound should be overtaxed and made to feel inadequate by the hare. The cardinal fault of barking while coursing—called 'opening up' in the lurcher parlance—is quite simply the result of a dog failing to come to terms with its quarry and giving tongue as a cry for help. It is a habit that is easily acquired. It is the very devil to eradicate, and is likely to worsen rather than improve. The seeds of the vice of 'opening up' (which reduces the value of a lurcher by three-quarters) are borne in faulty entering, starting a puppy either too young or in the wrong physical and mental condition. A hound, lurcher or longdog, cannot be expected to perform well if it is unfit—and the word fit should be a magnificent understatement when referring to the condition a hound needs to attain before coursing hares without damage to wind, limb or disposition. Six weeks of roadwork and light running should precede a run at a strong hare, for few dogs are fit enough, without a special conditioning programme. Southerd—a successful modern longdog courser—feeds ad lib for a period before a competitive coursing contest, and relies on hard five miles of roadwork at 15 mph to condition the dogs. Stonehenge, a mid-nineteenth century writer on coursing, advocated judicious deprivation—careful and measured feeding and 20 miles a day's exercise behind horses, though such training would be unsuitable for modern faster coursing greyhounds. To expect a dog to be in kennels day after day, only to be taken out and slipped at a hare—and one adds to experience success—is both ludicrous and ridiculously ambitious. A hare is a natural athlete, its very lifestyle is such that it is always pursued. Seldom does a day go by where it does not need to use its athletic ability to escape capture and usually it must travel great distances to eat the variety of plants it needs to sustain its body weight. No unfit dog is capable of catching a strong fit January hare, given even the shortest of law.

The pursuit of leverets is neither sporting nor sensible, however. The fully-grown hare is such a miracle of speed and endurance that it is sheer folly and almost sacrilege, to hunt down and kill immature specimens. Young hares display a certain suicidal lunacy after the corn is cut, a sort of madness which makes them easy prey for a week or so before they orientate to the change of landscape the autumn reaping brings. A moderately good dog will catch September hares and it requires no great athlete to be able to catch a reasonable number of them in the state of mind induced by the reaping of corn. Hares left until after Christmas become the greatest test of a sight hound. Coursing should not be considered as a means of bringing down a huge head of game—coursing, in fact, is an inefficient way of controlling hares in number if one compares the tally of hares taken to that of an organised shoot. The pleasure of coursing lies in the chase of the hare, in the attempts of the dog to unravel the windings and the devious route of the hare. It is the most thrilling of sights, the most testing of sports.

The Fox

Foxes are considered by some to be unsuitable quarry for sight hounds and many believe sight hounds are not the best of dogs for taking them. Normally such protests are levied by those who ride to hounds and criticisms are made simply because the catching of foxes with lurchers and the like is damaging to the quality of sport offered by the local foxhound pack. Frankly, a pair of good class lurchers will take more foxes than a pack of hounds costing up to £100,000 per annum to keep—though as has been mentioned the killing of foxes with lurchers is scarcely considered entertainment by those who ride to hounds! The morality of killing foxes with sight hounds is questioned by some, but a pair of them, even of small whippet-sized types, will despatch a fox with the same speed as would a pack of foxhounds.

The last wild dogs in Britain are foxes. Wolves vanished in the middle of the eighteenth century having led lonely 'hobo' existences in the remote areas of Scotland and the Lake District for a century or so before—scavenging on sheep carcasses, hurting no-one perhaps, but like Ishmail having everyone's hand against them. The marauding ways of wolves have always been exaggerated. True, they can be ferocious stock worriers, killing sheep and cattle alike, but contrary to the folk legends, wolves have no antipathy to mankind and if man-killers have been recorded, there is evidence to suggest that these man-killers are hybrids between dogs and wolves and not true lupine stock. Corto, the bob-tailed wolf of fifteenth-century Paris, was in all probability a wolf dog hybrid, as were the awesome Beasts of Gevauden which terrified eighteenth-century France.

Foxes are some of the most successful carnivores of all time and certainly one of the most successful and versatile members of the Canidae. There are huge fox populations—populations to make the Quorn country green with envy—in the centre of many large cities. Birmingham is literally plagued with foxes and though these foxes present no problem at present, should rabies appear once again in Britain, the fox population of inner cities will be a serious matter indeed, for foxes are both great travellers, and equally, great carriers of rabies. Foxes, which in rural conditions normally eat 15–25 per cent vegetable matter—roots, grain, and the contents of herbivores' stomachs—will take fairly readily to bakery waste and other pasta, with rats, mice and beetles providing the necessary animal protein to supplement an almost exclusively vegetable diet. Small domesticated livestock is seldom attacked if there is an abundant vole and mouse population, but in districts where rodents are relatively small in numbers, guinea pigs, rabbits and poultry have been snatched under the very noses of pet keepers.

As to whether the fox is a sheep worrier, or more to the point a killer of lambs, is a shade questionable. The appearance of a fox in the Scottish Highlands, particularly at lambing time is cause for much concern and so foxes are hunted down without mercy. The Lake District foxhound packs—the Lunesdale, the Melbreak, the Eskdale and Ennerdale, the Ullswater and the Blencathra hold special mid-week meets to placate the wrath of farmers who have had lambs killed by fox and hunt alleged lamb worrying foxes without mercy. It is argued that fox hunting will never be made illegal in the Lake District, but such a statement tempts providence—the same was once said of otter hunting!

Students of vulpine behaviour are less convinced about the damage wrought by foxes and state that there is little or no concrete evidence to suggest foxes worry lambs. True, afterbirths of sheep and dead lambs are eaten by foxes, but farm dogs display an equal predilection for fallen mutton. Farm dogs may well be the true culprits regarding the killing of newborn lambs and it has to be admitted that bad management may well be the principal cause of neo-natal mortality rather than damage by foxes. The presence of lamb tails and remains of the lamb pelts in fox earths is no real proof of the predations of foxes—the wool and tails may well have come from stillborn lambs. Thus a question mark must be placed over the role of the fox as a sheep worrier, despite claims by hill farmers to the contrary.

There can be no question as to the role of the fox as a poultry worrier, however, for foxes often wreak havoc on ducks, geese, chickens and turkeys alike. The havoc caused in a poultry pen by a wayward fox leaves little doubt as to vulpine habits! Poultry are sometimes chopped, maimed and left untouched by foxes and the hideous damage wrought by a raiding fox will cause serious antagonism to them in the poultry keeper. Turkeys suffer most from fox attacks, for the hysterical nature of turkeys tends to panic the survivors into forming heaps of birds, those at the bottom of which being suffocated and crushed. Pheasants are equally attractive to foxes which seem to be able to detect any weaknesses in release pens in order to perpetrate damage on the inmates.

Cats may not play an important part in the diet of foxes although kittens perhaps up to the size of half-grown female cats may be taken. A cat is a ferocious fighter and foxes usually fight shy of tackling them, but kittens are regularly found in the lairs of both urban and rural foxes. However feral cats are often notoriously remiss about caring for their first litters and hence the carcasses found in fox earths might well be victims of death through hypothermia rather than from fox attacks. Foxes are great scavengers and meat of any sort and in any state of decay seldom comes amiss. The gastric juices of foxes seem capable of coping with flesh that even vultures would find unpalatable. Nauseous messes, carcasses too decayed to allow identification by laymen are still considered edible by foxes, and thus it must be obvious that a wound created by a fox bite tends to become infected. Prior to the advent of Fleming and antibiotics, fox bites invariably festered, or 'went wrong' to use 'hunt' parlance. The bite is no less dangerous now than then, however, and if a fox bite—received by man or dog—is untreated it tends to fester and complications usually set in. Prior to Fleming, fox bites were treated by bathing the wound in methylated spirits, whisky and/or salt-water. Nowadays, bites, punctures, are more likely to fester than slashes, should be treated with a suitable antibiotic but they should also be bathed with a dilute solution of antiseptic.

The fox is seldom to ground after May when the earths become unpleasant and foetid with mange mites thriving in such conditions. Mange is a constant companion of the fox and few pelts of wild foxes do not manifest its ravages. Fox mange may be caused by one (or both) of two mites. *Sarcoptis scabii*—a mite that causes the maddening itching which accompanies scabies—and *Sarcoptis communis*—a mite which causes the same symptoms as does scabies, but is fairly resistant to many insecticidal dips. Foxes are plagued by these mites and it is estimated that far more foxes die of scabies, the sepsis introduced by these mites and the subsequent scratching of the fox, than are killed by fox hunts or motor vehicles. At one time hunt servants encouraged badgers in bad fox mange country—the Atherstone, the Meynell and the South Staffs hunt country were famous for their mangy earths—for, because of their constant excavating, badgers tend to remove the detritus which seems to abound in fox earths. This mange can, and probably will, infect both dogs and man and fox-hunting sight hounds should be watched for traces of mange at all times. Scabies is not unknown in hunt servants because of the handling of fox carcasses by them. This should also be borne in mind by those who would course foxes with sight hounds. An infestation of scabies mites is not difficult to eradicate perhaps—a single dip of appropriate insecticide will usually clear the most unpleasant case of scabies. The disease, however, is both embarrassing and unpleasant.

The treatment of an infected dog will be dealt with later in the book.

In summer foxes lie up above ground and return to the nursery earth—and other temporary abodes—only when fairly severe frosts threaten. Thus foxes may be found above ground in summer and can be run with hounds, but as the year progresses and foxes return to earth, terriers are needed to bolt the fox so that it can be coursed with sight hounds. Foxes sometimes run to ground in established badger earths and hereby lies the danger. Since 1973 the badger has received some protection by law, protection which was reinforced by the Wildlife and Countryside Act of 1981. Indeed, an amendment to the 1981 act passed in 1985, makes it necessary for a man with a terrier to ground to prove he is in pursuit of foxes and not badgers. As the habits of foxes and badgers are similar and the earths and sets of these creatures sometimes found in the same subterranean labyrinths of tunnels, clearly it is almost impossible to prove that a terrier to ground is not in pursuit of badger. Hence any earth which may also be a badger set should be avoided. Badger sets are not easy to differentiate from fox earths. The presence of a strong stench of fox is certainly not conclusive evidence that the hole is not a badger set, for foxes will at times inhabit the sub-chambers of one. Badger sets are usually fairly extensive, as the badger is a habitual digger, and the excavations of the badger may alter the topography of a landscape with the mounds of earth excavated from the depths of a set. Bedding outside the holes—dry straw, grass, and sometimes (though rarely) bracken—is a fair indication that badgers are or were at home and often very old bedding decayed and disintegrating is enough to secure a conviction against a person for badger digging. Sufficient to say that if an earth is inhabited by badgers or is likely to have once housed badgers, a terrier should not be entered.

Foxes are not beyond the catching capabilities of any sight hound. Large dogs such as wolfhounds and deerhounds are able, or should be able, to kill them at a bite, whereas even a whippet, the smallest, most fragile of the true sight hounds, will often make a fair show at bringing them down. The Irish saying that it is not the size of the dog in the fight that counts, but the size of the fight in the dog, should be borne in mind regarding the tackling of foxes with sight hounds, and while careful entering and early success will produce the best results, if a dog shows no inclination to tackle foxes there is little one can do to encourage it to do so. Frankly, there is no natural enmity between dogs and foxes, and while some dogs can be taught to initiate this enmity, some simply refuse to, and there is little anyone can do to kindle an interest in foxes in a sight hound which is patently unwilling to tackle them.

The catching of foxes is seldom an easy task and can be attempted in three ways:

- *(a)* daytime coursing;
- *(b)* night-time hunting;
- *(c)* bolting foxes from earths with terriers and coursing them with sight hounds or allied types.

Daytime coursing can be fairly unproductive, for foxes are often very furtive during daylight hours, lying up in fairly inaccessible places and earths. Woodlands, deciduous more than coniferous, often harbour foxes and few sight hounds (perhaps whippets and some lurchers are exceptions) are capable of performing well in such country. Foxes which are to be hunted in these woodlands should be driven out by systematic bush beating so that hounds stationed outside the copses and woods can course them. In open country, foxes might seem to have little chance against the faster, large sight hounds, but in reality this is far from the truth. A fox coursed in apparently earth-free country seems to be able to find gaps in fences and outsized rabbit warrens in which to dive. A running fox is deceptively fast and whereas its jinking action when coursed is not as spectacular and sophisticated as that of the hare, it is often sufficient to be able to throw off even an experienced coursing dog. Furthermore foxes enjoy the bonus of seldom venturing outside familiar territory. Every obstacle, every impediment to the running of a sight hound, every drain, every weakness in a fence, every slightly shaky stone wall is used to best advantage by the fox to throw off its pursuers.

A young dog should first be run at fox in the company of an experienced and preferably dextrous fox catcher. So much depends on the actual disposition of the young hound that it is impossible to make generalisations. Some of them which are badly bitten during their first skirmishes with fox may react unfavourably to the biting and 'quit', refusing to run and catch foxes ever again—though the majority will invariably run alongside a fox, simply refusing to make a strike. Likewise, a hound that is badly bitten may become furious and seize its fox, thus becoming wed to the quarry for life. Hancock, in his book *My Life With Lurchers*, makes the following observations about entering a dog to fox. At the time in question Hancock had a young blue merle lurcher, called Romulus, a gauche, rather silly puppy which Hancock's daughter was wont to dress in doll's clothes and treat very much as a pet. Hancock was at that time in the process of winding down his poultry farm and was plagued with foxes that pestered his poultry and broke into many of the sheds. To curb their ravages, Hancock set numerous snares and trapped a live healthy fox one morning. He found it while walking the farm with Romulus at his heels who sniffed the fox curiously, refusing to accept the beast as a foe, and receiving a ferocious bite for his inquisitiveness, whereupon he erupted, shaking the fox to death in seconds, and continued to savage the carcass for some time after the fox had died. Henceforth, he became wed to foxes and was literally frantic to chase and kill them. His brother Timmy, also owned by Hancock, was nipped during his first course and after this became cautious of foxes, preferring to come on a 'downed' prey, while another dog received punishment from the fox. Timmy would have been ruined by such accidental entering as Romulus had. Foxes caught by sight hounds should never be baited to death, nor be forced to experience agony or fear before their demise. Once a fox is taken it is the trainer's duty to despatch the fox quickly and cleanly. Dogs do not improve their coursing skills through protracted battles with foxes, nor do they benefit by receiving frequent painful bites during the combat. Despatch the foxes quickly and cleanly—a sharp blow or a shot to the head of the fox will stop the battle quickly. Lengthy battles between dogs and foxes witnessed by unsympathetic onlookers cause ill feeling between the general public and the hunting fraternity. Public opinion will eventually bring about the end of field sports—to assist that ending by perpetrating pointless cruelty is ridiculous.

General opinion is decidedly against hunting and it is wise to know the relevant laws and codes of conduct to prevent fanning the flames of public resentment. A fox is regarded as vermin and in a rural setting a person who kills a fox by any legal means available is committing no offence. Within the confines of a town it is a different matter. It is an offence to encourage a dog to kill a fox in urban surroundings and while it seems a little unlikely that police will bring a prosecution under an obscure, half-forgotten act, it is not worthwhile stirring up public antipathy.

The fox should be killed with speed and as few histrionics as possible. A protracted battle damages both the mask and the pelt of the fox and makes its killing a little less financially worthwhile. If the animal is required as a trophy or even if not, no benefit is achieved by allowing a lurcher to fight its fox to the death.

Foxes lying below ground may be bolted with terriers. A terrier which bays loudly and sharply is more effective at bolting a fox than one which wades in and gains a hold and, in a deep earth, a lurcher or sight hound can follow the progress of the battle if a dog bays at its fox rather than tackles it.

A sight hound intended to work with a terrier should not only be well-acquainted with the terrier to be used, but should be allowed to walk above the earth while the terrier works its fox, often yards beneath the hound's feet. Many hounds and particularly lurchers will develop a habit of freezing near a hole and remaining immobile until the fox decides to bolt. No hound or other dog for that matter should be allowed to push its head into a hole and snort its presence to a fox. A fox is unlikely to consider bolting if a dog's head seems to block its progress, and a fox so impeded or frightened will return to fight the terrier rather than attempt to bolt. A sight hound or hybrid must be kept under control, until it has learned to freeze by an exit to await the flight of the bolted fox. A steady dog is the only type of dog to work in these situations. A dog which erupts at the first sight of the mask of the fox is a liability, although such problems are temporary and can usually be ironed out by careful training. A sight hound will develop an affinity with a terrier fairly quickly if it realises the terrier is an ally and will follow its actions below ground, tracing the movement of battle by sound. This partnership between hound and terrier requires little training to develop it, but some training is essential, if a successful fox hunting team is to be formed.

A very productive method of catching foxes—though not considered particularly sporting by some—is lamping. Foxes are furtive creatures and far more difficult to lamp successfully than rabbits or perhaps even hares. The subject of lamping generally, and lamping foxes specifically, will be dealt with at a later stage, but basically foxes can be caught by lamping, only if they can be lured away from hedges or woodland and run on open country. A field where foxes are to be taken should be baited and the hunters positioned around the field, dogs on slips and kept in absolute silence until the fox is lured to the centre of the field by the bait. Fox pelts taken in mid-winter are in certain years quite valuable—up to £25 for a good standard red pelt sold 'wet'—taken off the fox without drying or added preservatives, but the market is variable and only top class pelts without tears, marks, or blemishes are worth selling to a furrier. The fur market is a fickle one. One month pelts are at a premium, the next they are scarcely worth the taking. A single dog must be run at fox if the skin is to be sold as a 'prime'. When two dogs engage a fox they are likely to rip or puncture the pelt. However the subject of lamping will be dealt with more fully at a later stage.

Deer

The pursuit of deer with dogs—sight hounds, lurchers and longdogs—is fraught with danger, although not particularly difficult to accomplish. In Scotland where the laws are often very different, the pursuit of deer with dogs, or for that matter, any method of taking them other than by shooting, is illegal and a violator of this code faces a very stiff sentence.

More to the point, however, few sight hounds are capable of finishing a deer cleanly and quickly, and the sound of a deer screaming piteously while trying to throw off a hound which is in the process of disembowelling it is sure to provoke outrage on the part of the general public.

Britain has a rich and varied population of deer, some indigenous, others the issue of escapees from imported stock, for Britain, although still regarded as a crowded country, still has sufficient secret places to absorb a population of fairly large exotic mammals.

Red deer are a truly British species, though the continent of Europe still has a fair-sized (though supposedly not thriving) population of them. However, in Britain, particularly in Scotland, they are often given sufficient protection to be able to increase in number. Red deer therefore fall into three categories:

(a) tame or farmed deer;
(b) wild deer which are still tame enough to accept supplementary feeding in winter;
(c) truly wild deer—accepting no supplementary feeding at any time.

The lot of the red deer is a tough one, be it farmed for its meat or roaming wild. Originally it was a creature of the forests, but the subsequent removal of trees and the pressure of population has forced this elegant creature to seek refuge in less clement conditions. In Scotland the deer is relegated to heather pastures, to seek a living on herbage that would not be nutritious enough to support black-faced sheep. Its digestive tract is efficient and examination of a gralloched deer's stomachs show a variety of seemingly inedible plants in a state of fine maceration prior to digestion.

Large deer are still taken from time to time—stags up to 18 stone in weight are found, though they are admittedly fairly rare. There is some evidence to suggest that the deer of the forests were considerably larger, possibly because of the more varied and richer diet, or possibly because trophy specimens may have been culled out, leaving only smaller, less regal looking deer to perpetuate their kind—although the latter theory has little credibility amongst authorities on this species. Certainly a large animal by today's standards would have caused little interest amongst the Norman and Angevin knights who pursued stags and hinds with a variety of hounds—both scent and sight hunting types.

As mentioned in the chapter on the deerhound, the ancients usually required two strong hounds to pull down a stag and the fate of these hounds was sometimes far from enviable. Perhaps the deer have decreased in size since the cessation of deer coursing with deerhounds, but it seems unlikely that any single modern sight hound is keen enough and strong enough to catch and hold a wild stag. Poachers using small packs of lurchers and longdogs (the most popular cross-bred for hunting or poaching deer is the deerhound/greyhound, known to Romanies as the 'staghound' because of its deer-killing qualities) do pull down red deer but the possibilities of these being truly wild deer and not farmed deer or partially farmed deer is remote. Genuine wild deer are difficult to approach and unless a series of mistakes are made by it, it is unlikely that a poacher with a pack of deer-hunting lurchers can come to terms with one.

Deer coursing with dogs of any breed is strictly forbidden in Scotland—although it is fair to state that there is perhaps more deer poaching taking place in Scotland than anywhere in Britain—so unless the sight hound trainer has farmer friends in the neighbourhood of deer moors, like Exmoor, where deer are frequent pillagers of crops, there seems little opportunity to hunt this species of deer legally with sight hounds. The majority of red deer caught by Scottish and English poachers are far from being wild, for most seem to be the inmates of some deer farm. Taking deer in these conditions is not only unlawful and unsporting, but, frankly, so easy, that the poacher or deer thief, for that is the true status of one who takes tame deer, would do as well to set his hounds on calves or sheep—as, alas, is often the case—for deer poachers have the reputation of being very catholic in their choice of quarry. A prosecution in Caithness in 1988 revealed that a red deer, killed by intruders at Phillip Mains, was a tag-eared tame female (tame deer are earmarked for identification purposes), foundation stock for a deer farm. Red deer stags are tough quarry for a single sight hound, or a pair for that matter, but the opportunity to course such a beast legally is remote. So to all intents and purposes the red deer must be described as unsuitable quarry for the sight hound.

Fallow deer, however, are not only more common, but well within the capabilities of a good strong sight hound, lurcher or longdog. Unlike the red deer—an indigenous British species—there is some evidence that the fallow deer was imported into this country, though when and where the importation took place is open to question. It seems likely that they retreated before the glaciers, disappearing when the land sank to create the area known as the North Sea. Rutter, in his book *An Ark In Our Midst* (1959) is of the opinion that possibly a land bridge existed for some time after the recession of the glaciers and fallow may have travelled from the continent to Britain to become trapped when the bridge, too, sank beneath the 'melt' of the glaciers.

Millais, *Mammals of Great Britain and Ireland*, (1904–1906) states that he believes that the Phoenicians, rather than the Romans, were responsible for bringing this deer to Britain, although he offers no proof for his opinion, other than that the Phoenicians seemed more adventurous in their trading exploits, but whoever was responsible for the introduction of the fallow deer, the species was well-established by Roman times.

Black fallow deer (they range between what appears to be jet black when viewed from a distance, to dark brown when the pelt becomes less dense through moult) may be an exclusively British variety bred by a process of deliberate selection of melanistic specimens or perhaps even a slightly different species, though they differ little if at all in outline, weight or habit from the more commonly seen deer throughout Britain, and are fairly rare.

The rare white fallow deer—the fabulous magical white hart (though the term hart is usually applied to the red deer) of the later books of the *Mabinogion* is still found in Britain. In 1900 the sixth Duke of Portland introduced white fallow deer to Berriedale, a district on the north-east coast of Scotland, from the nucleus of white fallow deer he was breeding at Welbeck Abbey Park—although these white fallow deer are seldom seen in Caithness today. Islay, on the west coast of Scotland has a justly famous collection of wild deer of different species, but there is a tale that these were imported from the mainland by tenth-century monks who developed a fondness for venison and deer hides while living on the mainland of Scotland.

The south of England harbours an enormous number of these deer, both in parks and roaming wild, though in some cases the latter are afforded the luxury of carted provender during hard winters, and it is these that are often run and captured by sight hound enthusiasts. Fallow deer are reputedly as fast as brown hares and have terrific acceleration. Hence a daytime course at such quarry is likely to be hard and testing, though the fallow certainly does not have the bulk and fighting ability of the red deer. The illegal night-time hunting of this type of deer is, of course, more fruitful (all pursuit of deer one hour after dark to one hour before light is illegal and night-time poaching carries a fairly weighty fine—although it is fair to add that such fines are rare when a night-time hunter has permission to take the deer) but the fallow deer are still a fairly testing quarry at any time of day or night.

Catching fallow deer is an art only some dogs learn. Indeed many hounds are reluctant to come to grips with a large animal of any sort. The majority of deer killed are usually run by motley hordes of lurchers—the south of England is plagued by itinerant bands with packs of sight hounds, pure and hybrid, that are as dangerous to sheep and calves as to the deer—and deer taken this way are usually badly lacerated before those in charge of the hounds assist by cutting their throats. These mob-handed hunts have done much to make the public dislike the lurcher or longdog, and, frankly, hunts of this kind have no place in a country like Britain. Single dogs certainly can and do bring down fallow deer well and learn a technique of either securing the deer by a throat hold or catching and holding it by the leg—the carcass of which is thereby still saleable as the meat does not bear the same bruising and lacerations as a deer killed by the worrying, ripping action of several dogs.

Fallow are usually gregarious, congregating in small single sex herds. A dog faced with cutting out a single deer from a fleeing herd is often baffled unless one deer decides to make a break from the herd. Should a herd stay together, however, many a single dog is confused by the very number of deer and the thunderous sound—'an avalanche of hooves'—such a herd makes when running. New Forest deer poachers of the last century tended to favour collie lurchers but the majority of New Forest itinerants today seem to keep only longdogs and pure sight hounds for the pursuit of deer. Collie lurchers, because of their herding dog ancestors, perhaps, are believed rightly or wrongly to be able to cut out a single deer from a single sex herd more skilfully than would a longdog. Many deer are poached by barbaric methods, however, the most popular of which is the running of herds of frightened deer by night and entangling the wretched creatures on barbed wire. Prosecutions of such poachers are not unknown, but the atrocities committed by such people and their hounds are seldom related in court.

Lurcher owners who claim to live by poaching cannot do so by hunting only rabbits or hares. At the time of writing, a rabbit will fetch perhaps a pound in England, and considerably less in Scotland, while brown hares (not to everyone's taste) will seldom fetch the price of two rabbits. Deer are large animals and a carcass with few lacerations on it will command a figure of about £30–£40, although the poacher has little negotiatory power should an unscrupulous game dealer decide to pay him less. A hard night's lamping of rabbits and hares will, therefore, net only a fraction of the money that a successful tilt at deer will provide. Hence fines for poachers who take only rabbits and hares are seldom really severe, but the punishment for the poaching or the theft of deer is often staggering.

Some of the most fascinating court cases have involved the prosecution of deer poachers. The famous Leighton Buzzard prosecution needs little elaboration, except to say that the accused pleaded guilty to the taking of 201 deer including the rare Père David deer, a species thought to be extinct in the wild for 3,000 years. However the Attingham Park slaughter—an expression used by the daily papers to describe the ill-fated poaching expedition in Attingham Park near Shrewsbury in the early 1980s—is more interesting still. The accused were caught red-handed stealing park deer, and after a fascinating, if bizarre, court case involving stinging and witty repartee on the part of the judge, the prosecution and the defence counsel, the perpetrators of the crime were sentenced to eighteen months imprisonment apiece. The case made national headlines, including a full feature in the *Police Gazette* and was certainly a landmark in the evolution of the complex deer protection laws.

Thus are the fines and punishments and thus is the prize for which the gauntlet must be run. Sufficient to conclude, concerning this species of deer with a mention of a Scottish law passed in 1424, designed to protect fallow deer from the ravages of poachers in a land that had recently endured famine and war, and was later to suffer the ravages of plague. 'Anyone found guilty of taking fallow deer shall be fined 40 shillings (£2) and their lairds £10'—a staggering fine for a Scottish peasant whose way of life would have ensured he would seldom have seen such monies, or coin of any sort for that matter.

Roe are truly British deer, not only smaller than red or fallow but also white-rumped and elegant as cherubs. Roe exist as solitaries, in pairs or occasionally in small parties of perhaps up to five in number, although herds or large families are seldom encountered. The species is wild and is seldom fed hay or turnips even during the most severe winter. Roe are shy furtive creatures preferring a nocturnal to a diurnal lifestyle whenever possible, and spending their sleeping hours in dense woodland if it is available. In the Highlands where trees of any sort, other than forestry plantations, are a rarity, roe tend to live in deep unburned heather, sheltering from wind and rain in peat hags or dry peat cuts. The roe is speedy and wonderfully agile but not as fleet as the fallow nor is it such a formidable fighter as the red deer. Roe are small enough to be held by most sight hounds. Indeed the introductory chapter of Standfast Press's *Coursing* describes how a roe was surprised by a show-bred whippet which hung on to its prize until help could arrive. This, coupled with the fact that roe are easily disposed of, has made the poaching of wild roe deer profitable. While the roe is described as no mean quarry, the illegal lamping of deer (one hour after dark, one hour before light, are the forbidden times for deer hunting) can produce a good haul in country where roe abound. The roe is not as speedy as the fallow, hence a dog learns the technique of securing a leg hold fairly quickly when coming to grips with it. Their venison is not to everyone's taste and is tough and indigestible unless cooked for a long period of time. A north country folk song describes the roe as being 'light on the hoof, heavy on the stomach', as apt a way to complete a description as any.

Sika deer are certainly escapee imports, although the species is spreading at a staggering rate, both as a hybrid type and as a pure bred. Three types of sika are at large in Britain—the Japanese sika, the most commonly seen sika, the Manchurian sika whose natural habitat is around Port Arthur, and the somewhat less common Formosan sika. All three forms will mate together, breeding fertile hybrids. Hybrids between sika and the British red deer have also been reported and these cross-breds, too, are reputed to be fertile—a fact that suggests that they may be related species. The sika rut takes place in September and the stag will gather perhaps five hinds to him, staying with them until March or April in North Sutherland, when the group will split up and the stag retire to grow antlers.

Sika are somewhat smaller than red deer however—a large stag weighing in at less than nine stone (an adult, though very large, red stag may be double that weight)—but whereas the red deer have the reputation of being reluctant to face a human being, sika, which have somewhat aggressive faces, will justify their expressions when challenged or surprised and are, in fact, described as some of the most pugnacious and aggressive deer in the world. They are, however, reputedly very dog-shy and while they will often face down a human being, a dog, particularly a vociferous dog (not a good quality in sight hounds, longdogs or lurchers) will cause them to panic. There are no recorded instances of them facing a dog, although park deer will sometimes refuse to be moved by sheep dogs.

The sika is not as fleet as the fallow but is a little more bulky. Their reputation of being dog-shy makes them difficult to approach with a dog on leash so as to ensure a good and profitable slip at them. When alarmed the thunder of their hooves may well deter all but the most enthusiastic deer-hunting sight hound, but unless pressed, and sorely pressed at that, they seldom retaliate against dogs. A sika can be brought down by most medium-sized sight hounds and sight hound hybrids, particularly if the dogs have a fairly tenacious disposition. Wild—or rather feral, in view of the fact that most herds are descended from escapee deer, brought into Britain by the German animal dealer, Johann Carl Jamrach, in 1860—are on the increase but the would-be hunter of sika would do well to secure written permission from farmers whose land is invaded by such deer. The venison of sika is almost identical to that of the larger red deer and sells for roughly the same price or perhaps a shade less.

Both Chinese and Indian muntjac deer are smaller—the Chinese type is scarcely 25 pounds in weight and 18 inches at the shoulder with antlers a little over $2\frac{1}{2}$ inches in length. The Indian species (known as *Kakar* in Hindustani after its strange bark which is said to indicate the presence of tiger) is slightly larger, with longer, more pointed antlers. Unlike sika, the muntjac can scarcely be considered dog-shy and, although over-matched by most sight hounds, a muntjac deer will often bite with great fury rather than rely on its antlers to defend itself. The small 'tusks'—actually the upper canine teeth of the deer—will inflict great damage to a dog, and tales of both species, particularly the Indian species, besting a small dog, are not uncommon. There are numerous hybrid muntjac in south-east England but there is no evidence of the pure or hybrid muntjac spreading beyond the south Midlands.

Muntjac live in woodlands, eating grasses and brambles and seldom venture out into open pastures. This deer is a natural solitary, living as a single or in pairs and seldom gives a hound a satisfactory course, disappearing into thickets and deep cover with the ease of a rabbit into a bramble patch. There are instances of enthusiastic hunters living adjacent to this shy and secretive deer for years without the presence of the muntjac being noticed.

The mysterious Chinese water deer is even more localised than the muntjac. This deer lives a secretive life north of London, around Ampthill and Flitwick, but is also to be seen around the borders of Wales. Slightly larger than the muntjac they possess an abnormal development of the upper canine teeth, which protrude as tusks $3\frac{1}{2}$ inches or so. These tusks, like all animal tushes, are reputed to have medicinal properties and find their way into Chinese herbalist shops where, after being ground up and added to thyme and balsam, they are sold as a cure for ailments ranging from gout to stomach ulcers. The habitat of the deer—they frequent downland as well as woodlands in England (in China they live exclusively in riverbeds and marshes)—makes them more suitable for hounds to course than the woodland-dwelling muntjac. Both muntjac and water deer move at great speed however—deceptively fast until one sees even a swift hound matched against one—and this speed allows many of them to escape capture. Only bucks seem to possess the tushed canine teeth and the absence of antlers or tushes on the doe probably accounts for the specific and generic name—the weaponless water drinker. Speed and shy disposition are the weapons of the doe, but bucks will on occasions fight off dogs, particularly small dogs. They present no serious problem for the smallest of sight hounds however, and whippets are often extraordinarily successful in bringing down water deer.

Hancock mentioned in his talks at Forest School in Walsall, in 1985, that dogs which grow up on intimate terms with sheep and goats are often reluctant deer coursers, unless started at deer in the company of another dog which shows enthusiasm. Conversely, many deer poachers note that dogs which are enthusiastic deer hunters, are frequently unsteady with sheep—although this is by no means always the case, for many deer poachers are foolish enough to regard the carcass of a sheep as an added bonus to a night's adventure and actively encourage their dogs to take them. This madness, coupled with the extraordinary cruelty sometimes used to bring down deer, has made the deer poacher almost a *persona non grata* amongst even the lurcher fraternity, and there are many genuine sportsmen who consider deer to be unsuitable quarry for sight hounds. If deer are to be taken they must be given fair law, run in suitable country and not despatched by barbaric methods. Deer poaching is always a questionable pursuit, and while the activity no longer merits the death sentence as it once did, it is certainly an activity which will eventually be used by those opposed to hunting to sway public opinion to outlaw field sports.

12. LAMPING

Lamping or spotlighting, as it is known in Scotland, has a totally baffling mystique about it. It is baffling because any sight hound, even the most excitable Afghan hound, the biggest Irish wolfhound and the most diminutive whippet can be taught to lamp, or lamp after a fashion, that is. It is also baffling because the most simple-minded hunters, the very worst dog trainers imaginable, can and do, teach a dog to lamp. Still the sport has this mystique about it, and is referred to as an art, a science and by other hyperbolic definitions. It is simply a technique of procuring rabbits, no more no less, and a very simple technique at that. Anyone can learn to train a dog to lamp and while it is obviously true that some people learn the technique more quickly and more professionally than others, it is such a simple skill that it is surprising that hunters boast of their ability as lampers.

Lamping is quite simply the shining of a beam of light around a field and encouraging a dog to run down that beam to pursue the animal thus illuminated. Running a dog to a lamping kit is probably a fairly recent practice—perhaps only a matter of 30 years old but running game in a beam of light, is an old hunting technique and it is likely that as soon as motor cars became fitted with headlamps someone realised their potential for hunting. Early lamping trips probably consisted of driving a car along a flat field in almost total darkness, flicking on the headlamps to full beam and slipping a dog at the rabbits sitting within the beam. One or two rabbits could be caught before the noise of the car put the game back for the rest of the night. Modern lamping devices are much more sophisticated but the principle is exactly the same.

There are a few cardinal rules which should be observed concerning lamping, and it should be added that since many lampers break these elementary rules, chaotic happenings occur. The first rule of lamping is like the Lewis Carroll rule, the most important. Never run more than one dog on a beam of light. Many lampers work two or more dogs and bizarre sights are not uncommon because of this. Yet the use of one dog is so totally logical that it is puzzling why it is not universal practice. Rabbits are the most commonly lamped game and any sight hound from whippet to wolfhound has speed enough to catch them. A single dog should therefore be used to lamp rabbits.

Sight hounds of all sorts from the tallest to the smallest can run at speeds up to 30 mph—a considerable speed by any standards and the cause of a considerable impact when two hounds collide, as they are wont to do in the darkness, either running down the beam or racing back into the glare of the lamp. Many lamping dogs sustain injury, sometimes fatal injuries this way. In fact, most lamping dogs treated by vets for fearful breakages, some of which incapacitate the dog for life, are injured because another one or two dogs were running loose at the time of the accident.

It is argued that the best way to start a puppy to lamp is to run it down the beam in the company of a grown dog, which is an experienced lamper. It is also a fact that such a method is a 100 per cent guaranteed way of stopping the grown dog working properly. Not only will the puppy usually jostle the adult as it runs, or perhaps do more than jostle, as any veterinary surgeon will probably attest, but the presence of a young dog, eagerly snatching a rabbit from the jaws of a mature, trained catch dog, will not improve the grown dog's retrieving ability. Nothing looks worse, nothing looks more amateurish than the sight of a dog carrying a rabbit back to hand with a puppy lunging at it and trying to snatch its prey. Nothing is as likely to ruin a good retriever as this and nothing is more certain to produce a damaged rabbit carcass than another dog plucking at it.

Running two dogs in a beam of light therefore, is little short of a recipe for disaster, a certain method of ruining one or both of the dogs. Yet it is amazing how many people adopt this method in order to secure the capture of one rabbit, as if two dogs are twice as likely to catch a rabbit as one dog. It just is not the case.

The second cardinal rule of lamping, and once again this rule is broken with great regularity, is 'never run unknown country after dark'. A daytime coursing dog not infrequently comes to grief, running country relatively well-known to it. Injuries such as broken legs, damaged shoulders and more complicated and dangerous accidents are relatively common in running dogs, for, as has been mentioned, when a 30 mph body meets an immovable object like a gatepost or a tree stump, something literally has to give and the something is always a portion of the dog's anatomy. Run the same dog over country unknown to it, though well known to the quarry, and the injuries are tenfold, for hares and rabbits alike, seek refuge in some strange places when pursued by a dog. Now take away the all-important element of daylight and run the dog after dark in a country unknown to it and the lamper, but familiar to the quarry, and the result can be both predictable and horrific. Electric fences may not be firmly fixed enough to actually behead a dog, but they will sometimes break the dog's neck. These fences will seem invisible at the end of a beam of light. Barbed-wire fences litter the countryside. A dog brushing against a tine will sustain a slight rip perhaps. At 30 mph he may sustain an injury so large as to disembowel him. Eyes are gouged out all too easily and some animals 'tangled in barb' will resemble the victim of an assault by a chainsaw.

The British countryside is seldom flat and uninteresting as guide books would have us believe. Houses have been built with stone from nearby quarries and seldom are they completely filled in. Sometimes a shallow crater in the earth marks the spot where a quarry once existed and this may provide a slight pitfall for a dog walking over the land after dark but to a dog travelling at full speed after a rabbit, which may have a burrow in the top of the quarry, it may prove a death-trap. Deep, unfilled quarries are almost certain to bring a dog to grief, while tangles of rubbish, intertwined with rusted barbed wire are almost certain to be refuge places for fleeing rabbits. After dark even familiar countryside becomes dangerous to running dogs and unfamiliar country becomes a nightmare, causing injuries which are horrendous, wounds which would need the technology found only in futuristic films to repair them.

Walk around an area, scheduled to be lamped, during the daylight hours, when it is sensible policy to ascertain the presence of dangerous obstacles which cannot be seen by simply flashing a light around a field. Worse still, they are obviously invisible if an excited dog runs out of the beam, as many dogs are prone to do. Running new land 'blind', to use a lamping term, is madness. It is simple logic to see that it takes at least two years, possibly more, to rear and train a first-class lamping dog. To ruin such an animal, to make a hideous cripple out of a first-rate athlete, is a moment's work, when accidents can often be prevented by a little time spent in exploring the land to be lamped.

A lamping kit can either be purchased for around £30–£40, at the time of writing, or made up from scrapyard equipment for considerably less. Obviously properly constructed kits are usually a lot more efficient than Heath Robinson devices, but once again it has to be stressed that lamping is a fairly strenuous and often accident-prone affair for both the dog and lamper, and damage to the kit is not unknown. Hence a cheap home-made affair, while it is not particularly efficient and foolproof, is nevertheless expendable and can usually be replaced by another visit to a scrapyard.

A simple lamping kit, devoid of frills and expensive extras, can be made by wiring up a quartz halide spotlamp to a battery of sorts. A 12-volt motorcycle battery is light and easy to carry, but only has a very limited life, needing to be recharged after an hour or so of use. A car battery has a considerably longer life but is so heavy that anyone carrying such a kit would need a course of steroids before embarking on a lamping trip. Motorbike batteries purchased new and ready to use cost in the vicinity of £20, at the time of writing, and modern ones are both light and robust. If kept topped up with distilled water (and spillage is frequent during lamping trips) they will last indefinitely, but allowed to empty of distilled water, soon corrode and become useless. Such a battery is best placed in a cut down gallon-sized plastic container packed with rolled up newspaper between the battery and the sides, to act as a buffer against shock. Spillage from a battery is acidic—albeit a dilute sulphuric acid—but corrosive enough to eat through a pair of jeans or a plastic-type anorak. A buffered plastic container prevents damage to the battery and damage to one's clothes. Frequent checks on the padding are needed as the newspaper becomes saturated with the battery acid and, covered in salts of sulphuric acid, ceases to be an effective buffer. The battery should be checked nightly for any drop in the level of the acidic solution and should be kept topped up with distilled water. Distilled water can be made from the ice covering the inside of a deep freeze, but the melting of the ice provides little water and is rather false economy, as distilled water can be purchased very cheaply from local garages. A battery does need constant checking to ensure a long life however, and at the end of the lamping season—roughly about March, for pregnant doe rabbits and hares tend to be caught after that date—the battery cannot be simply discarded. The plates within the battery need always to be covered with fluid to ensure that the battery functions properly.

Electrical connections must be checked regularly, particularly on home-made lamping kits. Lamping equipment sustains more bumps, knocks and damp conditions than most electricals and the connections often part company or corrode badly. The sight of a dog running an exciting chase after rabbit in a beam of light and the whole scene being reduced to inky blackness when connections fail, will convince the lamper how important regular checks on equipment are. It should also be noted that while a battery can be modified, replaced or repaired, a dog is a little more difficult to patch up after a collision in pitch blackness. Vigilance regarding the checking of a battery can prevent breakdown of services and also breakages to the limbs of one's dog.

To lamp regularly one requires not only a lamping kit, but also a battery charger. This must be attached to the battery and then plugged in at the mains. Avoid touching the terminals together when the battery charger is plugged in. The gas being released from the battery is an explosive mixture of hydrogen and oxygen, and while only a tiny amount of the gaseous mixture is generated, batteries have been known to explode from time to time. Leave the battery to recharge in a quiet place where it is unlikely to be damaged while it is charging.

Lamps have improved dramatically over the last few years and now immensely powerful beams are available, lamps which emit a light of 100,000 candle power. It is questionable if such a powerful beam is normally needed and claims that it can illuminate a spot nearly a mile distant are irrelevant to the issue. No dog would be sent to chase a rabbit that appeared so far away. The beam obviously has its advantages. It lights up the entire field with ease, but while it is essential to have such a beam when night ratting with a terrier pack one might question as to whether such a beam aids a single lamping sight hound chasing a rabbit which has a mere 40 yard advantage. A point against such a powerful beam must be the fact that it literally drains the battery of its power in minutes and can exhaust a heavy car battery in less time than one would imagine. As a security aid the lamp is a marvellous innovation, but its use as a lamping device for night hunting is somewhat questionable.

The less light a lamp emits, the slower it drains the power from a battery. Conversely the more powerful a beam, the more power the beam drains from the battery. Somewhere there has to be a happy medium; a lamp which is moderately powerful, but drains a battery fairly slowly. Such a lamping kit can give a good night's lamping if it is used carefully and allowed to charge up a little between 'runs'.

Some lampers tend to use a curbed beam for night-time hunting in preference to the conventional type lamps. This customised lamp is simply an ordinary lamp, the perimeter of which is either painted in with black lacquer or fitted with a circle of black card or plastic, the centre of which has been removed to allow light to pass only through a three-inch circle. Such a lamp emits a thin beam of light which illuminates the rabbit well enough to enable the dog to see it but the beam has little spread. This type of beam is said not to disturb the rest of the rabbits feeding nearby but to say that it reduces the disturbance somewhat, would be more accurate. Whether or not the sound of a dog running down the field causes more disturbance than a fine pencil-thin beam of light is a bit debatable, but some lampers swear by such 'customised' lamps. Many night-time poachers use such a piece of equipment, as the beam is said to attract less attention than a floodlit field. Again this point is open to question. Whereas a floodlit field may be the result of illumination by the headlamps of a car, a pencil-thin beam of light is such an unusual occurrence that many keepers would leave their beds to investigate the sight. However, a light of any sort flickering unevenly around a field is certainly not the least conspicuous of actions, and unauthorised lamping of any sort is usually investigated immediately by landowners these days.

Any breed of sight hound can be trained to lamp, or rather work with the lamp would be a more accurate statement. Small hounds, such as very tiny whippets, have only a limited vision because of their small stature, and allowance for this must be made, but they often make splendid lamping dogs. However, certain types of dogs are obviously better than others for this sort of work. If one is to elaborate on the qualities of the ideal lamping dog the following points must be considered. An ideal lamp dog must have the following qualities:

(a) some speed to outpace the quarry;
(b) rapid response reaction to return to the lamper immediately after the quarry is caught or missed;
(c) retrieving ability;
(d) stamina;
(e) a controllable nose—a curious quality that needs some explanation;
(f) a light running style, if possible;
(g) some intelligence to be able to predict and outsmart the quarry.

Lamping dogs do not require a phenomenal turn of speed to catch rabbits, though a somewhat more speedy dog is better if hares are to be caught. Breeds other than sight hounds do, in fact, make passable lamping dogs. Collies—long-in-the-leg-type hill collies—are easily able to outrun rabbits on the lamp and other dogs such as German shepherd dogs often make a reasonable, though not particularly good show of catching on the beam. Obviously there are horses for courses and sight hounds, particularly sight hound derivatives, do better than most breeds, but providing the rabbit to be run is chosen carefully—not too far out, not too close to the hedge or warren, reasonably athletic breeds and crosses make a passable show at lamping. Cunning or a sort of undefined acquired hunting intellect is perhaps a far more important quality than speed. Good hauls of rabbit are often made by very old dogs, dogs long past their best, simply because they have acquired some archaic knowledge of rabbit behaviour and more to the point, know how to cope with this. Rabbits usually run for home when danger threatens and head for their warrens fairly quickly. Some tend to squat, to sit ears back to the head, in the impression that if they remain motionless they will escape detection. If the land on which the rabbits live is lamped infrequently, the greater the incidence of these squatters. Conversely land lamped regularly is thinned of rabbits with this inclination, and a flash of light will cause most rabbits to head for the warren without further ado. Experienced dogs learn how to cope with squatters the presence of which is indicated only by an outline and a fiery red eye which glows in the beam of light. These are picked up easily and without much effort. Indeed, a dog which learns the technique of walking up to squatters and picking them up as they sit—before the rabbits decide that squatting is not such a good idea and run for home—will secure a good and easy catch in newly lamped territory. A fast dog, or a dog with more exuberance than sense, may well cause squatters to throw their ears upright and run for home. Squatters seldom perform the same caper more than once, for obvious reasons, and those which escape capture seem to learn from the experience. If a fast dog was all that was required in a lamping dog, the most obvious choice would be a pure-bred sprint-track greyhound. Other qualities are far more important than speed, however.

A rapid response to command is one of those qualities. Dogs which miss the quarry and spend minutes peering into a hedge, in which a warren is situated, are unproductive, as is a dog which runs, head down, following the scent of other rabbits and thwarted sight hounds of any breed can display very keen olfactory senses in such situations. The fault is perhaps inbred—salukis are often very reluctant to acknowledge the game has escaped and seem to believe it can be caught by a little extra effort. This 'switching off to command' mechanism which is fairly characteristic of salukis—the somewhat glazed stare which follows an urgent command by the trainer and the second or so delay before that command is obeyed—is difficult to eradicate in salukis or saluki hybrids and must be tolerated or, alternatively, the dog simply rejected as a hunting companion. Sagar of the Saluki Club believes that after a time the dyed-in-the-wool saluki addict tends to overlook such minor failings, but the slow return to hand certainly reduces the value of a dog as a lamping companion and often infuriates the lamper. A dog which misses its quarry should return to hand straight away. Puppies should be taught to return to command instantly and refresher courses given every day, particularly in areas where the heavy scent of game abounds. A dog, which seeks about after a fruitless run or runs head down on scent tracks, will put other rabbits back to ground by its actions. Instant response to command is essential in a first-rate lamping dog. Tension is usually fairly high during a night's lamping, and a recalcitrant dog is likely to produce a bad response from the lamper.

Retrieving is obviously of paramount importance amongst the qualities a good lamp dog should possess and an otherwise efficient lamp dog which kills or catches and stands over its quarry, refusing to return it to hand, is not to be prized. Retrieving is so easily taught to a puppy that a non-retrieving dog is symptomatic of bad training. Dogs which catch, start to return the quarry to hand only to circle the owner just out of reach, moving ever further out each time the owner tries to take the catch are equally annoying, though this behaviour is a little more understandable. Such dogs have usually been worked with other dogs which have at some time in their lives either snatched at the catch or menaced them. A reluctance to bring the catch to hand is a clear indication that the cardinal rules of retrieving training have been broken. It is a difficult fault to correct and an impossible one if the trainer persists in taking another dog along with the lamping party. Some dogs become so reluctant to retrieve that they will refuse to return the catch to anyone in the group except the trainer—a questionable quality, but an indication that the trainer should avoid lamping parties like a plague. A dog that displays these qualities is clearly a one person, one dog sort of animal and lampers other than the trainer should not try to make the dog relinquish its catch. Dogs which circle the owner or are slow to bring the catch to hand can sometimes be improved if the trainer walks away when the dog begins to circle him with its catch, but this method of correcting a fault is by no means infallible. Faults which begin to manifest themselves because of poor or misguided training are never easily put right. If possible avoid having another dog running loose or even kept on a slip when lamping. Despite the typical lamping element which tends to enjoy going everywhere as a group rather than singly, lamping is really a one person, one dog exercise.

The term stamina, its true meaning, its nature and the biological make-up of a dog which manifests it has always been debated and will continue to be so, as no real definition of the term has yet been offered. Some dogs put so much effort into running quarry on the lamp that they are exhausted after a few runs. Light-framed and also very heavy dogs tend to get really exhausted quite quickly, yet salukis have a reputation for having immense reserves and are amongst the most lightly built of all sight hounds. Style of running, or rather running style, perhaps has much to do with apparent stamina. A greyhound or a whippet, for instance, will propel itself like wildfire at any suitable quarry in a muscle-straining, fibre-testing burst of speed. No dog can run using this style of movement for a length of time; muscle tissue simply will not tolerate it. Salukis lope with an economic style of movement, a movement possibly developed over tens of thousands of years to facilitate the bringing down of gazelle, desert hare and other long distance athletic type mammals. A loping style of running can be sustained for a length of time without the dog collapsing with exhaustion. Greyhounds which manifested this style of running were certainly bred out when competitive coursing and racing began, as it was not conducive to winning a competitive event. How important stamina is to the lamping sight hound is another moot point. Lurcher breeders are often approached by lamping enthusiasts with demands for a dog which is capable of taking a hundred rabbits a night and tales of catches of this nature abound amongst the lurcher fraternity. However, once again it is wise to examine such tales in the light of reason. A catch of around 100 rabbits a night for a week or so requires either an unusually big and productive lamping area, or what is more likely, an incredibly fertile imagination. A haul of 500 rabbits a week would tax the resources of a very large estate, and estates which had such populations of rabbits would allow a keeper to obtain his perks from snaring and trapping such numbers rather than permit an amateur lamper to make nightly forays on the place. Perhaps hauls of 100 rabbits in a night can be taken just now and again, but catches of this nature would reduce a very productive area to a rabbit desert in no time. Consider yet another fact concerning these colossal hauls. Assuming a dog is required to run 100 yards to catch and retrieve each rabbit, and for the sake of argument, assume that such is the lamper's skill, and the dexterity of his dog, that it catches two out of every three rabbits he runs. A fascinating formula emerges; a dog takes 100 rabbits in 150 runs, each of 100 yards and so a night's catch entails a distance of 15,000 yards being run, a distance of roughly $8\frac{1}{4}$ miles run at roughly 30 mph. A greyhound is exhausted after long distance races of 800 yards, and a greyhound is run at a peak of physical fitness, a peak seldom achieved by amateur lurcher buffs. The '100 a night' claims come a little amiss at this point. A dog run at this pitch would not last long before collapsing and dying—as indeed it has to be admitted do a great many lurchers—but a great many more would suffer the same fate if 100 rabbits a night were run by dogs. Incidentally the figures and distances quoted do not allow for walking between fields or the exploration of unproductive fields by man and dog. Clearly claims of 100 a night belong to the realms of fairy tales. Few hauls exceed a dozen rabbits in the course of an entire night's hunting. At the time of writing, the country is grossly over-hunted by lurcher owners. At one time the presence of a lurcher in a district indicated that the owner was a man to be watched. Now so many lurchers are worked that it would require the vigilance of the Danites to watch lurcher owners. If each of these dogs killed only 30 rabbits in a season the reduction of the rabbit population would be more dramatic than it was at the advent of myxomatosis. In the light of all this it should be clear that while stamina might be a desirable quality in a sight hound it is by no means an essential feature. Most sight hounds have enough stamina to provide a good evening's entertainment and lamping is simply that—an entertainment, not a livelihood.

Some lampers seem to live in a world of extreme exaggeration and the most exaggerated claim is 'I live from the catches of my lurchers' or more fashionably, but even less exactly, 'my lurcher pays the mortgage'—a statement which when explored usually means, 'the DHSS pay my mortgage and I enjoy a night's lamping'. These extraordinary claims present a further mathematical improbability—namely the number of rabbits which need to be caught to allow the lamper to make a living. The majority of lampers who make such spurious or ridiculous claims are unemployed and in receipt of DHSS benefits, so that statements to the effect that this person 'lamps to live' are clearly a little awry. Britain is quite a pleasant country in which to live, for while the unemployment benefit certainly does not allow a claimant to trip the light fantastic, it is enough to prevent him from starving. Furthermore, the DHSS pay the interest on mortgages if the person is unemployed. Politics, jingoism and the activities of the DHSS aside, let us now explore the economics behind the statement, 'my lurcher keeps me and my family' or similar claptrap comments. Let us assume that the minimum basic income a lamper expects to make is £100 a week or £5,000 per annum, and let us disregard the money paid in by the DHSS, for few lampers declare the profits of their night's exploits anyway.

So the required income or salary set, the sale of rabbits (at £1 a head for convenience) automatic—which it rarely is—our first problem presents itself. Rabbits are unsaleable from March to September partly because of custom (the British public doesn't eat rabbits during the summer months) and partly because rabbits are often pregnant during this period (and the thought of eating a pregnant rabbit even divested of foetuses is repugnant to most Britons). Hence for perhaps six months of the year rabbits are unsaleable. So the lamper must secure his 5,000 rabbits in the remaining six months—well it is just possible, or is it? A haul of 5,000 rabbits has therefore to be taken in roughly 200 days of lamping, a matter of 25 rabbits a night—which perhaps doesn't seem too outrageous—that is until one goes one step further in the indepth examination of the subject.

Not every night is a suitable lamping night for lamping can only be conducted when there are reasonably good conditions and such conditions are usually bad conditions. If that sounds a shade Irish, it is necessary to elaborate. Lamping nights need to be dark moon-free nights preferably with a strong wind to deaden the sound of footfall and with a slight stinging rain to add to the physical discomfort and aid the lamper to be able to slip his dog at a suitable distance from the rabbit. Thus at least six nights of each month are going to be too light to run rabbits—a further 36 should be deducted from the 200 lampable days. Subtract perhaps a further 10 days for heavy snows or ground frozen so solid that it would be madness to run a dog in such conditions. Few lampers venture out in blinding rain and few rabbits are enthusiastic about feeding in these conditions either. So perhaps deduct a further 10 days from the original 200 lampable days. The lamper now has roughly 150 nights to catch the necessary 5,000 rabbits to make a living or to equal the income of the lowest paid worker in Britain. Well 5,000 divided by 150 works out at 33 rabbits a night, every night of the 150 days available. Dogs sometimes go lame, cars refuse to start and, horror of horrors, the dead nights, nights when no rabbits can be caught, are known to all lampers. Perhaps the 33 rabbits a night should be increased to perhaps 50 rabbits to make the sum more realistic, and it should be borne in mind that the lamper must be able to go each night and every night to places where this number are available. One small point that the arithmetic shown has not taken into consideration—some rabbits will be damaged and others so diseased as to be unsaleable—but let us be charitable and deny that carcass damage and rabbit disease will dog the footsteps of the lamper. The prospect of earning even a pittance from the lamping looks tough, the prospect of earning a living is unlikely. Thus tales of lurchers paying the mortgage are a little ludicrous and ridiculous or beyond belief, if the truth is told. A lamper will earn pocket-money through his hobby, no more, no less, but then as has been mentioned the state is seldom keen on inflicting hardship on a person. The myth of the professional lamper has now been exploded fully. Let us return to the qualities which a dog should manifest to be a satisfactory lamper and the reader will perhaps forgive the slight digression.

It now becomes necessary to explain the somewhat peculiar phrase—a controllable nose—and this will be a shade more difficult than the debunking of lurchermen's lies. Sight hounds are so called because they usually prefer to hunt by sight and not because they have little or no sense of smell. A lurcher, a composite of two or more breeds, will usually enter a field, sight hunt for a moment or so, gazing head high around the field before putting its nose down to sniff out the possible presence of huntable quarry. An all-purpose hunting dog of any sort must use both nose and eyes to seek out quarry. A sight hound which does not 'hunt up' can scarcely be classed as all-purpose, a lurcher which does not is only 'half complete'. A sight hound with a good nose is useful, but the use of that nose must be regulated by the trainer. A dog which runs game by scent after dark may or may not be successful, but a dog which exercises the same skill while lamping is certainly not required. A beam illuminates the quarry and straightway the hound must forget hunting with its nose and concentrate on the quarry revealed by the beam of light. A dog which is still sniffing at a scent when held on a leash, while the beam is switched on, is neither efficient nor to be desired. Many hunters who specialise in lamping, rather than daytime hunting, prevent a dog from using its nose, deterring it from scent hunting, keeping it on a leash most of the time and nudging it with a knee movement should it show any inclination to use its sense of smell. Longdogs are more easily curbed than true lurchers however, for lurchers are, by definition, sight hounds ameliorated with other blood to create a more versatile animal (i.e. to give intelligence, nose and tractability). More irritating still is the sight of a dog which, having lost its prey, runs head down to seek out other quarry running each and every rabbit back to cover for the rest of the night. It has been said that a good lamping lurcher never 'hunts up'. 'Never' is a terribly exacting word which should always be used sparingly. An all-round hunting dog of course 'hunts up', but a night hunter or lamper does not or rather should not. A lamping dog must be under control before and after it runs and must obey commands to return to hand immediately and without question. To train a dog to this level is not easy and is certainly a very lengthy process. It can be done, however, although its reinforcement does require control and frequent refresher courses. A dog kept exclusively for lamping could theoretically be trained never to use its nose. Daytime hunting then becomes a matter simply of slipping the dog at quarry as soon as it is sighted. The prospect of owning a dog that is kept exclusively for sight hunting is not a particularly exciting one though.

A light running style is a statement that also needs a little explaining. Most sight hounds run exceedingly fast but make a considerable noise while running. Size or weight seems to have little to do with this, but the sound of pounding feet certainly telegraphs the presence of a dog to the rabbits feeding in a field. Oddly enough no lurcher enthusiast seems to pay much attention to the style of running favoured by a dog, but it must have considerable bearing on the amount of quarry taken. Puppies from the same litter develop an amazing variety of styles of running, ranging from the light-footed dog that moves with a series of silent bounds to the heavy-footed dog which moves equally as fast but more noisily. Strangely enough some of the finest competitive coursing longdogs generate a fair amount of noise while running, yet come upon the quarry quickly and efficiently. Nevertheless a silent runner must obviously be the best type of lamping dog, particularly if the lamper is not exactly welcome on the land he is running!

To define canine intelligence is certainly not easy, and while sight hounds do not occupy the upper IQ bracket of the canine intelligentsia, after a while they begin to understand the quarry they are encouraged to chase and catch in an almost uncanny way. A saluki longdog gets on the wavelength of the hares it pursues after a year or so (longdogs are rarely early starters or should never be allowed to be early starters when coursing), predicting the way it turns and learning to strike and pick up that most elusive quarry. A lamp dog from any breed of sight hound worked regularly by a sane and sensible lamping enthusiast anticipates the ways of rabbits and hares in the most amazingly perspicacious way. It is strange how many lurcher enthusiasts ('enthusiasts' is a bit of a questionable word) will willingly sell a slightly over-the-hill dog as soon as they consider it is getting a shade too long in the tooth. As a lamp dog ages, it acquires startling skills to compensate for its increasing age. Some learn to cut off rabbits before they reach sanctuary, others learn the technique of walking up the beam to pick up squatters—this strange walking-stalking movement cannot be taught. It is a skill dogs either acquire or do not. Ironically dogs with a lot of sight hound blood (pure-bred sight hounds or longdogs) seem to acquire this unique method of catching as quickly as collie-bred lurchers—perhaps it is the racial memory of times when the ancestors of sight hounds walk-stalked quarry on some savannah or steppe.

Dogs which are over the hill, however, often develop a hard mouth or more simply damage the quarry they retrieve to hand, although hard mouths can be developed in other ways. A hound run to a state of exhaustion is likely to kill and damage its catch, as it learns that an inert and lifeless creature is less trouble to carry than a live and kicking one. On the subject of kicking, hares are seldom retrieved alive by dogs. The very effort a dog exerts to hold a violently kicking and struggling hare usually kills the creature. A hard mouth should be avoided if at all possible, for the value of a carcass diminishes if the flesh is bruised or punctured. Running an elderly dog, an unfit dog, a tired dog suffering from the effects of too many runs that night, all conspire to produce a dog that realises that it is easier to kill its catch than to retrieve it live and unharmed to hand.

It is possible to secure a large haul of rabbits by lamping, a far larger haul than can be caught during daylight hours as a rule. This is not because the rabbits sit mesmerised in the beam allowing themselves to be picked up by the dog, though this seems to be the opinion of the general public, whose knowledge of night hunting techniques seems to be a brief encounter with a panic-stricken rabbit illuminated by the headlights of a car. Rabbits simply do not wait around to be caught. When danger threatens they run for home, daytime or night, and as rabbits are more nocturnal than diurnal, their velocity at night must easily equal that of a daytime run. The fact is that few rabbits feed far from their warrens during daylight hours. Some may chance a morning or an afternoon feeding session, but these rabbits usually nibble the dry grass stalks near the warren possibly to obtain bulk rather than nutritious grass. After darkness the rabbits stroll out of their warrens to feed on better provender and, more to the point, further afield—100 yards is not too far from a warren for a rabbit to seek a new supply of food. There is little chance of a sight hound catching many rabbits during the daylight hours (though a few can be taken)—as rabbits are very dexterous at racing the few yards near the warren to sanctuary. After darkness, the spurt to home is sometimes considerably longer and here a hound gains advantage points. Few hounds have the speed of a rabbit over a short distance—to use modern automobile parlance 0–24 mph in a few seconds flat—but, once the dog has attained his top speed, few sight hounds are out-paced by rabbits—although it must be stressed many dogs are clearly out-manoeuvred. Hence, during the hours of darkness, hounds are able to gather full speed to pursue rabbits which are feeding a fair way from home. Dogs will often catch rabbits after dark without the aid of a lamp, though most runs are invariably unproductive and sometimes very hazardous for rabbits are well-adapted to a nocturnal way of life. To obtain even a respectable catch of rabbits, a lamp has to be used to assist the hound to make its catch. Despite the claims of lurcher enthusiasts, many of whom cherish the image of the competent Victorian poacher and his esoteric skills, lamping can be learned by anyone with half the intellect of a gibbon. It simply is not the great skill that many stalwarts claim it to be, though it can involve one or two adjacent skills to enable the lamper to make a larger catch.

LAMPING

In its simplest form, lamping consists of finding a place where rabbits are known to feed, waiting for a moonless windy night for obvious reasons, going to the fields where the rabbits are feeding, shining a beam around the field and allowing the dog to chase and possibly catch the rabbits illuminated by the lamp. This is clearly an over-simplification of matters, but it is certainly not a gross over-simplification. Lamping is not a complex skill and, if further proof is needed, a conversation with a typical lamper will convince the reader that lamping is neither a great skill or an art. Anyone can learn it, and more to the point, anyone can teach any physically capable breed of dog to catch rabbits on the lamp.

Young sight hounds are, in fact, best started on the lamp. Game is more abundant by night, feeding further from home and therefore more likely to afford the hound a run, if not a catch. It may take several nights to convince the hound that game is more likely to appear in the beam than in the heavily scented grass around its feet, but once the hound understands that this is so, basic lamping skill is virtually complete. Once the dog is prepared to follow the beam with its eyes and pursue the game in the beam then 90 per cent of its training is over.

To get the dog to accept that the beam of light is its ally is perhaps a shade more difficult. Some dogs, even bright, normally fast-learning lurchers, tend to prefer to sniff around rather than watch the beam. Hence lamping, or, at least, preliminary lamping training, should be conducted with the dog on a quick release slip which can consist of either an elaborate coursing slip or a piece of binder twine under the dog's collar or around its neck for collars should not be worn by a dog which is running after quarry. A dog worked free, or more accurately, an untrained dog worked free, is likely to chase every rabbit in sight, regardless of its chance of catching them. Hence a dog about to start lamping should be kept in 'tight' with a slip lead until it has learned to stay at heel until it is required to chase. Elaborate coursing slips are not really necessary and are so easily lost that the majority of experienced lampers invariably use cheap and inexpensive equipment. It is said that tyro golfers start out golfing with every conceivable club and aid to golfing, but as time goes on discard most of their equipment and treat it as superfluous; likewise the typical lamper. The loss rate of lamping accoutrements is staggering, and expensive to replace. Thus the lamper should start out cheaply and add only that which is totally necessary to facilitate a night's lamping.

A young dog is most easily started if it is allowed to see another dog chase and preferably catch within the beam of light. The sound of running feet, however light, is bound to interest any running dog and the dog will invariably watch the beam which is the source of the activity. The disadvantage is, of course, that the dog chasing the quarry in the beam is required to catch and bring back its quarry to the lamper, who has an eager or perhaps a frantic puppy on the slip. If a grown dog is allowed to be used as a training aid for any length of time, it is almost inevitable its retrieving qualities will suffer. The adult may, in extreme circumstances, simply refuse to retrieve—though this is fairly uncommon. What is more likely is that the older training dog will simply return almost to hand and tantalisingly circle the trainer, who with his puppy on slip is faced with the problem of trying to divest the training dog of its catch while not releasing the straining eager puppy. To allow the dog on the slip a lunge or worse still a snatch at the rabbit (this is not unknown as a quasi-training method) is utter madness. Nothing is more likely to create a bad relationship between hounds of the chase than deliberately fermenting jealousy. The circling action, the most maddening of all hunting dog faults, is almost certain to result. The whole process looks bad, messy, untidy and should not be allowed to develop, let alone tolerated.

Sooner or later a young dog will be frantic to run quarry that appears in the beam of light and should be allowed to chase and, with luck, catch the rabbits.

The correct age for starting a dog depends a lot on the breed. Large sight hounds are gangling giants until their second birthday, so perhaps eighteen months would be the correct age to consider teaching such a sapling the use of the lamp. A lurcher may be started younger, about twelve months of age seems to be the optimum time to start a collie or Bedlington terrier hybrid. Longdogs may display the desire to chase considerably earlier, but a dog of this breeding is likely to get physically damaged (heart and lung injuries are common) if allowed to strain itself at this age. The reader must shut his ears to talk at lurcher shows of four-month-old dogs catching well on the lamp. Such prodigies are usually offered for sale within their first year and have developed physical disorders and mental hang-ups because of their early entering. A working sight hound should be a dog for life. There is no merit in starting a dog too young if its working life is to be curtailed by physical and mental injuries. Conversations heard during a visit to a lurcher show should be treated with some reservation. Much bad advice is proffered there and many are the lies that are told.

A lamping dog should be run sparingly during its first season no matter how available the quarry, no matter how tempting it is to take one more rabbit. A hound is simply not a machine, capable of an indefinite number of runs night after night. Once a dog shows signs of weariness while out lamping, the night's work for that dog, at least, is over. Physical fitness, according to Kurt Hahn, can be measured by the length of time an animal or man takes to recover from a set of physical exercises. If a dog is panting heavily and is slow to recover, stop—and do not restart that night. Should a hound obviously be strained by its attempts to pick up a rabbit which is illuminated by the beam, do not continue. Simply pack up and go home. Do not run the dog again that night. A wheezing sound from the dog's thoracic cavity should indicate the lamper has run the dog too hard and done damage—an indication that he should have ceased running the dog minutes before. No dog should be run until it passes out or keels over while hunting on the lamp and a trainer who allows this to happen is a poor one indeed. Lurcher training is at a very low level in Britain and many of the people who own such hounds are not really fit to keep dogs of any sort. Boasts of having run dogs to death are all too commonly heard. Such stories may elevate the teller in his fellow fools' eyes but, to the thinking man, such a person is a crass and brutal amateur, unable to read the tell-tale signs, which indicate a running dog has had enough and is far from well.

Lamping dogs should be run with empty bellies—a dog should have had its last meal 12 hours before a gruelling lamping session. A dog run on a full stomach is at a serious disadvantage when trying to keep up with a fleeing rabbit, or worse still, a hare. Lurchers should be fed on arrival from a lamping session as soon as the dog has recovered from its exertions and is behaving and breathing normally. This is perhaps the very best time to tell how the exertions of the night have affected the dog. A dog, which has been run hard but sensibly, should eat its food voraciously before sleeping soundly—a sleep of the just perhaps! A dog which is unenthusiastic about its food after a night's lamping is ill and needs rest, and possibly veterinary attention. A lamping dog will usually sleep soundly for a few hours before leaping about enthusiastically in its kennel. A dog, which sleeps the day through, scarcely moving a muscle, but breathing deeply, is not ready for another night's lamping and is, in fact, decidedly unwell. Avoid, at all costs, spontaneous lamping trips planned on the spur of the moment, ventures when the dog has been fed or is obviously tired. Many dogs are injured as the result of these ill-planned ventures. If one is invited to a lamping session, it is the trainer's duty to make sure his dog will give of its best. If the dog is unwell or recently fed the trainer should say so, and decline the offer no matter what the outcome of his refusal.

It is staggering how many lamping dogs are bought and sold simply because they have sustained injuries while lamping. Dogs which are apparently hale and hearty, but which pass out after a hard run, are all too commonly sold as 'sound' only to be killed as a result of the first strenuous lamping session. Blown dogs—a curious euphemism for dogs, which have sustained injury because of heart, lung or diaphragm damage—are also regulars on the transfer list and once again sold as 'sound'. Bad management becomes all the more obvious when one realises that sight hounds are perhaps the most physically perfect of all types of dogs and consequently fairly easy to condition and run at physical peak. Some lurcher enthusiasts are amongst the least capable of dog trainers and simply pass on dogs as soon as they are damaged by mismanagement. More amazing still is the sale of a lamping lurcher, which is past its best, but has given half a lifetime of good service. Such a dog, once sold, is destined to pass from home to home, each home more seedy than the last, each owner less caring. Dogs which serve well have the right to an old age lived in some comfort and dignity.

Lamping dogs of course can really only be made totally fit by actual lamping work although the body building adage 'there is no gain without pain' should certainly be treated with some care, for once a dog strains a muscle, rest is necessary and during that period of rest a dog loses its original fitness. A few days of exercise chasing a ball, playing with the trainer or another dog in a large field will usually get a dog well enough to start the season at some level of physical fitness. Lure chasing—running a dog at a mechanical hare—may be advantageous, but a far better piece of equipment to exercise a dog is a rubber ball. The ball thrown at the ground bounces and the dog will usually enjoy catching it. The bouncing action of a ball is attractive to most dogs and the hound's attempts to catch the ball will improve its coordination as well as its physical fitness. A wall adjacent to a grass field is an ideal training spot for the grass surface then buffers any injury the dog might receive when leaping after the ball.

Rabbits, of course, are the lampers' meat and hares are regarded as mixed blessings by some. Second-rate lamping dogs, or rather second-rate coursing dogs which would not so much as 'bend' a hare (cause it to exert itself) will catch them if assisted by a lamp. A strong hare, one which has bettered the very best coursing dogs during a season, is often brought down by an indifferent lurcher aided by a lamp. Hares seem to run berserk in the beam, often heading for the lamper's beam when a dog gets behind them. Most lampers can relate tales of hares crashing into their legs or feet while being chased and few have not caught a hare by simply pushing out a foot in front of the passing creature. The circuitous route followed by hares is often their downfall and if hares pass through a hedge when pursued by the lamper's dog the chances are that if the lamp is held on the hedge the hare will usually return to the field on which it has been run.

Hares are hardly the most profitable creatures to lamp even though a second-rate coursing dog can catch one 'on the lamp'. A really top-rate hare scarcely injured by a dog will fetch perhaps £2.50 from a domestic sale and less from a game dealer, whereas the same dealer may offer as much as £1 a piece for rabbits which can be captured with only a fraction of the physical effort. Hare meat is rich and bloody (the reasons for this have been explained) and it is not to everyone's taste and hence it is not easy to find a domestic buyer for a carcass. Rabbits are now becoming quite easy to dispose of, though after myxomatosis the meat became very unfashionable. More to the point, hares exhaust dogs which capture them, and after taking two hares many dogs look as if they would prefer to be at home. The same dogs would still be ready to run again after catching perhaps a dozen rabbits. Thus, some lampers simply switch off the lamp and deny the dog the run when a hare becomes illuminated by the beam. There is a lot to be said for leaving hares for daytime coursing when they give the best sport and almost always escape capture. Indifferent dogs can catch hares when aided by a lamp.

Deer, as has been mentioned, are strictly forbidden quarry after dark. In other words the hunting of deer must cease one hour after dark until one hour before light—the terms dark and light are indicated by official lighting-up times. Deer are not difficult animals to bring down with a lamping lurcher if that lurcher is so inclined, but the subject of taking deer—and the subsequent punishment for offenders—is a shadowy one. Indifferent coursing dogs are certainly capable of slaying deer 'after dark' though there are very obvious problems regarding the right to take deer on certain areas of land. Poachers who stick to rabbit and hare catching are seldom treated too harshly by magistrates, even if apprehended in the act. The odd deer or so added to the night's bag makes a lot of difference to the way the courts treat offenders. The Attlingham Park slaughter of the early 1980s brought punishments of 18 months imprisonment apiece to the offenders and it should be noted that in Scotland, where deer are not regarded as legal quarry for dogs either by day or by night, punishments are likely to be even more severe. It is ludicrous to take a moralistic approach concerning the hunting of deer with a lamp or spotlight. Sufficient to say that a man may well lose 18 months of his freedom for a deer, the carcass of which is worth about £35!

Foxes are legal quarry, although the BFSS and allied bodies seem to regard their catching as the prerogative of registered fox hound packs. This anachronistic attitude was voiced by them in August 1981 and the statement issued was certainly no membership booster for the society. Since that date there seems to have been no official condemnation of the taking of foxes with lurchers.

Foxes are fairly taxing quarry for a lurcher, longdog or any breed of sight hound to tackle, though most breeds of running dog produce individuals which tackle them with great enthusiasm. Even the smaller sight hounds—the diminutive whippet for example—will often course them with great enthusiasm and spirit, although it is only fair for the lamper to race to the assistance of a small sight hound and despatch the captured fox quickly. Large sight hounds, such as borzois (which are reputed to have an in-built dislike of lupine and vulpine types alike) deerhounds and wolfhounds will usually despatch foxes fairly quickly, but even such large sight hounds should be assisted lest a course at a fox degenerates into a slogging match which can not only maul a fox but damage a hound quite badly.

The size of a sight hound is a mixed blessing and frankly the great size of some sight hounds is a little superfluous with regard to the catching of fox and other British quarry. Small lurchers and longdogs—23-inch dogs and smaller are often excellent fox catchers—and the courage of the dog, the very persistence of the hound counts a lot more than the pursuer's size. In fact the chasing of a fox along a narrow beam of light in a pitch black field is a pursuit that would favour a dog somewhat smaller than the giant hounds. A 25-inch hound is easily capable of taking a fox, providing the dog is so inclined.

Foxes are furtive creatures and their shy, cautious nature is often confused with intelligence. When pursued with a lamping beam and hound they simply turn their heads out of the beam, an action which causes their saucer-like eyes to disappear and unless the lamper plus hound is fairly nimble on his feet the fox will seem to disappear into thin air. A fox must be kept in view during the entire course if it is to be taken by the hound, but foxes are natural hedge skulkers, seldom keen to venture into the middle of the field unless it is obviously necessary or advantageous to the fox. It is therefore the lamper's duty to ensure the fox finds it to its benefit to explore the centre of the field and thereby offer a sporting course for the hound. Unless this sporting chance can be offered, dogs lamping foxes become rather frustrated.

Foxes can be persuaded to leave the sanctuary of the edges of the field by one of two methods. 'Squeaking in' is a popular way of encouraging foxes to come near enough to ensure a satisfactory slip. They react to a variety of calls, ranging from the squeal of a stricken rabbit to the call of a frightened hen. It seems doubtful if foxes are deceived by these cries, despite claims to the contrary and the fact that fox calls are sold commercially. A low rhythmic, repetitive clicking noise made by the lamper sucking air into his cheeks is equally effective. Foxes are naturally curious and investigate all unusual and repetitive sounds, providing the sound is not likely to indicate the presence of danger, or so loud that foxes are frightened by its decibel level. Clearly a human voice is likely to indicate the presence of danger and a shot is so loud as to frighten. A variety of sounds attract foxes to investigate, the click of two plastic bottles struck together at regular intervals attracts, whereas the tapping of a spoon on a glass vessel seems to fascinate, yet not quite enough to ensure the fox approaches closely to investigate. The mouth clicking action or the stricken rabbit cry is almost certain to bring in foxes, but a fox needs only to be fooled a few times to become extremely wary of such cries. An anxious fox, one which is curious but wary of approaching, is nearly impossible to run with hound and beam, but foxes can be drawn as close as 10 feet from the lurcher, providing the sound made by the caller is consistent and does not range too much in pitch and volume. At all times the dog must not only be controlled but kept silent, and this is easier said than done, where excited sight hounds are concerned. Dogs which have developed or acquired aversion to foxes are bound to become excited when they see their quarry actually approaching. This excitment may not manifest itself by barking, but the slightest squeal or the smallest murmur from the dog will frighten away the fox and before the beam can be flicked on the fox will have turned tail to run for safety.

Another way of persuading them to leave the shelter of the hedges is to spread evil-smelling flesh in the middle of the field, far from the protection of hedgerows. This really attracts foxes from a great distance and often amazes the hunter, when he realises how many foxes live in a seemingly fox-free district. Twelve or 13 foxes does not seem to be an excessive number to be attracted by thoroughly rank-smelling offal or a mixture of fish heads and meat. Other decoctions are used by hunters, including chemical fox attractants, which are popular in the USA. A pencil beam of light—an ordinary lamp (quartz halogen) painted in—should be flashed around the field to test the efficacy of the attractant, but the run must be accomplished with the use of a broad beam of light, for as stated, once a fox turns its head it becomes invisible in the beam.

Foxes will often follow a 'rabbit' for a mile or so, attracted not so much by the imitation squeals as by the curious sounds of the lamper and his dog. A lamp flashed behind the lamper from time to time will often illuminate the eyes of foxes. In country where lamping is uncommon, foxes will often run into the field to investigate the imitation squeals and, indeed, approach the dog until they realise the error of their ways. Few will come close enough to allow themselves to be caught, however, but some do make that error from time to time. No matter how often the land is lamped, foxes seem to follow to investigate the sight of a man lamping rabbits, but curiosity, while it apparently has a devastating effect on cats, seldom gets the better of a fox.

At one time, fox catching was fairly profitable as there was a good sale for top quality pelts, though inferior soiled, ragged or punctured pelts were worth little or nothing. During 1983 the European market for wild red fox pelts soared and wet skins (skins not dried board-hard or salted down with saltpetre, salt or other supposed cure-alls) sold for up to £25 a piece. Lamping foxes often became profitable, but the hunting of pelts is a desperately hard way of earning pocket-money, let alone a type of living. Very inclement weather is best for hunting foxes, nights of stinging sleet and desperately cold winds, and such weather devitalises dog and man producing a curious inertia at the end of the night's hunting, an inertia and a physical apathy not assuaged or alleviated by the success of the night's hunting.

One dog is necessary for procuring good pelts from foxes, and two or more dogs are a decided nuisance. Pelts are ragged and pulled apart by the combined effort of several dogs and torn or shredded pelts are worth little or nothing to the furrier. A dog required to catch 'pelts' must be quick off the mark, certain of strike and able to catch, pin and hold the fox for the hunter to race in and despatch the quarry. A running battle between dog and fox will usually result in the escape of the latter and damage to the dog, so the hunter much despatch the fox quickly, quietly and with the minimum cruelty or histrionics. A sharp hard blow on the neck will kill any fox, but the blow must be delivered deftly, not an easy task when it is writhing and biting and the hound is endeavouring to continue the battle. Still, the killing must be done humanely. The killing of foxes with lamp and sight hound is not favoured by the RSPCA or the BFSS, though the latter disapprove of the practice simply because the pursuit of foxes by sight hounds is furiously efficient and leaves little for registered packs to hunt. Indeed, in 1982, many packs of hounds outside the Lake District had very bad years, simply because the fox was literally exterminated from hunt country by lampers with fox-killing lurchers. The RSPCA have a somewhat better reason for disliking fox hunting with sight hounds. If the fox is not despatched quickly then some fairly savage scenes result and damage to dog and fox can be extreme.

Whatever, the best bait for luring foxes so that they may be lamped is certainly the cadaver of another fox. Cannibalism may be the reason for the fatal attraction of such carcasses to others of their kind. What is more likely is their natural curiosity for objects which they consider strange or odd smelling. A carcass of a fox killed by a fairly strenuous physical battle will emit a strong odour which must alert others for perhaps a mile from the scene of the battle, which certainly seem to wish to investigate the cause of the stink. Their attitude to the carcass of a fallen cousin is strange. Many will walk around the cadaver for a moment or two and then attempt to pull the corpse away. Others will lift a leg and spray the dead fox. Some approach, belly to the earth, cat-like, as though suspecting a trap. However, whatever the attitude to the dead body, live foxes find the corpse irresistible and come close enough to investigate. The result of such curiosity should be fairly predictable if the lamper is astute and the lurcher keen, sharp and, above all, silent. Rabbits will often race half-hearted for home once a dog yelps, but sometimes return to feed in minutes. Hares will high tail it into the night to run a circuitous trail only to return to the field an hour later, when they are startled by the yelp of a dog. Foxes seem much more sensitive to danger and once disturbed by a barking dog will often shun the spot for a night or so.

Unless the dog is extremely lucky, extremely quick and delivers the *coup de grâce* with amazing precision, it will sustain bites from the fox. These bites can vary from minor scratches to severe punctures and fairly hideous rips. The incidence of these bites can be reduced by terminating the battle swiftly, but foxes are capable of dealing out tremendous bites when retaliating, so it is almost inevitable that a sight hound, used for running foxes, will sustain injury of this nature which should be treated as soon as the lamper reaches home and even before he starts to recharge his lamp. Smooth-coated hounds such as greyhounds, salukis and smooth-coated lurchers seldom have enough fur to mask the bites. Hairier species such as wolfhounds, deerhounds and some rough-coated lurchers have enough fur to conceal bites and a careful examination of muzzles and legs must be made if the wounds are not to fester. Muzzle bites which cannot be cleaned by licking (though sight hound kennel mates, particularly epsilon peck-order females, are often great nurse dogs with a tendency to lick and clean every wound). Nevertheless, canine saliva, rich in antiseptic as it is, is seldom enough to stop a fox puncture festering. Antibiotics are the only certain way of treating a bad fox bite and herbal remedies for wounds must be treated with caution at all times. Foxes are scavengers and hence their bites introduce an amazing spectrum of infections. Oxytetracyclin tablets are a good standby if one intends to hunt foxes regularly.

A word of warning should be given at this point. If one lamps regularly, it is almost inevitable that badgers will appear in the beam. A badger is far from the harmless creature described by writers of children's fiction. If allowed to go unmolested it will never attack a dog, but if run, attacked or merely pestered, it can retaliate with great ferocity. Badgers are capable of tearing huge pieces of flesh from a dog and of breaking limbs and jaws in a manner quite out of proportion to their body size. More to the point, it is a serious offence to take badgers on the lamp, or in any manner for that matter, and the fines imposed by courts on those found guilty of hunting these creatures are staggering. A badger, no matter how easy a prey it provides, when outlined by the beam, should be left alone and unharmed. If one appears in the spotlight, and they often do, and the lurcher and longdog or sight hound runs them, the beam should be switched off to allow the creature to escape into the sanctuary afforded by the night. Badgers present apparently easy victims to a sight hound. In fact, they are deceptively ferocious as are the laws protecting them.

On the subject of the law it would be foolish not to mention the subject of poaching in a chapter concerned with lamping and the sight hounds, for lamping is the most popular form of poaching in use today. Few pure-bred sight hounds are used for poaching, though it would be a very pure and holy sort of person who has not allowed a hound to run on country where the owner is not exactly welcome. Lurchers which are more tractable than either longdogs or pure-bred sight hounds are, of course, the obvious choice of the poacher, though there are tales of incredible and audacious atrocities committed by poachers who have tried every conceivable sight hound to hunt quarry from rabbit to deer on land where no permission for lamping has been granted.

The golden age of poaching, if such an expression is applicable, was undoubtedly the time of Queen Victoria, when the 1831 Act and its subtle ramifications, was designed to protect game, and by doing so, cheapened regard for human life was passed. Tales of poachers facing imprisonment for taking rabbits and deportation for taking hares and feathered game are not uncommon. The lot of the Victorian poacher, however, is not nearly as difficult as the situation of his modern equivalent. Tales of poachers beating up police officers, gamekeepers or anyone falling foul of them, are common in Victorian poaching books, and the transgressors invariably escape to live in true fairy-tale fashion, happily ever after. This is simply not the case today. Sophisticated electronic devices monitor game estates. Police are seldom out of radio contact with their headquarters and the possibility of a criminal escaping to anonymity in a big city is remote. Britain is a country where human freedom is carefully guarded, but the rights of man heavily monitored. Victorian poachers would have survived only months in such conditions. Police out to apprehend poachers are advised never to set out without first phoning through their locations. An officer out of touch for minutes after such a call is usually checked on by other officers. Gamekeepers too, are aided by telephones and are seldom out of contact with the police when a poaching expedition occurs on their sites. A Victorian poacher took his chance on foot against adversaries also on foot, keepers aided by bullmastiffs perhaps, (the breed was created as a deterrent against poachers), but on foot, nevertheless. The poacher had but to disappear into the night, escape detection by the dogs, remain silent about his misdeeds and live happily ever after. Nowadays, a sophisticated police officer and a gamekeeper go out against the poacher and all odds are against the miscreant. Yet strangely, poaching is on the increase.

The reasons why poaching is becoming more popular have, as yet, not been clearly explained. Most poaching is done by lamping and the spectrum of quarry, from partridge to deer, is taken by lampers. To the uninitiated (and lamping by its very nature is an esoteric practice, regarded by many as symptomatic of insanity) the sight of a beam of light shone around a field is a clear indication to gamekeepers and police alike that a poacher is abroad and not only abroad but avoiding his presence. Keepers have but to search out the source of the beam to bring about an arrest, although the arrest of a lamper is far from plain sailing.

A lamp, shone around the field, makes the denizens within the beam clearly visible. However, the very intensity of the light renders the lamper invisible to anyone approaching him. Some of the very high powered spotlights actually hurt the eyes of anyone walking towards it. Thus, poachers have simply to keep the keeper in the beam until the very last moment, call in the dogs, shut off the lamp and disappear into the darkness, now made tenfold by the absence of the bright eye-dazzling light. A poacher has only to find a convenient spot, keep his dog quiet and hole up until daylight, when he can walk home, picking up his haul by car later in the day—preferably secreting it under a hedge until it is 'all clear'. Poaching, particularly rabbit poaching with a lamp, is normally carried out in bad weather in the coldest, most severe conditions. A keeper would need to be hell-bent on an arrest to seek out a poacher in such weather. Few keepers are so keen, and a few nights under these conditions usually deters the most enthusiastic keeper from further investigation. Police officers are singularly unlikely to enjoy a trek across mile after mile of mud to catch a poacher, and so most of them simply phone in and ride around the lanes happy, if they find the poacher, or better still, his car.

Cars are usually the 'giveaway' of poachers for all a keeper must do is wait by the car for him to return. A phone call to Swansea made by the police officer will usually ascertain the owner of the vehicle who, though he may be able to say that the reason the vehicle was there was that it was stolen, will seldom be believed. Hence, cars are usually parked miles away from the hunting ground and the poachers walk to the estate, returning to the car once the deed is done, and collecting the swag later. An element of risk is always present, but one supposes this lends spice to an otherwise cold and damp enterprise.

The sale of one's catch is always a problem, particularly if the dealer knows the source of the 'loot'. Absurdly low prices are offered for poached rabbits, hares, pheasants, partridge and deer, and the dealer has the seller over a barrel for, not only is the game stolen but it is also perishable. Unless the poacher has a commercial freezer he has to take whatever price he is offered for his wares—particularly as a call from dealer to police usually results in the poacher's house being searched and the game confiscated. Dealers who receive game, which they know to be poached, are not likely to have qualms about behaving in a manner best described as 'a shade underhand'. Still, a person who steals game—and that's just about what a poacher is, if one analyses the nature of the word,—is obviously running the gauntlet of being caught and swindled from the moment he sets out on his illegal caper.

The bench seems to make a distinction between types of poacher, the most innocuous being the poacher of rabbits and hares who is sometimes regarded (particularly if this is the poacher's first offence) as a sort of anachronistic, but gentle lunatic. Pheasants and other game are considered to be more valuable and so the poaching of this quarry is considered to be a lot more heinous an offence. The bench deal out stinging fines for the taking of just one pheasant, while the rabbit poacher often escapes with a caution. Deer poachers can expect to have the book thrown at them, particularly if they brought the deer down with a sight hound and lamp combination. To repeat: the Attingham Park poachers received 18 months apiece for the slaughter of fallow deer using such a combination. Poachers who set out to take deer know the rules, understand the laws and must expect the punishment.

Sociologists have debated the reason why men poach since the scientific study of criminology was first started in the nineteenth century. The concept of the poacher with a large family of starving children being supported by the haul of game was laughable even in Victorian times, for other endeavours would net a better haul for less work. Even when the punishment for such activities was hanging, the prospect of death did little to deter even the petty poacher from his pursuit of a rabbit or so, so that punishment seems to have little deterrent value to dissuade the poacher. Heavy fines, therefore, have no deterrent value whatsoever. The fact is that, if society makes rules of any sort, then there are those who will seek to break those rules regardless of the punishment. This is certainly equally true of poaching. Even respectable people, who would shudder at the thought of being accused of shoplifting, will encourage a dog to chase a rabbit on forbidden ground. Every piece of land in Britain belongs to someone. It is a thought to bear in mind when allowing a dog to chase a rabbit!

13. COURSING

For some reason, falconers claim that their sport is as ancient as coursing but, on examination, this premise seems illogical. The sight hound is a fairly early type of domesticated dog, whether the type is monophyletic (derived from one species of wild dog) or polyphyletic (derived from several species of such), whereas the taming rather than the domestication (for it has been found practicable to breed hawks in captivity only in the last 40 years) of hawks, eagles and falcons must have been a relatively recent event.

Coursing, in its widest definition, is the pursuit of game, especially the brown hare, with dogs which hunt by sight rather than scent and all sight hounds can be used for coursing—though admittedly with varying degrees of success. Coursing under rules—the testing of the merits of two dogs during the pursuit of a single hare—is a relatively recent sport but it would be harder to find a more emotive and controversial subject than competitive coursing.

The pursuit of a single hare with one dog in what is often called 'best of three', or 'best of five, or six, or seven' hares, is said to be a popular event amongst longdog enthusiasts, though where such numbers of hares exist and can be run without interruption by owners of the land is a mystery. In these contests a hare is given law of 40 to 80 yards, or even 100 yards, according to individual rules, and a single dog is slipped on a hare. The winner of the event is the dog which brings down the hare by any means, once the agreed law has been granted the quarry. In late summer, it may be possible to catch four or five hares with a single dog, for the hares are immature and foolish, apt to panic and liable to even crouch when coursed. Hares taken after Christmas are a different matter and it requires something better than an indifferent coursing dog to bring down any January hare. The truth is that very few dogs, pure-bred sight hounds, lurchers or longdogs are capable of putting up a good show against three strong hares in one day. The speed required to turn a hare once it has been given fair law is incredible. The effort to catch it is exhausting and the complex running pattern of hares is hard for any dog to comprehend and unravel. A strong hare makes the majority of coursing dogs look foolish and the majority of these three, five or seven hare contests usually result in a loose chaotic coursing event, where such has been the lack of success of the competitors, that finally several dogs are slipped and run simultaneously at the hare.

According to sporting fiction, itinerants are fond of such contests and are known to bet incredible sums on the outcome of these single dog coursing contents, but this is simply gross exaggeration. A coursing dog required to bring down a succession of hares in a single day needs to be as finely conditioned as a Derby winner, to be fed as carefully as a prize fighter and to lead a regulated, carefully exercised lifestyle. The unsettled lifestyle of the itinerant—however caring he may be with his dogs (and the majority of itinerants are something less than caring, as a trip to any caravan site will indicate)—is unlikely to produce the quality of dog required for this sort of contest, but, once again, whether or not these much acclaimed contests take place is a matter for speculation.

Don Southerd of Burton-on-Trent did much to debunk the notion of these much vaunted itinerant-owned hare-killing dogs (though some dogs of this calibre must occur, as one changed hands at Appleby Fair for £3,800 in 1980 and there is a tale that this sum has been exceeded since then). The Gaskin family reputedly paid £4,500 for such a dog. Southerd started a strain of longdog by mating a

Springer spaniel with a greyhound and while the offspring had incredible nose and a lurcher's turn of speed (qualities enough for the average lurcher enthusiast) Southerd was not content with it. Walsh, in *Lurchers and Longdogs* was somewhat disparaging about these early hybrids, and Southerd agrees whole-heartedly with the colonel's condemnation of his initial experiments. Further crosses with greyhounds and saluki/greyhound hybrids did much to improve the coursing potential of these longdogs (though little, one should add, to improve the working ability of what would have been a very useful lurcher type) and an incredibly rigorous selection started to produce very serviceable competitive coursing hounds. Southerd seldom deviated far from the saluki hybrid, as he believes that the saluki stride, that effortless, cantering, flowing movement, coupled with the typical thrust and reliability of the good coursing greyhound produces the best hare killers. As the strain progressed and improved, Southerd sought out training methods to bring his hybrids to a sufficient peak of physical condition to produce athletic prowess enough to bring down a succession of hares. Finally, he embarked on a system of lightly exercising his dogs in early summer, increasing the level of training until they were scarcely winded by 15 mph for 15 minutes running behind a pick-up truck along country lanes. Such dedication to both eugenics and conditioning, Southerd reasoned, would produce the required result and now all Don needed were opponents to compete in these events.

Southerd had by now befriended a sporting farmer, whose land held a fair number of hares, and he fired the landowner with enthusiasm for the sport. Both drew up a set of rudimentary rules for coursing events, and the farmer agreed to officiate when these events took place. Thus, Southerd had now obtained a suitable strain of dog, training methods to condition the strain of hound produced by him, and land on which to stage these contests. All he required were enthusiasts of a like ilk to test his hounds. In this he was to be somewhat disappointed.

Southerd stimulated, or attempted to stimulate, interest in such an event by writing letters to the sporting press eulogising on the sporting prowess of the brown hare and remarking that there were perhaps less than a dozen dogs alive which could bring down hares regularly. His letters produced a predictable result and a host of hare coursing enthusiasts, with a variety of orthodox and exotic crosses ranging from saluki/greyhound hybrids to otterhound/greyhound crosses, replied, agreeing with Southerd and questioning where the other 11 dogs might be! The boasts of these people were predictable and the hyperbole regarding their own dogs was to be expected. Southerd's next letter to the sporting press provoked less response, however.

The next letter was in the form of a challenge, inviting the owners of the mythical 12 dogs to a best of three hare coursing contest for sums between £200 and £1000. His challenge received scant response and only one contestant with the famous bitch, Anna, a saluki/greyhound lurcher hybrid, came forward to compete. Southerd's dog ran twice against this bitch, winning one event and losing the other, in what in sporting circles must be classed as fairly close contests. Tales of best of three hare contests, gambling lorries, cars and huge sums of money clearly belong in the realms of fiction.

Yet competitive lurcher coursing does of course exist, though here the event involves the use of two dogs run under rules similar to those of the National Coursing Club. A particularly popular meet is at Drax Power Station in Yorkshire and this event must be classed as the lurcher equivalent of the Waterloo Cup. Despite the reputation of lurcher enthusiasts, (one newspaper described these people as the canine equivalent of the soccer hooligan element) few unpleasant events occur at Drax. The event is well organised, reasonably well timed (no coursing meet is run to the minute) and there is little gambling and few bad losers. Events of this quality should be encouraged, but such is the ill-repute of the lurcher fraternity (and the memory of the Lambourn Lurcher Show at Four Burrows dies hard) that few seem likely to be staged. Perhaps the National Lurcher Racing Club, which has a reputation for organising well run shows, agility events and obedience tests, may arrange such meets at a future date, though in view of the riff-raff an event of this nature may attract, an 'invitation only' rule may have to be implemented.

More conventional, if not more acceptable (coursing is a pursuit seldom considered as acceptable by the public at large) coursing, is staged by the National Coursing Club and the various breed clubs, the Saluki, the Deerhound and the Whippet Clubs. Coursing meets have been organised by the Irish Wolfhound Club and various Borzois Clubs, often with a somewhat mixed response from the members and an even more mixed enthusiasm from the hounds. Basically, the coursing rules are the same for all breeds, though minor variations in breed club regulations do occur.

The only acceptable quarry involved in British coursing events is the brown hare *Lepus timidus*. Rabbits are scarcely acceptable quarry as they provide few runs of sufficient length to test a sight hound, before diving into the sanctuary of the burrow. Likewise the blue hare is an inferior athlete, ill-designed to survive a hard-pressing course, though meets involving the pursuit of the blue hare do occur. Furthermore the altitude at which they seem to thrive does not suit the conventional coursing spectator and the terrain over which the hares are run is usually too rugged and damaging to be favoured by the owner of the hounds. Thus the brown hare, the strongest of all European species, the fastest and most elusive of all hares is considered the only animal suitable for coursing in conventional coursing events.

Contrary to public opinion and the views voiced by the British press, which since 1948 have become increasingly anti-field sport, the hare is not boxed or caged to be released in front of the hounds. Such a hare, off country, unaware of the lie of the land, ill-versed in the nature of every hedge, wall and pitfall, would fall easy prey to an indifferent dog and, if pursued, would be inclined to crouch so as to avoid detection. To allow a hound to course a captured and released hare would be counter-productive to the pursuance of coursing and would certainly not provide a sporting course. Hares used for competitive events are afforded some protection inasmuch as landowners do not encourage dogs on the land while hares are breeding and obviously seldom allow hares to be shot on their estates. Otherwise the hare used in coursing is totally wild. Furthermore, because of the hare's tendency to run a circular territorial route, hares are never intentionally driven off country to be coursed. So they are assured of all the advantages and every possible chance of evading the dogs and escaping. Few courses—at least where greyhounds are concerned—last longer than a minute and by that time some greyhounds are 'running at a walk'. In contrast to which the hare is not only a superb sprinter, but also a formidable middle-distance runner. The odds strongly favour the hare in conventional coursing events.

The object of coursing is not to bring about the death of a hare—or rather the killing of the hare is not the reason why dogs are run at this creature. Coursing, or the act of two dogs striving desperately to overtake and possibly capture a hare, is an art form in motion and, if the morality of such a practice is in question, not only the excitement of the chase, but also the beauty of two hounds matched against each other certainly provides a stimulating scene. Coursing enthusiasts are often aesthetically inclined and are seldom the blood-crazed beasts they are purported to be by the national press. The pursuit of a hare has been the subject of writing since antiquity. Still, the morality of coursing, the ethical considerations of causing pain and massive and perhaps unnatural exertion will be debated as long as coursing is practised.

Two hounds are released simultaneously at a hare by a slipper, using a double slip lead which allows both hounds to be freed at the same instant. A slipper's job is a skilled one and requires qualities other than simply strength to hold both hounds until the hare has been allowed sufficient law to give a fair and testing run. He must be able to assess distance accurately and must be able to gauge exactly the moment when to release both hounds. Hounds released too soon will often catch and kill a hare before the creature has had time to gain a velocity suitable to test the mettle of the hounds. Should they be slipped too late they may not come to terms with the fleeing quarry. A slipper must work unobtrusively and remain hidden in the 'shy' until the time is right to release the hounds.

Coursing judges are usually mounted, as not only does the use of a horse allow the judge to follow the pursuit of the hare more closely, but the added elevation afforded by a horse, enables the judge to see more clearly and to reach a decision more fairly. Coursing judges, like judges and referees everywhere, are invariably wrong in the decisions they make, or the verdicts they pass—at least that is the opinion of the audience! A mounted judge is able to see more clearly and assess more accurately the flow of the course.

Not all judges at coursing meets are mounted, however. In parts of Scotland, where some of the meets of the Saluki and Deerhound Coursing Clubs are held, it would be impracticable to employ a mounted judge for the terrain is heather-covered and the presence of rocks and peat hags would make riding a monumental task in itself. Here a judge achieves a vantage point, if possible, and follows the course by the use of binoculars. Such meets, devoid of the spectacle of colourfully mounted judges, may lack pageantry perhaps, but the sight of elegant loping salukis and towering hirsute deerhounds pursuing hares over taxing ground compensates for this. The enthusiasm of the competitors at such meets is infectious. Few of the entries have been professionally trained and the money wagered on such events is minimal, but the sheer exuberance of amateur coursing enthusiasts out to try their dogs at the most taxing and difficult of sports is as exciting as the event itself. No feeling generated by a show can match it. No win at Crufts brings greater pleasure than seeing one's hound perform well at coursing and frankly, the sheer 'amateur' excitement of such a meet transcends any of the thrills of the Waterloo Cup.

In a conventional coursing meet, dogs wear white or red collars during a course and the judge signals a win by holding a cloth of the appropriate colour aloft. The time between the release of the hounds and the signalling of the winner seems like an eternity for the owners of the hounds (and possibly the hare) but, in point of fact, is seldom more than 60 seconds. Ironically, it is often the hare, escaping after a taxing run, which inspires the adulation of the crowd, rather than a tremendous effort by the hounds.

The hound making the kill is awarded fewer points, if any, than the hound bringing the hare to turn. Speed, ability and coursing sense (a difficult expression to define) must all be assessed by the judge. The overall winner of a course is the hound which has contributed most to the capture of a hare, even though the hare was not caught — a statement which not only seems paradoxical, but also sets the judge a difficult problem to solve. Experienced, well-respected judges, whose lot is certainly a very difficult one, are not easy to come by.

Failure to mention the fabulous Waterloo Cup would be a very serious omission in any chapter on the subject of coursing. It is an event which is the highlight of the coursing calendar, a spectacle which brings together some of the finest coursing hounds in the world. It is a pageant from start to finish, colourful as a scene from *The Arabian Nights*, and there is something to interest everyone, be they an enthusiast of the chase, student of humanity or merely out to protest about the iniquity man perpetrates on hares. Throughout the three-day meet staged at Altcar near Liverpool there is scarcely a moment when the spectator or the competitor is not occupied and entranced with a kaleidoscope of activities.

In 1825 the Altcar Club was formed by a great British sportsman, Lord Molyneux, an enthusiastic and generous supporter of the ring, the turf and the leash, as *Blackwood's* magazine describes boxing, horseracing and coursing. The club, an elite group of some of the best British sportsmen ever, met at the Waterloo Hotel, Liverpool, for Waterloo Hotels had sprung up like autumnal mushrooms since the Napoleonic War. A Mr Lynn, the proprietor of the hotel and a casual sportsman, became interested in coursing and requested that he be allowed to take some of his friends coursing over the Altcar Estate. Lord Molyneux was more than a little amused by the request and lent Mr Lynn a dog to compete in an eight-dog stake, which was to bear the name of the hotel and which became known as The Waterloo Cup.

Lord Molyneux's red bitch, Milanie, won the first of these cups (merely a sum of money placed in a cup—no trophy was presented until later events in the early twentieth century, one should add). So successful was the meet that a few months after the event the Waterloo Club was formed and the stake enlarged to include 16 dogs. Later the stake was to enlarge still further to become a 32-dog and then a 64-dog stake.

The Waterloo Cup was an important democratic breakthrough as much as a coursing event. Prior to the creation of the Waterloo Club, the sport of coursing was an elitist one. The Roman Camp (Midlothian) Club disbarred any member with a social rank lower than a baronet. Seemingly the Canute Forest Law of 1016 which states that no mean man may own a greyhound was obviously believed by some. However, the Waterloo Club is open to anyone with an interest in coursing, no matter what his rank or financial status. It should also be added that once the liberalising effect of the formation of the club spread, the greyhound improved dramatically, though it has to be mentioned that the advent of greyhound racing in 1926 accelerated its evolution to such an extent that the speed and height of the breed increased considerably. Just as it is likely that the illustrious Mick the Miller would have been outpaced by the modern flapping trap dog, so it is likely that coursing aces, such as Fullerton, would have been made to look a shade stale and slow compared to modern coursing greyhounds. If competitive coursing has done anything, it has accelerated the improvement of the coursing greyhound dramatically. No organisation has encouraged this acceleration more than the Waterloo Club.

To take a kennelled dog and run it at hare without first conditioning it is not good policy and could result in permanent damage to the dog. The chop-and-change world, in which the lurcher and longdog find themselves, is very destructive to the sight hound. Dogs are traded, swapped and sold on a fancy, rejected as useless, sold in poor condition and invariably finish up in the hands of a dealer. Here the dejected animals reside a while, in conditions less than ideal before being sold to a less than meticulous buyer and tested perhaps on the first day after the purchase. Few dog dealers have any idea of how to condition a dog. Fewer still have facilities to exercise their charges, and seldom are the dogs that come into their hands of prime quality. The result of immediately testing dogs bought from such an environment, on a hare is usually unpleasant, though totally predictable. Most coursing dogs, and that includes sight hounds, lurchers and longdogs, will chase instinctively and the effort and exertion required by an unfit dog to 'close' with a hare given a fair slip is destructive. Muscle tissue is torn, and feet—the most vulnerable of all parts of a sight hound—are often damaged irreparably. More serious still, both heart and lungs can suffer during a course and so are easily damaged if a dog is run unfit. Lurchers and longdogs change hands frequently and a condition known as 'blown' exists in many of these oft-traded unfortunates—a condition, one should add, seldom if ever found in well-trained, well-exercised greyhounds. 'Blown' is a collective term in connection with dogs with serious damage to heart, lungs and diaphragm—and none of these organs are capable of repairing themselves completely when damaged. A 'blown' dog will appear hale and hearty even when subjected to light exercise. A hard testing course is a different matter. Once the damaged organs are subjected to serious physical stress they deteriorate swiftly. Blown dogs often keel over after a severe course and display symptoms similar to those manifested by a 'fitting' dog. As often as not, blown dogs die as a result of testing exertion—or, worse still, are traded again until they are literally run to death. The Environmental Health Acts need gearing to cope with the existence of the backyard dog dealers who trade in unfortunate waifs and strays, and breeders of lurchers and longdogs should vet buyers carefully lest the puppies finish up in the same way as the dogs just described.

Conditioning any sight hound for coursing is an art, and a skilled trainer can almost produce a silk purse out of a sow's ear, or at least produce an astonishingly good result from an indifferent dog. Likewise, in the hands of an indifferent trainer, a poor stockman, even the very best dog will fail to 'shine'. Stockmanship, particularly that which is required to care for coursing dogs is an indefinable quality and owners can often plot the success rate of their hounds by noting the difference certain kennelmen make. Some will achieve magical results with the same food and facilities that have produced losers in the hands of less efficient kennelmen.

A dog required to show well in the coursing field needs to be reared well and the diet that suits some hounds, certainly does not suit others. *Stonehenge* (E.H. Walsh) once told an audience that an hour spent simply watching the occupants of a kennel is well spent and productive. Good doers with a tendency to put on fat need restricting in their diets, poor doers and dogs which look less than well, need carefully watching at the food plate and may need cleansing of external or internal parasites before they begin to thrive. However, as the time of the coursing season draws near, dogs need a slightly different diet from their ordinary maintenance rations.

A dog, or any animal, required to exert itself strenuously, requires a ration that is higher in protein than his usual day-to-day food. To accomplish this, biscuit or meal should be reduced and protein in the form of flesh substituted. Almost any flesh is suitable, although pork is not advised by many coursers because of its high fat content, but, at the time of a meat shortage, pork is more than acceptable. Thus as soon as increased exercise begins, a higher meat diet should be fed.

Before embarking on coursing training most competitive kennels consider a health programme. Dogs should be checked for cracked pads, and feet or wrist weaknesses, for once training in earnest begins these will be sorely tested. Most trainers worm and de-flea dogs immediately prior to the coursing season, repeating the process two weeks later. Some veterinary surgeons are of the opinion that tapeworms do little harm to a dog. Perhaps there is scientific evidence to suggest that worms in moderation are harmless. Certainly the segments adhering to the tail of infected dogs are unpleasant to see and appear to be symptomatic of neglect.

As training progresses the hounds are usually groomed and massaged daily. If at first the reader considers that massage and grooming are simply affectations, it should be noted that many trainers consider that attention of this sort means the difference between fielding a winner or a loser. Certainly, dogs seem to glow with health if massaged after exercise and a groomed dog seems to radiate health far more than an ungroomed one. The majority of athletes are massaged before and after competing and there seems to be some indication that massage does improve muscle tone and general well-being.

Exercise must certainly be an important factor in conditioning a dog. Dogs must be taken up 'out of rest' and conditioned gradually with increasing amounts of exercise daily. It is a mistake to think that a crash course to get a dog fit will pay off. It is more likely that such a course will strain and tear muscle fibres leaving the dog sore, lame and unwilling to try hard at a hare. Start exercising gradually, increasing the exercise daily but keeping a careful watch on the dog while exercise is being given. A tired dog, a listless dog after a spell of strenuous exercise, may indicate the animal is unwell. The condition may also indicate that the rate of exercise is too great or the quality of exercise too strenuous. Dogs allowed to exercise free in paddocks should be watched for condition several times a day and their general well-being, or lack of it noted. There are no hard and fast rules regarding the exercising of sight hounds prior to coursing. Each one will need personal attention and their individual needs are vastly different. Some top class hounds are lazy in kennels though they excel on the coursing field. Others are full of energy and are willing to exercise long after the trainer is ready to cry, 'halt'. A lazy dog is not automatically a bad coursing prospect. Neither is a hyperactive dog a good prospect. However, a trainer should be able to assess the needs of his wards, both food and exercise-wise and act accordingly.

Perhaps the only hard and fast rule concerning exercise should be that it must be gradual until the dog has reached a state when it literally glows with health and is exultant at the prospect of a course. Watch the dog after a long course. Fitness, according to Hahn, can be ascertained by the time that an animal takes to recover from a set exercise. After exercising, a dog should never be exhausted and, if it is, it is either ill or was unready for the ordeal it has endured. Ordeal just about summarises a hard course, for every muscle, every organ is taxed to capacity. It is all the more remarkable that a novice will often buy a dog from a dealer and test the animal forthwith on a hare!

The morality of coursing is questionable, and it is calculated that 72 per cent of the public disagree with it. To offer a defence for it is not only difficult but fraught with danger. The truth is that one cannot really justify any form of hunting that either terrifies or results in the death of an animal. To do so by the statement that the hare is to be used as food would certainly bring the retort that the flesh of the hare (or arguably of any animal) is not essential for human beings to live.

That coursing improves the quality and pace of the greyhound is true. Likewise it can be argued that the race-track where no live animal is hurt, frightened or killed is an even better place to develop pace. As for the improvement engendered in coursing skill by the art of coursing, it can be counter-argued that, should coursing be banned, this improvement in coursing skills would not be necessary or desirable for that matter. Without the sport of coursing one would not need a hound capable of coursing.

That the hare is seldom killed during coursing meets is offered as a sort of oblique type of defence for coursing. Alternatively, no hare that is not coursed will meet its death in the jaws of a coursing dog! That the course only results in pain or fear for a mere 40 seconds or so, also does not hold water. No hare needs to experience even 40 seconds of pain or fear. Again it is argued that a hare has always been pursued and has always had everyone's hand against it, so coursing is no new and terrifying experience to it. Likewise the argument can be countered by the fact that there is little point in adding to the hare's plight by giving it the dubious distinction of being the quarry of sight hounds

All hunting involves cruelty. All hunting involves pain and fear. No beast enjoys being chased, if the consequence of being caught is to be hurt or killed. Perhaps the only logical defence of coursing is that it is a way of life, a pursuit which is an integral part of country living. To air one's views publicly in its defence at the present time is inadvisable.

14. FERRETING

Ferreting can certainly not be classed as everyone's cup of tea. At times it can be as slow and unproductive as salmon fishing in a muddy river, and others as exhilarating as the Cresta run. A rapid succession of bolters can be the most exciting of events, a 'lie up' as dull as ditch water. The ferreter must be able to cope with both, and above all, must have the patience of a latter-day Job. One thing is certain, ferreting is the very best way of allowing a sight hound a chance to run and perhaps catch rabbits.

All sight hounds will work with ferrets, though admittedly with varying degrees of success. Irish wolfhounds are usually too large to be first-rate rabbit catchers, whereas salukis, Afghans and borzois usually lack the powers of concentration needed to stay poised over an earth in which a ferret is lying up on a rabbit it has killed, though Paul Sagar from Manchester does work his salukis to ferret. Whippets are an ideal type for ferreting—they are quick, mercurial, fast of foot and reaction, with a fairly good attention span—and some greyhounds also have the ability to be able to stay fixed above an earth. Lurchers—a variable type admittedly—are usually excellent ferreters, particularly collie-blooded dogs which, because of their collie ancestry, have a high attention span and are extremely tractable. Longdogs too are a variable mix and certainly do work with ferrets, but few longdogs have a high attention span, for longdogs are simply sight hound composites, though they do gain an extra 'something' through hybrid vigour perhaps. So what exactly are the qualities that are desirable in a dog to be used for ferreting?

Firstly, a hound must have nose to be able to mark an inhabited earth. Many earths look well-worked but are simply play holes perhaps used for night-time forays by rabbits, but seldom found to be inhabited during daylight hours. The presence of rabbit dung at the mouth of an earth is an indication that the earth or warren, call it what you will, is simply a play earth and unlikely to be inhabited. Still a dog with a good nose, and some sight hounds do have such a nose, will determine if an earth is worth ferreting. To ferret a 30 hole earth or warren is a tedious and often lengthy task, particularly if such earths are in deep cover which has to be chopped or cleared before nets can be set. For such an earth to be uninhabited, after all the nets have been set and a ferret allowed to work it thoroughly, is annoying. Coupled with this, considering that ferreting is an exclusively wintertime pursuit, standing around or netting up holes in freezing conditions may be tolerable if there is a catch at the end of the tedium, but is very disenchanting when an earth or warren proves to be empty. A dog with a good accurate nose will detect the presence of a rabbit in a very deep earth and distinguish between a heavily scented, but empty earth and one with occupants.

Never encourage a dog to mark every hole—some dogs will equate marking an earth with the praise given by the owner and soon mark every earth, inhabited or not, simply to please him. False marking is easy to 'train in', it is a very difficult habit to break. Allow a dog to make up its own mind and learn to interpret the language of the dog when it wants to indicate whether the earth is inhabited. Some will stand, paw raised like a pointer, others will snort down the earth and indicate the presence of rabbits with a wag of the tail. Restrain the dog which insists on snorting its presence down the hole and digging madly at the mouth of the warren—it is difficult enough for ferrets to persuade some rabbits to bolt without this sort of deterrent. A dog with a good nose makes ferreting a pleasure.

Attention span is an important factor in determining the value of a ferreting dog. A dog is required to stay over an earth in which a ferret has been entered and not to wander off in pursuit of game, excitedly tracking other scents. It must remain in situ and not indulge in pursuing other quarry. True, it is easier to fix a dog by making it sit near an earth—and this is an admirable way of ensuring a dog does not wander off. It is, however not a particularly economic method in terms of movement. A sitting dog needs two distinct movements to become a pursuing dog. By far the best method of ensuring that a dog stays at the mouth of an earth is to cause it to freeze—to remain in a frozen stance—, or the half-panther crouch, as the rabbit bolts. A dog, frozen in this position, gets into stride instantly and does not need to rise to its feet to follow the rabbit—as would a sitting dog. Perhaps only a hundredth of a second is needed for a sitting dog to get into its stride, likewise the same length of time is all that is needed to allow a rabbit to escape down another burrow. Here however is the rub. A sitting dog is easily kept sitting—one frozen to the spot is not so co-operative—and it requires an animal with a fairly high attention span to remain immobile above an earth while a rabbit is worked by the ferret. Sight hounds are not the most patient of dogs—few have the ability to maintain any degree of concentration for long. Here, however, a collie lurcher comes into its own. A dash of collie—apparently not liked by all lurcher enthusiasts—ensures that the lurcher is bright, sensible and has a high attention span.

A good ferreting dog should be quick off the mark, able to galvanise into movement, and rapid movement at that, in a split second. A whippet mentality or a 25-yard dog is the ideal type for the ferreter. A large longdog, a dog capable of a long enduring course with bottomless stamina and courage to face an agonising chase, has its place, but certainly not as a ferreting dog. Few rabbits bolted from a warren by a ferret will run further than 30 yards or so before seeking refuge in a hole, hedge or thicket. Furthermore, although a rabbit lives in a relatively small territory, it knows every inch of that territory and can exploit it to its advantage. A dog required to take such a rabbit needs little stamina and even less courage. What it does need is instant reaction and a short, sharp turn of speed to match that of the rabbit. Pure-bred whippets seem to be the ideal type of dog,

FERRETING

and in fact, there seems to be no reason why small whippet lurchers are bred. Few can perform any task of which a purebred whippet is incapable. Bedlington whippet lurchers are often believed to be the very best rabbiting dogs—in point of fact a good whippet is a considerably better prospect. Whippets are infinitely faster, equally as game, and despite a smooth coat, seldom reluctant to plunge into bramble and cover to take a rabbit. There seems little case for breeding a whippet-based lurcher. However a fast-thinking, fast-moving dog is the ideal ferreter's associate.

This opinion is not shared by everyone. Walsh, in his masterly *The English Whippet* (written together with Mary Lowe), states categorically that to ferret efficiently it is necessary to 'leave the dog at home'. Walsh has his reasons. A ferreter must concentrate wholly on the job in hand—fixing a dog to a freeze position and checking on it from time to time, can be a distracting practice for him. Furthermore, when a rabbit bolts, he needs to concentrate on the task of getting it out of the net. Here, once again, the dog, and controlling it can be an unwanted distraction. A dog passing over nets, however careful it is moving, 'snags up' nets with its feet and it requires iron control to fix a dog, when a rabbit is struggling in the net. Walsh clearly does not think that a dog poised ready for the escapee—the rabbit that throws a net, the second rabbit that follows before the net can be replaced—is really worth the trouble of training, and there is no denying that he could be right. If one wishes to be a devil's advocate, however, how does one detect an inhabited earth without a dog, and rabbits do escape, for nets like the best laid plans of mice and men 'gang aft aglae'. There are points for and against taking a dog ferreting, and the most obvious argument in favour of it is that the presence of a canine companion makes the day fun, or more fun than usual, for ferreting can be a fascinating hobby by any standards.

No dog should ever be taken out with ferrets, unless the owner is absolutely certain that the animal is not only trustworthy with ferrets, but also knows its role and that of the ferret. If it is not properly broken to ferret, no amount of training ever puts a ferret killer right again—indeed one can add the tyro trainers' oft repeated statement, 'I'm sure he'll be all right with ferrets' to that massive tome, 'Famous Last Words'. Equally dangerous is the trainer who boasts of over familiarity 'twixt dog and ferret, an example of tales of this kind is, 'he'll carry the ferret back in his mouth'. Fine, so he will carry the trainer's ferret back in his mouth, but not all ferrets are tolerant of dogs carrying them about in this way, and most will panic and retaliate. The least that can happen is that the dog gets a nipped tongue, the worst is a very dead ferret. Before ferreting with an unknown dog, place a dish of milk before both ferret and dog and watch carefully. The properly trained dog will drink alongside the ferret with a decided lack of concern. Edgy behaviour at the milk dish will not improve with the excitement of the hunt. If a stranger's dog displays any alarm, animosity or mistrust of one's ferret, leave one of them at home. Do not hesitate to offend the owner of the dog. His assurances that all will be well should count for nothing if his dog displays the slightest antipathy. A good reliable ferret is a treasure and takes a year or so to train. The same ferret takes a split second to die—and always bear in mind sight hounds may not be the height of the canine intelligentsia, but nevertheless they react extremely quickly!

Dogs should be ferret broken at an early age. Eight weeks is not too young, and such training at this age is simplicity itself. Simply place the ferret on the ground and allow the sight hound to sniff it. Should the puppy display too active an interest, the ferret will, like as not, nip not the pup but also precocious behaviour in the bud. Some ferrets are very tolerant and need protecting from a forward puppy, so if the latter becomes too boisterous a slap (no more is usually necessary, as sight hounds are amongst the most sensitive of dogs) accompanied by the command, 'No', will usually stop the puppy in its tracks. The singularity of the word 'puppy' should be noted—it is possible to break two or more puppies to ferret simultaneously, but it is certainly not advisable, since they gain courage when a number of other whelps are also present and a fairly nasty incident involving ferret and the rest of the litter can easily result. In fact it is good policy to train only one hound at a time for any task. Two trained together will invariably become either jealous retrievers or, worse still, spasmodic retrievers, showing great enthusiasm for the task at times and a blank total disdain for it later. It takes a very skilled trainer indeed—there are few about—to have command over a pair of hounds while ferreting. Teamwork simply does not apply with sight hounds, for next to terriers perhaps, the sight hound is certainly one of the most jealous workers.

Breaking an older dog to ferret can be a shade more difficult, particularly if it is already catching rabbits and has never seen ferrets before. A puppy has to be simply convinced that the ferret will not be hostile to it, a grown dog has to be made aware that it is not fair quarry. Fortunately, once more it has to be stressed, sight hounds are sensitive creatures, and a sight hound on a slip allowed to sniff a ferret will usually learn to understand that the ferret is not to be killed if the lead is jerked sharply, a slap being given to the more recalcitrant hound, and the deterrent command of 'No', uttered. Once a sight hound has killed ferrets or shown antagonism towards them, the training is far more difficult, but once again, due entirely to the sight hound's sensitive disposition, good results can be obtained even by gentle restraint of the hound.

A sight hound trainer should, in fact, always be aware of the type's gentle disposition and react accordingly. There are few recalcitrant, or totally recalcitrant sight hounds, despite the type's limited attention span and most of them become upset if punished severely, rebuked a little too strongly or frightened in any way. Sight hound puppies are easily ruined—which incidentally explains why so many longdogs and lurchers change hands regularly, an action which usually exacerbates the problems it is experiencing until it becomes a useless nervous wreck. A heavy hand is seldom necessary with an adult sight hound—it is never necessary with a puppy. Once more to compare them with terriers, also 'seek out and catch/kill dogs'—a terrier puppy may be a recalcitrant bully by the time it is 12 weeks old, eager to fight and prepared to cock a snoot at obedience training. A sight hound is usually a shrinking violet at this age, slightly cringing by nature, gentle and very submissive. Hence treatment, which would not offend a terrier puppy, usually reduces a sight hound whelp to a gibbering wreck. To over-punish or over-train, once the puppy is confused or upset is a certain way to ruin it, but it is wrong to assume that this gentle disposition is an indication of cowardice or lack of courage. Hancock in *My Life With Lurchers* tells the tale of a three-quarter bred puppy, a collie x greyhound x greyhound whelp called Timmy, who was sold to a rather heavy handed buyer. Before long Timmy was returned at 10 weeks of age with the comment that the dog was not 'hard' enough to become a good worker. The buyer had, in fact, written off the puppy because it had behaved like a typical sight hound whelp—sycophantic, gentle and frantic to please. Timmy grew up to be a first rate coursing dog, an excellent lamper and a good all-round worker. The buyer was clearly not experienced enough to accept and tolerate typical sight hound puppy disposition.

To return to ferreting and the training of a ferreting dog. Once the dog has been totally broken to ferret, both should be worked together without delay—though the operative phrase in the sentence should be 'totally broken'. Haphazard, incomplete training is useless. A dog may react relatively favourably to ferrets on its home ground. When heated up by the activity of the hunt, in a state of excitement at the proximity to quarry, a sight hound (or any dog for that matter—a terrier in particular) may once again decide the ferret is fair quarry and react accordingly. The speed of a sight hound's reactions when off a slip is electrifying, hence there is little a person can do to prevent a partially broken sight hound killing a ferret. One should be absolutely certain that one's dog is absolutely steady with ferrets. It may take a little extra time, but the effort is well worthwhile.

There are two ways of catching rabbits bolted by ferrets. Firstly, the hound can be kept by a burrow entrance and a ferret inserted, driving out the rabbit and thereby allowing the sight hound to chase and possibly capture it. This is not a particularly productive method of taking rabbits, as sight hound puppies make frequent mistakes, and will lose many rabbits before becoming even fairly proficient. A rabbit is familiar with its surroundings, the puppy is a stranger to the area the rabbit will run. Still if a sight hound puppy is to be trained to catch ferreted rabbits, these losses, these misses, are part of the training and without them the puppy will never become a proficient rabbit hunter. The trainer who jealously treasures every caught rabbit and curses the dog for every rabbit it misses, would do better to buy his rabbits at a supermarket and forget hunting. The rabbit is always an odds-on favourite even when driven from its lair. A variety of events will certainly conspire to make a young hound look foolish on its first time out. Rabbits may reach the sanctuary of another hole before the hound has time to gather speed—an action that results in it looking down a hole with a puzzled look on its face, an all too common sight—but it is a sight that must be accepted and tolerated for there are no short cuts to training a dog to catch rabbits efficiently. Similarly two rabbits may bolt simultaneously but far from being advantageous, this will only confuse him. For a split second he is unsure as to which rabbit to pursue and a fraction of a second is all that a rabbit usually needs to reach sanctuary. Likewise a youngster may snatch too soon at a rabbit bolting from a burrow—and this can be a heinous fault if not corrected—causing it to dart back to safety. Few rabbits will consider bolting a second time after a dog has struck at them, missed and allowed the rabbit to escape back into its home warren. Most will simply find a blind-hole end, push their heads into the end, hump their hind-quarters to fill the hole, thus protecting the vulnerable nape of the neck, and invite the ferret to do its worst, death below ground often being preferable to them to bolting a second time and facing a dog! Actually this is one time when a puppy needs chastising—preferably verbally—though a slap and muttered threats is the order of the day, lest another rabbit, unaware of the presence of dog and man, be alerted. A sharp glance is often enough to cause a hound puppy to realise its mistake. Savage punishment of any sort is not only inadvisable but also destructive to the training programme. Still a sight hound puppy which strikes too soon at a rabbit, causing it to double back into a warren, should be made aware of its error. Watch its face and body in these circumstances. A puppy, which having been cautioned for its mistakes, shows no remorse, and blindly continues with the pursuit of the rabbit, perhaps diving after the rabbit into a hole, needs further chastising or admonishing. A puppy which looks quite pitiful and resorts to sycophantic gestures and glances has learned its lesson and needs praise for its efforts, once it has tried hard to catch the next rabbit that bolts. There are no hard and fast rules about how much a dog has to be checked for its mistakes, and this absence of hard and fast rules makes it possible for one trainer to be a failure with a sight hound and another to become a resounding success with the same animal.

A word concerning ferrets and their disposition will not come amiss before dealing with the taking of rabbits with purse nets. The sight of a hound standing poised at the mouth of a rabbit earth, a look of nerve-tingling anticipation on its face, a ferreter set back out of sight of a rabbit which may be about to bolt, and a ferret working feverishly within a warren, may cause an uninitiated bystander to think that the team is the perfect symbiotic group, each member working to secure the rabbit for its fellows. Nothing could be further from the truth (though the combined actions of the team members do allow rabbits to be taken). Dogs may work to please humans, but a ferret works simply to please itself, entering a warren with the express purpose of killing a rabbit and eating a portion of the kill. That the rabbit bolts rather than stays to be killed, is an indication of the ferret's personal inefficiency though it does help ensure that a rabbit can be caught without having to dig for the corpse. A ferret is not concerned with the symbiotic nature of a group and is indifferent to praise or criticism. Most will kill rabbits if they can, and as they become older and more warren-wise, most will succeed in this. The essence of ferreting is that the ferret goes to ground to attack and possibly kill a rabbit. A rabbit that bolts is considered by the ferret to be one that has escaped and, should it encounter this rabbit frozen to immobility at the mouth of the earth, deciding whether to bolt or not, the ferret will pull it back into the earth in order to slay it. Some ferrets kill a rabbit and simply leave the carcass, others will gnaw a fragment of the meat before seeking out another rabbit to kill. They have no loyalty to man and would be astonished by any form of chastisement from a human being. Should ferrets display a habit of pulling the rabbit they have killed out of an earth rather than into the earth—the action is purely accidental and in no way indicates that it is trying to secure a carcass for the dog or its owner. Most prefer to pull the carcass into the sanctuary and peace of the burrow to worry it a little or possibly eat a small portion of the carcass.

It is sound policy to feed ferrets before working them, and even better policy to offer a ferret a saucer of milk before it goes hunting. A well-fed, well-watered ferret will hunt simply because it is its nature to hunt and if it kills its rabbit it does so simply because its nature compels it to do so. It will kill its prey, shake it a little, bite the carcass a few times, and then, tiring of the activity, either come out of the burrow or seek another occupant of the warren to kill. A hungry ferret also seeks out and kills rabbits, but it then assuages its appetite by eating the rabbit and like most carnivores, after it eats its fill, it sleeps off the effect of the meal, lying up on the cooling body of its prey until it decides to hunt again. A hungry ferret is often a liability. It will simply kill and stay underground spoiling the day's sport. Male ferrets are called hobs and are bigger, stronger and usually more dextrous at killing a rabbit than the smaller jills, which, because they lack the power to kill quickly often make better bolting ferrets. However once one has learned the knack of killing a rabbit, and it usually becomes proficient in its second year, it is more likely to kill than to bolt its quarry. Some ferrets never learn the technique of killing a rabbit and while these are prized by the ferreter, they are biological failures which would certainly not survive to propagate their kind in the wild. Nevertheless they are joys to own, though they are seldom encountered.

A hunter out to secure a haul of rabbits rather than to provide runs for his dog would do best to consider the use of purse nets. Like many supposedly complex country skills the setting of a purse net is child's play. A purse net is designed to close on the rabbit when the rabbit touches it and the more the captive struggles, the more it tangles in the meshes of the net. Nets are made of either hemp—hemp nets are always made by hand—or else nylon—most nylon nets are machine-made. Both nylon and hemp are strong materials but neither are resistant to the effect of a dog tearing at them with its teeth. Hence all ferreting dogs should be net broken and should refuse to attack or pick up a rabbit enveloped by a net. A dog which allows a purse net to envelop a rabbit and refuses to touch it gives the trainer the reputation of being an expert, but the dog easily learns the skill. Each time a rabbit hits the nets and tangles, a sharp word, 'No', 'Leave' or something similar, will cause the dog to stop snatching at the rabbit. A mere day or two's training is usually sufficient for a lurcher, though a longdog or sight hound may need a slightly longer period. A net-worrying dog is a nuisance and its presence not conducive to a good haul of saleable rabbits. Furthermore a dog of this sort causes upset and anxiety to a ferreting group and spoils an otherwise pleasant day. Sight hounds are so easily prevented from indulging in this annoying habit that it is ridiculous not to break them to nets.

Any trainer of sight hounds, lurchers or longdogs would do well to close his ears to the boasts of lurcher enthusiasts at lurcher shows. Few will admit to any difficulty while starting a dog at hunting. It is rare indeed to find a dog that is not a brilliant ferreting dog! Likewise, most boast that their dogs catch most of the rabbits they see, and are competent to do so at six months of age. Few will admit to owning dogs that have missed rabbits, even while the dog is a puppy, and all are totally capable trainers. These self-same experts are usually conspicuous by their absence at obedience tests or competitive jumping events, although they will have glib excuses for not competing. The truth is that sight hounds are not difficult to train to basic obedience standards, but most dogs miss a great many rabbits before they develop the technique of catching them. There is no quick or easy way of starting a dog at rabbit catching and experience and practice is the only answer. That there is a sight hound or lurcher training mystique is hogwash.

15. Exhibiting Sight Hounds

Xenophobia, the fear of, dislike and ridicule of foreigners, is not an exclusively British malaise and while it is common knowledge that the French are over-sexed, the Belgians brutish and Germans humourless, the British are regarded as a rather curious group of nations best kept isolated by that convenient strip of water, the English Channel. During Bismarck's regime, a popular Prussian quip regarding the English was that while an Englishman might forgive his wife being referred to as unfaithful, and his mother as a slattern, the conformation of his pointer must never be criticised. All the more remarkable therefore that it was in Britain, where some of the first organised dog shows were staged, that the British dog breeder invited the man in the street to publicly criticise the exhibits.

Prior to 1850, dog breeding was at a low ebb throughout the western world. Numerically, the species was strong, for hordes of cur dogs, owned by no-one it seemed, when redress against an owner was sought, roamed the countryside and towns. Canine nutrition was relatively unexplored and training methods were often bizarre and disgusting, but dogs were always news in British newspapers and periodicals and, despite political events at the turn of the century, the spectacle of the greyhound, Bang, leaping 30 feet was front-page news in many papers.

Eugenic stock improvement by selection was in its infancy in the canine world in 1850, despite the works of Bakewell and the fame of British cattle, sheep and pigs, and while an enterprising entrepreneur, James Spratt, saw an opening in providing dog cake, and a properly balanced diet for dogs, the majority of dogs in Britain were probably suffering from some form of malnutrition. True, the lot of the mid-nineteenth-century dog was not a happy one—although, judging from reports from abroad, the lot of the British dog was superior to that of dogs elsewhere.

Dog thefts had been widespread for 200 years or so, so rampant in fact that Charles II wrote to *Mercurius Publicus* to complain that so common were such thefts within his palace that it seemed as though he would never be able to keep a dog. By 1850, so organised were dog stealers that a system of ransoming dogs with fixed prices for their return had long been going on amongst the more degraded elements of city life. Elizabeth Barrett Browning's spaniel, Flush, was thus abducted and ransomed and the theft of the popular and gentle, (hence easily captured) Newfoundland dog was quite a profitable business. Tales of beheaded Newfoundlands left on doorsteps, when owners had been a shade remiss about the payment of ransoms, occupied front pages of the press and invoked the same sympathy as do tales of child abuse today.

It was almost inevitable therefore, that in this dog-orientated country, enthusiasts should become interested in creating competitions between dogs, for the British in addition to being besotted with dogs are also aggressively competitive. The first Act to effectively outlaw baiting and cruelty appeared in 1835, and the same year saw the first successful prosecution for cruelty to dogs. But fighting competitions between bulldog-blooded animals experienced a revival of interest and rat pits, where dogs killed a number of hapless rodents in competitions against the clock, were popular in both town and country public houses. On a less sleazy note, in 1858 the National Coursing Club was formed and stringent rules of fair play applied to what was already a fairly controversial sport. Thus one supposes that the first British dog show staged in 1859 was a fairly logical progression for a country so dog orientated and fiercely competitive.

In 1859, W R Pape, a gunsmith from Newcastle on

Tyne, organised a dog show for setters and pointers, offering a set of guns as prizes. The affair was possibly considered as a 'one off' advertising campaign, but his choice of venue (Newcastle was and still is a hotbed of successful dog breeders), his choice of judge, J H Walsh, who, as *Stonehenge*, wrote, (perhaps none too accurately one should add) on the subject of dogs the world over and the very nature of the event made the first dog show an overwhelming success. So much so, in fact, that, in 1859, a successful foxhound exhibition was staged in Cleveland and in 1863 a well-organised multi-breed show was held at Chelsea. The aesthetic qualities of dogs were thus catered for, but even in the 1860s there were those who perhaps realised that the breeding of dogs for exhibition, and exhibition alone, would be destructive to the working qualities of dogs, for in 1865 *The Field Magazine*, long the best written and most accurate magazine appertaining to field sports, suggested a field trial for gun dogs, the event being held at the Whitbread Estate at Southill, near Bedford, the same year. So common were the shows hereafter that a club to monitor these shows, the Kennel Club, was formed in 1877 under the patronage of Edward, Prince of Wales.

The Kennel Club has become a much criticised body, accused unjustly and mindlessly, of ruining the working qualities of dogs, but the Kennel Club is a faceless body of people and simply undertook the publication of the *Stud Book* and lifted the breeding of dogs out of the quagmire of the disreputable. Victorians had long considered the dog enthusiasts to be 'doggy men who congregated in the doorways of clubs'. The Kennel Club gave the dog breeder the aura of respectability and one of its first tasks was to lobby Parliament and bring about the cessation of ear and lip cropping, for fighting dogs had their ears cropped close to prevent a purchase hold by the opponent, and several other breeds, the Manchester terrier, the bull terrier and the toy black and tan were cropped to follow fashion. The RSPCA prosecuted many who cropped ears but the fines were not enough to deter the practice. Eventually Landseer refused to paint a cropped animal, thereby indicating the public disapproval of the mutilation, but it was left to the Kennel Club to forbid the awarding of prizes to any cropped animal and this brought about the cessation of ear cropping in 1859. In recent months (1988) a revival of ear cropping has appeared in Britain. Breeders consider it worthwhile to take litters of Dobermann puppies to southern Ireland where their ears can be cropped prior to their return. These puppies could not win under Kennel Club rules, but another Act now seems necessary to prevent this unnecessary cruelty.

Sight hound types followed hounds, setters and terriers into the *Stud Book* and there are now classes for most breeds of registered sight hounds at the majority of shows. Fortunately, the committees involved in drawing up the standards for sight hound types very wisely chose the working type of dog as a standard of excellence, and there is little tendency to promote the sort of physical exaggeration that has now ruined the bulldog, and perhaps the fox terrier. Dog shows are certainly not everyone's cup of tea, but the dog show is just as certainly the shop window for the would-be buyer and Britain is justly famous the world over for the quality of dogs it produces. Exports of dogs amount to perhaps millions of pounds in value, for the standard of British dogs is considered superior to the stock produced by much of the rest of the world. Certainly some of the best sight hounds in the world are bred in Britain—though the loss of bloodstock through export may well undermine Britain's position concerning the production of pedigree sight hounds.

The Kennel Club sanctions and promotes many shows, the most prestigious of which is Crufts. The origin of this illustrious dog show is interwined with that of Spratts, the oldest of the dog food manufacturing companies. Spratt began a 'one horse' factory in Holborn, but the factory and its products became so successful that Spratt was forced to take on another helper, a young gentleman with the same entrepreneurial skill as Spratt, a young man called Charles Cruft. Cruft travelled widely selling Spratt's products and was impressed by livestock shows staged on the Continent, shows so well managed that he realised that British dog shows, still in their infancy perhaps, left much to be desired. Furthermore, he hit upon a sales technique for selling Spratt's dog cakes as a food for pedigree dogs.

Cruft returned to Britain after his continental sales campaign and organised the first Crufts Dog Show at the Royal Aquarium in Westminster in 1886, a hall which, in spite of its name, was famous for its somewhat notorious music hall acts. Cruft's first show catered only for terriers, but it attracted an entry of 600 exhibits. He was a master organiser and not only arranged special rates at railway stations for the transport of dogs, but commissioned a special dog van to be used to assist in their movement.

Later the show became more popular and had to be moved to the Central Hall, Holborn, a stone's throw from the factory where Cruft started work as Spratt's assistant. Class 220 of this show, incidentally, catered for a stuffed dog in a glass case, but the exhibition of stuffed dogs was fortunately a short-lived peculiarity. More to the point, early in 1890, Cruft decided to print detailed descriptions of each breed, written by various experts, and thus the first authentic standards were created, skeletal and perhaps embryonic standards, but guidelines for breeding committees and judges nevertheless. The dog show, despite much criticism, did much to improve the lot of the dog, for it provided the vital ingredient of competition. Nutrition improved dramatically, though scientifically prepared complete dog foods are credited to an American stud dog breeder called Milton Seeley, rather than to the work of Spratt.

Various types of dog show catered for dogs of all standards, shows ranging from quite ordinary pet stock class dog exhibitions, to the more physically perfect specimens which are catered for by championship dog shows. Here, dogs and bitches, compete for the prestigious Challenge Certificates, three of which, awarded by different judges, allow the winner to bear the title Champion. Entries for these shows are normally arranged several weeks in advance and the judging of exhibits is to the very highest standard, the appropriate breed standard of specific breeds being a guideline by which the judge must assess the relative qualities of the exhibits. Renegade judges, those who refuse to conform to the breed standard, or who make decisions totally without regard to it, are subject to disciplinary measures being taken by the Kennel Club, and there have been occasions where judges' decisions have been overruled. Kennel Club regulated shows are, of necessity, very serious affairs. The production of top class pedigree dogs is big business, and money is always a very serious subject!

Country shows catering for sight hounds, but primarily sight hound derivatives such as lurchers and longdogs, are entirely different matters. In 1973 a group of enthusiasts with an interest in that Ishmael of canine types, the lurcher, got together and ran a lurcher show at Lambourn, Berkshire. It was a quiet and informal show, but such was the expertise of organisers and publicity personnel that it was well-attended and passed without a hiccough. Lurcher racing followed, an extremely well-run set of classes for lurchers of all sorts, and though there was a slight criticism that only longdog types, rather than lurchers, were picked for the winners (the longdog is usually aesthetically more pleasing than the traditional lurcher), the reports of Lambourn were so favourable that in 1974, and henceforth until 1982, the show was well-attended and, next to the Game Fair, became the highlight of the countryman's year.

The show attracted several stalls, stalls which sold sporting equipment, country clothing, books and a variety of other country sport products and, of course, encouraged the inevitable dog dealers who bought and sold dogs, (oblivious to the regulations concerning pet dealing) but the presence of these added to the piquancy of the show so there were no objections to them. In 1978 the show was marred to some extent by the fact that a band of itinerants decided to settle a quarrel amongst themselves in a manner best kept for Appleby Fair, but the show was still a success although one or two stallholders did notice an increase in pilfering from the stalls. However, such traders usually accept shrinkage (a curious euphemism) as being an occupational hazard of running a stall at a country show. Although, from 1978 onwards a number of people noticed that the carefree easy going, good loser attitude of the early days of the show was not as evident as it had been. The first Sunday in September (the traditional day for Lambourn) 1979, saw several people camping on the grounds of the show and in nearby fields, and some of the villagers were more than a little concerned about the curiously dressed people who converged on the village during the first days of September—figures who often resembled hybrids between out-of-date Hell's Angels' members and Stonehenge-frequenting hippies. Some were inoffensive, though their presence must have caused concern, while others were less so, and regarded the well-farmed area around Lambourn as simply a right of way to be used for exercising unruly lurchers, illicit coursing and a certain amount of stock worrying. The organisers were presented with the monumental task of preventing entry by disreputables and were obviously unable to prevent attracting sleazy individuals, some of whom must have manifested curious mental disorders, if the stories published by the press were true.

Many of the tales simply were not true and 1982, which saw the last Lambourn Lurcher Show, was a time when the press, both local and national, enjoyed a field day at Lambourn. Photographs of a bare-knuckle battle staged between two itinerant contestants were carried by most papers—the battle had obviously been arranged in advance by the travelling bands, but was certainly not condoned by the show organisers. Reports of a badger bait and cock fighting taking place at the show were ridiculous and totally untrue, but the villagers of Lambourn had had enough, for once again the curious band of campers had returned to the village causing all manner of nuisance. With many regrets, but probably with many a sigh of relief, the organisers decided to abandon the show and thus one of the best-organised country shows in history came to an end. There was little the organisers could do and the natives of Lambourn were not prepared to tolerate the sort of behaviour which the inhabitants of Appleby must consider fairly average. The loss of the Lambourn Lurcher Show was indeed a tragedy and, frankly, organisers of other shows must have learned a lesson from the happenings at Lambourn.

The success, or rather the early success, of the Lambourn Lurcher Show prompted other country fairs, fund-raising committees and hunt supporters to stage lurcher shows, for the sum of money raised by Lambourn, and incidentally paid to worthy charities (which made the cessation of the show doubly sad) was considerable and many shows decided to run lurcher classes along with working terrier classes, as fun events.

Some of these country shows, Whaddon Chase, Heythrop and the majority of the north east of England shows were successful, trouble free and well-organised. A few were less so, and there were unsettling stories of families having had family pets stolen. Such functions should be boycotted by spectators for though there is no way organisers can be held to blame, they need to be closed down as a way of expressing that thugs, louts and maladjusted miscreants are not welcome. However, shows where unpleasantness takes place are relatively uncommon though it has to be said that the presence of lurchers tends to attract some rather odd individuals.

A well-organised lurcher show is an excellent and relatively cheap day's outing for the family and is often action packed from the time the show opens until the time when the shutters are drawn. Stalls, tents, activities, some odd, others hilarious, such as Hit the Rat and catapult displays make the shows of all-round interest, and while the quality of the dogs is very variable from show to show, there is so much general interest that a family is seldom disappointed. It is also a meeting place for lurcher enthusiasts, eager to meet and 'talk dogs' with people of a similar ilk, and while a few dog dealers ply their wares in amongst the stalls, the presence of such people is tolerated because it adds colour to the show.

Lurcher shows are seldom for lurchers alone as longdogs are not only frequent competitors but also often feature among the winners in such shows. Most shows usually run classes for greyhounds, whippets, sometimes for salukis, and less frequently for other sight hounds as well as lurchers and longdogs, and at times some very unusual dogs appear. Entries to these shows are usually taken on the field and thus a show can be quite badly organised when members of the committee are late, absent or lethargic. Seldom does this mar the interest of the day, however, and most country shows are enjoyed by all.

Lurchers, traditionally collie (or perhaps Bedlington crosses qualify as lurchers) seldom win against longdogs, simply because the greyhoundy shape which is so aesthetically pleasing is marred by the addition of collie blood. Short necks, frames which are too heavy to be eye-catching are common, if collie blood is included in a sight hound mix. Bedlington terriers now have a considerable proportion of whippet in their make-up. This whippet blood tends to help a Bedlington hybrid appear more elegant and hence it is not uncommon to find Bedlington terrier hybrids amongst the winners. Longdog hybrids win most of the events, however, and justly so, for being a mixture of sight hounds they possess none of the less appealing elements imparted by a cross which involves non-sight hounds. The truth is that some longdogs are extraordinary handsome, more so by far than even some of their pure-bred sight hound parents, and against these beauties, collie lurchers are seldom placed.

Lurcher owners are seldom good losers and comments, some vitriolic, others simply inane, are heard around the show ring, particularly if a fairly hefty monetary prize is offered, and £200 is not an abnormal amount to be offered to the outright winner of a lurcher show. However, there is absolutely no redress for a lurcher judge's most absurd decisions, and no standard exists to which a lurcher judge must adhere. Thus Saturday afternoon lurcher shows must be taken for what they are intended—a day's entertainment for the family—not a carefully organised and very formal Kennel Club type show.

Generally speaking, lurcher shows are divided into two main categories:-

(a) classes for lurchers under 23 inches;
(b) classes for 23-inches and over lurchers.

As a rule, the quality of small lurchers is fairly poor, for whippets mingled with non-sight hound breeds often produce quite unpleasing results. Whippets certainly do not 'gel' when mated to collies, for fairly unsightly animals can result from the cross. Quite a pleasant type of small lurcher can be produced by mating a Bedlington terrier with a whippet although this hybrid is certainly not as versatile or as pleasing to the eye as the Bedlington/greyhound hybrid, and Bedlington/greyhound hybrids are usually only slightly less popular than collie lurchers.

Judging a lurcher show, many of the competitors in which are poor losers, is an unenviable task, and amazing allegations of bribes, placing only friends' dogs, judging the wrong end of the lead (favouring only friends, attractive women or influential people) are made. Allegations of the judge being blind, and only choosing a particular type (not a bad fault actually) also abound. The absence of a breed standard—a dubious quality where lurchers are concerned as there is no fixed type for a pot-filling dog—allows all manner of odd decisions to be made and, unless a lurcher show can be regarded as 'a bit of fun', some contestants are apt to get upset by what they consider to be foolish or unjust decisions. It is an old adage, but a sensible one, that if a judge is appointed, it is his opinion that is sought. If the contestants or the spectators do not agree with that opinion, then that too is their prerogative, but it is the judge that has been asked for his or her decision, not the exhibitors or the spectators. If the competitor does not like the judge's decision it is his or her right not to show under him or her again. It can be argued that the discontent, the back-biting and the protestations of, 'we was robbed', are all as much a part of the show as the stalls and such comments may be regarded as part of the entertainment.

Fascinating events at many a country show are the lurcher obedience tests. Strangely enough, or perhaps not so, these draw a host of competitors but only a limited number of observers. On first glance, this lack of enthusiasm on the part of the lurcher-orientated audience is mystifying, but perhaps this will be explained by the nature of the events. The obedience tests for lurchers are relatively simple and in no way are they equal to the CD, TD, UD and PD tests set for non-sight hound breeds. Lurcher obedience events involve simple retrieving skills, some jumping and basic obedience such as expecting the dog to sit, lie and stay. They do not test the training standards of the owner very far, nor are they intended to do so, for the event is simply a lot of fun and meant to be.

Showable large lurchers are a lot easier to produce, possibly because the type is usually deerhound saturated, or at least most winning lurchers seem to be, and show-bred deerhounds are usually of a very high standard of conformation. There is no optimum size for a lurcher or longdog hybrid, though over-large specimens of 29 inches upwards are seldom placed, although a few years ago the winners all seemed to be very large hounds. Today a lurcher winning Best at Show and coming in at above 26 inches at the shoulder can cause some raised eyebrows, though some very useful and beautiful large animals do just that and are no less dextrous in the field than their smaller brethren. However, it is fair to say that the day of the large almost pure-bred deerhound type is long past.

Collie hybrid crosses are now fairly common, largely due to the influence of E G Walsh, an erudite man who foresaw the popularity of the type as early as 1978. Their classes are very variable and few good shapely specimens are seen, unless the proportion of collie in the hybrids is very small indeed, having been practically bred out by liberal crossing with deerhounds, greyhounds and sometimes whippets. This type of lurcher is not particularly popular in the show ring and breeders of it usually advise potential buyers who are purely show enthusiasts, to 'look elsewhere'.

Sour grape comments around the show ring are common, one of the most enigmatic of which seems to be, 'the judge is, or isn't putting up a working lurcher type'. What exactly is a 'working lurcher type' is never explained, and this seems to be a comment applied to a loser's animal, which the owners think should have won. Very few longdog hybrids will not work, given a chance, and an aesthetically pleasing one may be equally as good, or better, as a worker than a rather unshapely animal. Judging is simply personal choice, no more, no less, and it is impossible to tell which dogs are good workers and which are unentered.

Only quite a small proportion of the dogs at shows compete in the obedience tests and the dogs which do are subject to sneers and quips from non-competitors, comments meant to indicate that the ownership of an obedience-trained lurcher is indicative that the owner is less than truly masculine and the dog is not suitable for work in the field. This is clearly ridiculous as a dog is required to be more obedient in the field than in the showground, for the dog is more likely to encounter distractions in the hunting field than anywhere else. The truth is that the majority of lurcher owners are unable to train dogs to a high standard, and the back-biting attitude of non-competitors is a little easier to understand when viewed in this light. Whatever the reason, a visitor is likely to see a higher level of lurcher management at obedience tests than in the general show ring, as dogs are never asked to perform any task in the show ring. So spectators may air their envious views with impunity, without fear of being asked to perform any feat with their own dogs.

Jumping and speed hurdling events are staged at some of the better lurcher shows, although once again, presumably for the reasons explained, the winning of a jumping or hurdling rosette is not considered to be as prestigious as the rather meaningless beauty competitions. Once again the truth is that lurcher enthusiasts are seldom even proficient dog trainers and managers, let alone capable of training a dog to competitive levels. Scorn is usually heaped on the successful trainer, regardless of his ability in the field, and sadly, the owner of a series of dogs, a dog merchant, a dealer, a meddler, is often considered more expert than a person who trains a lurcher to a high standard and keeps the animal until it dies. Jumping or hurdling requires only a basic training to ensure a dog clears the hurdles against the clock, yet few expert lurcher men seem to want to watch such a contest, let along compete in one. The would-be competitor must be prepared to accept these comments and this attitude before entering these events, for the majority of lurcher owners are not the stuff of which dog trainers are made. Regular attacks on obedience trainers are made in the sporting press by people who would be totally unable to train animals themselves but who relegate the performances of obedience-trained dogs to 'tricks'.

High jumping is excellent fun and not only lurchers, but salukis, whippets and greyhounds have been known to compete well in these events. Salukis are superb athletes and while they seem unable to perform satisfactorily in obedience tests, or carry out any task consistently, they are certainly capable of doing well as high jumpers. Once again few dogs compete in these contests, as supposedly the tests are considered to be demeaning to the working lurcher enthusiast—until one wonders exactly what a working lurcher should be able to do, and just what constitutes a working lurcher owner. The competitor must close his ears to the ringside barracking and realise that the shouters and the braggarts, who are raining down abuse on the competitors, are conspicuous by their absence from such trials. 'Disregard any comments made by ringside experts', is good advice ideed.

The visitors to a lurcher show should not be surprised by competitors who seem unable to jump a dog over a four feet obstacle—quite clearly a five-bar gate would be well beyond such supposed working lurchers, whose owners often excuse the dog's lack of jumping ability by stating that the dog is a 'lamper' (for it is tradition, but only a tradition, that lamping dogs are not expected to jump, though the truth should be a lot more apparent!). However, some excellent jumping dogs do exist, for sight hounds and sight hound hybrids are outstanding athletes, and true lurchers are so incredibly willing to please an owner or trainer by demonstrating their jumping ability, that serious competitors can often persuade their dogs over obstacles that are seemingly far too high for any dog to scramble over. Collie crosses usually do best in these events as their intelligence and willingness to please makes them the best competition dogs available. Longdogs may perform well at jumping—most are certainly athletic enough to clear any suitable hurdle—but are seldom, if ever seen at obedience tests. Longdogs, strictly sight hound crosses, are not particularly gifted brainwise, nor are they particularly keen to please, and it can be argued that the longdog is exclusively a type of dog bred for coursing hares and little more. They certainly do not win well in the obedience tests, nor are they well-represented in the hurdling or high jumping events.

Since the early 1980s, the National Lurcher Racing Club has organised many events and staged many excellent, well-run shows. (It has to be admitted that the better organised the show, the more likely the competitor seems to take the event and the outcome of the event seriously.) The Club has done much to draw up obedience tests—even tests suitable for that enigma, the working lurcher. Though the club was created to promote lurcher racing—a dubious and much criticised type of contest—the organisation has long since ceased to be solely a group eager to promote the racing of lurcher and longdogs. Many new events like obedience testing and hurdling, are being included by the Club and their shows are amongst the best staged in the country.

Lurcher racing is indeed a double-edged sword. While it provides an interest for lurcher enthusiasts of all types, it is also taken very seriously by competitors, hence the majority of lurcher races are won by longdog hybrids which are, of course, faster than true lurchers as they have no base blood, no non-sight hound blood in their veins. Whether or not the bonhomie (and some club meets are highly entertaining, to say the least) of the racing will be ruined by the deliberate breeding of whippet/greyhound hybrids (ideally suited for a short sharp dash) or whether participants will simply recognise that lurcher racing is simply a lot of fun and not just a poor relation of greyhound racing, is debatable. Dogs are certainly advertised at stud simply because they are capable of winning these races and other qualities such as nose, brain, retrieving skills, absolutely vital in a lurcher, are seldom mentioned. Perhaps there is even a danger that the lurcher is in the process of dividing up into specific categories; the show-bred dog, the obedience lurcher, the racing lurcher, and that most mysterious of dogs, the working lurcher (which apparently by definition is a dog incapable of winning shows, obedience classes or racing). Nevertheless lurcher racing does add some extra spice to a show. The races are seldom long enough to prove anything and wins should be treated as being no more than an indication that the owner has raced his dog on a particular day. Sadly many competitors take the events very seriously and place great value on the 200-yard dash wins, the task of a whippet rather than a lurcher. To breed from a dog, simply because it is capable of a win of this type is not good policy. There are far too many lurchers being bred as it is, and selective breeding to establish nose, brain and hunting ability is needed. Speed should not be the most important consideration in breeding. It is to be hoped that good sensible strains will not degenerate or lose ground to sight hound crosses (the whippet/greyhound is a classical example and is being created in great numbers to win at whippet races) bred only to win the 200-yard dash.

Nevertheless, despite the spitefulness of the image makers and the bad losers attending such places, a lurcher show or a Kennel Club show is an excellent day's entertainment. Furthermore, the more entertainment a dog gives its owner, the more the dog itself receives. Shows certainly have their uses.

16. First Aid and the Sight Hound

Evolution and the most stringent selection have conspired to produce the most physically perfect of dogs in the sight hounds. Seldom is one troubled by hip dysplasia (though in the larger dogs, such as the Irish wolfhound, such abnormalities are not unknown). Heart defects, the curse of some of the larger breeds, are rare and epilepsy and hereditary nervousness almost unknown. A sight hound must make the most desirable of canine pets, for once the puppy has been inoculated for the four major canine maladies, parvo virus, distemper, hepatitis and leptospirosis, it is seldom that the hound will need medical attention throughout its life. The lot of the typical lurcher or longdog attests this soundness.

Lurchers have been known to produce live and healthy litters when the dam is 16 years of age—though in fairness to the animal, breeding from a bitch of this age is inadvisable. One tale will certainly illustrate the physical toughness of the lurcher, and while the story is quite well-known and often repeated, it is still well worth relating. In the late 1960s there was a temporary revival in the rabbit population and many considered that rabbits had become immune to myxomatosis, though this proved not to be the case. From 1953 to 1960 the lurcher had waned in popularity due to the near extinction of the rabbit, although longdogs had become more popular for the hare, the traditional quarry of the longdog, was not effected by the ravages of the disease. Indeed most workable strains of lurcher had become hopelessly bastardised by the addition of more and more sight hound blood, so that the reappearance of the rabbit and the subsequent revival of interest in working lurchers, found few strains of true lurchers still being bred. A variety of curious crosses were made to produce suitable lurchers once again and one of these strange hybrids, an English bull terrier to greyhound mix was bred in a village near the Grand National race-course close to Liverpool.

A bitch from this litter would have made a suitable canine counterpart of the 'My Life By A Penny' composition, once popular in junior schools. After a reasonable start in life the bitch changed hands countless times often passing through the kennels of many Midland dog dealers four or five times a year. Her condition varied from portly to emaciated according to the whims of her current owner. Two toes on each foot were eventually damaged so badly as to necessitate amputation and a variety of ills, caused by running the animal unfit, had caused the bitch to be 'blown'—a damaged heart, lungs or diaphragm will cause an animal to collapse when it is subjected to a hard testing course. A glance at the animal's coat indicated that she had received numerous rips and tears, some of which had been stitched professionally although others bore the hallmarks of having healed naturally—broad coarse scar tissue—or having been stitched by an amateur and non-too-meticulous surgeon. Both ears had parted company with the head, probably as a result of battles in the all-too-crowded kennels of dog dealers and there was scarcely a bone which had not broken or splintered. The bitch's jaw had healed badly, pushing the teeth out of alignment and giving the face a curious vicious appearance akin to the *rix sardonicus* manifested by some corpses. Despite the injuries and ill-treatment the animal lived to nearly 22 years of age and is buried in an allotment near Lichfield.

However, the very work a sight hound is required to do makes it injury-prone and coursing or even rabbit hunting becomes more perilous by the year. Barbed wire, reputedly a device designed by a woman, but certainly the devil's own machination, becomes more and more common by the year—gouging, ripping, even disembowelling a dog unfortunate enough to entangle itself at high speed. Farm machinery left idle and overgrown with grasses is more dangerous still and hares seem to know instinctively that these often-rusted piles of oddly assorted scrap iron are sanctuaries for the pursued and hell on earth for the pursuer. Collisions with gateposts or stumps of trees probably bring more dogs to grief than even the dreaded barbed wire, while running a dog after dark is almost certain to result in some terrific injury if the animal is run regularly. Sprains, breaks, punctures, tears of unbelievable proportion are part and parcel of coursing and a sight hound is a very lucky animal if it can survive a lifetime's coursing without needing some veterinary attention or first aid.

A sight hound is a rather special sort of dog with a very special sort of constitution and hence it deserves a very special sort of veterinary surgeon. The common or garden practitioner deals with creatures the size of gold finches to cattle and seldom has a chance to specialise in treating the injuries a sight hound is likely to sustain during its work. There are however, those who do specialise in their ailments. A visit to the local greyhound track and a chat to the owners and punters (and most regular punters have had fairly intimate contact with greyhounds) is well worthwhile. Not only are some tips concerning veterinary treatment obtained—some good, though some simply ludicrous, one should add—but the name of vets who specialise in the treatment of greyhounds can be obtained. Many of these have attended courses concerned with the treatment of greyhounds (and greyhound breeding and training is surprisingly big business in Britain) while others through long association with track greyhounds and the injuries these dogs incur will have an excellent knowledge of them. Drabble in *Of Pedigree Unknown* tells a story about the difference that two vets will make, one a general practitioner type—an ' 'oss and cow man' as Drabble puts it—the other a greyhound specialist. Drabble's deerhound/greyhound longdog had been troubled with persistent toe injuries and his local vet—an ' 'oss and cow man' had advised that the only cure was the amputation of two of the offending toes. This would impede the dog's coursing career (though one should add, this seldom ruins the dog as a useful lurcher). Drabble was upset by the prospect of the operation and subsequent mutilation and was advised by a coursing enthusiast to see a greyhound vet who promptly advised another course of action which not only prevented the amputation but cleared the persistent lameness. A vet is no less professional for being an ' 'oss and cow' man, it is simply that one specialising in the ailments and injuries which are common in running dogs is undoubtedly the best vet to treat such a dog.

Injuries to the feet are common when a dog is coursed regularly and the stronger and more powerful the coursing dog the more frequent the injuries it tends to receive. Advocates of the saluki hybrid longdog suggest that these hybrids are less prone to foot injuries than other lurchers and longdogs and perhaps this is true, for salukis have feet quite unlike those of a coursing greyhound and the peculiar 'spread' of the saluki's toes might well have been developed for running across rugged *zeugen* and *yardang* type deserts. However, few dogs which course regularly—no matter what the breed or hybrid mix—will not sustain toe injuries from time to time, injuries which manifest themselves when the dog limps badly or looks pained by the slightest effort. Toe injuries will frequently respond to kennel rest—no work or strenuous exercise, or even walking—and will usually heal quite well without veterinary treatment. Should the injury recur or should the limp and obvious pain persist then it is time to consult a vet. Lamping dogs have a bad reputation for sustaining injuries; the very nature of their work is such that injuries are bound to occur. Likewise the seemingly expendable nature of a lamping dog—the majority of lurchers are swapped and sold for the merest fault, real or imagined—ensures that the majority of lamping lurchers seldom receive proper rest and veterinary treatment and hence are permanently crippled by poor stockmanship. This is a bewildering state of affairs. The majority of lamping enthusiasts make spurious boasts that their dogs keep them in money, often eulogising on the merits of the animal and its phenomenal catch rate. Yet the majority of lamping enthusiasts seem remiss about giving their dogs treatment for injuries received during their work and prefer to offer the dog for sale in a damaged condition, trading it for another whole or sound dog, rather than having a perfectly good dog properly treated. The cavalier attitude of typical lampers seems to be decreasing, however, and fewer lamping dogs are chopped and changed than hitherto.

Wrist injuries sustained while coursing over rough or frosted ground are all too common. It is, in fact, excellent policy not to run dogs over ground which is frozen hard or worse still puckered with ice ridges. A lamper, since the temperature at night falls and hence the ground is invariably more likely to be frozen then than by day, should be constantly on the lookout for ground which is unsuitable for his dog to run. The soil in frost hollows sometimes remains hard and refuses to melt throughout the winter. Places like this produce ridges of soil and ice which cut or jar toes and wrists.

The treatment of damaged wrists can vary considerably. If the bones are broken, the dog will show pain when the paw is bent or allowed to touch the ground as the dog walks. Home-made remedies will not work particularly if a wrist bone is fractured, so that a veterinary surgeon's advice should be sought, immediately. No dog which favours a foot—carries a paw, displays a reluctance to put the paw to the ground—should be exercised until the foot is well and truly healed. Minor wrist problems—slight soreness or slight swelling of the joint after running—may be treated by the layman, and an experienced kennelman seldom needs to run to the vet at the slightest sign of trouble. Poulticing joints with hot bandages or cloths is now out of fashion as a treatment for wrist injuries or bruised and damaged joints. Ice in the form of a short-lived poultice or simply blocks or chunks of ice held against the damaged joint seems to reduce the swelling and help with the general healing programme. However, should the wrist injury simply not improve, leaving the dog lame or simply favouring a foot, or if the problem manifests itself again without obvious injury or cause, then a vet must be consulted without delay. The feet or legs of a lurcher, or any type of running dog, are like a carpenter's saw—the dog cannot perform without them! Never exercise a damaged dog. Few dogs of any breed display restraint when at exercise, and because sight hounds delight in running, and all of them display a crazy exuberance when out at exercise, injury is temporarily forgotten when the dog is playing, but will be evident again with a vengeance when a dog is at rest or in kennels.

There is such a lot written about the almost magical properties of the plant known as Russian comfrey. Comfrey is reputed to be a medicinal plant and its leaves, roots and sterile flowers are used as cures for scrofula, bronchitis, intestinal upsets, headaches and to assist as a healing agent for bone injuries. The plant was originally sent to Britain by a Russian gardener who noted that comfrey grew lushly in good soil and that when animals could be induced to eat certain varieties of the plant (and not all comfrey is relished by any animals) they grew well and developed a healthy glow. Henry Doubleday who received the plant from the Russian gardener probably believed that the plant could be developed until it produced tons of foliage which was high in nitrogen and a strange alkaloid called allantoin and had possibilities of being developed as a high-grade food plant to feed the increasing numbers of the world's population. Doubleday's comfrey was to be eaten as spinach—it resembles spinach in taste—or could be fed to animals, the flesh of which became human food.

The medicinal properties of the plant were described by various herbalists and the plant received various nicknames such as Healing Herb, Knit Back, Knit Bone, etc. Dr Kadans describes almost magical healing results in his *Encyclopedia of Medicinal Herbs*, when a compound fracture was treated with powdered comfrey, and tells of deep cuts having healed at a fast rate after fresh and powdered comfrey was poulticed on the wound. Many running dog enthusiasts swear by the plant, growing it in gardens and drying both leaves and roots for winter use.

Alternative medicine, herbalism, osteopathy and chiropractice are bound to attract scepticism from both orthodox medical and veterinary schools of thought and, until the properties of the plant have been explored more fully, the reader would be well-advised to treat the reports about the plant with some reserve. Yet comfrey has unusual properties, of which there seems little doubt, and anyone interested in it would do well to consult Lawrence Hills at the Henry Doubleday Research Association for further information. Deep wounds and serious injuries should not be in the domain of the amateur herbalist, however, and are best treated by qualified veterinary surgeons. In fact, amateur dabbling may well constitute an offence if the animal is caused to suffer as a result of home doctoring.

Some of the gashes made by barbed wire are horrendous and need stitching. The legality of stitching a dog's wounds constitutes one of the grey areas of the law and sooner or later an action is bound to be tested by the RSPCA or by private prosecution. Strictly speaking, stitching should be done by a qualified practitioner using proper antiseptics and proper equipment. All too often it is done by amateurs and done very badly indeed. A coursing tear, stitched by an amateur with no knowledge of dog doctoring, will heal and leave a huge unsightly scar. A similar wound stitched and treated by a competent veterinary surgeon will usually heal, leaving little or no scar tissue to attest to the presence of the wound. Amateur stitching certainly causes pain, unnecessary pain at that, and hence the action probably constitutes an offence. A defence for the action might be that the dog was in need of immediate surgery and the owner had to stitch its wound to prevent death. However, unless the owner lived in remote Sutherland, and few places are remote even in Sutherland, it could be argued that vets are readily available in any part of the country.

Badly stitched wounds look nasty and are symptomatic of neglect and lack of care. True, most sight hounds' cuts and tears heal, even if stitched by a crass amateur, for sight hounds seldom die of shock even when suffering from wounds, which would kill most other breeds, and hideous wounds kept clean and free of infection will knit together—after a fashion! Nevertheless, a home-doctored wound rarely heals as well, or as quickly as one treated by a veterinary surgeon. If a dog is badly torn, whether or not the wound is stitched professionally, keep it inside until the gash has healed. The public's aversion to coursing and the sight of rips, tears, gashes and ill-treated wounds gives ammunition to those who would end field sports. It is bad policy to parade a damaged dog in public, anyway, and such action invites criticism.

FIRST AID AND THE SIGHT HOUND

Still, the layman must have some knowledge of both antibiotics and antiseptics if he is to regularly work his dog, and yet not incur vets' bills which resemble the national debt figures. Antiseptics such as TCP, Dettol, Milton and a dozen other commercial brands are as efficacious for the treatment of sight hounds as they are for humans. The instructions should be read carefully and the dogs treated with the same strength of dose recommended for human treatment. Remove filth, grit and pieces of waste material, adhering to the wound before using a fresh solution to douse and finally clean the wound. Foreign bodies and mangled tissue are the very worst sources of infection and must be removed if the wound is to heal well.

Antibiotics seal off potential infections and prevent various types of bacteria spreading to infect other tissues. Unlike antiseptics, antibiotics cannot be bought over the counter at the local chemists, and must be prescribed by a doctor or veterinary surgeon. Some are wide ranging in their effects—treating a great many infections as well as the infection they were intended to treat. It is said that syphilis became extinct, or at least very rare, because dentists and doctors alike prescribed penicillin for lesser diseases and the antibiotics attacked the syphilis spirochaete as well. Likewise, some antibiotics are designed to treat certain ailments such as infections of the gut and lungs and these antibiotics do little good for the treatment of infected wounds. Old or out-of-date antibiotics, and most containers of drugs are date stamped, are of little use and may even be dangerous. There are good reasons why they cannot be purchased at chemists and pet shops—Harry Lime the anti-hero of *The Third Man* could attest to this—and a visit to the vet will secure good, properly dated antibiotic tablets. Antibiotics are not only a belt-and-braces type of treatment to be used in conjunction with antiseptics, they present a totally different method of treatment of infection and should never be used indiscriminately.

Alternative medicine offers different treatment for wounds, but once again must be treated with some reserve. Some 20 years ago the book of Juliette de Baïricli Levy was held in some regard by pet keepers and students of human illnesses alike. Critics of her work believe her theories constitute no more than herbal hocus-pocus and for a while she became discredited and almost forgotten. Recently the Baïricli Levy cult has had an incredible revival. According to her book, honey poured into deep wounds promoted healing in much the same way that comfrey was said to do. In 1985 an American TV programme showed an operation on a human being's infected chest tissue which was treated by pouring neat untreated cane sugar into the chest cavity and some weeks later removing the surplus sugar from the now-cleansed tissue. The American magazine *Grit and Steel* made much of this television production, as apparently it was the custom of Oklahoma cock fighters to treat 'rattled' cock birds (birds which had been struck with spurs through the lungs, chest and throat) with neat cane sugar. Honey is simply a mixture of various sugars extracted from the nectar of plants, and thus, perhaps the methods of Juliette de Baïricli Levy might have some credibility. Approach such theories with care however. Not one of the good lady's theories has been tested under laboratory conditions and there is not a shred of real scientific evidence to suggest that she is correct about her treatments. Despite the revival of interest in her work—and it is believed there is a move afoot to try to republish her book—deep, infected wounds need proper veterinary treatment. A hard-working, dearly beloved dog needs better treatment than simple guess work remedies, and these herbal remedies are often just that—guess work remedies.

It seems almost absurd that, while sight hounds must be some of the most placid animals of dogdom, seldom biting and rarely provoking a fight, kennel fights involving sight hounds are some of the most awesome and injurious of battles. Sight hounds are difficult to rouse to anger but, when they are roused, they fight with great intent. Greyhounds can be terrible battlers and will almost dismember each other when a pair, or worse still, a trio start to fight. Despite the almost fragile appearance of their jaws (fragile that is compared to those of a bull terrier and related dogs), they can perpetrate havoc.

If kennels are close to the house, the noise of a kennel fight will alert the owners, particularly if there are other dogs living in adjacent kennels, for while the actual antagonists fight almost silently, other dogs eager to join in the battle will be most vociferous. Heed all barking emanating from kennels, it is always meaningful, though the melancholy howling from a group of kennel dogs is simply a cry of the pack, a sound of unity and translated into simply human terminology means, 'I am here'. Frenzied barking is another matter entirely and always indicates something is wrong.

It is impossible to prevent kennel fights or to understand their cause. A pair of hounds may live amicably for many years only to engage in a bloody battle which alienates them for ever after. One hound with a foot trapped may utter a cry of panic and pain only to find an old friend attacking, madly excited beyond belief by the panic stricken cry. The presence of food triggers off many disagreements and it is wise, when feeding chunks of meat, to stay inside the kennels until the meat is eaten. Growling and snarling may occur but this should be allowed, as it is part and parcel of pack behaviour, and in open country seldom followed up by conflict, but in kennels where the dogs cannot avoid one another to feed elsewhere, conflict may occur. There is, in fact, much to be said for the feeding of dogs in a kennel yard or a field where any of them can run for sanctuary when problems seem imminent. It is good practice to watch dogs feeding, anyway. Poor eaters, odd mannerisms, which can be indicative of the fact that all is not well, can be observed and gluttons and vomiters—nauseating habits but perfectly natural—can be observed and a note made of the various food intake. Above all, kennel skirmishes can be stopped before they progress to fully fledged, bloody affrays. Hints of future trouble can often be detected at the food bowl and suitable action taken. However this will not stop fighting completely, for as has already been mentioned, the causes of kennel fights are not only manifold but also baffling to the human observer. Develop a rapport with one's dogs, integrate if possible into the pack system which regulates a dog's behaviour. Lorenz once said that there was an Arab legend that Solomon had a magic ring which enabled him to talk to animals in their own languages. Perhaps fanciful but it is the duty of kennelmen to acquire a basic knowledge of this very rudimentary dog language.

Fights will almost certainly arise when two or more sight

hounds are kennelled together and the kennelman/trainer must know how to treat the wounds which result from such fights. Two types of wound seem to result from kennel fights—the rip or tear, and the puncture. Rips and tears in the skin and muscle often look horrendous, with great pieces of red raw muscle showing under the wound. Punctures are the results of wounds by carnassial teeth or fangs and are seldom obvious but are, in fact, far more serious than the most awesome tears. Some punctures are deep and give rise to the very worst sorts of infections, particularly if such wounds are found on the dog's abdomen—a gut bite is frequently far more serious than first impressions indicate.

As for treatment, in true Mrs Beaton style, first part your antagonists; this can be done by a frenzied banging of a metal container, throwing a bucket of water over them or pulling the combatants away from each other. Be careful, however, for a dog involved in a fight, particularly a frightened loser in danger of its life, can bite savagely and inflict serious damage on its handler. When separated, allow a few seconds or so cooling off time before handling the opponents, then forthwith take both out of the pens and examine them.

Minor wounds need cleaning if they are not to become infected. Tiny punctures should never be overlooked and filth, blood and foreign bodies such as shavings, removed immediately, but continue to watch out for bites from the animal being treated. Once calm, most sight hounds will allow anyone to take outrageous liberties when treating them, but when 'heated' by a fight, or frightened, they can be very dangerous to handle. Clean wounds carefully, possibly muzzling the hound before this is done, if the creature is in the least bit suspect. It is argued that muzzling can frighten a hound and increase its reaction to shock. It can also be pointed out that a hound left unmuzzled can wreak havoc on its handler. This is a very real danger when treating the results of a kennel fight. No dog with the biting power of a sight hound should be trusted in these circumstances.

Once wounds are cleaned and the full extent of the damage wrought by the fight assessed, wounds must be treated both internally and externally. A few oxytetracycline tablets, antibiotics specifically designed for the treatment of wounds, will usually help prevent the spread of infection and a mild antiseptic can be used to clean up wounds. Avoid iodine, however efficient it may be (and, frankly, there are more efficient aids to the healing of wounds)—the stinging burning pain it causes will help promote further shock rather than alleviate the condition and shock kills a surprising number of dogs injured in kennel fights. Once its wounds have been treated for possible infection, the animal should be treated for shock immediately.

Shock kills a large number of dogs if they are not treated immediately. Dog fighters of old—there has been an unfortunate revival of interest in this activity recently—were aware of the dangers brought about by shock and it is estimated that more dogs died of this than infection directly resulting from injuries sustained in the pits. Dog fighting cannot be condoned, but in the USA the treatment of badly damaged fighting dogs has led science to understand the full implications of shock and allied secondary problems in canines generally. Both pit dogs and sight hounds are in fact very resistant to shock, but this fact should not allow the kennelman to neglect his wards. Place the injured animal under a heat lamp and leave it there until it is able to regain its feet again. Offer water, either by holding a bowl close to its mouth, or on the other side of the pen, but do not leave bowls under the lamp or close to the dog where it could be upset and cause the dog further discomfort by soaking it. A dog kept warm stands a fair chance of recovering—the same dog left to its own devices may die from seemingly insignificant injuries.

Clean wounds on a regular basis and dose with antibiotic tablets until either the veterinary surgeon decides it is no longer necessary to do so, or the dog has quite clearly recovered. To discontinue the administration of antibiotics before the dog has completely recovered is very bad policy and relapses are common if this irresponsible attitude is taken. Furthermore, if re-infection occurs it is likely that the antibiotic, originally used to treat the wound, will no longer be effective for the particular strain of bacterium will have developed some immunity to that particular antibiotic. Always complete a course of antibiotics and never keep back a tablet or so for some future emergency. There is considerable evidence to suggest that the use of out-of-date antibiotics as well as not being beneficial, can also increase the immunity which some bacteria acquire.

Curious illnesses result from over exertion during coursing, and mention should be made of dogs suffering from some disorders, the presence of which label the dog as 'blown'. A dog said to be 'blown' has sustained damage to either heart, lungs, diaphragm or all three organs. Injuries of this nature result from running the dog repeatedly after it has shown signs of distress; by running the dog unfit; and by running a dog that has shown signs of distress prior to this particular course.

A dog that is 'blown' will manifest its problems in a variety of ways. Dogs will sometimes collapse and thrash around as though seized by an epileptic fit. Some will simply fall while running and remain on their sides, sometimes breathing deeply, others scarcely breathing at all. Others may return home from a day or a night's coursing, apparently unwell, refusing to eat, and remain ill for days, often displaying a glazed and terrified look.

Blown dogs, particularly lurchers and longdogs, are often sold by unscrupulous owners, often for a good price, to a buyer who is unaware of the problems which have beset the dog, but such problems will become obvious when the dog is subjected to violent, taxing exertion. The problems will certainly reappear and, if the dog is run extremely hard, it may die as a result of failure of any of the organs mentioned. The answer is quite simple. Do not buy a grown dog unless it has been examined by a veterinary surgeon who is familiar with disorders of sight hounds—and many are not. Even a veterinary certificate stating the animal is sound is likely to be of little value, for sometimes these problems will only show up if it has been run hard or subjected to violent and exciting exercise. Greyhound vets, or those who specialise in the treatment of coursing dogs, will usually ask for a dog to be subjected to a violent and strenuous testing period and make their examination before and after the exercise. Registered greyhounds should always be bought subject to a veterinary certificate anyway, and the same rule should apply to lurchers, longdogs or any other sight hound.

Buying a grown or tried and tested lurcher or longdog is always a risky business, a transaction into which no sensible buyer should enter without a lot of thought. So many injuries can be sustained through coursing and these injuries are easily masked if the dog is allowed to rest up for a week or so. A dog with a heart defect will often appear not only sound but quite lively and will not display its affliction until a hard grinding course either cripples or even kills it. Animals with toes that are 'shot', damaged so badly that a dog will limp and become very lame after a hard course, are also sold off by unscrupulous sellers, as are dogs with suspect wrists.

If a dog is purchased, it is absolute madness to take the dog and run it at a hare without any training or conditioning programme, yet the majority of flash-in-the-pan merchants do just that. One tale is well worth repeating. A well-known Midland dog meddler who sometimes had over 100 dogs pass through his hands each year, saw an advertisement for a collie/greyhound lurcher bitch, bred in the purple, but just over weaning a litter of puppies. The bitch's normally svelte shape had not been improved by the fact that she was a shade overweight and at the time of sale still had milk. The man bought the bitch and despite the fact that the vendor stated that the bitch had been kept off exercise for 10 weeks he ran her at hare a half mile from the house of the person from whom he had purchased it, only to return the animal and ask for his money back since the bitch had not performed well. During the half hour or so following her acquisition he had run her hard at two hares, 'blown' her and knocked up two of her toes, rendering her useless, but the distressed vendor willingly repaid the money to rectify the mistake he had made selling the dog to such a person. There are no happy endings to such tales. The bitch collapsed and died later that evening.

A dog run unfit, particularly a gutsy dog, a real tryer, will often come to grief if matched with a strong hare. Dogs, even unfit dogs, excited by a course will quite often crash through the pain barrier and continue with a course to their own detriment. Comments like, 'I dislike collie greyhounds; they don't try hard enough', are all too often heard and coursing dogs are often required to run themselves to a standstill before they are considered to be worthy of being called 'honest' coursers. In point of fact, such a dog seldom lives long enough and will come to grief very early in its life particularly if owned by an uncaring person. Crazy courage is fine in a very fit, properly conditioned dog, it is a dangerous quality in an animal that is run a shade below par.

If any dog is to run a hare it should be conditioned properly before it is coursed, gently exercising the dog at first and gradually increasing its exercise periods, making each day harder and more testing. When a dog shows little sign of fatigue after a lengthy exercise period and when it recovers completely from exercise, quickly and thoroughly, it is then ready to put up a show against a hare, but not before that physical peak has been reached. The average lurcher man seldom produces that wonderful, if ephemeral, peak in his dog and hence many lurchers are damaged by coursing and those self-same dogs then join the circus, paraded around by the dealers, suffering both mentally and physically through these experiences.

The real answer to the question, 'what do I do if the dog I've bought is blown?' is, of course, avoid the dog dealer, with his crop of adult sight hounds, like the plague. These dogs are in his kennel for a reason. They have been passed on by an enthusiast because they were unsuitable for his requirements or had failed at some task they had been required to fulfil. That, of course, is the reason dog dealers exist, to act as a stop gap between consumers, to occupy a niche between sellers and buyers. Few serious breeders or trainers consider a dog dealer worth contacting if they have wares to sell and the majority of dogs found at a dog dealer's kennels are simply misfits which no serious trainer would consider. It is impossible to determine if a running dog is sound in wind and limb without a medical examination conducted by a competent veterinary surgeon, preferably one attached to a greyhound track or one with strong running dog connections. Few dog dealers will allow such examinations which may be costly as well as embarrassing for him. The answer is, of course, to avoid purchasing any unknown grown dog and to train one's own hunting or coursing dog, rearing the animal from a puppy, giving it every chance, never over-matching it and never over-running it. Each dog has its own foibles, despite the high level of physical fitness of sight hounds in general. A trainer who rears a puppy will, or at least should, be aware of these little failings and make allowance for them. Dogs become damaged, blown, call it what you will, simply because their trainers are unaware of these shortcomings, and the physical limitations of their wards. Some saplings will run well and hard at hare before they are eighteen months old and suffer no physical damage from the effects of a hard course. Others, even whelps in the same litter, will be physically and mentally damaged beyond repair by the effect of such efforts, although there are few enough saplings of any breed/blend or straight hybrid that are capable of putting up a fair show against a January hare before their second birthday.

Most physical injuries that a running dog may sustain can be avoided with a little care and it is sheer lunacy to believe that only dogs with unhealed gashes wrought by barbed wire are real coursing dogs. If there is danger on the coursing field—and wire is certainly the most dangerous of obstacles—don't run the dog. If there are large expanses of concrete or tarmac—material which plays havoc with a dog's feet and stops—avoid coursing the animal. A dog has only to chase a rabbit along a gravel path to ruin its feet and render its stops a bloody pulp. A hare coursed across or along an airstrip will often cripple a hound pursuing it. Stops, unlike ears, seldom bleed copiously when damaged and often the damage passes unnoticed. A dog suffering from this sort of injury is seldom well however, and never gives of its best during the next course unless it is allowed to rest and recover with time given for its feet and stops to heal.

No dog should be run impromptu, without proper conditioning, at a hare—the hare is too great an athlete for such a dog. A visit from a friend, dog on slip, inviting one's dog to a course at hare without giving prior warning of the visit can invite tragedy. A dog just fed, just exercised, just recently hunted, is simply not ready for a feat of endurance such as a course on a strong hare presents. Any dog run hard, immediately after a meal, comes unstuck in no uncertain manner and damage to the diaphragm is almost inevitable if it is run fully gorged. Coursing enthusiasts seldom feed a dog less than 24 hours before a meet and simply feed an egg and honey mixture perhaps 12 hours before it is required to run. This mixture is often advocated by best of three hare coursers and consists of an egg and a tablespoonful of honey mixed in a third of a pint of milk.

It should be added that the hound must be accustomed to this preparation several weeks before a course as any gastric problems created by feeding unfamiliar substances will certainly not enhance the dog's prospects of putting up a satisfactory show on the coursing field. The glass of sherry, once advocated by some greyhound buffs just prior to the advent of greyhound racing, should be regarded as an affectation and certainly does not improve a dog's performance in the field. It is often argued that greyhound racing brought the greyhound into disrepute as races involved gambling and large sums of money being offered as prizes. Likewise these large sums of money have prompted much serious scientific research into the metabolism, anatomy and performance of the sight hound. The improvement in racing techniques and the research which has enabled such improvements to take place has done much to debunk old wives' tales regarding coursing dogs. Edwards Clark was once asked if sherry was of use to the conditioning of a running dog and replied, 'No, but certainly give the sherry to the trainer!'

It is inevitable that even an excellent coursing companion will age and become less and less useful as time goes by. The somewhat heartless Abbess of Sopwell believed that after its seventh year, a dog was no longer useful and should be killed and its hide sold to a tanner to make leather. However, the fate of many ageing lurchers is less pleasant, for once they fail to give of their best and become less useful, they are allowed to change hands with all the callousness one should never associate with the keeping of sporting dogs. Such dogs are usually sold 'under-stated', sold as younger than they actually are and expected to perform as would a much younger dog. Once again the fate of such a dog is predictable, it passes from hand to hand, experiencing physical and mental distress in the process and finishes its life, having worked damnably hard during its sporting days, to die in some out of the way spot in less than salubrious conditions.

Such happenings are best illustrated by an actual example. Jade was bred near Preston in 1975 by a black brindle Staffordshire bull terrier out of a pied-track greyhound bitch from the Silver Hope line. It was sold via an advertisement in *Exchange and Mart* to an enthusiast in the north east of England and for four years it had but one home, was worked quite well and moderately well-trained. It changed hands as a saluki/greyhound in 1979 and was somewhat less than well treated by a Midland meddler who bought and sold dogs with the sympathy and understanding of a used car dealer. The dog was badly used, run excessively by a number of owners, who bought the animal on trial, ran it enthusiastically for a night or two's lamping, returned it as useless, and left it to the next owner to further run, damage and bewilder.

Jade stayed in the Midlands until 1981 and was sold to a Lancashire-based dealer who took the dog once again 'on trial', despite the fact that the Midland owner and his associates had so ill-treated the animal that it had now developed a bad rupture of the groin and ran, displaying obvious pain. Amazingly, it found a temporary base in Newcastle, less than a dozen miles from its original owner who was astonished at the reappearance of the dog and more than likely a little upset at its deterioration and condition. Jade stayed in Newcastle for less than a year, changing hands twice during that time, its groin rupture worsening by the week until it ran more pain-wracked than ever. In September 1983, it appeared near Lichfield in Staffordshire with its feet in bad condition and the rupture so apparent that only a fool would have bought the animal and expected it to work. However, fools abound in the lurcher fraternity. Jade saw little work that year and was regularly seen scrounging along the streets favouring different feet by the day, and so swollen had the groin rupture become, that the dog by now had developed roach back to compensate for it.

The dog changed hands once again in 1984, now nearly 10 years of age and in such bad condition that even the tanner advocated by the *Book of St Albans* as the last port of call for a hound, would have questioned the value of the hide, and this time the dog came to rest in Leicester—on trial. The trial was short-lived and no doubt agonising, for within weeks, Jade was once more foraging amongst the bins in Lichfield looking more emaciated, less cared for, even more pained than ever. That summer an RSPCA/Department of Environment enquiry brought about an end to the succession of dogs which were brought to and from the house near Lichfield and Jade appeared, living rough, a dozen miles from the dealer's house. A 10 year-old dog is not of an age to cope with such treatment and the winter of 1984 brought an end to the misery of the wretched animal, the cadaver of which remained unburied on the verge of the A38, for a month or so. This tale is quite a well-known one, but the fate of this lurcher is not exceptional, nor are the characters who own and deal in discarded dogs even slightly misrepresented by the tale.

Perhaps viewed in the light of the sad fate of Jade, the advice given by the Abbess Juliana Berner is excellent, if perhaps a trifle premature, since a good sight hound, kept in fine condition, is still useful at seven years of age, though getting a shade over the top, perhaps. However, be that as it may, once a lurcher, or any dog, is no longer wanted, and a permanent and kind home cannot be obtained for it, it is as well to put the dog down—humanely and quickly—allowing the dog to die with dignity.